Lecture Notes in Computer Science 16590

Founding Editors

Gerhard Goos
Juris Hartmanis

Editorial Board Members

Elisa Bertino, *Purdue University, West Lafayette, IN, USA*
Wen Gao, *Peking University, Beijing, China*
Bernhard Steffen, *TU Dortmund University, Dortmund, Germany*
Moti Yung, *Columbia University, New York, NY, USA*

Roberto Casadei · Fatemeh Ghassemi

Editors

Coordination Models and Languages

28th IFIP WG 6.1 International Conference, COORDINATION 2026
Held as Part of the 21st International Federated Conference
on Distributed Computing Techniques, DisCoTec 2026
Urbino, Italy, June 8-12, 2026
Proceedings

 Springer

Editors
Roberto Casadei (ID)
University of Bologna
Cesena, Italy

Fatemeh Ghassemi (ID)
University of Tehran
Tehran, Iran

ISSN 0302-9743   ISSN 1611-3349 (electronic)
Lecture Notes in Computer Science
ISBN 978-3-032-28357-3   ISBN 978-3-032-28358-0 (eBook)
https://doi.org/10.1007/978-3-032-28358-0

This Springer imprint is published by the registered company Springer Nature Switzerland AG
The registered company address is: Gewerbestrasse 11, 6330 Cham, Switzerland

If disposing of this product, please recycle the paper.

Preface

This volume contains the proceedings of the 28th International Conference on Coordination Models and Languages (COORDINATION 2026), held on June 8–12, 2026, in Urbino (Italy), hosted by the University of Urbino Carlo Bo, as part of the 21st International Federated Conference on Distributed Computing Techniques (DisCoTec 2026).

The COORDINATION conference series has a long history of contributions related to the study and engineering of coordinated systems. Interaction is a fundamental dimension in systems. Modern information systems increasingly rely on combining concurrent, distributed, mobile, adaptive, reconfigurable, and heterogeneous components. New models, architectures, languages, and verification techniques are necessary to cope with the complexity induced by the demands of today's software development. Coordination languages have emerged as a successful approach, in that they provide abstractions that cleanly separate behavior from communication, thereby increasing modularity, simplifying reasoning, and ultimately enhancing software development. Building on the success of the previous editions, COORDINATION 2026 provided a well-established forum for the growing community of researchers interested in models, languages, architectures, and implementation techniques for coordination.

COORDINATION 2026 solicited contributions in three different categories: (1) *regular papers* describing thorough and complete research results and experience reports; (2) *survey papers* describing important results and success stories related to the topics of COORDINATION; and (3) *tool papers* describing technological artifacts in the scope of the research topics of COORDINATION, and requiring the submission of the associated artifact via a separate procedure.

There were 28 paper submissions sent for peer-review distributed over the different categories: 23 regular papers, and 5 tool papers. The selection of the papers was entrusted to the Programme Committee (PC), consisting of 32 members from 15 different countries (with gender balance F/M = 12/20). The selection of the papers was done electronically, in two phases. In the first phase, each submission was single-blind reviewed by at least three PC members, in some cases with the help of external reviewers. During the second phase, the papers were thoroughly discussed. The decision to accept or reject a paper was based not only on the reviews and scores but also on these in-depth discussions. In the end, 13 papers were selected to be presented at the conference, for an acceptance ratio of 47%: 11 regular papers, and 2 tool papers.

The authors of the submitted tool papers were requested to participate in the EAPLS artifact badging, which instead was optional for all the other paper categories. There were 13 artifact submissions. The 9 members of the Artifact Evaluation Committee (AEC), chaired by Gianluca Aguzzi, awarded the Available and Reusable Badge to 3 artifacts, and the Available and Functional Badge to 4 artifacts.

We organized the accepted papers into five groups according to the topics they address.

Theoretical foundations and models for distributed systems. This group, containing three papers, focuses on formal reasoning about distributed system properties.

- The paper "Timed Scenario Expressions and Realisability" introduces the notion of timed scenarios expressions to tackle the problem of realisability of global models of distributed systems denoted as sets of sequential timed scenarios.
- The paper "HistMSO: a Logic for Reasoning on Consistency Models with MONA" reasons on the consistency of replicated data systems modeled by sequences of data operations.
- The third paper "Motif Refinement for the Hierarchical Control of Structured CPSs" introduces a refinement-based modeling and development approach for cyber-physical systems which preserves control stability.

Distributed algorithms for collective adaptive systems. This group contains two papers which propose collective distributed algorithms within the aggregate programming framework with specific guarantees.

- The paper "Aggregate Indoor Localisation" reformulates existing localisation algorithms in aggregate computing settings, provides stabilisation guarantees, and proposes improved algorithmic variants that are experimentally studied w.r.t. resilience and performance.
- The paper "A Self-Stabilizing Min-Max Consensus via Path-Loop Detection" proposes a novel min-max consensus algorithm, proves its self-stabilization property, and experimentally assesses its Collektive implementation for correctness and resilience by simulation.

Coordination languages, frameworks, and patterns. This group includes contributions centered on the design and implementation of coordinated systems through programming languages and middleware support.

- The paper "ScalaTropy: Multiparty Coordination with Monadic Communication Primitives" provides a design and Scala-internal DSL that combines choreographic and multi-tier programming to support multiple coordination patterns.
- The paper "Bach4Popper: Towards Federated Inductive Logic Programming using Coordination" proposes a distributed framework and architecture for federated inductive logic programming, to support learning while ensuring explainability and privacy.
- The paper "Runtime adaptation as a programming pattern in service composition" addresses the dynamic reconfiguration of service-oriented applications by proposing an adaptation pattern leveraging behavioral contracts and semantic-based dynamic discovery and binding of services.
- The tool paper "Phyelds: A Pythonic Framework for Aggregate Computing" provides a Python library for aggregate programming, paving the path for integration of this collective computing paradigm into the Python and machine learning tool ecosystem.

Formal verification in coordination languages. This group focuses on the static verification of two classes of coordination languages.

- The paper "Proof of Delivery: Mechanized Mailbox Types" introduces a machine-checked foundation for programming languages, specifically Pat, that incorporate a mailbox type system to reason about the contents of mailboxes.
- The paper "Deductive Verification of Legal Contracts" enables deductive verification of contracts specified by Stipula through their translation into Java programs annotated with Java Modeling Language specifications preserving the dynamic features of the original programs – most notably the scheduling of events at future times.

Simulation tools and methodologies for collective adaptive systems. This group focuses on the simulation of systems consisting of a multitude of devices or agents.

- The paper "Simulation and Analysis of Indoor-Air-Quality Measuring Devices with YODA" provides an experience report on the design of an Internet of Things system using the agent-based language YODA and the Sibilla simulator for collective systems.
- Finally, the tool paper "High-Fidelity Simulation of Aggregate Computing Systems with Collektivity" presents an integration of Collektive and Unity for the simulation of aggregate computing systems.

Furthermore, as Programme Chairs, we actively contributed to the selection of the three keynote speakers of DisCoTec 2026:

- Mehdi Dastani (Utrecht University, The Netherlands);
- Paolo Romano (NESC-ID, Portugal);
- Nathalie Bertrand (Inria, France).

We are most grateful to Mehdi Dastani for accepting our invitation as the COORDINATION-related keynote speaker. This volume includes the abstract of his keynote talk: "Efficient Communication and Coordination in Multiagent Reinforcement Learning".

As is traditional in DisCoTec, a joint session with the best papers from each main conference was organized. The best paper of COORDINATION 2026 was "Runtime adaptation as a programming pattern in service composition" authored by Carlos Gustavo Lopez Pombo, Pablo Montepagano, and Emilio Tuosto.

We are grateful to all the persons involved in COORDINATION 2026. In particular, we thank the authors for their submissions, the attendees of the conference for their participation, the PC members and external reviewers for their work in reviewing submissions and participating in the discussions, the AEC chair Gianluca Aguzzi and the AEC members for their effort in the evaluation of the artifacts, and the Steering Committee, chaired by Michele Loreti, for their guidance and support. We are also grateful to the Organizing Committee, chaired by Claudio Antares Mezzina, for their effort in organizing the conference. We also thank the providers of the EasyChair Conference Management System, which was of great help in the submission and reviewing process and in the preparation of the proceedings. We would also like to acknowledge the prompt and professional support from Springer, which published these proceedings in printed and electronic volumes as part of their LNCS book series.

April 2026   Roberto Casadei
                                                                   Fatemeh Ghassemi

Organization

DisCoTec General Chair

Claudio Antares Mezzina   University of Urbino, Italy

DisCoTec Organizing Committee

Sara Montagna (Gender Equality)	University of Urbino, Italy
Pierluigi Graziani (Local Organizer)	University of Urbino, Italy
Andrea Esposito (Satellite Events Chair)	University of Urbino, Italy
Claudio Antares Mezzina (General Chair)	University of Urbino, Italy
Martin Vassor (Publicity Chair)	Université de Lorraine, France

DisCoTec Steering Committee

Simon Bliudze	Inria Centre at the University of Lille, France
Rocco De Nicola	IMT School for Advanced Studies Lucca, Italy
Adrian Francalanza (Chair)	University of Malta, Malta
Ivan Lanese	University of Bologna, Italy
Alberto Lluch Lafuente	Technical University of Denmark, Denmark
Michele Loreti	University of Camerino, Italy
Luís Veiga	INESC-ID, Universidade de Lisboa, Portugal
Gianluigi Zavattaro	University of Bologna, Italy
Carla Ferreira	NOVA University of Lisbon, Portugal
Jorge A. Pérez	University of Groningen, The Netherlands

COORDINATION Steering Committee

Gul Agha	University of Illinois Urbana-Champaign, USA
Farhad Arbab	CWI and Leiden University, The Netherlands
Simon Bliudze	INRIA Lille, France
Laura Bocchi	University of Kent, UK

Ilaria Castellani	INRIA, France
Ferruccio Damiani	University of Turin, Italy
Ornela Dardha	University of Glasgow, UK
Wolfgang De Meuter	Vrije Universiteit Brussel, Belgium
Rocco De Nicola	IMT School for Advanced Studies Lucca, Italy
Giovanna di Marzo Serugendo	Université de Genève, Switzerland
Tom Holvoet	KU Leuven, Belgium
Jean-Marie Jacquet	University of Namur, Belgium
Sung-Shik Jongmans	Open University of the Netherlands, The Netherlands
Christine Julien	University of Texas at Austin, USA
Eva Kühn	Vienna University of Technology, Austria
Alberto Lluch Lafuente	Technical University of Denmark, Denmark
Antónia Lopes	University of Lisbon, Portugal
Michele Loreti (Chair)	Università di Camerino, Italy
Mieke Massink	CNR-ISTI, Pisa, Italy
José Proença	University of Porto, Portugal
Marjan Sirjani	Mälardalen University, Sweden
Carolyn Talcott	SRI International, USA
Maurice ter Beek	CNR-ISTI, Italy
Francesco Tiezzi	Università di Firenze, Italy
Emilio Tuosto	Gran Sasso Science Institute, Italy
Vasco T. Vasconcelos	University of Lisbon, Portugal
Mirko Viroli	Università di Bologna, Italy
Gianluigi Zavattaro	Università di Bologna, Italy

COORDINATION Program Committee Chairs

Roberto Casadei	University of Bologna, Italy
Fatemeh Ghassemi	University of Tehran, Itan

COORDINATION Program Committee

S. Akshay	IIT Bombay, India
Duncan Paul Attard	University of Malta, Malta
Giorgio Audrito	University of Turin, Italy
Simon Bliudze	INRIA, France
Roberto Casadei	University of Bologna, Italy
Valentina Castiglioni	Eindhoven University of Technology, The Netherlands

Mariangiola Dezani-Ciancaglini	University of Turin, Italy
Cinzia Di Giusto	Université Côte d'Azur, France
Francisco Ferreira	Imperial College London, UK
Fatemeh Ghassemi	University of Tehran, Iran
Silvia Ghilezan	University of Novi Sad, Serbia
Susanne Graf	Université Joseph Fourier / CNRS / VERIMAG, France
Ludovic Henrio	CNRS, France
Thomas Hildebrandt	University of Copenhagen, Denmark
Ping Hou	University of Oxford, UK
Eva Kühn	Vienna University of Technology, Austria
Ivan Lanese	University of Bologna, Italy
Carlos Gustavo Lopez Pombo	National University of Río Negro, Argentina
Michele Loreti	University of Camerino, Italy
Stefano Mariani	University of Modena and Reggio Emilia, Italy
Hernan Melgratti	University of Buenos Aires, Argentina
Fabrizio Montesi	University of Southern Denmark, Denmark
J. Garrett Morris	University of Kansas, USA
Rumyana Neykova	Brunel University London, UK
José Proença	University of Porto, Portugal
Violet Ka I Pun	Western Norway University of Applied Sciences, Norway
António Ravara	NOVA University Lisbon, Portugal
Marjan Sirjani	Mälardalen University, Sweden
Carolyn Talcott	SRI International, USA
Maurice ter Beek	ISTI-CNR, Italy
Francesco Tiezzi	University of Florence, Italy
Nils Timm	University of Pretoria, South Africa
Emilio Tuosto	Gran Sasso Science Institute, Italy
Frank Valencia	École Polytechnique de Paris, France

COORDINATION Artifact Evaluation Committee Chair

Gianluca Aguzzi	University of Bologna, Italy

COORDINATION Artifact Evaluation Committee

Davide Domini	University of Bologna, Italy
Nicolas Farabegoli	University of Bologna, Italy
Matteo Magnini	University of Luxembourg, Luxembourg

Mário Pereira	NOVA University Lisbon, Portugal
Marco Quadrini	University of Camerino, Italy
Corentin Reuther	University of Namur, Belgium
Lorenzo Rossi	University of Camerino, Italy
Gerard Tabone	University of Malta, Malta
Laura Voinea	University of Glasgow, UK

COORDINATION Additional Reviewers

Davide Basile	ISTI-CNR, Italy
Nicola Del Giudice	University of Camerino, Italy
Masoud Ebrahimi	Mälardalen University, Sweden
Gabriele Genovese	Université Côte d'Azur, France
Ramchandra Phawade	IIT Dharwad, India
José Ignacio Requeno Jarabo	Complutense University of Madrid, Spain
Volker Stolz	Hø gskulen på Vestlandet, Norway

Efficient Communication and Coordination in Multiagent Reinforcement Learning (Invited Talk)

Mehdi Dastani

Utrecht University
`M.M.Dastani@uu.nl`

Abstract. Multiagent reinforcement learning (MARL) is a powerful framework for learning effective policies in complex multiagent environments. A key challenge in MARL is to learn coordinated policies efficiently in a decentralised manner. Prior work has explored a range of communication and coordination mechanisms to address these challenges. In this talk, I will present our recent contributions towards improving the efficiency and performance of MARL systems through principled communication and coordination mechanisms. First, I introduce a decentralised communication scheduling approach that leverages supervised learning to construct a message estimation model. This model enables individual agents to selectively decide when sharing local information is beneficial, thereby reducing unnecessary communication. Empirical results show that this approach significantly decreases communication overhead while improving overall learning performance. Second, I present two logic-based methods for synthesising multiagent reward machines and action-masking artefacts. These methods provide formal guarantees that the resulting policies are both coordinated and safe, while also improving sample efficiency.

Contents

Theoretical Foundations and Models for Distributed Systems

Timed Scenario Expressions
and Realisability

Neda Saeedloei[1]([✉]) and Feliks Kluźniak[2]

[1] Towson University, Towson, USA
`nsaeedloei@towson.edu`
[2] Towson, MD, USA

Abstract. We introduce expressions formed from distributed timed scenarios. Such expressions allow us to specify complex distributed behaviours in a hierarchical fashion. We define the semantics and consistency of a scenario expression. We then address the problem of realisability of sets of sequential timed scenarios as scenario expressions and present an efficient algorithm which produces a non-trivial scenario expression that preserves the semantics of the original set of scenarios. Our method directly handles explicit time constraints and produces a scenario expression whose time constraints are inferred from those of the realised set.

1 Introduction

The problem of realisability of global models, e.g., global (session) types [1–4], global choreographies [5], global labelled transition systems [6] and global languages has attracted many researchers over the past several years. A realisation of a global model is a set of collaborating computing entities which are executed concurrently, and whose behaviours, obtained from their (synchronous or asynchronous) interactions, are exactly those that are obtained from the global models. For example, a global model can be the parallel composition of a set of labelled transition systems, each of which models the local behaviour of a component. An interesting, but challenging question is how to determine whether a global model is realisable and, if so, how to obtain a realisation.

We are interested in the problem of realisability for global models that take the form of sets of sequential timed scenarios. Given such a set, our goal is to obtain a *timed scenario expression* that realises the set.

In earlier work we developed the notions of sequential timed scenarios (scenarios for short) [7] and distributed timed scenarios [8]. A scenario is a sequence of (names of) events along with a set of constraints on the times at which these events occur (see Sect. 2.1 for more details). A distributed timed scenario (DTS) is a collection of components, each of which is a timed scenario (see Sect. 2.2 for more details). Each component performs its specified actions, represented as a sequence of events, concurrently with other components. Components can

© IFIP International Federation for Information Processing 2026
Published by Springer Nature Switzerland AG 2026
R. Casadei and F. Ghassemi (Eds.): COORDINATION 2026, LNCS 16590, pp. 3–25, 2026.
https://doi.org/10.1007/978-3-032-28358-0_1

communicate or synchronise with each other by performing the same action simultaneously. A DTS, Ξ, is viewed as a parallel composition of its components and its semantics is defined as a set of distributed behaviours, i.e., the set of all possible interleavings of events in the components of Ξ that satisfy the constraints and the synchronising requirements of Ξ.

Given a set, $\mathcal{S}$, of scenarios over a set of events, $\Sigma_\mathcal{S}$, the stable distance relation [8] of $\mathcal{S}$ is $\mathcal{DR}_\mathcal{S} = (\prec_\mathcal{S}, \mathcal{DF}_\mathcal{S})$. The partial order $\prec_\mathcal{S}$ captures all the ordering dependencies between events in $\mathcal{S}$, while the distance function, $\mathcal{DF}_\mathcal{S}$, expresses constraints on the time between every pair of events e and e', where $e \prec_\mathcal{S} e'$. A projection of $\mathcal{DR}_\mathcal{S}$ is a scenario over $\Sigma_\mathcal{S}$ whose sequence of events agrees with $\prec_\mathcal{S}$ and whose constraints satisfy the constraints captured by $\mathcal{DF}_\mathcal{S}$.

In the current paper we introduce *timed scenario expressions* and solve the problem of realisability of sets of scenarios as scenario expressions. So our contribution is twofold:

First, we introduce a limited form of timed scenario expressions (expressions for short), as a means of constructing hierarchical models of complex systems, whose constituent parts are distributed systems (Sect. 3). Intuitively, an expression is built by repeatedly applying three operators, namely choice, concatenation and parallel composition (denoted by $|$, $\circ$ and $||$[1], respectively), to distributed scenarios. In its simplest form an expression is just a single DTS. Given an expression E, we define its semantics, denoted by $[\![E]\!]$, in terms of the set of distributed behaviours that are expressed by E.

Second, we tackle the problem of realisability of sets of (sequential) scenarios as expressions (Sect. 4). Given a finite set, $\mathcal{S}$, of scenarios, we produce a scenario expression, E, that realises $\mathcal{S}$, i.e., $[\![E]\!]$ is identical to the union of the sets of behaviours specified by the members of $\mathcal{S}$.

We identify two criteria for realisability of $\mathcal{S}$ as a single DTS: $\mathcal{S}$ is realisable by a DTS iff (i) it is *order-closed*, and (ii) all its members are *compatible*, in terms of their constraints, with $\mathcal{DR}_\mathcal{S}$. Intuitively, $\mathcal{S}$ is order-closed if, for every projection of $\mathcal{DR}_\mathcal{S}$, there is a scenario in $\mathcal{S}$ with that exact sequence of events, and vice versa. A scenario $sc \in \mathcal{S}$ is compatible with $\mathcal{DR}_\mathcal{S}$ if its set of constraints is equivalent to the set of constraints of the projection of $\mathcal{DR}_\mathcal{S}$ that has the same sequence of events as sc.

If $\mathcal{S}$ is not realisable by a single DTS, then it must be divided into partitions, in such a way that each partition is order-closed and all its members are compatible with the distance relation of the partition. Once every partition is realisable by a single DTS, the resulting expression will be a choice between these distributed scenarios.

The novelty of our work is primarily in the use of (stable) distance relations [8] as a linchpin of an efficient method for the realisation problem. By identifying the necessary and sufficient conditions for the realisability of a set of scenarios as a DTS, we address the problem that was left open in our earlier work [8].

---

[1] We do not consider the Kleene star ($*$) operator here, as its introduction opens up interesting questions that cannot be addressed in the confines of the current paper.

Related Work. In our earlier work [8] we developed an algorithm for solving the problem of realisability of sets of (sequential) scenarios as distributed scenarios. Given a set of scenarios, our algorithm determines whether the set is realisable by a *single* DTS, i.e., whether there is a DTS whose semantics is identical to the union of the behaviours described by the members of the set. If so, the algorithm produces such a DTS. Despite some similarities, the problem that we tackle in the current paper is fundamentally different.

The comparison of our sequential timed scenarios with simple temporal networks (STNs) [9], as well as with message sequence charts (MSCs) [10,11], is presented elsewhere [8]. Similarities between the distributed behaviours of distributed timed scenarios and the timed traces of Balaguer et al. [12] are also discussed in our earlier work [8].

The problem of realisability has been investigated in a variety of settings, e.g., for message sequence charts [13], global session types [1–4], pomsets [14], global labelled transition systems [6], choreography languages [5] and team automata [15]. Unlike in all these works the realisability of our sets of sequential scenarios as scenario expressions is determined by precise time analysis enabled by our distance relations. That is, in our setting we are able to directly reason about realisability of models that include explicit time constraints and produce realisations that involve time constraints.

2   Preliminaries

This section briefly recounts our earlier work [7,8].

2.1   Sequential Timed Scenarios

Let Σ be a finite set of symbols called *events*. A *behaviour*[2] over Σ is a non-empty sequence $(e_0,t_0)(e_1,t_1)(e_2,t_2)\ldots$, such that $e_i \in \Sigma$, $t_i \in \mathbb{R}^{\geq 0}$ and $t_{i-1} \leq t_i$ for $i \in \{1,2\ldots\}$. For a finite behaviour $\mathcal{B} = (e_0,t_0)(e_1,t_1)\ldots(e_{n-1},t_{n-1})$ of length n $(n \in \mathbb{N}^{>0})$, and for any $0 \leq i < j < n$, the *distance*, in time units, of event j from event i in $\mathcal{B}$ is denoted by $t_{ij}^{\mathcal{B}}$. That is, $t_{ij}^{\mathcal{B}} = t_j - t_i$.

A *sequential timed scenario* (*scenario* for short) of length $n \in \mathbb{N}$ over Σ is a pair $(\mathcal{E},\mathcal{C})$, where $\mathcal{E} = e_o e_1 ... e_{n-1}$ is a non-empty sequence of events from Σ, and $\mathcal{C} \subset \Phi(n)$ is a finite set of constraints. A constraint in $\Phi(n)$ is of the form $b \sim a$, where b is the symbol $\tau_{i,j}$ (for some integers $0 \leq i < j < n$), $\sim \in \{\leq,\geq,=\}$[3] and $a \in \mathbb{Q}$ is a constant. The interpretation is that $\tau_{i,j}$ is the time distance between the i-th and the j-th events in the behaviours described by a scenario. The constraints $\tau_{i,j} \geq 0$ and $\tau_{i,j} \leq \infty$ are called *default constraints*.

We use $\Sigma_{\mathcal{E}} = \{e_0, e_1, \ldots, e_n\} \subseteq \Sigma$ to denote the set of events in $\mathcal{E}$.

---

[2] The notion of "behaviour" is equivalent to that of Alur's "timed word" [16].

[3] To keep the presentation compact, we do not allow sharp inequalities. They are mostly of theoretical interest: in practice we can measure time only with some finite granularity γ, so $x < c$ is for all practical purposes equivalent to $x \leq c - \gamma$.

A behaviour $\mathcal{B} = (e_0, t_0)(e_1, t_1) \dots (e_{n-1}, t_{n-1})$ over Σ is *allowed* by scenario $\xi = (\mathcal{E}, \mathcal{C})$ iff $\mathcal{E} = e_0 \dots e_{n-1}$ and every $\tau_{i,j} \sim a$ in $\mathcal{C}$ evaluates to true after $\tau_{i,j}$ is replaced by $t_{ij}^{\mathcal{B}}$. The *semantics* of scenario ξ, denoted by $[\![\xi]\!]$, is the set of behaviours that are allowed by ξ. A scenario ξ is *consistent* iff $[\![\xi]\!] \neq \emptyset$.

For example, $\xi = (abc, \{\tau_{0,1} \geq 3, \tau_{0,2} \leq 7\})$ is a consistent scenario: $[\![\xi]\!] = \{(a, t_0)(b, t_1)(c, t_2) \mid t_0 \leq t_1 \leq t_2 \wedge t_1 - t_0 \geq 3 \wedge t_2 - t_0 \leq 7\}$.

2.2 Distributed Timed Scenarios

The scenario $\xi = (\mathcal{E}, \mathcal{C})$ is in *normalised form* iff every event of $\mathcal{E}$ has only one occurrence in $\mathcal{E}$[4]. If ξ is in normalised form, then each event is uniquely identified by its name. If event i in ξ is a, we will use t_a (instead of t_i) to refer to the time of a in a behaviour $\mathcal{B} \in [\![\xi]\!]$. If event j $(i < j)$ in ξ is b, we will use $\tau_{a,b}$ (instead of $\tau_{i,j}$) in a constraint that restricts the time distance between a and b, and $t_{ab}^{\mathcal{B}}$ (instead of $t_{ij}^{\mathcal{B}}$) to represent the time distance between a and b in $\mathcal{B}$. Naturally, the sequence $\mathcal{E} = e_o e_1 \dots e_n$ of a normalised scenario ξ induces a total order on Σ_ξ. We use $<_\xi$ to denote this total order: for two events e_i and e_j in $\mathcal{E}$, $e_i <_\xi e_j \iff i < j$.

A *distributed timed scenario* (*DTS* or *distributed scenario* for short) over Σ is a finite collection of (sequential) scenarios, denoted by $\Xi = \mathcal{D}(\xi_1, \dots, \xi_n)$, such that each ξ_j $(1 \leq j \leq n)$ is consistent and is in normalised form. We refer to each ξ_j as a *component of* Ξ. We use $\Sigma_\Xi = \Sigma_{\xi_1} \cup \dots \cup \Sigma_{\xi_n} \subseteq \Sigma$ to denote the set of events of Ξ. We say Ξ is *well-formed* iff $\prec_\Xi \subseteq \Sigma_\Xi \times \Sigma_\Xi$, defined as the transitive closure of $\bigcup_{\xi \in \Xi} <_\xi$, is a strict partial order on Σ_Ξ.

For $\mathcal{B}$, a behaviour over Σ, and ξ, a scenario, such that $\Sigma_\xi \subseteq \Sigma$, the *restriction* of $\mathcal{B}$ to ξ, denoted by $\mathcal{B}_\xi$, is the maximal subsequence of $\mathcal{B}$ such that every event of $\mathcal{B}_\xi$ is in Σ_ξ. If $\Xi = \mathcal{D}(\xi_1, \dots, \xi_n)$ is a DTS over Σ, then behaviour $\mathcal{B}$ over Σ is *allowed* by Ξ iff, for every component ξ_i of Ξ $(1 \leq i \leq n)$, $\mathcal{B}_{\xi_i} \in [\![\xi_i]\!]$. Clearly, if Ξ is not well-formed, then it allows no behaviours. The *semantics* of Ξ, denoted by $[\![\Xi]\!]$, is the set of behaviours that are allowed by Ξ. A DTS Ξ is *consistent* iff $[\![\Xi]\!] \neq \emptyset$. For a DTS Ξ, and $e \in \Sigma_\Xi$ if $|\{\xi \in \Xi \mid e \in \Sigma_\xi\}| > 1$, then e is called a *synchronising event* for Ξ[5].

For example, $\Xi_1 = \mathcal{D}(\xi_1, \xi_2)$, where $\xi_1 = (habc, \{\tau_{h,a} \leq 3, \tau_{a,b} \leq 4\})$ and $\xi_2 = (hefbd, \{\tau_{h,e} \geq 4\})$ is a consistent DTS: behaviour $\mathcal{B} = (h, 0)(a, 3)(e, 5)(f, 6)(b, 7)(c, 9)(d, 10)$ is in $[\![\Xi_1]\!]$. This is because $\mathcal{B}_{\xi_1} = (h, 0)(a, 3)(b, 7)(c, 9)$ is in $[\![\xi_1]\!]$ and $\mathcal{B}_{\xi_2} = (h, 0)(e, 5)(f, 6)(b, 7)(d, 10)$ is in $[\![\xi_2]\!]$. Notice that $\mathcal{B}$ consists of an interleaving of the timed events of ξ_1 and ξ_2, except that the events h and b occur only once. These events, which occur simultaneously in ξ_1 and ξ_2, are the synchronising events of Ξ_1. One can think of the behaviours of the components of Ξ_1 as taking place concurrently, but synchronising on the shared events ("rendezvous" synchronisation). In other words, Ξ_1

---

[4] If there is more than one event with the same name, say a, in a scenario of length n, the kth $(1 < k \leq n - 1)$ occurrence of a can be replaced with a_k.

[5] We assume that any renaming of the synchronising events necessitated by normalising the components of a DTS is performed consistently across all the components. This does not pose any practical limitations.

$$\begin{aligned}
l_{e_1e_2} + l_{e_2e_3} > l_{e_1e_3} &\longrightarrow l_{e_1e_3} := l_{e_1e_2} + l_{e_2e_3}\\
l_{e_1e_2} + h_{e_2e_3} > h_{e_1e_3} &\longrightarrow h_{e_2e_3} := h_{e_1e_3} - l_{e_1e_2}\\
l_{e_1e_3} > l_{e_1e_2} + h_{e_2e_3} &\longrightarrow l_{e_1e_2} := l_{e_1e_3} - h_{e_2e_3}\\
h_{e_1e_2} + l_{e_2e_3} > h_{e_1e_3} &\longrightarrow h_{e_1e_2} := h_{e_1e_3} - l_{e_2e_3}\\
l_{e_1e_3} > h_{e_1e_2} + l_{e_2e_3} &\longrightarrow l_{e_2e_3} := l_{e_1e_3} - h_{e_1e_2}\\
h_{e_1e_3} > h_{e_1e_2} + h_{e_2e_3} &\longrightarrow h_{e_1e_3} := h_{e_1e_2} + h_{e_2e_3}
\end{aligned}$$

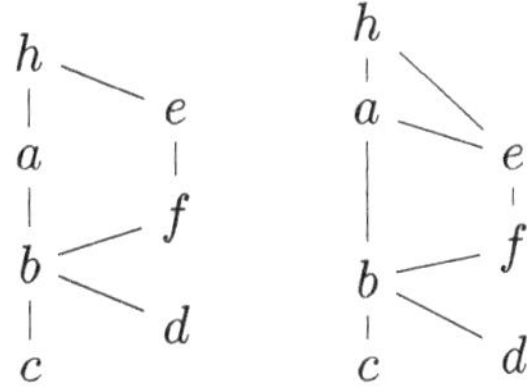

Fig. 1. Rules for stabilising a distance relation.   **Fig. 2.** $\prec_{\varXi_1}$ and $\prec^x_{\varXi_1}$.

can be viewed as a *parallel composition* of its components. If $\varXi = \mathcal{D}(\xi_1, \ldots, \xi_n)$, then we often write $\varXi = \xi_1 \| \cdots \| \xi_n$.

Distance Relations. If $\varXi = \mathcal{D}(\xi_1, \ldots, \xi_n)$, where $\xi_i = (\mathcal{E}_i, \mathcal{C}_i)$ $(1 \leq i \leq n)$, then let $\mathcal{C}(\varXi) = \bigcup_{1 \leq i \leq n} \mathcal{C}_i$. If $\varXi$ is a well-formed DTS, for $(e_1, e_2) \in \prec_\varXi$, we define $L_{e_1e_2} = \{l \mid \tau_{e_1,e_2} \geq l \in \mathcal{C}(\varXi)\}$ and $H_{e_1e_2} = \{h \mid \tau_{e_1,e_2} \leq h \in \mathcal{C}(\varXi)\}$. The distance relation of $\varXi$ is $\mathcal{DR}_\varXi = (\prec_\varXi, \mathcal{DF}_\varXi)$, where $\mathcal{DF}_\varXi : \prec_\varXi \mapsto \mathbb{Q} \times \mathbb{Q}$ is a total function and $\mathcal{DF}_\varXi(e_1, e_2) = [l_{e_1e_2}, h_{e_1e_2}]$, such that (i) if $L_{e_1e_2} \neq \emptyset$, then $l_{e_1e_2} = \max(L_{e_1e_2})$, otherwise $l_{e_1e_2} = 0$ and (ii) if $H_{e_1e_2} \neq \emptyset$, then $h_{e_1e_2} = \min(H_{e_1e_2})$, otherwise $h_{e_1e_2} = \infty$. $\mathcal{DR}_\varXi$ is *stable* iff for every $e_1 \prec_\varXi e_2$, $l_{e_1e_2} \leq h_{e_1e_2}$, and for every $e_1 \prec_\varXi e_2 \prec_\varXi e_3$, the following inequalities hold

$$l_{e_1e_2} + l_{e_2e_3} \leq l_{e_1e_3} \leq \left\{ \begin{matrix} l_{e_1e_2} + h_{e_2e_3} \\ h_{e_1e_2} + l_{e_2e_3} \end{matrix} \right\} \leq h_{e_1e_3} \leq h_{e_1e_2} + l_{e_2e_3} \tag{1}$$

If $\varXi$ is consistent, $\mathcal{DR}_\varXi$ can be stabilised by iteratively applying the rules shown in Fig. 1. We use $\mathcal{DR}^s_\varXi = (\prec_\varXi, \mathcal{DF}^s_\varXi)$ to denote the stable distance relation of $\varXi$. $\mathcal{DF}^s_\varXi$ maps (e, e') in $\prec_\varXi$ to an interval which corresponds to the lower and upper bounds on the time distance between e and e' in all the behaviours of $\varXi$.

We represent a partial order by its maximal chains, visually represented by a Hasse diagram. For $\varXi_1$, $\prec_{\varXi_1}$ is shown in Fig. 2, $\mathcal{DF}^s_{\varXi_1}$ is represented by $\{(h, a, 0, 3), (h, b, 4, 7), (h, c, 4, \infty), (h, d, 4, \infty), (h, e, 4, 7), (h, f, 4, 7), (a, b, 1, 4), (a, c, 1, \infty), (a, d, 1, \infty), (e, b, 0, 3), (e, f, 0, 3), (f, b, 0, 3)\}$. Tuples of the form $(e, e', 0, \infty)$ (indicating default constraints) will not be included in our examples.

Extended Distance Relations. The *extended partial order* of $\varXi$, $\prec^x_\varXi : \varSigma_\varXi \times \varSigma_\varXi$, is the smallest relation that satisfies the following conditions: (i) if $e \prec_\varXi e'$, then $e \prec^x_\varXi e'$; (ii) if there exists $o \in \varSigma_\varXi$ such that $o \prec^x_\varXi e$, $o \prec^x_\varXi e'$ and $M_{oe} < m_{oe'}$ in $\mathcal{DF}^s_\varXi$, or $e \prec^x_\varXi o$, $e' \prec^x_\varXi o$ and $M_{e'o} < m_{eo}$ in $\mathcal{DF}^s_\varXi$, then $e \prec^x_\varXi e'$; (iii) if $e \prec^x_\varXi e'$ and $e' \prec^x_\varXi e''$, then $e \prec^x_\varXi e''$. The *initial* extended distance relation of $\varXi$ is $\mathcal{DR}^x_\varXi = (\prec^x_\varXi, \mathcal{DF}^x_\varXi)$, where $\mathcal{DF}^x_\varXi(e, e') = [0, \infty]$ if (e, e') in $\prec^x_\varXi \setminus \prec_\varXi$, and $\mathcal{DF}^x_\varXi(e, e') = \mathcal{DF}^s_\varXi(e, e')$ if (e, e') in $\prec_\varXi$. The *stable extended distance relation* of $\varXi$, denoted by $\mathcal{DR}^{xs}_\varXi = (\prec^x_\varXi, \mathcal{DF}^{xs}_\varXi)$, is obtained by stabilising $\mathcal{DR}^x_\varXi$.

In $\varXi_1$, $M_{ha} = 3 < m_{he} = 4$ in $\mathcal{DF}^s_{\varXi_1}$, so $\prec_{\varXi_1}$ can be extended with (a, e) (see $\prec^x_{\varXi_1}$ in Fig. 2) and $\mathcal{DF}^{xs}_{\varXi_1} = \mathcal{DF}^s_{\varXi_1} \cup \{(a, e, 1, 4), (a, f, 1, 4)\}$.

To avoid visual clutter we will use $\mathcal{DR}_\Xi = (\prec_\Xi, \mathcal{DF}_\Xi)$ for the stable extended distance relation of Ξ. A (sequential) scenario, ξ, can be seen as a trivial DTS, $\mathcal{D}(\xi)$. We use $\mathcal{DR}_\xi = (\prec_\xi, \mathcal{DF}_\xi)$ for its stable distance relation, where $\prec_\xi$ is $<_\xi$.

Realisability of (Sequential) Scenarios as Distributed Scenarios. Let $\mathcal{S} = \{s_1, \ldots, s_n\}$, such that each $s_i \in \mathcal{S}$ has a different sequence of events, and each event in $\Sigma_\mathcal{S}$ occurs exactly once in each s_i. If there exists a DTS Ξ over $\Sigma_\mathcal{S}$, such that $[\![\Xi]\!] = \bigcup_{1 \leq i \leq n} [\![s_i]\!]$, we say $\mathcal{S}$ is *realisable* by Ξ.

Projections of Distance Relations. Let $\mathcal{DR} = (\prec, \mathcal{DF})$ be a stable distance relation over Σ. A *projection* of $\mathcal{DR}$ is a scenario $\xi_p = (p, \mathcal{C}_p)$, where (i) p is a permutation of events in Σ that agrees with $\prec$, and (ii) $\mathcal{C}_p$ is a set of constraints: for every e and e' such that e appears before e' in p, if $e \not\prec e'$, then the default constraints $0 \leq \tau_{e,e'} \leq \infty$ are added to $\mathcal{C}_p$, otherwise the constraints $l \leq \tau_{e,e'} \leq h$ are added to $\mathcal{C}_p$, where $\mathcal{DF}(e, e') = [l, h]$. When we create $\mathcal{DR}_{\xi_p}$, we must, of course, stabilise it. In the rest of the text we assume the distance relations of all the projections are stabilised.

The set of all the projections obtained in this way is realisable by any DTS for which $\mathcal{DR}$ is the extended distance relation. Moreover, given the extended distance relation $\mathcal{DR}$ for a DTS Ξ, the set of projections of $\mathcal{DR}$ uniquely determines the semantics of Ξ: every behaviour in $[\![\Xi]\!]$ is allowed by one projection.

3   Timed Scenario Expressions

In this section we introduce the notion of timed scenario expressions (expressions for short). Expressions allow us to construct models of behaviours of complicated systems whose constituent parts are distributed systems. They provide a hierarchical way of specifying systems, where distributed scenarios are used as the building blocks. First, we introduce a few operations for manipulating scenarios.

Definition 1. *Let $\xi = (\mathcal{E}_1, \mathcal{C}_1)$ and $\eta = (\mathcal{E}_2, \mathcal{C}_2)$ be two normalised scenarios over Σ_ξ and Σ_η, respectively.*

– The *concatenation* of ξ and η, denoted by $\xi \circ \eta$, is defined if $\Sigma_\xi \cap \Sigma_\eta = \emptyset$. If defined, $\xi \circ \eta$ is the scenario $(\mathcal{E}, \mathcal{C}_1 \cup \mathcal{C}_2)$ over $\Sigma_\xi \cup \Sigma_\eta$, where $\mathcal{E}$ is the concatenation of $\mathcal{E}_1$ and $\mathcal{E}_2$. The semantics of $\xi \circ \eta$, denoted by $[\![\xi \circ \eta]\!]$, is $[\![\xi]\!] \circ [\![\eta]\!]$, that is, every behaviour of $\xi \circ \eta$ is a concatenation of some behaviour of ξ and some behaviour of η.
– The *choice* between two alternatives, ξ and η, is denoted by $\xi | \eta$. Its semantics is defined by $[\![\xi | \eta]\!] = [\![\xi]\!] \cup [\![\eta]\!]$.

If ξ and η are two scenarios, then $\xi | \eta$ is consistent if ξ or η is consistent. If $\xi \circ \eta$ is defined, then it is consistent if ξ and η are both consistent.

Definition 2. *Let $\Xi_1 = \mathcal{D}(\xi_1, \ldots, \xi_n)$ and $\Xi_2 = \mathcal{D}(\eta_1, \ldots, \eta_m)$ be two distributed scenarios over Σ_{Ξ_1} and Σ_{Ξ_2}, respectively.*

- The *concatenation* of Ξ_1 and Ξ_2, denoted by $\Xi_1 \circ \Xi_2$, is defined if $\Sigma_{\Xi_1} \cap \Sigma_{\Xi_2} = \emptyset$. If defined, $\Xi_1 \circ \Xi_2$ is the DTS $\Xi = \mathcal{D}(\gamma_{11}, \ldots, \gamma_{1m}, \ldots, \gamma_{n1}, \ldots, \gamma_{nm})$ over $\Sigma_{\Xi_1} \cup \Sigma_{\Xi_2}$, where $\gamma_{ij} = \xi_i \circ \eta_j$ (for $1 \leq i \leq n$ and $1 \leq j \leq m$), and $[\![\Xi_1 \circ \Xi_2]\!] = [\![\Xi]\!]$.
- The *parallel composition* of Ξ_1, and Ξ_2, denoted by $\Xi_1 \| \Xi_2$, is the DTS $\Xi = \mathcal{D}(\xi_1, \ldots, \xi_n, \eta_1, \ldots, \eta_m)$ over $\Sigma_{\Xi_1} \cup \Sigma_{\Xi_2}$ and $[\![\Xi_1 \| \Xi_2]\!] = [\![\Xi]\!]$.
- The *choice* between two alternatives, Ξ_1 and Ξ_2, is denoted by $\Xi_1 | \Xi_2$. Its semantics is defined by $[\![\Xi_1 | \Xi_2]\!] = [\![\Xi_1]\!] \cup [\![\Xi_2]\!]$.

If Ξ_1 and Ξ_2 are two distributed scenarios, then $\Xi_1 | \Xi_2$ is consistent if Ξ_1 or Ξ_2 is consistent. If $\Xi_1 \circ \Xi_2$ is defined, then it is consistent if Ξ_1 and Ξ_2 are both consistent. It is worth pointing out that, except for the case of concatenation, Ξ_1 and Ξ_2 might share some event names. In that case, the event names in $\Sigma_{\Xi_1} \cap \Sigma_{\Xi_2}$ will be synchronising events in $\Xi_1 \| \Xi_2$. If Ξ_1 and Ξ_2 are both consistent, $\Xi_1 \| \Xi_2$ might not be well-formed, and, if well-formed, might not be consistent.

For example, $\Xi_1 = \mathcal{D}(\xi_1, \xi_2)$, where $\xi_1 = (abc, \{\tau_{a,b} \geq 2\})$ and $\xi_2 = (eb, \{\tau_{e,b} \leq 3\})$ is a consistent DTS, so is $\Xi_2 = \mathcal{D}(\xi_3)$, where $\xi_3 = (efb, \{\tau_{e,b} \geq 4\})$. But $\Xi_1 \| \Xi_2$ is inconsistent. Observe that b is a synchronising event in Ξ_1, while both b and e are the synchronising events in $\Xi_1 \| \Xi_2$. Because the constraints $\tau_{e,b} \leq 3$ in Ξ_1 and $\tau_{e,b} \geq 4$ in Ξ_2 cannot be satisfied simultaneously, $\Xi_1 \| \Xi_2$ is inconsistent.

Definition 3. *A* timed scenario expression *(expression for short) is one of the following:*

- a DTS,
- $(E_1 \circ E_2)$, where E_1 and E_2 are expressions,
- $(E_1 \| E_2)$, where E_1 and E_2 are expressions, or
- $(E_1 | E_2)$, where E_1 and E_2 are expressions.

Recall that a scenario ξ can be seen as the DTS $\mathcal{D}(\xi)$, so it is an expression.

It should be obvious that the three operators, $\circ$, $|$ and $\|$, are associative. The first one is not commutative, while the other two are.

The following observation follows directly from the definitions.

Observation 1. *Distributive laws for expressions:*

- $E_1 \circ (E_2 \| E_3) = (E_1 \circ E_2) \| (E_1 \circ E_3),\ (E_1 \| E_2) \circ E_3 = (E_1 \circ E_3) \| (E_2 \circ E_3)$
- $E_1 \circ (E_2 | E_3) = (E_1 \circ E_2) | (E_1 \circ E_3),\ (E_1 | E_2) \circ E_3 = (E_1 \circ E_3) | (E_2 \circ E_3)$
- $E_1 \| (E_2 | E_3) = (E_1 \| E_2) | (E_1 \| E_3),\ (E_1 | E_2) \| E_3 = (E_1 \| E_3) | (E_2 \| E_3)$

Definition 4. *An expression, E, is in* normal form *if E is either a DTS Ξ, or of the form $\Xi_1 | \ldots | \Xi_k$, where each Ξ_i $(1 \leq i \leq k, 1 < k)$ is a DTS.*

Using the distributive laws an expression can be converted into normal form. It should be obvious that the normal form of an expression is unique.

Observation 2. *Let E be an expression. The semantics of E, denoted by $[\![E]\!]$, is*

- $[\![\Xi]\!]$, if E is an expression with normal form Ξ,
- $[\![\Xi_1]\!] \cup \cdots \cup [\![\Xi_k]\!]$, if E is an expression with normal form $\Xi_1 | \ldots | \Xi_k$ $(1 < k)$.

Definition 5. *An expression, E, is* consistent, *if $[\![E]\!] \neq \emptyset$.*

If E is a consistent expression, we say $[\![E]\!]$ is the set of behaviours that are *described* or *expressed* by E.

Example 1. Consider a system in which two runners compete with each other in a race managed by a controller [6]. The race begins with the controller issuing a signal **start**, which is received by both the runners simultaneously. Upon completing the run, runner i sends a **finish$_i$** signal to the controller. So there are two alternative outcomes, depending on which runner finishes first. This can be modeled by the expression $(C_1|C_2)||R_1||R_2$, in which C_1 and C_2 correspond to the two outcomes, each specified by a DTS: $C_1 = ($**start finish$_1$ finish$_2$**$, \emptyset)$, $C_2 = ($**start finish$_2$ finish$_1$**$, \emptyset)$, while R_1 and R_2 capture the behaviours of the runners: $R_1 = ($**start finish$_1$**$, \emptyset)$, $R_2 = ($**start finish$_2$**$, \emptyset)$. Observe that **start** is a synchronising event between all the components, **finish$_1$** is a synchronising event between the controller (specified by $(C_1|C_2)$) and R_1, while **finish$_2$** is a synchronising event between the controller and R_2.

In the rest of the paper our examples will not feature the operator $\circ$, as it plays no role in the problem of realisation.

4   Realisation of Sequential Scenarios as Expressions

In our earlier work [8] we addressed the question of whether a set $\mathcal{S}$ of normalised (sequential) scenarios, whose sequences of events are different permutations of the same set, can be realised as a single DTS that is semantically equivalent to $\mathcal{S}$, i.e., describes the same set of behaviours as $\mathcal{S}$. This can be done only if there is a distance relation whose set of projections is the same as $\mathcal{S}$. We showed how to obtain such a distance relation and a corresponding DTS [8].

In this section we tackle the problem of realisability of scenarios *as expressions*: given a set, $\mathcal{S}$, of scenarios, we want to find an expression that realises $\mathcal{S}$. Despite similarities, there is a fundamental difference between this problem and the one previously solved [8]: the members of $\mathcal{S}$ could be projections that are obtained from extended distance relations of different distributed scenarios, in which case $\mathcal{S}$ cannot be realised by a single DTS, but by a choice expression that involves more than one DTS. The challenge is to divide $\mathcal{S}$ in such a way that each partition could be realised by a DTS, while trying to avoid the trivial solution in which every member of S is a separate alternative. More precisely:

Given a finite set $\mathcal{S} = \{s_1, \ldots, s_n\}$ of scenarios of *possibly different lengths* over Σ, such that (i) $eseq(s_i) \neq eseq(s_j)$ (for $1 \leq i, j \leq n$ and $i \neq j$)[6], and (ii) each event of s_i $(1 \leq i \leq n)$ has a unique occurrence in s_i, we want to obtain an expression E over Σ, such that $[\![E]\!] = [\![\mathcal{S}]\!] = \bigcup_{1 \leq i \leq n} [\![s_i]\!]$. In general, $\mathcal{S}$ can be realised by more than one expression. Our goal is to find an expression with a reasonably small number of alternatives, while decreasing the number of trivial alternatives.

We say $\mathcal{S}$ is *realisable by E*, or E is a *realisation* of $\mathcal{S}$, if $\mathcal{S}$ is realised by E.

Example 2. Given the set, $\mathcal{S} = \{s_1, s_2, s_3, s_4\}$, of scenarios, where
$s_1 = (\texttt{start finish}_1 \texttt{ finish}_2 \texttt{ flag}_1, \emptyset)$, $s_2 = (\texttt{start finish}_1 \texttt{ flag}_1 \texttt{ finish}_2, \emptyset)$, $s_3 = (\texttt{start finish}_2 \texttt{ finish}_1 \texttt{ flag}_2, \emptyset)$, $s_4 = (\texttt{start finish}_2 \texttt{ flag}_2 \texttt{ finish}_1, \emptyset)$, there is no DTS that realises $\mathcal{S}$. But $\mathcal{S}$ can be divided into two sets $\mathcal{S}_1 = \{s_1, s_2\}$ and $\mathcal{S}_2 = \{s_3, s_4\}$ based on the sets of events of its members. The set $\mathcal{S}_1$ can be realised by DTS $E = \mathcal{D}(\xi_1, \xi_2) = \xi_1 || \xi_2$, where $\xi_1 = (\texttt{start finish}_1 \texttt{ flag}_1, \emptyset)$ and $\xi_2 = (\texttt{start finish}_1 \texttt{ finish}_2, \emptyset)$. Similarly, $\mathcal{S}_2$ is realised by DTS $E' = \xi_3 || \xi_4$, where $\xi_3 = (\texttt{start finish}_2 \texttt{ flag}_2, \emptyset)$ and $\xi_4 = (\texttt{start finish}_2 \texttt{ finish}_1, \emptyset)$. So $\mathcal{S}$ is realised by the expression $E|E' = (\xi_1 || \xi_2)|(\xi_3 || \xi_4)$.

Definition 6. *Let $\mathcal{S} = \{s_1, \ldots, s_n\}$ be a finite set of normalised scenarios and $\{\mathcal{DR}_{s_1}, \ldots, \mathcal{DR}_{s_n}\}$ be the set of corresponding stable distance relations, where $\mathcal{DR}_{s_i} = (\prec_{s_i}, \mathcal{DF}_{s_i})$ $(1 \leq i \leq n)$. The distance relation of $\mathcal{S}$, $\mathcal{DR}_{\mathcal{S}}$, is the pair $(\prec_{\mathcal{S}}, \mathcal{DF}_{\mathcal{S}})$, where $\prec_{\mathcal{S}} = \bigcap_{1 \leq i \leq n} \prec_{s_i}$ and, for every (e, e') in $\prec_{\mathcal{S}}$, $\mathcal{DF}_{\mathcal{S}}(e, e')$ is the smallest interval that includes each $\mathcal{DF}_{s_i}(e, e')$.*

The first step in solving the problem posed at the beginning of this section is to divide $\mathcal{S}$ in such a way that all the members of each partition are scenarios of equal lengths over the same set of events. Then we solve the problem for each partition, independently. Our general strategy is the following: whenever a partition is not realisable by a single DTS, we divide it repeatedly, so that at the end each partition will be realised by a DTS and will correspond to one alternative in the overall choice expression. This process is guided by the results of our analysis based on $\prec_{\mathcal{S}}$ and $\mathcal{DF}_{\mathcal{S}}$, described in Sects. 4.1 and 4.2. Additionally, some divisions are simply necessary, as described below.

Gaps. Let $S_{(e,e')} = \{s_i \in \mathcal{S} | e \prec_{s_i} e'\}$. Let $s_1, \ldots, s_m$ be a sequence of members of $S_{(e,e')}$ such that, for every $1 \leq i \leq m$, $[l_i, h_i] = \mathcal{DF}_{s_i}(e, e')$ and $l_i \leq l_{i+1}$. Let $H_r = \max\{h_j | 1 \leq j \leq r\}$. If there is a k, $1 \leq k < m$, such that $H_k < l_{k+1}$, $\mathcal{DF}_{\mathcal{S}}(e, e')$ contains a gap. Then $\mathcal{S}$ is said to be *with gaps*. An $\mathcal{S}$ with gaps cannot be realised by a single DTS: this is because the interval between e and e' in $\mathcal{DF}_{\mathcal{S}}$ would be $[l_1, H_m]$, which would allow also behaviours in which the time distance between e and e' is between H_k and l_{k+1}. Such behavious are allowed by none of the members of $\mathcal{S}$. So $\mathcal{S}$ must be divided into partitions with no gaps.

---

[6] In Sect. 4.4 we show how to relax the assumption.

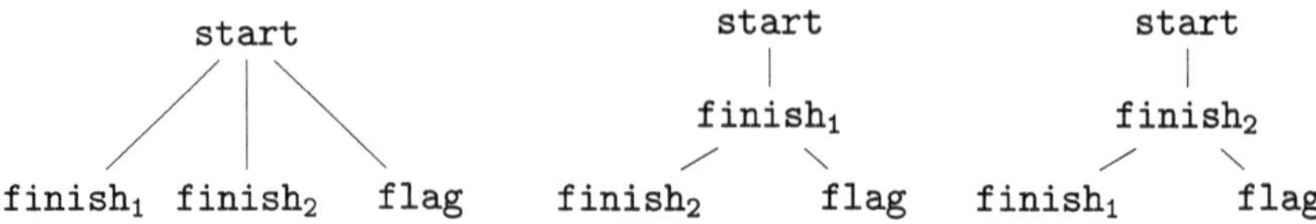

Fig. 3. Maximal chains (Example 3)

Fig. 4. Maximal chains for $\prec_{S_1}$, $\prec_{S_2}$ (Example 3)

Whenever a partition is divided into finer partitions (see Sect. 4.1 and Sect. 4.2), we must check for the existence of gaps in any newly formed partition.

In the rest of the paper we assume that all scenarios in S are over the same set, Σ_S, of events, and that each $s \in S$ contains all the events from Σ_S. Moreover, we assume that any divisions necessitated by gaps have already been carried out, so that S is without gaps. We describe our method in two steps: first, we tackle the problem *without accounting for constraints*. Because constraints will not play a role, in our examples we will discuss scenarios with only default constraints.

4.1   Partitioning a Set of Sequential Scenarios Based On Ordering

Let $S = \{s_1, \ldots s_n\}$ be a set of normalised scenarios over Σ_S, such that, for every $1 \leq i \leq n$, $s_i = (\mathcal{E}_i, \emptyset)$, where $\mathcal{E}_i$ contains all the events from Σ_S. Moreover, let S be without gaps. We are interested in obtaining an expression that realises S.

Example 3. Let $S = \{s_1, s_2, s_3, s_4\}$, where $s_1 = (\texttt{startfinish}_1\texttt{finish}_2\texttt{flag}, \emptyset)$, $s_2 = (\texttt{startfinish}_1\texttt{flagfinish}_2, \emptyset)$, $s_3 = (\texttt{startfinish}_2\texttt{finish}_1\texttt{flag}, \emptyset)$ and $s_4 = (\texttt{startfinish}_2\texttt{flagfinish}_1, \emptyset)$. The set S cannot be realised by a single DTS, as will be explained below. Unlike in Example 2, S cannot be divided according to sets of events: each member contains the same set of events. So we need another criterion for partitioning S.

Definition 7. *Two (sequential) scenarios, s and p, match if $eseq(s) = eseq(p)$.*

Definition 8. *Let S be a finite set of scenarios and $\mathcal{DR}_S$ be its distance relation. The set of projections of $\mathcal{DR}_S$ (see Sect. 2.2) is denoted by $\mathcal{P}_S$.*

Definition 9. *Let S be a finite set of scenarios. We say S is order-closed iff every member of $\mathcal{P}_S$ matches one scenario in S and vice versa.*

Intuitively, if S is order-closed, then extending it with a scenario that has a new sequence of events will change $\prec_S$.

Observation 3. *Let S be a finite set of scenarios. If $|S| = |\mathcal{P}_S|$, then S is order-closed.*

As mentioned at the beginning of Sect. 4, S can be realised as a single DTS only if $S = \mathcal{P}_S$. This leads to the following observation:

Observation 4. *Let S be a finite set of scenarios. If S is not order-closed, then it cannot be realised by a single DTS.*

In Example 3, $\prec_S$ is represented by the maximal chains $\mathtt{start}-\mathtt{finish}_1$, $\mathtt{start}-\mathtt{finish}_2$ and $\mathtt{start}-\mathtt{flag}$ (see Fig. 3). The distance function of S, $\mathcal{DF}_S$, has only default constraints. The set of projections of $\mathcal{DR}_S = (\prec_S, \mathcal{DF}_S)$, includes four projections that match the scenarios in S. Additionally, $\mathcal{P}_S$ includes two projections whose sequences of events are $\mathtt{start}$ $\mathtt{flag}$ $\mathtt{finish}_1$ $\mathtt{finish}_2$ and $\mathtt{start}$ $\mathtt{flag}$ $\mathtt{finish}_2$ $\mathtt{finish}_1$. So, by Definition 9, S is not order-closed.

In general, $\prec_S$ captures the ordering relations that are identical between all the members of S. If S is not order-closed, there are certain subtle similarities between some of the members, similarities that cannot be explained by $\prec_S$. For instance, in Example 3, $\prec_S$ does not reflect the fact that $\mathtt{flag}$ does not occur immediately after $\mathtt{start}$ in any member of S: $\mathtt{flag}$ is preceded by $\mathtt{finish}_1$, $\mathtt{finish}_2$, or both in all the members of S.

Intuitively, if S is not order-closed, $\prec_S$ is *too permissive*. So $\prec_S$ would have to be made stricter, somehow, to reflect *all* the ordering relations that exist between the members of S. But this cannot be achieved without partitioning S. Our goal is to divide S in such a way that each partition is order-closed. To achieve this we investigate the relations between events of Σ_S that are not related by $\prec_S$.

Definition 10. *Let S be a finite set of scenarios over Σ_S, such that S is not order-closed. Let $e, e' \in \Sigma_S$, such that $(e, e') \notin \prec_S$. The order-based division (OBD for short) of S with respect to (e, e'), denoted by $obd_S(e, e')$, is the unordered pair (S_1, S_2), where $S_1 = \{s_1 \in S \mid e \prec_{s_1} e'\}$ and $S_2 = \{s_2 \in S \mid e' \prec_{s_2} e\}$.*

Observe that all scenarios in S contain e and e', but not all in the same order. Clearly, an OBD (S_1, S_2) is a partitioning, i.e., $S_1 \neq \emptyset$, $S_2 \neq \emptyset$ and $S_1 \cup S_2 = S$.

Observation 5. *Let S be a finite set of scenarios, such that S is not order-closed and $|S| > 1$. Then there is at least one OBD.*

In Example 3 $\mathtt{finish}_1 \nprec_S \mathtt{finish}_2$ and $obd_S(\mathtt{finish}_1, \mathtt{finish}_2) = (S_1, S_2)$, where $S_1 = \{s_1, s_2\}$ and $S_2 = \{s_3, s_4\}$. Notice that $\mathtt{finish}_1$ occurs before $\mathtt{flag}$ in all members of S_1, while in all members of S_2 $\mathtt{finish}_2$ occurs before $\mathtt{flag}$. So $\prec_{S_1} = \prec_S \cup \{(\mathtt{finish}_1, \mathtt{finish}_2), (\mathtt{finish}_1, \mathtt{flag})\}$ and
$\prec_{S_2} = \prec_S \cup \{(\mathtt{finish}_2, \mathtt{finish}_1), (\mathtt{finish}_2, \mathtt{flag})\}$.

Figure 4 shows the maximal chains representing $\prec_{S_1}$ and $\prec_{S_2}$. Observe that both S_1 and S_2 are order-closed. Indeed, S_1 can be realised by the DTS $\xi_1 \| \xi_2$, where $\xi_1 = (\mathtt{start}$ $\mathtt{finish}_1$ $\mathtt{flag}, \emptyset)$ and $\xi_2 = (\mathtt{start}$ $\mathtt{finish}_1$ $\mathtt{finish}_2, \emptyset)$. Similarly, S_2 is realised by the DTS $\xi_3 \| \xi_4$, where $\xi_3 = (\mathtt{start}$ $\mathtt{finish}_2$ $\mathtt{flag}, \emptyset)$ and $\xi_4 = (\mathtt{start}$ $\mathtt{finish}_2$ $\mathtt{finish}_1, \emptyset)$. So S is realised by $(\xi_1 \| \xi_2) | (\xi_3 \| \xi_4)$.

In this example there are two other ways to divide S:
$obd_S(\mathtt{finish}_1, \mathtt{flag}) = (\{s_1, s_2, s_4\}, \{s_3\})$, from which we obtain the expression $(\xi_5 \| \xi_6) | s_3$, where $\xi_5 = (\mathtt{start}$ $\mathtt{finish}_1$ $\mathtt{flag}, \emptyset)$ and $\xi_6 = (\mathtt{start}$ $\mathtt{finish}_2, \emptyset)$.

$obd_\mathcal{S}(\texttt{finish}_2, \texttt{flag}) = (\{s_1, s_3, s_4\}, \{s_2\})$, which results in $(\xi_7 \| \xi_8) | s_2$, where $\xi_7 = (\texttt{start finish}_2 \texttt{ flag}, \emptyset)$ and $\xi_8 = (\texttt{start finish}_1, \emptyset)$. But such solutions do not align with our goal: our algorithm (see Sect. 4.3) will produce the first solution.

Definition 11. *The* o-ranking *of* $(\mathcal{S}_1, \mathcal{S}_2)$, *a division of* $\mathcal{S}$, *is* $o_1 * \frac{|\mathcal{S}_1|}{|\mathcal{S}|} + o_2 * \frac{|\mathcal{S}_2|}{|\mathcal{S}|}$, *where* o_i *(*$i \in \{1, 2\}$*) is 0 if* $\mathcal{S}_i$ *is order-closed, and 1 otherwise.*

This ranking will be used to choose between several possible divisions: lower o-ranking should give more satisfactory results. The intuition is that an order-closed partition is likely to require less additional partitioning. Moreover, the larger the order-closed partition, the better.

Observe that in Example 3 all the OBDs have equal o-ranking. So in order to choose the best division we must find another criterion that looks more deeply into the partitions of OBDs.

The following definition is an adaptation of *Kendall tau distance* [17].

Definition 12. *Let* s_1 *and* s_2 *be two normalised scenarios of equal length over the same set of events. The* K-distance *of* s_1 *and* s_2, *denoted by* $d_K(s_1, s_2)$, *is* $|\{(e, e') \mid e \prec_{s_1} e' \wedge e' \prec_{s_2} e\}|$.

The larger the K-distance, the more dissimilar are the sequences of events.

Definition 13. *Let* $\mathcal{S}$ *be a finite set of scenarios. The* K-ranking *of* $\mathcal{S}$, *denoted by* $r_K(\mathcal{S})$, *is the average of all pairwise K-distances between the members of* $\mathcal{S}$.

Since $d_K(s_1, s_2) = d_K(s_2, s_1)$, the average is taken over the number of unordered pairs in $\mathcal{S}$, i.e., $\frac{|\mathcal{S}| * (|\mathcal{S}| - 1)}{2}$.

Definition 14. *Let* $\mathcal{S}$ *be a finite set of scenarios and* $D = (\mathcal{S}_1, \mathcal{S}_2)$ *be an OBD of* $\mathcal{S}$. *The* K-ranking *of* D, *denoted by* $r_K(D)$, *is given by* $r_K(\mathcal{S}_1) * \frac{|\mathcal{S}_1|}{|\mathcal{S}|} + r_K(\mathcal{S}_2) * \frac{|\mathcal{S}_2|}{|\mathcal{S}|}$.

It turns out that the K-rankings of divisions provide us with the crucial information that we need in order to choose the best division when there are multiple divisions that all agree with each other on their o-ranking.

Example 4. Let $\mathcal{S} = \{s_1, s_2, s_3, s_4, s_5, s_6\}$, where $s_1 = (adbc, \emptyset)$, $s_2 = (dabc, \emptyset)$, $s_3 = (acdb, \emptyset)$, $s_4 = (acbd, \emptyset)$, $s_5 = (abcd, \emptyset)$ and $s_6 = (abdc, \emptyset)$. The set $\mathcal{S}$ is not order-closed, so it cannot be realised by a single DTS. The relation $\prec_\mathcal{S}$ is represented by the maximal chains $a - b$, $a - c$ and $a - d$. There are four pairs of events that are unrelated by $\prec_\mathcal{S}$: (a, d), (b, c), (b, d) and (c, d). The divisions with respect to these pairs are shown in the second column of Table 1, the third column shows whether each partition of a division is order-closed or not, while the fourth column shows the o-rankings. Observe that $obd_\mathcal{S}(b, c)$ and $obd_\mathcal{S}(c, d)$ have equal and lowest o-rankings. So we compute their K-rankings.

For $obd_\mathcal{S}(c, d)$, $r_K(\{s_1, s_2, s_6\}) = \frac{d_K(s_1, s_2) + d_K(s_1, s_6) + d_K(s_2, s_6)}{3} \approx 1.33$. Similarly, $r_K(\{s_3, s_4, s_5\}) \approx 1.33$. So $r_K(obd_\mathcal{S}(c, d)) = 1.33 * \frac{3}{6} + 1.33 * \frac{3}{6} \approx 1.34$. Similarly, $r_K(obd_\mathcal{S}(b, c)) \approx 1.44$. So we choose $obd_\mathcal{S}(c, d)$ that has a lower K-ranking. The resulting expression is shown in the last row, last column of the table: $\{s_1, s_2, s_6\}$ is realised by $\xi_1 \| \xi_2$, while $\{s_3, s_4, s_5\}$ is realised by $\xi_3 \| \xi_4$.

Table 1. Divisions, their o-rankings, K-rankings and resulting expressions (Example 4)

pair	OBD	order-closed	o-rank	K-rank	expression
(a,d)	$\{s_1, s_3, s_4, s_5, s_6\}$ $\{s_2\}$	No Yes	0.83	1.5	$(\xi_1\|\|\xi_2)\|(\xi_3\|\|\xi_4)\|s_2$ $\xi_1 = (abc, \emptyset), \xi_2 = (ad, \emptyset)$ $\xi_3 = (acb, \emptyset), \xi_4 = (acd, \emptyset)$
(b,c)	$\{s_1, s_2, s_5, s_6\}$ $\{s_3, s_4\}$	Yes Yes	0	1.44	$(\xi_1\|\|\xi_2)\|(\xi_3\|\|\xi_4)$ $\xi_1 = (abc, \emptyset), \xi_2 = (d, \emptyset)$ $\xi_3 = (acb, \emptyset), \xi_4 = (acd, \emptyset)$
(b,d)	$\{s_1, s_2, s_3\}$ $\{s_4, s_5, s_6\}$	No Yes	0.5	1.67	$(\xi_1\|\|\xi_2)\|s_3\|(\xi_3\|\|\xi_4)$ $\xi_1 = (abc, \emptyset), \xi_2 = (dbc, \emptyset)$ $\xi_3 = (abd, \emptyset), \xi_4 = (ac, \emptyset)$
(c,d)	$\{s_1, s_2, s_6\}$ $\{s_3, s_4, s_5\}$	Yes Yes	0	1.34	$(\xi_1\|\|\xi_2)\|(\xi_3\|\|\xi_4)$ $\xi_1 = (abc, \emptyset), \xi_2 = (dc, \emptyset)$ $\xi_3 = (ab, \emptyset), \xi_4 = (acd, \emptyset)$

The K-rankings of the other two divisions are shown in the fifth column, while the last column shows the corresponding expressions. Notice that those partitions of $obd_{\mathcal{S}}(a, d)$ and $obd_{\mathcal{S}}(b, d)$ that are not order-closed must be further partitioned. Observe that $obd_{\mathcal{S}}(b, c)$ would have also resulted in an expression with two alternatives. In general, divisions with lowest K-rankings produce more satisfactory results, unless their o-rankings differ.

In our algorithm (see Sect. 4.3) we choose a division with the lowest o-ranking. We break a tie by choosing a division with the lowest K-ranking. In order to further break a tie we introduce a new ranking, called l-ranking, that takes into account whether the distance functions of the partitions of a division include gaps or not, and how balanced the partitions are with respect to their sizes. For a division D, its l-ranking is computed by $100 * g + b$, where g is the number of partitions of D that include gaps, and b is the difference between the sizes of the two partitions of D. The aim is to give higher priority to divisions whose partitions are without gaps. Parameter b can be used to discard trivial partitions, in favour of non-trivial ones. (We assume $|S| < 100$.)

4.2 Partitioning a Set of Sequential Scenarios Involving Constraints

In this section we fully tackle the problem of realisability of sets of scenarios as expressions, that is we account also for constraints. We begin with an example.

Example 5. Let $\mathcal{S} = \{s_1, s_2, s_3\}$ over $\Sigma = \{a, b, c, d\}$, where $s_1 = (cdab, \{\tau_{c,b} \leq 3\})$, $s_2 = (cadb, \{\tau_{c,d} \leq 1, \tau_{c,b} \leq 3\})$ and $s_3 = (cabd, \{\tau_{c,d} \leq 1\})$. The set $\mathcal{S}$ is order-closed, but, as will be explained below, it is not realisable by a single DTS. Therefore, $\mathcal{S}$ must be partitioned, somehow. The pairs of events not related by

$\prec_{\mathcal{S}}$ are (a,d) and (b,d), based on which two different OBDs, $(\{s_2, s_3\}, \{s_1\})$ and $(\{s_1, s_2\}, \{s_3\})$, could be formed. The divisions have not only equal o-rankings, but also equal K-rankings and l-rankings. So a division must be chosen randomly. Choosing the second division results in the trivial expression $s_1|s_2|s_3$. But, in fact, a satisfactory result can be obtained from the first division.

This example shows that in the presence of non-default constraints, when $\mathcal{S}$ is order-closed, but not realisable by a single DTS, reasoning based on orderings alone does not provide us with enough information to properly partition $\mathcal{S}$. Next, we investigate how the constraints can be used to effectively partition $\mathcal{S}$.

Definition 15. *Let $\mathcal{S}$ be an order-closed set of scenarios. Let $sc \in \mathcal{S}$ and $p \in \mathcal{P}_{\mathcal{S}}$, such that sc matches p. We say sc is* compatible with $\mathcal{DR}_{\mathcal{S}}$ *if $\mathcal{DF}_{sc} = \mathcal{DF}_p$.*

Notice that if all the members of $\mathcal{S}$ have only default constraints, then they are all compatible with $\mathcal{DR}_{\mathcal{S}}$.

In Example 5 $\prec_{s_1}$ is represented by $c - d - a - b$, while $\prec_{s_2}$ and $\prec_{s_3}$ are represented by $c - a - d - b$ and $c - a - b - d$, respectively. The distance functions of members of $\mathcal{S}$ are shown below:

$\mathcal{DF}_{s_1} = \{(a,b,0,3), (c,a,0,3), (c,b,0,3), (c,d,0,3), (d,a,0,3), (d,b,0,\ 3)\}$,
$\mathcal{DF}_{s_2} = \{(a,b,0,3), (a,d,0,1), (c,a,0,1), (c,b,0,3), (c,d,0,1), (d,b,0,3)\}$,
$\mathcal{DF}_{s_3} = \{(a,b,0,1), (a,d,0,1), (b,d,0,1), (c,a,0,1), (c,b,0,1), (c,d,0,\ 1)\}$.

The stable distance relation of $\mathcal{S}$ (see Definition 6) is $\mathcal{DR}_{\mathcal{S}} = (\prec_{\mathcal{S}}, \mathcal{DF}_{\mathcal{S}})$, where $\prec_{\mathcal{S}} = \prec_{s_1} \cap \prec_{s_2} \cap \prec_{s_3}$ is represented by $c - a - b$ and $c - d$, and $\mathcal{DF}_{\mathcal{S}}$ is represented by $\{(a,b,0,3), (c,a,0,3), (c,b,0,3), (c,d,0,3)\}$. Observe that, for example, $\mathcal{DF}_{\mathcal{S}}(a,b) = [0,3]$ is the smallest interval that includes $\mathcal{DF}_{s_1}(a,b)$, $\mathcal{DF}_{s_2}(a,b)$ and $\mathcal{DF}_{s_3}(a,b)$. The set of projections of $\mathcal{DR}_{\mathcal{S}}$ (see Sect. 2.2) is $\mathcal{P}_{\mathcal{S}} = \{p_1, p_2, p_3\}$, where p_1, p_2 and p_3 match s_1, s_2 and s_3, respectively. The distance functions of the projections in $\mathcal{P}_{\mathcal{S}}$ are shown below:

$\mathcal{DF}_{p_1} = \{(a,b,0,3), (c,a,0,3), (c,b,0,3), (c,d,0,3), (d,a,0,3), (d,b,0,\ 3)\}$,
$\mathcal{DF}_{p_2} = \{(a,b,0,3), (a,d,0,3), (c,a,0,3), (c,b,0,3), (c,d,0,3), (d,b,0,3)\}$,
$\mathcal{DF}_{p_3} = \{(a,b,0,3), (a,d,0,3), (b,d,0,3), (c,a,0,3), (c,b,0,3), (c,d,0,\ 3)\}$.

Notice that $\mathcal{DF}_{s_1} = \mathcal{DF}_{p_1}$, so s_1 is compatible with $\mathcal{DR}_{\mathcal{S}}$, but s_2 and s_3 are not. This observation can be immediately used to divide $\mathcal{S}$ into $\mathcal{S}_1 = \{s_1\}$ and $\mathcal{S}_2 = \{s_2, s_3\}$. The set $\mathcal{S}_2$ is order-closed, its distance relation is $\mathcal{DR}_{\mathcal{S}_2} = (\prec_{\mathcal{S}_2}, \mathcal{DF}_{\mathcal{S}_2})$, where $\prec_{\mathcal{S}_2}$ is represented by the maximal chains $c - a - b$ and $c - a - d$, and $\mathcal{DF}_{\mathcal{S}_2}$ is represented by $\{(a,b,0,3), (a,d,0,1), (c,a,0,1), (c,b,0,3), (c,d,0,1)\}$. The set of projections of $\mathcal{DR}_{\mathcal{S}_2}$, $\mathcal{P}_{\mathcal{S}_2}$, includes two projections, p_2' and p_3', that are identical to s_2 and s_3, respectively, so $\mathcal{DF}_{s_2} = \mathcal{DF}_{p_2'}$ and $\mathcal{DF}_{s_3} = \mathcal{DF}_{p_3'}$: s_2 and s_3 are compatible with $\mathcal{DR}_{\mathcal{S}_2}$. The set $\mathcal{S}_2$ is realised by DTS $\xi_1 || \xi_2$, where $\xi_1 = (cab, \{\tau_{c,a} \leq 1, \tau_{c,b} \leq 3\})$ and $\xi_2 = (cad, \{\tau_{c,d} \leq 1\})$. So $\mathcal{S}$ is realised by $s_1 | (\xi_1 || \xi_2)$ (compare this with the trivial solution shown in Example 5).

In Example 5 we partitioned $\mathcal{S}$ into scenarios that are compatible with $\mathcal{DR}_{\mathcal{S}}$, and those that are not. But sometimes none of the members of $\mathcal{S}$ will be compatible with $\mathcal{DR}_{\mathcal{S}}$, so we need another criterion for partitioning.

Definition 16. *Let $\mathcal{S}$ be an order-closed set of scenarios and $sc \in \mathcal{S}$. The constraint-based disagreement between sc and $\mathcal{DR}_\mathcal{S}$ is $dsg_\mathcal{S}(sc) = \{(e, e') \mid e \prec_{sc} e' \wedge \mathcal{DF}_{sc}(e, e') \neq \mathcal{DF}_p(e, e') where p is the projection of \mathcal{DR}_\mathcal{S} that matches sc\}$.*

Definition 17. *Let $\mathcal{S}$ be an order-closed set of scenarios over $\Sigma_\mathcal{S}$, such that none of its members are compatible with $\mathcal{DR}_\mathcal{S}$ and $|\mathcal{S}| > 1$. Let $e, e' \in \Sigma_\mathcal{S}$. The constraint-based division (CBD for short) of $\mathcal{S}$ with respect to (e, e'), denoted by $cbd_\mathcal{S}(e, e')$, is the unordered pair $(\mathcal{S}_1, \mathcal{S}_2)$, such that*

(1) $\mathcal{S}_1 = \{sc \in \mathcal{S} \mid (e, e') \in dsg_\mathcal{S}(sc)\}$ and $\mathcal{S}_2 = \mathcal{S} \setminus \mathcal{S}_1$, or
(2) $(e, e') \notin dsg_\mathcal{S}(sc)$ for any $sc \in \mathcal{S}$ and there exists some $sc' \in \mathcal{S}$, where $e \prec_{sc'} e' \wedge \mathcal{DF}_{sc'}(e, e') \neq [0, \infty]$, then $\mathcal{S}_1 = \{s \in \mathcal{S} \mid e \prec_s e'\}$ and $\mathcal{S}_2 = \mathcal{S} \setminus \mathcal{S}_1$.

Intuitively, if $cbd_\mathcal{S}(e, e') = (\mathcal{S}_1, \mathcal{S}_2)$ is formed by case (1) of Definition 17, then all the members of $\mathcal{S}_1$ disagree with their respective matching projections on the interval for (e, e'), i.e., on $\mathcal{DF}(e, e')$. In this case, if $s_2 \in \mathcal{S}_2$, then either $\mathcal{DF}_{s_2}(e, e') = \mathcal{DF}_{p_2}(e, e')$, where p_2 is the projection that matches s_2, or $e \not\prec_{s_2} e'$. Notice that $\mathcal{S}_1 \neq \emptyset$, but $\mathcal{S}_2$ can be empty. If $\mathcal{S}_2 = \emptyset$, then $(\mathcal{S}_1, \mathcal{S}_2)$ is *not* a CBD.

If $cbd_\mathcal{S}(e, e') = (\mathcal{S}_1, \mathcal{S}_2)$ is formed by case (2), then all the members of $\mathcal{S}_1$ agree with their respective matching projections on the interval for (e, e'), however, at least one of them has a non-default interval on (e, e').

Example 6. Let $\mathcal{S} = \{s_1, s_2\}$, where $s_1 = (abc, \{1 \leq \tau_{a,b} \leq 2\})$ and $s_2 = (acb, \{2 \leq \tau_{a,b} \leq 3\})$. The partial order in $\mathcal{S}$, $\prec_\mathcal{S} = \prec_{s_1} \cap \prec_{s_2}$, is represented by $a - b$ and $a - c$. The distance functions of the members of $\mathcal{S}$ are $\mathcal{DF}_{s_1} = \{(a, b, 1, 2), (a, c, 1, \infty)\}$ and $\mathcal{DF}_{s_2} = \{(a, b, 2, 3), (a, c, 0, 3), (c, b, 0, 3)\}$.

Observe that the smallest interval that includes $\mathcal{DF}_{s_1}(a, b) = [1, 2]$ and $\mathcal{DF}_{s_2}(a, b) = [2, 3]$ is $[1, 3]$, so $\mathcal{DF}_\mathcal{S}(a, b) = [1, 3]$. Similarly, $\mathcal{DF}_\mathcal{S}(a, c) = [0, \infty]$ is the smallest interval that includes $\mathcal{DF}_{s_1}(a, c) = [1, \infty]$ and $\mathcal{DF}_{s_2}(a, c) = [0, 3]$. Therefore, $\mathcal{DF}_\mathcal{S}$ is represented by $\{(a, b, 1, 3)\}$ (recall that we do not show the default intervals).

The projections of $\mathcal{DR}_\mathcal{S}$ yield $\mathcal{DF}_{p_1} = \{(a, b, 1, 3), (a, c, 1, \infty)\}$ and $\mathcal{DF}_{p_2} = \{(a, b, 1, 3), (a, c, 0, 3), (c, b, 0, 3)\}$, where s_1 matches p_1 and s_2 matches p_2. None of the members of $\mathcal{S}$ are compatible with $\mathcal{DR}_\mathcal{S}$: $dsg_\mathcal{S}(s_1) = dsg_\mathcal{S}(s_2) = \{(a, b)\}$. By case (1) of Definition 17, $cbd_\mathcal{S}(a, b) = (\{s_1, s_2\}, \emptyset)$. However, $\mathcal{DF}_{s_1}(b, c) = [0, \infty]$ and $\mathcal{DF}_{s_2}(c, b) = [0, 3] \neq [0, \infty]$, so, by case (2) of Definition 17, $cbd_\mathcal{S}(b, c) = (\{s_1\}, \{s_2\})$.

Theorem 1. *Let $\mathcal{S}$ be an order-closed set of scenarios, such that none of its members is compatible with $\mathcal{DR}_\mathcal{S}$ and $|\mathcal{S}| > 1$. Then there is at least one pair of events e and e' such that $cbd_\mathcal{S}(e, e') = (\mathcal{S}_1, \mathcal{S}_2)$, where $\mathcal{S}_1 \neq \emptyset$ and $\mathcal{S}_2 \neq \emptyset$.*

In general, $\mathcal{S}$ might have more than one CBD, so we need a criterion for comparing them.

Definition 18. *Let $\mathcal{S}$ be an order-closed set of scenarios and $s_i, s_j \in \mathcal{S}$ $(i \neq j)$. The c-distance of s_i and s_j, denoted by $d_c(s_i, s_j)$, is $|\{cbd_\mathcal{S}(e, e') = (\mathcal{S}_1, \mathcal{S}_2) \mid \mathcal{S}_1 \neq \emptyset \wedge \mathcal{S}_2 \neq \emptyset \wedge ((s_i \in \mathcal{S}_1 \wedge s_j \in \mathcal{S}_2) \vee (s_i \in \mathcal{S}_2 \wedge s_j \in \mathcal{S}_1))\}|$.*

Intuitively, the c-distance between s_i and s_j is the number of times that s_i and s_j would wind up in different partitions of CBDs. The smaller the c-distance, the more similar are the constraints of the scenarios.

Definition 19. *Let $\mathcal{S}$ be an order-closed set of scenarios. The* c-ranking *of $\mathcal{S}$, denoted by $r_c(\mathcal{S})$, is the average of all pairwise c-distances between its members.*

Definition 20. *Let $\mathcal{S}$ be an order-closed set of scenarios and $D = (\mathcal{S}_1, \mathcal{S}_2)$ be a CBD of $\mathcal{S}$. The* c-ranking *of D, denoted by $r_c(D)$, is given by $r_c(\mathcal{S}_1) + r_c(\mathcal{S}_2)$.*

Example 7. Consider the set $\mathcal{S} = \{s_1, s_2, s_3\}$, where $s_1 = (acdb, \{\tau_{d,b} \geq 2\})$, $s_2 = (adbc, \{\tau_{d,c} \geq 2\})$ and $s_3 = (adcb, \{\tau_{d,b} \geq 2\})$. The set $\mathcal{S}$ is order-closed, but not realisable by a DTS. The distance functions of its members are $\mathcal{DF}_{s_1} = \{(a,b,2,\infty), (c,b,2,\infty), (d,b,2,\infty)\}$, $\mathcal{DF}_{s_2} = \{(a,c,2,\infty), (d,c,2,\infty)\}$ and $\mathcal{DF}_{s_3} = \{(a,b,2,\infty), (d,b,2,\infty)\}$.

The partial order in $\mathcal{S}$, $\prec_{\mathcal{S}}$, is represented by $a-d-b$ and $a-c$, while $\mathcal{DF}_{\mathcal{S}}$ has only default intervals. The projections of $\mathcal{DR}_{\mathcal{S}}$ are $p_1 = (acdb, \emptyset)$, $p_2 = (adbc, \emptyset)$ and $p_3 = (adcb, \emptyset)$. So none of the members of $\mathcal{S}$ are compatible with $\mathcal{DR}_{\mathcal{S}}$.

The constraint-based disagreement between members of $\mathcal{S}$ and $\mathcal{DR}_{\mathcal{S}}$ are $dsg_{\mathcal{S}}(s_1) = \{(a,b), (c,b), (d,b)\}$, $dsg_{\mathcal{S}}(s_2) = \{(a,c), (d,c)\}$ and $dsg_{\mathcal{S}}(s_3) = \{(a,b), (d,b)\}$, while $cbd_{\mathcal{S}}(a,b) = cbd_{\mathcal{S}}(d,b) = (\{s_1, s_3\}, \{s_2\})$, $cbd_{\mathcal{S}}(a,c) = cbd_{\mathcal{S}}(d,c) = (\{s_2\}, \{s_1, s_3\})$ and $cbd_{\mathcal{S}}(c,b) = (\{s_1\}, \{s_2, s_3\})$.
This analysis leads to divisions $D_1 = (\{s_2\}, \{s_1, s_3\})$ and $D_2 = (\{s_1\}, \{s_2, s_3\})$, which have equal o-rankings and K-rankings, so we compare their c-rankings: $r_c(\{s_2\}) = 0$, $r_c(\{s_1, s_3\}) = d_c(s_1, s_3) = |\{cbd_{\mathcal{S}}(c,b)\}| = 1$, $r_c(\{s_1\}) = 0$ and $r_c(\{s_2, s_3\}) = d_c(s_2, s_3) = |\{cbd_{\mathcal{S}}(a,b), cbd_{\mathcal{S}}(a,c), cbd_{\mathcal{S}}(d,b), cbd_{\mathcal{S}}(d,c)\}| = 4$. So $r_c(D_1) = 0 + 1 = 1$ and $r_c(D_2) = 0 + 4 = 4$.

In D_1, $\{s_1, s_3\}$ is realisable by the DTS $\xi_1 \| \xi_2$, where $\xi_1 = (acb, \{\tau_{a,b} \geq 2\})$ and $\xi_2 = (adb, \{\tau_{d,b} \geq 2\})$. So $\mathcal{S}$ is realised by $(\xi_1 \| \xi_2) | s_2$. If we choose D_2 (which has the higher c-ranking), even though $\{s_2, s_3\}$ is order-closed, its members would not be compatible with the distance relation of the set. So we would have to divide the set once more and end up with the trivial expression $s_1 | s_2 | s_3$.

As shown above, if none of the members of an order-closed set, $\mathcal{S}$, are compatible with $\mathcal{DR}_{\mathcal{S}}$, then we compute all the CBDs of $\mathcal{S}$ and choose the one with the lowest o-ranking. We break a tie by choosing the CBD with the lowest K-ranking. If K-rankings cannot break a tie, we choose a division with the lowest c-ranking, and if necessary we use l-rankings to break a tie.

Theorem 2. *A finite set, $\mathcal{S}$, of sequential scenarios is realisable by a single DTS iff it is order-closed and every member of it is compatible with $\mathcal{DR}_{\mathcal{S}}$.*

We now present an algorithm that solves the problem of realisability of a set of scenarios as a scenario expression.

Function realise(a set of scenarios $\mathcal{S}$)

---

  if $|\mathcal{S}| = 1$ **then**

    $\lfloor\ E := s$, where $\mathcal{S} = \{s\}$;   /* trivially realisable by DTS s */

  else if $\neg order\text{-}closed(\mathcal{S})$ **then**

    $(\mathcal{S}_1, \mathcal{S}_2) := partition\text{-}order(\mathcal{S})$;

    $E := realise(\mathcal{S}_1)|realise(\mathcal{S}_2)$;

  else /* $\mathcal{S}$ is order-closed */

    $C := compatible(\mathcal{S})$;   /* compatible members of $\mathcal{S}$ */

    if $C = \mathcal{S}$ **then**

      $\lfloor\ E := realise\text{-}DTS(\mathcal{S})$;   /* Thm 2: a DTS realises $\mathcal{S}$ */

    else

      if $C \neq \emptyset \wedge C \neq \mathcal{S}$ **then**

        $\lfloor\ E := realise(C)|realise(\mathcal{S} \setminus C)$;

      else

        $(\mathcal{S}_1, \mathcal{S}_2) := partition\text{-}const(\mathcal{S})$;

        $E := realise(\mathcal{S}_1)|realise(\mathcal{S}_2)$;

  return E;

4.3   The Algorithm

Our algorithm is implemented as function *realise*, which takes a set of normalised scenarios, $\mathcal{S}$. The sequences of events in all members of $\mathcal{S}$ contain the same events, but each sequence is unique. The function iteratively performs the following:

- If $\mathcal{S} = \{s\}$, i.e., a singleton, then *realise* returns the expression s.
- If $\mathcal{S}$ is not a singleton and is not order-closed, then *realise* invokes function *partition-order*, which returns the best OBD. Then *realise* is recursively invoked on each partition of the division.
- If $\mathcal{S}$ is order-closed, and
  - all its members are compatible with $\mathcal{DR}_{\mathcal{S}}$, then $\mathcal{S}$ is realisable by a DTS (Theorem 2). In that case, *realise-DTS* [8] is invoked, which returns the DTS that realises $\mathcal{S}$.
  - some, but not all of its members are compatible with $\mathcal{DR}_{\mathcal{S}}$, then $\mathcal{S}$ is divided into two partitions of compatible and not compatible scenarios. Then *realise* is recursively invoked on each partition.
  - none of its members are compatible with $\mathcal{DR}_{\mathcal{S}}$, then function *partition-const* is called, which returns the best CBD (by Thm. 1 there is such a CBD). Then *realise* is recursively invoked on each partition of the CBD.

To avoid additional clutter we do not show the details of dealing with gaps (see Sect. 4, p. 9). Before every invocation of *realise* the argument is partitioned, if necessary, into sets with no gaps: *realise* is then called on each of these partitions separately, and the results are combined in a choice expression.

    The function *order-closed* checks whether a set of scenarios is order-closed.

Function partition-order(a set of scenarios $\mathcal{S}$)

$not\text{-}ordered := \{(e, e') \in \Sigma_{\mathcal{S}} \mid e \not\prec_{\mathcal{S}} e' \wedge e' \not\prec_{\mathcal{S}} e\};$
$D := (\emptyset, \emptyset, \infty, \infty, \infty);$ /* best OBD, so far */
foreach $(e, e') \in not\text{-}ordered$ **do**
$\quad$ $\mathcal{S}_1 := \{s \in \mathcal{S} \mid e \prec_s e'\};$
$\quad$ $\mathcal{S}_2 := \{s \in \mathcal{S} \mid e' \prec_s e\};$
$\quad$ $k\text{-}obd := g_k\text{-}rank(\mathcal{S}_1) * |\mathcal{S}_1|/|\mathcal{S}| + g_k\text{-}rank(\mathcal{S}_2) * |\mathcal{S}_2|/|\mathcal{S}|;$
$\quad$ **if** $better\text{-}ok(\mathcal{S}_1, \mathcal{S}_2, D, k\text{-}obd) \vee better\text{-}l(\mathcal{S}_1, \mathcal{S}_2, D, k\text{-}obd)$ **then**
$\quad\quad$ $D := (\mathcal{S}_1, \mathcal{S}_2, o\text{-}rk(\mathcal{S}_1, \mathcal{S}_2), k\text{-}obd, l\text{-}rk(\mathcal{S}_1, \mathcal{S}_2));$

return $(p_1(D), p_2(D));$

Function compatible(a set of scenarios $\mathcal{S}$)

$C := \emptyset;$ /* the set of compatible scenarios in $\mathcal{S}$ */
foreach $sc \in \mathcal{S}$ **do**
$\quad$ **if** $\mathcal{DF}_{sc} = \mathcal{DF}_p$, where $p \in \mathcal{P}_{\mathcal{S}}$ and sc matches p **then**
$\quad\quad$ $C := C \cup \{sc\};$

return $C;$

Function better-ok(set $\mathcal{S}_1$, set $\mathcal{S}_2$, division D, int k)

---

return $o\text{-}rk(\mathcal{S}_1, \mathcal{S}_2) < o\text{-}rk(p_1(D), p_2(D)) \vee$
$(o\text{-}rk(\mathcal{S}_1, \mathcal{S}_2) = o\text{-}rk(p_1(D), p_2(D)) \wedge k < K\text{-}rk(p_1(D), p_2(D)));$

Function better-l(set $\mathcal{S}_1$, set $\mathcal{S}_2$, division D, int k)

---

return $o\text{-}rk(\mathcal{S}_1, \mathcal{S}_2) = o\text{-}rk(p_1(D), p_2(D)) \wedge k = K\text{-}rk(p_1(D), p_2(D)) \wedge$
$l\text{-}rk(\mathcal{S}_1, \mathcal{S}_2) < l\text{-}rk(p_1(D), p_2(D));$

Function better-c(set $\mathcal{S}_1$, set $\mathcal{S}_2$, division D, int k, int c)

---

return $o\text{-}rk(\mathcal{S}_1, \mathcal{S}_2) = o\text{-}rk(p_1(D), p_2(D)) \wedge k = K\text{-}rk(p_1(D), p_2(D)) \wedge$
$c < c\text{-}rk(p_1(D), p_2(D));$

Function better-cl(set $\mathcal{S}_1$, set $\mathcal{S}_2$, division D, int k, int c)

---

return $o\text{-}rk(\mathcal{S}_1, \mathcal{S}_2) = o\text{-}rk(p_1(D), p_2(D)) \wedge k = K\text{-}rk(p_1(D), p_2(D)) \wedge$
$c = c\text{-}rk(p_1(D), p_2(D)) \wedge l\text{-}rk(\mathcal{S}_1, \mathcal{S}_2) < l\text{-}rk(p_1(D), p_2(D));$

In function *partition-order* variable D keeps track of the best OBD found so far. It is a five-tuple, $(\mathcal{S}_1, \mathcal{S}_2, r_o, r_k, r_l)$: the items are the two partitions, the o-ranking, the K-ranking and the l-ranking, respectively. In function *partition-const* the variable D, which is a six-tuple $(\mathcal{S}_1, \mathcal{S}_2, r_o, r_k, r_c, r_l)$,

---

Function partition-const(a set of scenarios $\mathcal{S}$)

```
/* invoked when |S| > 1 and none of the members of S is compatible
   with DR_S. */
```

$ordered := \{(e, e') \in \Sigma_\mathcal{S} \mid e \prec_s e' \text{ for some } s \in \mathcal{S}\};$

$CBDs := CDGs := \emptyset;$

foreach $sc \in \mathcal{S}$ **do**
$\quad\lfloor\ CDGs := CDGs \cup dsg(sc);$

foreach $(e, e') \in CDGs$ **do**
$\quad\mid\ \mathcal{S}_1 := \{s \in \mathcal{S} \mid e \prec_s e' \wedge \mathcal{DF}_s(e, e') \neq \mathcal{DF}_p(e, e')(s \text{ matches } p \in \mathcal{P}_\mathcal{S})\};$
$\quad\mid\ \mathcal{S}_2 := \mathcal{S} \setminus \mathcal{S}_1;$
$\quad\mid\ \textbf{if } \mathcal{S}_2 \neq \emptyset \textbf{ then } \texttt{/* } \mathcal{S}_1 \neq \emptyset \texttt{ */}$
$\quad\mid\quad\lfloor\ CBDs := CBDs \cup \{\{\mathcal{S}_1, \mathcal{S}_2\}\};$

foreach $(e, e') \in ordered \setminus CDGs$ **do**
$\quad\mid\ \textbf{if } there\ exists\ sc \in \mathcal{S},\ such\ that\ (e \prec_s e' \wedge \mathcal{DF}_s(e, e') \neq [0, \infty]) \textbf{ then}$
$\quad\mid\quad\mid\ \mathcal{S}_1 := \{s \in \mathcal{S} \mid e \prec_s e'\};$
$\quad\mid\quad\mid\ \mathcal{S}_2 := \mathcal{S} \setminus \mathcal{S}_1;$
$\quad\mid\quad\lfloor\ CBDs := CBDs \cup \{\{\mathcal{S}_1, \mathcal{S}_2\}\};$

$D := (\emptyset, \emptyset, \infty, \infty, \infty, \infty);$ $\qquad\qquad\qquad$ `/* best CBD, so far */`

foreach $\{\mathcal{S}_1, \mathcal{S}_2\} \in CBDs$ **do**
$\quad\mid\ k\text{-}cbd := g_k\text{-}rank(\mathcal{S}_1) * |\mathcal{S}_1|/|\mathcal{S}| + g_k\text{-}rank(\mathcal{S}_2) * |\mathcal{S}_2|/|\mathcal{S}|;$
$\quad\mid\ c\text{-}cbd := g_c\text{-}rank(\mathcal{S}_1) + g_c\text{-}rank(\mathcal{S}_2);$
$\quad\mid\ \textbf{if } better\text{-}ok(\mathcal{S}_1, \mathcal{S}_2, D, k\text{-}cbd) \vee better\text{-}c(\mathcal{S}_1, \mathcal{S}_2, D, k\text{-}cbd, c\text{-}cbd) \vee$
$\quad\mid\ \ better\text{-}cl(\mathcal{S}_1, \mathcal{S}_2, D, k\text{-}cbd, c\text{-}cbd) \textbf{ then}$
$\quad\mid\quad\lfloor\ D := (\mathcal{S}_1, \mathcal{S}_2, o\text{-}rk(\mathcal{S}_1, \mathcal{S}_2), k\text{-}cbd, c\text{-}cbd, l\text{-}rk(\mathcal{S}_1, \mathcal{S}_2));$

$return\ (p_1(D), p_2(D));$

---

keeps track of the best CBD found so far. The additional item is the c-ranking. Given a tuple D, functions p_1 and p_2 return $\mathcal{S}_1$ and $\mathcal{S}_2$. Functions o-rk, K-rk, l-rk and c-rk return the o-ranking, K-ranking, c-ranking and l-ranking of $(\mathcal{S}_1, \mathcal{S}_2)$; g_k-$rank$ and g_c-$rank$ are the K-ranking and the c-ranking of a partition.

Let N be the number of scenarios in $\mathcal{S}$ and L be the length of each scenario in $\mathcal{S}$. In the worst case the number of divisions constructed by the algorithm is $O(N)$. For each partition of a division the worst-case time complexity of constructing the distance relation is $O(N * L^2)$ (for the construction of the partial order) plus $O(L^3)$ (for the stabilisation of the distance function). The overall cost of creating the projections of the distance relation is $O(N * L^3)$. Checking the compatibility of each member of the partition with the distance relation of the partition costs $O(N * L^2)$. So the cost of treating one partition is $O(N * L^3)$. Since there are at most $O(N)$ divisions, the overall worst-case time complexity of the algorithm is $O(N^2 * L^3)$.

4.4 Revisiting an Assumption

In Sect. 4 we assumed that every member of the set of realised scenarios has a different sequence of events. In this section we discuss how to relax that assumption. Our method is best explained by an example.

Assume that we have already performed the initial partitioning (see p. 8), and that our current task is to realise the set of scenarios S, such that, for every $\xi, \eta \in S$, $\Sigma_\xi = \Sigma_\eta$. Moreover, $S = S_A \cup S_B \cup S'$, where

- $S_A = \{A_1, A_2, A_3\}$ and $eseq(A_1) = eseq(A_2) = eseq(A_3)$;
- $S_B = \{B_1, B_2\}$ and $eseq(B_1) = eseq(B_2) \neq eseq(A_1)$;
- every member of S' has a sequence of events that is unique in S.

Each projection of a DTS has a unique sequence of events, so the expression that realises S must have at least three alternatives: one for each member of S_A. However, it is possible that, say, A_2 and B_1 are projections of the same DTS. The question is how to pair the right A with the right B.

A way to address this question is to investigate all the combinations of members from S_A and S_B. More concretely, we create six sets of scenarios: $S_1 = \{A_1, B_1\} \cup S'$, $S_2 = \{A_1, B_2\} \cup S'$, $S_3 = \{A_2, B_1\} \cup S'$ etc. In each of these six sets every scenario has a unique sequence of events, so we can run our realisation algorithm separately for S_1, S_2 etc., to obtain six scenario expressions. From each of those scenario expressions we remove alternatives that realise only members of S', then find the best of the remaining expressions, i.e., one with the fewest alternatives. Let us say that it is an expression whose only alternative realises $\{A_3, B_2, D, F\}$ (where $D, F \in S'$). We retain this expression as a partial solution to the problem of realising S, and then repeat the process for $S \setminus \{A_3, B_2, D, F\}$ to find the other alternatives of the solution for S.

The problem with this approach is that the number of combinations to be investigated grows exponentially with the number of scenarios that have identical sequences. But as long as the number of combinations is not prohibitively large, the approach is quite effective.

5 Experimental Results

In Table 2 we show some experimental results for our realisation algorithm.

We have performed experiments for sets of scenarios with three different kinds of sizes, shown in the first column. For each size we considered three categories of scenarios according to their length, shown in the top row. For each kind of size and length we tried 5 different examples. Table 2 shows the minimum, maximum and average number of alternatives of the expressions generated for that set of examples, as well as the approximate running time of our entire program.

We compared these results with those from a program that performs a breadth-first search for an optimal solution (i.e., one with the minimum number of alternatives and as well-balanced as possible): in some of the cells those results are shown to the right of the vertical line. We were unable to do this for all the examples: for larger data the complete search becomes prohibitively long.

In two examples our algorithm yields 8 and 11 alternatives as opposed to the optimal 6 and 10 (see the second row of column one and column two).

Our experimental results confirm that our approach is very effective in identifying the divisions that lead to satisfactory realisations of sets of timed scenarios.

Table 2. Experimental results

$|\mathcal{S}|$	$5 \leq |sc| \leq 10$		$10 < |sc| \leq 15$		$15 < |sc|$	
	$2, 0.2$ s	$2, \quad 10.0$ s	$2, 0.2$ s	$2, \quad 0.5$ s	$3, \quad 3$ s	$3, 284.8$ s
≤ 10	$6, 0.4$ s	$6, \quad 51.4$ s	$8, 1.8$ s	$8, 278.2$ s	$7, \quad 5$ s	$7, \ 52.3$ s
	$4.2, 0.3$ s	$4.2, \quad 23.6$ s	$5.2, 1.1$ s	$5.2, \ 65.4$ s	$4.8, 3.8$ s	$4.8, 171.1$ s
	$3, 0.4$ s	$3, 1287.2$ s	$3, 2.0$ s	$3, \quad 7401.7$ s	$2, \ 2.6$ s	$2, \ 17866.5$ s
≤ 20	$8, 0.8$ s	$6, 1477.0$ s	$11, 2.9$ s	$10, 147597.7$ s	$10, 10.8$ s	$10, 251865.8$ s
	$4.8, 0.5$ s	$4.4, 4703.8$ s	$5.4, 2.2$ s	$5.2, \ 32438.6$ s	$6.8, 15.1$ s	$6.8, \quad 92812$ s
	$3, 0.9$ s		$3, \ 2$ s		$3, \quad 4.4$ s	
> 20	$10, 1.6$ s		$12, 4.8$ s		$17, 642.9$ s	
	$5.8, 1.2$ s		$6.6, 3.2$ s		$8.25, 247.6$ s	

6   Conclusions

We introduced the notion of timed scenario expressions (expressions for short) and their semantics. A distributed timed scenario (DTS) is an expression. Expressions are also built by applying three operators, $|$, $\circ$ and $\|$, to expressions. The operator $|$ specifies a choice between two alternatives, while $\circ$ and $\|$ indicate the concatenation and the parallel composition of two expressions. We defined $[\![E]\!]$, the semantics of expression E, in terms of the set of behaviours that are specified by E, and defined the consistency of E in terms of its semantics.

We tackled the problem of realisability of sets of (sequential) scenarios as scenario expressions. We developed an algorithm that, given a set of scenarios, $\mathcal{S}$, produces an expression E that realises $\mathcal{S}$, i.e., $[\![\mathcal{S}]\!] = [\![E]\!]$.

The set $\mathcal{S}$ can sometimes be realised by a single DTS. But, in general, realising $\mathcal{S}$ involves dividing it into partitions, in such a way that each partition can be realised by a single DTS. The choice expression whose alternatives are these distributed scenarios would realise $\mathcal{S}$.

We investigated the fundamental reasons when $\mathcal{S}$ is not realisble by a DTS. This investigation resulted in developing two methods for effectively dividing $\mathcal{S}$. One is based on reasoning about the underlying partial order in $\mathcal{S}$, and the other is based on the time constraints of $\mathcal{S}$. We identified the necessary and sufficient conditions for realisability of a set of scenarios as a single DTS (Theorem 2), and thereby solved the problem that was left open in our earlier work [8].

To illustrate the effectiveness of our approach we compared our algorithm with one that performs a complete breadth-first search to find an optimal solution, i.e., one with the minimum number of alternatives. Our experimental results confirm the effectiveness and efficiency of our algorithm.

As our future work we plan to incorporate the Kleene star operator in scenario expressions, and to explore the usefulness of machine learning for solving the problem of realisability.

References

1. Bejleri, A., Yoshida, N.: Synchronous multiparty session types. Electron. Notes Theoret. Comput. Sci. **241**, 3–33 (2009). Proceedings of the First Workshop on Programming Language Approaches to Concurrency and Communication-centric Software (PLACES 2008)
2. Castagna, G., Dezani-Ciancaglini, M., Padovani, L.: On global types and multiparty sessions. In: Bruni, R., Dingel, J. (eds.) Formal Techniques for Distributed Systems, pp. 1–28. Springer, Berlin, Heidelberg (2011)
3. Honda, K., Yoshida, N., Carbone, M.: Multiparty asynchronous session types. J. ACM **63**(1), 9:1–9:67 (2016)
4. Hüttel, H., et al.: Foundations of session types and behavioural contracts. ACM Comput. Surv. 49(1), 3:1–3:36 (2016)
5. Barbanera, F., Lanese, I., Tuosto, E.: Formal choreographic languages. In: ter Beek, M.H., Sirjani, M. (eds.) Coordination Models and Languages, pp. 121–139. Springer Nature Switzerland, Cham (2022)
6. ter Beek, M.H., Hennicker, R., Proença, J.: Realisability of global models of interaction. In: Ábrahám, E., Dubslaff, C., Tarifa, S.L.T. (eds.) Theoretical Aspects of Computing - ICTAC 2023, pp. 236–255. Springer Nature Switzerland, Cham (2023)
7. Saeedloei, N., Kluźniak, F.: Timed Scenarios: Consistency, Equivalence and Optimization. In: Massoni, T., Mousavi, M.R. (eds.) SBMF 2018. LNCS, vol. 11254, pp. 215–233. Springer, Cham (2018). https://doi.org/10.1007/978-3-030-03044-5_14
8. Saeedloei, N., Kluźniak, F.: Distributed timed scenarios. In: Damiani, F., Farrell, M. (eds.) Integrated Formal Methods - 20th International Conference, iFM 2025, Paris, France, November 19–21, 2025, Proceedings, Vol. 16194 of Lecture Notes in Computer Science, pp. 487–508. Springer, Cham (2025). https://doi.org/10.1007/978-3-032-10794-7_24
9. Dechter, R., Meiri, I., Pearl, J.: Temporal constraint networks. Artif. Intell. **49**(1), 61–95 (1991)
10. Harel, D., Thiagarajan, P.S.: Message Sequence Charts, pp. 77–105. Springer, US, Boston, MA (2003)
11. ITU-T recommendation Z.120. Message Sequence Charts (MSC'96), ITU Telecommunication Standardization Sector (1996)
12. Balaguer, S., Chatain, T., Haar, S.: A concurrency-preserving translation from time petri nets to networks of timed automata. Formal Methods Syst. Des. **40**(3), 330–355 (2012)
13. Alur, R., Etessami, K., Yannakakis, M.: Inference of message sequence charts. IEEE Trans. Softw. Eng. **29**(7), 623–633 (2003)
14. Guanciale, R., Tuosto, E.: Realisability of pomsets. J. Logical Algebraic Methods Program. **108**, 69–89 (2019). https://doi.org/https://doi.org/10.1016/j.jlamp.2019.06.003
15. ter Beek, M.H., Hennicker, R., Proença, J.: Team automata: Overview and roadmap. In: Castellani, I., Tiezzi, F. (eds.) Coordination Models and Languages, pp. 161–198. Springer Nature Switzerland, Cham (2024)

16. Alur, R., Dill, D.L.: A theory of timed automata. Theor. Comput. Sci. **126**(2), 183–235 (1994)
17. Kendall, M.G.: A new measure of rank correlation. Biometrika **30**, 81–93 (1938)

HistMSO: a Logic for Reasoning About Consistency Models with MONA

Isabelle Coget[1] and Etienne Lozes[2(✉)][ID]

[1] Institut Polytechnique de Paris, Palaiseau, France
[2] Université Côte d'Azur, CNRS, I3S, Sophia Antipolis, France
`etienne.lozes@univ-cotedazur.fr`

Abstract. Reasoning about consistency models for replicated data systems is a challenging task that requires a deep understanding of both the consistency models themselves and a large part of human inputs in mechanized verification approaches.

In this work, we introduce an approach to reasoning about consistency models for replicated data systems. We introduce HistMSO, a monadic second-order logic (MSO) for histories and abstract executions, the formal models of executions of replicated data systems introduced by Burckhardt. We show that HistMSO can express 39 out of 42 consistency models from Viotti and Vukolic hierarchy. Moreover, we develop a method for reducing HistMSO satisfiability and model-checking to the same problems for MSO over words. While doing this, we leverage the MONA tool for automated reasoning on consistency models.

Keywords: Replicated data systems · Consistency models · Automated verification

1 Introduction

Replicated data systems consist of multiple agents (or processes) that maintain copies (replicas) of shared data objects. These agents perform operations, such as reads and writes, on the replicas. Due to network delays and the asynchronous nature of distributed systems, these operations may not be immediately visible to all agents, leading to potential inconsistencies among replicas. The replicated data system abstraction is widely used in various applications, including distributed databases, cloud storage systems, or fully decentralized storage systems such as blockchains or peer-to-peer networks. To some extent, consistency models are also related with weak memory models employed in hardware design [22]. An important aspect of replicated data systems is that they often prioritize availability and partition tolerance over strong consistency guarantees. Since the strongest consistency model, linearisability [16], is too costly to implement in many practical applications, replicated data systems often implement weaker consistency models (often called *isolation level* in the database community).

R. Casadei and F. Ghassemi (Eds.): COORDINATION 2026, LNCS 16590, pp. 26–46, 2026.
https://doi.org/10.1007/978-3-032-28358-0_2

Monotonic reads, monotonic writes, read my writes, eventual consistency, etc. are among the most popular ones of the lush jungle of consistency models. Viotti and Vukolić [24] inventoried 42 consistency models in 2016, and formally established the complex hierarchy they form (see Fig. 1 in [24]).

Following Burckhardt [6], a consistency model is a property that an execution of a replicated data system must satisfy. The model of execution of a replicated data system introduced by Burckhardt, called a *history*, bases on a collection of *operations*, each located on a precise process. Each operation also lasts on a time interval that may partially overlap the time interval of another operation located on a different process. Like a Gantt diagram, a history therefore combines a partial order on operations and a continuous model of time. The history model is however often too simple for grounding a consistency model. Indeed, several consistency models rely on a logical justification of the way how the operations that compose a given history are related to each others. This justification may contradict the partial order and the timings of the operations. Burckhardt [6] therefore also introduced *abstract executions*, that enrich histories with two binary relations among operations, called *visibility* and *arbitration*.

In this work, we address the problem of automated reasoning on consistency models. Due to the combination of partial orderness and continuous time we just mentioned, it is not obvious which verification models, techniques and tools are the most appropriate for histories and abstract executions (see discussion in conclusion). Our proposal in this work is to leverage MONA [20], and more generally MSO-to-automata translations, for automated reasoning on consistency models. MONA models, which are words over a finite alphabet, do not have a lot in common with histories. As a consequence, this requires a significant work for encoding the latter in the former. The choice of MONA also enforces some finiteness limitations, like a bounded, fixed, number of processes, or finitely many values (see conclusion for a detailed discussion on the limitations), which might be compensated by further applications of the automata-based approach (see also discussion in conclusion).

This work stems from an attempt to draw a parallel between communication models and consistency models. This work indeed is partly influenced by previous works of the second author on tree decompositions of message sequence charts for some weakly-synchronous communication models [13]. Taking a step back in abstraction, we may address the question of automated reasoning on consistency model by transferring the tree decomposition techniques developed for message-passing concurrency to the realm of replicated data systems.

To sum up, we make the following contributions.

1. We introduce HistMSO, the monadic second order logic of histories and abstract executions.
2. We show that HistMSO can express 39 out of the 42 consistency models studied by Viotti and Vukolić [24]; remarkably, this result is quite straightforward, and follows from a translation of the meta logic used by Viotti and Vukolić into HistMSO, based on rather standard MSO encoding techniques

for expressing transitive closures, finiteness of sets defined by set comprehension, etc.

3. We show that the HistMSO theory of histories is decidable, by reducing the satisfiability problem of HistMSO to the one of MSO over infinite words. Moreover, our reduction also leverages MONA [20] as a practical theorem prover for the (weak) HistMSO theory of finite histories.
4. We introduce k-transient visibility, a restriction on the visibility relation, and we show that the HistMSO theory of real-time, k-transient abstract executions is decidable.
5. We show that the partial order defined by the timings of the operations of a given history is the transitive closure of a graph whose cutwidth is bounded by the square of the number of processes; since the treewidth is bounded by the cutwidth, this result induces in particular a tree decomposition of histories bounded by the number of processes and draws a parallel with the second author's previous work.

Outline. Section 2 recalls the models of histories and abstract executions. In Sect. 3 we introduce HistMSO logic and show on a few representative examples how to axiomatise the majority of consistency models studied by Viotti and Vukolic. Section 4 develops the translation of HistMSO to MONA, first for histories, then for k-transient real-time abstract executions. Section 5 constructs a graph from an history whose transitive closure captures the returns before partial order over operations, and establishes a bound on the cutwidth of the graph that only depends on the number or processes. Due to space constraints, some details and proofs are omitted and can be found in the full version of the paper [8].

Related Works. Logical axiomatisations of communication models can be found in [7,13,14]. Recent works on histories try to remove the arbitration relation from abstract executions [2]. MONA was already applied to a wide range of applications, including reactive systems [19], pointer programs [18], hardware verification [3], or parsing [10]. There are several other automated verification techniques and tools that could have been considered instead of MONA, each with its own drawbacks (MONA being the finiteness assumptions we already mentioned). Several model-checking tools are well suited for discrete time, with an interleaving semantics of parallelism (like SPIN [17] or TLA+ [26], to quote a very few), but they miss continuous-time. Timed automata [1] and the model-checking tools based on them [4,5], on the other hand, do not handle any partial

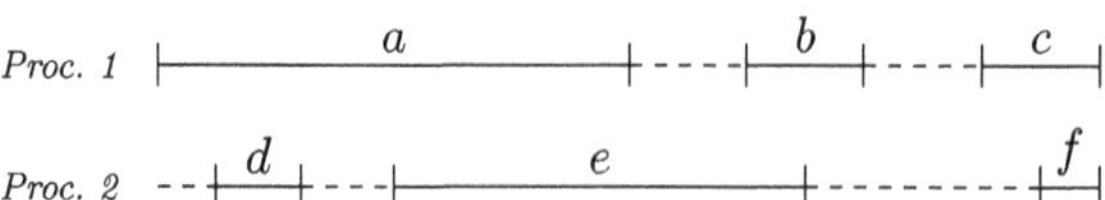

Fig. 1. A history on two processes, with operations a, b, c, d, e and f.

order beyond the total order of events defined by their timings. Automated theorem provers [21, 25] and SMT solvers [11] are quite versatile, but with a limited support of quantifiers, specifically when quantifying over a binary relation. Interval Temporal Logics aim at automated reasoning on Gantt diagrams, but the strong theoretical results developed in this research community are not so well tools supported. That said, it is unclear to us whether some of these techniques, and the recent advances in each of these research communities, could not compete with our MONA-based approach, either on satisfiability and automated reasoning, or on runtime, distributed monitoring and model-checking.

2   Background

Tracking the sequence of computed actions in replicated data systems can be achieved through various methods. In this paper, we base our approach on the notion of histories defined in [24]. A history of a program execution is defined as a set of *operations* that represent all the actions performed during the computation.

Histories can be visualized as timelines, where each process is represented by a horizontal line aligned to a global clock (see Fig. 1). The execution of an operation is shown as a solid segment, while dashed segments indicate periods when the process is idle. These timelines are read from left to right. Each operation has the following attributes: the process running the operation, the invocation time, the return time, the type[1] of operation, the object on which the operation takes effect, the input value of the operation and the output value of the operation. Since our objective is to encode these histories as words over a finite alphabet, for analysis using MONA, we make the assumption that the non-temporal attributes belong to finite sets of possible values. Without this finiteness assumption, the encodings presented in this paper would only work with an infinite alphabet.

Thereby we assume a set $\mathbb{P}$ of processes from which operations are launched, a set $\mathbb{T}$ of types of operations, and a set $\mathbb{O}$ of objects, which are the data to be modified or read by operations (objects can be registers or variables for instance). Also, we define the set of values as $\mathbb{V} \cup \{\nabla, \Phi\}$ where $\mathbb{V}$ is the set of values that can be read or written on objects. Symbol Φ represents a non-relevant or not needed value. For instance, we can claim that for a write operation, the input value is the value to be written, and the output value is Φ; as a write operation does not necessarily need to return anything. Finally, ∇ stands for the "output value" of an operation that never returns. Concretely, ∇ represents the absence of a return value due to a never ending operation.

As explained above we assume $\mathbb{P}, \mathbb{T}, \mathbb{O}, \mathbb{V}$ finite.

Invocation and return times are defined in $\mathbb{R}_{>0} \cup \{+\infty\}$. We include $+\infty$ to represent operations that never return. Assigning $+\infty$ as a return time reflects

---

[1] following [24] terminology; however, it might be more accurate to think about it as the *method name* of the replicated object; in this paper we consider that operations are of type either *read* or *write*.

that, beyond a certain point, the operation is considered to never terminate; invocation time however is always finite. These timestamps refer to an ideal and global notion of time that we use to reason about histories a posteriori, although it may not be accessible by processes during executions.

We recall the attributes from [24] along with their respective domains. The set of operation attributes is

$$\text{Attributes} = \{proc, stime, rtime, type, obj, ival, oval\}$$

An operation o is thus defined as a record containing these attributes, with values taken from the following domains (throughout the paper, we use the notation $o.a$ to denote the value of a given attribute a of an operation o):

* $o.proc \in \mathbb{P}$ is the process on which the operation o is executed
* $o.stime \in \mathbb{R}^+$ is the invocation time of o
* $o.rtime \in \mathbb{R}^+ \cup \{+\infty\}$ is the return time of o, $+\infty$ if the operation never returns (we assume that for any operation o, it holds that $o.stime < o.rtime$)
* $o.type \in \mathbb{T}$ is the type of operation o
* $o.obj \in \mathbb{O}$ is the object on which the operation o takes effect
* $o.ival \in \mathbb{V}$ is the input value of o, Φ if the operation is a *read*
* $o.oval \in \mathbb{V}$ is the output value of o, Φ if the operation is a write, and ∇ if the operation does not return

Two operations a and b are said to be *concurrent* if their execution times overlap, *i.e.* if $a.stime \leq b.rtime$ and $b.stime \leq a.rtime$. Otherwise, the operations are *sequential*. Note that if an operation never returns, it is concurrent with all operations that start after its invocation time. We assume in this paper that two concurrent operations cannot run on the same process.[2] We say that a *returns-before* b, denoted as $a \xrightarrow{rb} b$, if a returns before b starts, i.e. $a.rtime < b.stime$. We say that a is in the *same session* as b, denoted as $a \approx_{ss} b$, if a and b are running on the same process, i.e. $a.proc = b.proc$; we also say that a and b are in the *session order*, $a \xrightarrow{so} b$, if $a \approx_{ss} b$ and $a \xrightarrow{rb} b$.

Example 1. In Fig. 1, operations a and d are concurrent, whereas operation a returns before operation f; operations a and b are in the same session.

We say that two operations a and b are extremity-disjoint if $a.stime$, $a.rtime$, $b.stime$ and $b.rtime$ are pairwise distinct.

Definition 1 (History). *A history over $\mathbb{P}$, $\mathbb{T}$, $\mathbb{O}$, and $\mathbb{V}$ is a finite set H of operations such that for every pair of distinct operations $a, b \in H$, (1) a and b are extremity-disjoint, and (2) if $a \approx_{ss} b$, then a and b are sequential.*

---

[2] This is important for the translation of histories to words over a <u>finite</u> alphabet we present later. We could however relax this assumption by bounding the number of concurrent operations per process, which would serve modeling multi-threaded processes or operation/method calls inside an operation.

A history is finite if it contains a finite number of operations. The set of finite histories over $\mathbb{P}$, $\mathbb{T}$, $\mathbb{O}$, and $\mathbb{V}$ is denoted by $\mathcal{H}^*(\mathbb{P}, \mathbb{T}, \mathbb{O}, \mathbb{V})$. An ω-history is an infinite countable set of operations with no *Zeno behavior*[3]: for all time $t \in \mathbb{R}^+$, there are finitely many operations that start before time t. The set of ω-histories over $\mathbb{P}$, $\mathbb{T}$, $\mathbb{O}$, and $\mathbb{V}$ is denoted by $\mathcal{H}^\omega(\mathbb{P}, \mathbb{T}, \mathbb{O}, \mathbb{V})$.

In Sect. 5.1, we will study the oriented graph $(H, \xrightarrow{rb})$ of the operations of a history H. The $\xrightarrow{rb}$ relation will be "too redundant" for the purpose of bounding some complexity measure of the graph, there we will consider a more restrictive relation, which we call *direct succession*.

Definition 2 (Direct Successor). *Let $H \in \mathcal{H}^*(\mathbb{P}, \mathbb{T}, \mathbb{O}, \mathbb{V})$ and $\xrightarrow{rel}$ a binary relation over H. We say that an operation b is the direct successor of a on process p, written $a \xrightarrow{rel}_p b$, if b is the first operation on process p such that $a \xrightarrow{rel} b$.*

Note that the relation $a \xrightarrow{rb}_p b$ holds information about the process of b (namely, p), but does not reveal any information about the process on which a is executed. Additionally, we say that b is a direct successor of a, written $a \xrightarrow{rb} b$, if there exists a process p such that $a \xrightarrow{rb}_p b$.

Abstract executions are an enrichment of histories with two relations over operations: arbitration and visibility. Observe that a history does not contain enough information about operations to assess its consistency. Indeed, if two operations are concurrently executed, there is no way of knowing which operation should be considered as "logically before" the other. Thus, histories are traditionaly enriched with two relations over operations: arbitration and visibility.[4]

Definition 3 (Abstract Execution [24]). *An abstract execution is given by a triple $(H, \xrightarrow{ar}, \xrightarrow{vis})$ where H is a history, $\xrightarrow{ar}$ is an arbitration relation, and $\xrightarrow{vis}$ is a visibility relation such that:*

* $\xrightarrow{ar}$ *is a total order over H;*
* $\xrightarrow{vis}$ *is an acyclic relation[5] over H.*

---

[3] We could also relax this assumption and translate arbitrary infinite histories to transfinite words indexed by ordinals, see e.g. [12].

[4] Quoting [6], page 46: *Visibility tells us about the relative timing of update propagation and operations. It is an acyclic relation. If an operation a is visible to b (written $a \xrightarrow{vis} b$), it means that the effect of a is visible to the client performing b. In a system where updates are communicated by messages, this may mean that the message about operation a reached the client that performed operation b before the operation b was performed. Arbitration is used to indicate how the system resolves update conflicts, i.e. how it handles concurrent updates that do not commute. It is a total order on operations. If an operation a is arbitrated before b (written $a \xrightarrow{ar} b$), it means that the system considers the operation a to happen earlier than operation b..*

[5] with no look-ahead, see Definition 4 below.

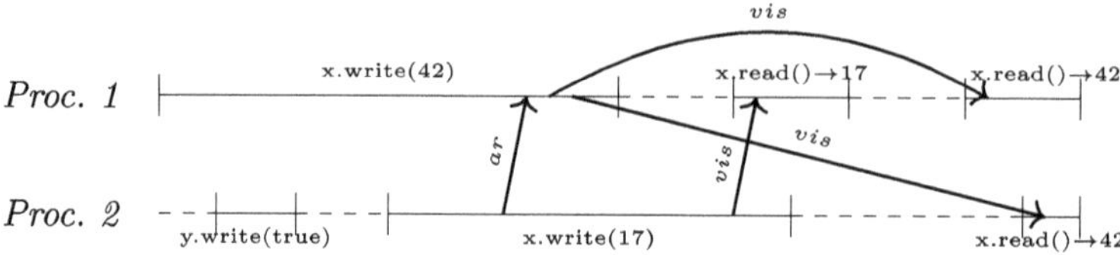

Fig. 2. An abstract execution over the history of Fig. 1, with arbitration and visibility relations.

Example 2. In Fig. 2, we illustrate an abstract execution over the history of Fig. 1. The arbitration relation $\xrightarrow{ar}$ is represented by arrows going from an operation to another one. We only depict an arrow $a \xrightarrow{ar} b$ if a and b are on different processes and if b is the first operation after a in the arbitration order on process $p = b.proc$ (we later write $a \xrightarrow{ar}_p b$ when this is the case). The visibility relation $\xrightarrow{vis}$ is represented similarly, as well as the direct succession relation $a \xrightarrow{vis}_p b$.

Note that Burckhardt's model of abstract executions is quite general, and does not make any assumption on the relations between $\xrightarrow{ar}$, $\xrightarrow{vis}$, and $\xrightarrow{rb}$ beyond the ones explicitly stated in Definitions 1 and 3. To conclude this section, we try to hint why abstract executions are defined in this way, and introduce a new property, absence of look-ahead, that seems to us rather reasonable to assume for all abstract executions.

Remark 1. Visibility does not imply arbitration. This property is sometimes enforced by some consistency models (for instance, by the SingleOrder property used to define linearizability, see below), but it is not the case for all consistency models. Arbitration, that corresponds to a global consensus on the order of operations, may deviate from visibility in some scenarios: for instance, with three processes and arbitration based on majority, if two processes perform `x.write(0)` and the third one performs `x.write(1)`, they may collectively arbitrate `x.write(1)` before the two `x.write(0)` in order to reflect majority voting and "drop" the `x.write(1)`, even if both `x.write(0)` were visible to the third process when he performed `x.write(1)`.

Remark 2. Visibility does not imply returns-before. Indeed, an operation can be visible to another operation even if it has not yet returned. In Fig. 2, for instance, `x.write(17)` on process 2 is visible to `x.read(17)` on process 1, even if `x.write(17)` has not yet returned when `x.read(17)` started. Intuitively, process 2 sent a message about `x.write(17)` to process 1 before `x.write(17)` finished, and this message reached process 1 before `x.read(17)` finished.

Remark 3. At a process-local scale, visibility does not imply session order. This is weird if we stick to the intuition that visibility is related to message passing, because it would mean a process can receive a message from itself that it will send in the future. If we do not stick to the message passing intuition, we can think about visibility in a broader sense, and allow processes to rely on some look-ahead on the operations they will execute.

For simplicity, we later exclude this look-ahead behavior[6] and assume the following property (that expresses the absence of look-ahead at the process-local scale and further restricts visibility accross distinct processes, seen as a message passing relation, to allow receiving messages that are sent in the future).

Definition 4 (No Look-ahead). *We say that an abstract execution* $(H, \xrightarrow{ar}, \xrightarrow{vis})$ *satisfies the no look-ahead property if for all operations a and b, if* $a \xrightarrow{rb} b$, *then* $b \xnrightarrow{vis} a$.

In the rest of the paper, we implicitly assume that this property is part of Definition 3. We conclude with two further remarks about the fact that $\xrightarrow{ar}$, $\xrightarrow{vis}$, and $\xrightarrow{rb}$ relations are independent of each other.

Remark 4. Session order (and more generally, $\xrightarrow{rb}$) does not imply visibility. For instance, in Fig. 2, on process 1, `x.write(42)` is not visible to `x.read(17)`. This would however be enforced by consistency models such as ReadYourWrites, that require that an operation is visible to all subsequent operations in the same session.

Remark 5. Session order (and more generally, $\xrightarrow{rb}$) does not imply arbitration. This is the case for instance when a write operation is dropped by the system, arbitrating it before other writes, see discussion in Remark 1 above.

3   A Logical Formalism for Consistency Models

In this section we introduce HistMSO, a logic that allows to express properties of histories and abstract executions in distributed systems. We first define the syntax of the logic, then we show how to express consistency models in this logic.

3.1   Definition of HistMSO

We define HistMSO, the Monadic Second-Order (MSO) logic of histories and abstract executions as expected. MSO logic is the restriction of second-order logic where second-order quantifications are limited to quantifications over sets (of operations). Formally, the grammar of the MSO formulas ϕ over histories and abstract executions is the following, with a and b ranging over first order variables (interpreted as operations), and A ranging over second order variables (interpreted as sets of operations), and $attr$ ranges over operation attributes.

$$
\begin{aligned}
t & :: = \mathsf{a}.stime \mid \mathsf{a}.rtime \\
f & :: = \mathsf{a}.attr = \mathsf{b}.attr \mid t < t \mid \mathsf{a}.proc = p \\
g & :: = \mathsf{a}.ival = \Phi \mid \mathsf{a}.oval = \Phi \mid \mathsf{a}.oval = \nabla \\
\phi & :: = f \mid g \mid \phi \vee \phi \mid \neg\phi \mid \forall \mathsf{a}. \ \phi \mid \forall A. \ \phi \mid \mathsf{a} \in A \\
& \quad \mid \ \mathsf{a} \xrightarrow{ar} \mathsf{b} \mid \mathsf{a} \xrightarrow{vis} \mathsf{b}
\end{aligned}
$$

---

[6] we could probably cope with a finite look-ahead, but this would complicate the translation to MSO, and it is unclear how relevant it would be.

The formulas $\phi_1 \wedge \phi_2$ (conjunction), $\phi_1 \Rightarrow \phi_2$ (implication), $\exists a.\ \phi$ (first order quantification), guarded quantification $\forall a \in X.\ \varphi$, and so on are defined as macros as expected. Formulas that do not contain $\xrightarrow{vis}$ and $\xrightarrow{ar}$ are interpreted over histories, while formulas that do contain these relation symbols are interpreted over abstract executions. The satisfaction relation $(H, \xrightarrow{ar}, \xrightarrow{vis}), v \models \phi$ between an abstract execution $(H, \xrightarrow{ar}, \xrightarrow{vis})$, a variable assignment v, and a formula ϕ is defined as usual, with the obvious interpretations for the $\xrightarrow{ar}$ and $\xrightarrow{vis}$ predicates. The set of free variables of a formula ϕ is defined as usual, and a formula is closed if the set of free variables is empty.

Remark 6. The relations $\xrightarrow{rb}$ and $\approx_{ss}$ introduced in Sect. 5.1 can be defined in the logic. For instance, $a \xrightarrow{rb} b \overset{\text{def}}{=} a.rtime < b.stime$. The direct successor relations $\xrightarrow{rb}, \xrightarrow{rb}_p, \xrightarrow{ar}_p$, etc. introduced in the previous section can also be defined in the logic. For instance,

$$a \xrightarrow{rb}_p b \quad \overset{\text{def}}{=} \quad b.proc = p \wedge a \xrightarrow{rb} b \wedge \neg \exists c.c \approx_{ss} b \wedge a \xrightarrow{rb} c \wedge c \xrightarrow{rb} b$$

3.2 Expressing Consistency Models in HistMSO

In this section we exercise the expressive power of HistMSO by formally defining several consistency models from Viotti and Vukolic classification [24]. Our finding is that almost all of the 42 models formalized by Viotti and Vukolic (see [24] Fig. 1) can be expressed in our logic. The only exceptions[7] are the few models based on exact timing constraints: *Timed Visibility* [23], *Timed Causality*, and *Timed Linearizability*. Due to space constraints, we only present a very short selection of consistency models here, showing by some examples how to reformulate in HistMSO the meta logic used by Viotti and Vukolic. The reader may consider looking first at Viotti and Vukolic formalisation of the consistency models in their meta logic, see page 41 of [24].

Return value consistency ensures that all operations return the appropriate and correct values. In this work, this means that any read operation should output the most recent value written to the corresponding object by a visible operation. The following formula intuitively captures this behavior: it holds if all *writes* return the empty value Φ, and if every *read* either accesses an object that has not been written to before, or retrieves the last (in the sense of arbitration) value visibly written to that object.

Before expressing these with formulas, let us first recall the notion of context of an operation, introduced by Viotti and Vukolic. An operation b is part of the context explaining a read operation a if it is a write on the same object that is visible to a.

---

[7] even those models could be approached by moving to a discrete time semantics.

$$b \in \mathsf{ctxt}(a) \quad \overset{\text{def}}{=} \quad b \xrightarrow{vis} a \wedge b.type = write \wedge b.obj = a.obj$$

It becomes then easy to express return value consistency in HistMSO.

$$\text{RVAL} \overset{\text{def}}{=} \forall a.\ W(a) \wedge R(a)$$
$$W(a) \overset{\text{def}}{=} a.type = write \Rightarrow a.oval = \Phi$$
$$R(a) \overset{\text{def}}{=} a.type = read \Rightarrow a.oval = \mathsf{lastWrite}(\mathsf{ctxt}(a))$$
$$v = \mathsf{lastWrite}(C) \overset{\text{def}}{=} \forall b.\ \big(b \in C \wedge b.ival \neq v\big) \Rightarrow \exists c \in C.\ b \xrightarrow{ar} c$$

Real time guarantees that any two operations not concurrently executed are ordered by *arbitration* according to absolute time. In Viotti and Vukolic meta logic, this is expressed as $rb \subseteq ar$. In HistMSO, this becomes
$$\text{REALTIME} \overset{\text{def}}{=} \forall a.\forall b. a \xrightarrow{rb} b \Rightarrow a \xrightarrow{ar} b.$$

Linearizability states that "each operation shall appear to be applied instantaneously at a certain point in time between its invocation and its response" [16]. Following Burckhardt [6], Viotti and Vukolic formalize linearisability as the conjunct of return value consistency, real time, and a third notion, called single order: LINEARIZABILITY $\overset{\text{def}}{=}$ SINGLEORDER $\wedge$ REALTIME $\wedge$ RVAL. Intuitively, single order tights toghether visibility and arbitration. In Viotti and Vukolic meta logic, this is expressed as $\exists H' \subseteq \{op \in H : op.oval = \nabla\} : vis = ar \setminus (H' \times H)$. In HistMSO, this becomes

$$\text{SINGLEORDER} \overset{\text{def}}{=} \exists X.(\forall x.x \in X \Rightarrow x.oval = \nabla) \wedge$$
$$\forall a.\forall b.(a \xrightarrow{vis} b \Leftrightarrow a \xrightarrow{ar} b \wedge \neg(a \in X))$$

Quiescent Consistency requires that if all objects stop receiving updates (i.e., become quiescent), then the execution is equivalent to some sequential execution containing only complete operations. Although this definition resembles eventual consistency, it does not guarantee termination: a system that does not stop receiving updates will not reach quiescence, thus replicas convergence. Following Viotti and Vukolic[8], we can express quiescent consistency in HistMSO based on set finiteness.

$$\text{QUIESCENTCONSISTENCY} \overset{\text{def}}{=} \mathsf{Finite}(\{a \mid a.type = write\}) \Rightarrow \mathsf{FiniteInconsistency}$$
$$\mathsf{FiniteInconsistency} \overset{\text{def}}{=} \exists a.\ a.type = read$$
$$\wedge \mathsf{Finite}\big(\{b \mid b.oval \neq \mathsf{lastWrite}(\mathsf{ctxt}(a))\}\big)$$

---

[8] We slightly simplified their formula for presentation purposes. Their formula was $|H_{|wr}| < \infty \Rightarrow \exists C \in \mathcal{C} : \forall [f] \in H/\approx_{ss} : |\{op \in [f] : op.oval \neq \mathsf{lastWrite}(C)\}| < \infty$. In this formula, C is a context and $[f]$ is the set of operations of some process. Due to the finiteness of the set of processes, it is equivalent to $|H_{|wr}| < \infty \Rightarrow \exists C \in \mathcal{C} : |\{op \in H \mid op.oval \neq \mathsf{lastWrite}(C)\}| < \infty$.

On arbitrary structures, set finiteness is not MSO definable. However, since ω-histories are non-Zeno and involve a finite number of processes, a subset O of an ω-history H is finite if and only if there is a time t such that all operations of O starts before t.

$$\mathsf{Finite}(O) \stackrel{\text{def}}{=} (\neg \exists a \in O) \vee \exists a \in O.\, \forall b \in O.\, b.stime \leq a.stime$$

All together, we have that quiescent consistency is expressible in HistMSO.

4   Translation to MONA

In this section we show how to translate HistMSO to MSO over natural numbers. This translation allows us to leverage MONA's decision procedures to verify properties of finite histories and abstract executions in distributed systems. We first recall some background on MONA, then we present our translation for histories, and finally we discuss how to extend this translation to abstract executions.

4.1   Background on MONA

MONA deals with the following logical formalism:

$$\varphi ::= x < y \mid x \in X \mid \neg\varphi \mid \varphi \wedge \varphi \mid \exists x.\varphi \mid \exists X.\varphi$$

where x, y are first-order variables ranging over natural numbers, and X is a second-order variable ranging over sets of natural numbers. A model of a formula φ with free (first and second order) variables $v_1, \ldots, v_n$ (the order of the enumeration matters) is a word over the alphabet $\{0, 1\}^n$. Each position i of the word corresponds to a natural number, and the j-th bit of the letter at position i is 1 if and only if the j-th order-1 (resp. order 2) variable is interpreted as equaling to (resp. containing) i (see [20] for more details).

Our goal in the following is to define an encoding function Enc that takes as input a finite history $H \in \mathcal{H}^*(\mathbb{P}, \mathbb{T}, \mathbb{O}, \mathbb{V})$ and outputs a word of bitvectors $\mathsf{Enc}(H) \in (\{0, 1\}^n)^*$ (for some n depending on the meta parameters $\mathbb{P}, \mathbb{T}, \mathbb{O}, \mathbb{V}$) and a translation $T(\varphi)$ of a formula φ of the MSO logic of histories and abstract executions defined in Sect. 3.1 into a MONA formula $T(\varphi)$ such that

$$H \models \varphi \qquad \Longleftrightarrow \qquad \mathsf{Enc}(H) \models_{\mathsf{MONA}} T(\varphi) \tag{1}$$

4.2   Encoding Histories to Words

Each letter of $Enc(H)$ represents the operations and relations of H at a certain point in time: the word $Enc(H)$ forms a sequence of snapshots of H over time, quite similar to a discrete sampling of a continuous signal. To define the encoding function we follow these steps: coding the timeline, then adding information about types and values.

Coding the Timeline. Let us first fix some enumeration $\mathbb{P} = \{p_1, ..., p_m\}$ of the (finite) set of processes. For a finite history (resp. an ω-history) H, and for a timestamp $t \in \mathbb{R}_{\geq 0}$, let $\mathsf{snapshot}(H, t) \in \{0, 1\}^{|\mathbb{P}|}$ denote the bitvector whose i-th coordinate is 1 if and only if process p_i is active in H at timestamp t; for an increasing sequence $\mathbf{T}$ of timestamps $t_0 < t_1 < ...$ we define $\mathsf{snapshots}(\mathsf{H}, \mathbf{T})$ as the sequence of snapshots $\mathsf{snapshot}(H, t_i)$. The timeline encoding $\mathsf{Enc}_{tl}(H)$ is $\mathsf{Enc}(H, \mathbf{T}_H)$ where $\mathbf{T}$ denote the enumeration of all starting and ending times of operations in H.

Example 3. The construction is illustrated on Fig. 3. The history H on this figure is run on three processes. We therefore have $Enc(H) \in (\{0, 1\}^3)^*$. Each time an operation starts or returns, we take a snapshot.

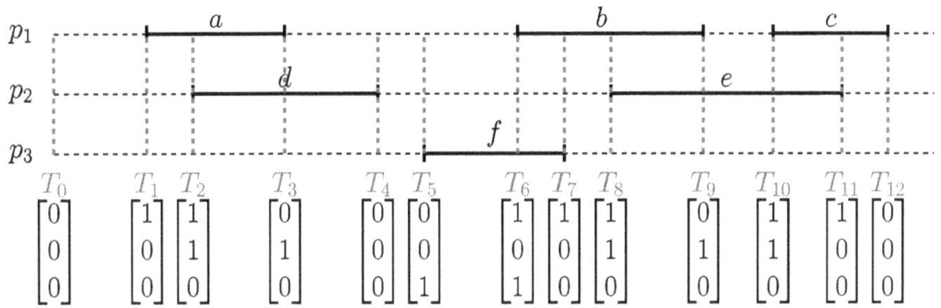

Fig. 3. A finite history H and its timeline encoding $\mathsf{Enc}_{tl}(H)$

Remark 7. We assumed in Definition 1 that the histories we consider are such that every timestamp occurs in at most one operation extremity, and no operation starts at $t = 0$. This ensures that every two consecutive vectors in $\mathsf{Enc}_{tl}(H)$ differ at exactly one coordinate and help identify the process on which an operation starts or stop at a given timestamp (see for instance the formula $\mathsf{isStart}$ we later define).

Adding Information About Types, Values, and Objects. For now the only information encoded are the start and return times. We want to enrich the encoding with the *type*, *ival/oval* and *obj* attributes. We will do so by adding coordinates to the vectors we just used to define $\mathsf{Enc}_{tl}(H)$. Remember that we assumed the meta parameters $\mathbb{T}$, $\mathbb{V}$ and $\mathbb{O}$ are finite sets. We can therefore assume that a type, a value, or an object identifier can be coded on a number of bits that can be determined in advance. For instance, we assumed above for simplicity that $\mathbb{T}$ contains only **read** and **write**. We can simply code a **read** as a 0 and a **write** as a 1. For *Values*, we can stick to their machine representation. To encode $\mathbb{O}$ we can fix an enumeration $o_1, ... o_n$ and represent the object identifier o_i by the binary encoding of i of $\lceil \log_2(n) \rceil$ bits.

In $\mathsf{Enc}_{tl}(H)$, two successive vectors differ in only one coordinate. This means, in particular, that when introducing a new operation a on a vector w, we only need to encode data about a.

Each vector of $Enc(H)$ is of the following form. The m first coordinates are used as explained above in the definition of $\mathsf{Enc}_{tl}(H)$. The following coordinates encode the attributes of the operation that either starts or stop at this timestamp: the $m+1$ coordinate encodes the type of the operation (0 for *read*, 1 for *write*), the next $\lceil \log_2 |Values| \rceil$ coordinates are dedicated to encoding either the input or the output value[9], and the last $\lceil \log_2 |Objects| \rceil$ to the encoding of the object identifier. The very first vector is the null vector.

Translating Formulas. Finally, we sketch the definition of the translation $\varphi \mapsto T(\varphi)$ of MSO formulas over histories to MONA formulas. Each line ℓ of a bitvector of $\mathsf{Enc}(H)$ is associated with a second order variable X_ℓ. The translation otherwise maps each first order variable a (ranging over an operation) to a first order variable ranging over a column of $\mathsf{Enc}(H)$, that we also write a. Similarly, second order variables are mapped to second order variables. More precisely, we define the translation inductively as follows:

$$T(\varphi \vee \psi) \overset{\mathrm{def}}{=} T(\varphi) \vee T(\psi) \qquad T(\neg\varphi) \overset{\mathrm{def}}{=} \neg T(\varphi)$$
$$T(\exists \mathsf{a}.\ \varphi) \overset{\mathrm{def}}{=} \exists \mathsf{a}.\ \mathsf{isStart}(\mathsf{a}) \wedge T(\varphi) \qquad T(\mathsf{a} \in A) \overset{\mathrm{def}}{=} \mathsf{a} \in A$$
$$T(\exists A.\ \varphi) \overset{\mathrm{def}}{=} \exists A.\ (\forall \mathsf{a}.\ \mathsf{a} \in A \Rightarrow \mathsf{isStart}(\mathsf{a})) \wedge T(\varphi)$$

where $\mathsf{isStart}(\mathsf{a})$ is a MONA formula stating that the vector at position a corresponds to the start of an operation (that is, $a \neq 0$ and the only bit that differs between $a-1$ and a is equal to 1 at a). The atomic formulas are translated as expected from the encoding defined above. For instance $T(\mathsf{a}.obj = p) = \mathsf{a} \in X_p$, where X_p is the free variable associated with the line of p in $\mathsf{Enc}_{tl}(H)$. The translation of $\mathsf{a}.tattr < \mathsf{b}.tattr'$ is $\exists \mathsf{a}', \mathsf{b}'.\ tattr(\mathsf{a}, \mathsf{a}') \wedge tattr'(\mathsf{b}, \mathsf{b}') \wedge \mathsf{a}' < \mathsf{b}'$, with $stime(\mathsf{a}, \mathsf{a}') \overset{\mathrm{def}}{=} \mathsf{a} = \mathsf{a}'$, and $rtime(\mathsf{a}, \mathsf{a}')$ expressing that a' is the first position after a where the bit on the line of the process of a is null. We omit the full definition of the translation for brevity. We also omit the definition of the formula $\mathsf{isEncoding}$ that checks that a word is indeed an encoding of a history, i.e. $w \models_{\mathsf{MONA}} \mathsf{isEncoding}$ if and only if there exists $H \in \mathcal{H}^*(\mathbb{P}, \mathbb{T}, \mathbb{O}, \mathbb{V})$ such that $w = \mathsf{Enc}(H)$.

Theorem 1. *For every closed formula φ of $HistMSO \backslash \{\overset{ar}{\longrightarrow}, \overset{vis}{\longrightarrow}\}$, for every finite history $H \in \mathcal{H}^*(\mathbb{P}, \mathbb{T}, \mathbb{O}, \mathbb{V})$ (respectively ω-history $H \in \mathcal{H}^\omega(\mathbb{P}, \mathbb{T}, \mathbb{O}, \mathbb{V})$), it holds that*

$$H \models \varphi \qquad \Longleftrightarrow \qquad \mathsf{Enc}(H) \models_{\mathsf{MONA}} T(\varphi)$$

Corollary 1. *The HistMSO theory of finite histories and the HistMSO theory of ω-infinite histories are decidable.*

---

[9] A *read* operation does not have an input value and a *write* operation does not have an output value.

4.3   Extension to Abstract Executions

In this section we explain how to extend the encoding defined for histories to abstract executions. It is not clear how to encode the relations $\xrightarrow{vis}$ and $\xrightarrow{ar}$ directly in the word encoding of an abstract execution, as they are not directly related to the timeline of operations. Therefore, we propose a few assumptions that can be made on these relations, and then exploit them to extend our encoding technique.

Representing Arbitration in Real-Time Histories. Remember that arbitration is *any* total order on operations. Without any further assumption, the two relations $\xrightarrow{rb}$ and $\xrightarrow{ar}$ could be used to define a grid, and the logic would be undecidable even at first order.

However, in practice, arbitration is not completely independent of the timeline. We therefore make the assumption that the abstract executions we consider are real-time[10] (see formula REALTIME in the previous section).

With this restriction, the only pairs of operations (a, b) for which our encoding should specify whether a is arbitrated before b or the converse are those pairs of concurrent operations. To encode this information, we add $|\mathbb{P}| - 1$ extra bits to the vectors we used in the definition of $\mathsf{Enc}(H)$. If t is the starting time of an operation a on process p_i, then the j-th extra bit (for $j \neq i$) indicates whether $a \xrightarrow{ar} b$, where b is the last operation started on process the jth process (skipping p_i if $j > i$) before time t.

This coding allows us to define a binary relation $\xrightarrow{arc}$ such that $\xrightarrow{arc} \cap \xleftarrow{arc} = \emptyset$ and $a(\xrightarrow{arc} \cup \xleftarrow{arc})b$ iff a and b are concurrent. We then just need to define $\xrightarrow{ar}$ as $(\xrightarrow{rb} \cup \xrightarrow{arc})^+$, and assert in the formula isEncoding that $\xrightarrow{ar}$ is acyclic.

Representing Visibility Under Real-time and k-transient Visibility Assumptions.

Visibility is even more versatile and challenging to encode. We again rely on the real-time assumption to restrict the possible visibility relations, which enforces that $\forall a, b, a \xrightarrow{rb} b \Rightarrow \neg(b \xrightarrow{vis} a)$. We can therefore decompose the visibility relation into two parts: the visibility between concurrent operations, which can be encoded as we did for arbitration, and the visibility between operations a and b such that $a \xrightarrow{rb} b$, two relations we denote respectively by $\xrightarrow{visc}$ and $\xrightarrow{visrb}$, with $\xrightarrow{vis} = \xrightarrow{visc} \cup \xrightarrow{visrb}$. We therefore add an extra bit to the vectors of $\mathsf{Enc}(H)$ to encode $\xrightarrow{visc}$ as we did for arbitration.

In order to encode $\xrightarrow{visrb}$, we need to make further assumptions on visibility. We cannot make too strong assumptions, as we want to be able to tell apart all consistency models defined in [24]. For instance, it would be problematic to make the assumption that once an operation a is visible to another operation b, then it is also visible to all operations started after b on the same process.

---

[10] Weaker forms of this assumption, like "boundedly deviating from real-time", could be worth exploring.

Indeed, this assumption, known as PRAM, or FIFO, subsumes some prominent consistency models like *monotonic reads, monotonic writes*, or *read my writes*.

Remember that $a \xrightarrow{rb}_p b_0$ if b_0 is the first operation on process p that starts after the return time of a. Given a fixed a and p, consider $b_0, b_1, \ldots, b_i, \ldots$ such that $b_0 \xrightarrow{rb}_p b_1 \xrightarrow{rb}_p \cdots \xrightarrow{rb}_p b_{k-1}$. We say that a is k-transient to process p if for all $i \geq k$, $a \xrightarrow{vis} b_i$ iff $a \xrightarrow{vis} b_{k-1}$. Intuitively, this means that the visibility of an operation a to operations on a given process p stabilises after a bound k to either always visible or always invisible.

Definition 5 (k-transient Visibility). *Let $k \geq 0$. An abstract execution $(H, \xrightarrow{ar}, \xrightarrow{vis})$ has k-transient visibility if for all operations $a \in H$, for all processes $p \in \mathbb{P}$, a is k-transient to process p.*

We therefore add an extra meta parameter k, and add $k \cdot |\mathbb{P}|$ bits to the vectors of $\mathsf{Enc}(H)$. These bits are used to encode, for each process timestamp corresponding to the start of an operation a, the visibility of a to the first k operations started on each process p after the return of a. With this encoding, we can define a formula for $\xrightarrow{visrb}$ in MONA, and impose in the formula isEncoding that $\xrightarrow{vis} = \xrightarrow{visc} \cup \xrightarrow{visrb}$ is acyclic.

Theorem 2. *For every closed formula φ of HistMSO for every finite (resp. ω-infinite) abstract execution $(H, \xrightarrow{ar}, vis)$, it holds that*

$$H \models \varphi \qquad \Longleftrightarrow \qquad \mathsf{Enc}(H) \models_{\mathsf{MONA}} T(\varphi)$$

Corollary 2. *The HistMSO theory of finite (resp. ω-infinite) abstract executions with real-time arbitration and k-transient visibility is decidable.*

5   Cutwidth Complexity of Histories

In this section we show that the partial order $\xrightarrow{rb}$ among operations of a given finite history is the transitive closure of a graph whose cutwidth is bounded by the square of the number of processes; since the treewidth is bounded by the cutwidth, this result induces in particular a tree decomposition of histories bounded by the number of processes. We refer the interested the reader to second author's previous work [13], and more generally to Courcelle's theorem [9], to better understand how this question is related to the decidability of satisfiability checking or to local, PTIME model-checking. Proofs omitted here can be found in the of [8]. In this section, all histories are implicitly assumed to be finite.

5.1   Problem Statement

We adopt the conventional notation for a graph $G = (V, E)$ with V the set of vertices and E, where E is a subset of $V \times V$, or equivalently a binary relation on V. The rb-graph G_H associated with an history H is $G_H = (H, \xrightarrow{rb})$.

The rb-graph of an history is overly dense, with redundant information. This redundancy makes it impractical to define a bounded tree decomposition of such a graph. We therefore aim to define a new binary relation $\rightarrow$ on operations with the two following properties.

* $\xrightarrow{rb}$ is the transitive closure of $\rightarrow$. As a consequence, the MSO theory of G_H can be reduced to the one of $G = (H, \rightarrow)$.
* $(H, \rightarrow)$ admits a tree decomposition whose width is bounded by a number n that only depends on the meta parameters (more precisely, it will only depend on $\mathbb{P}$)

The graph $(H, \rightarrow)$ is called a generator of $(H, \xrightarrow{rb})$. We will achieve something even stronger than what we just stated, as we will instead show that the generator $G = (H, \rightarrow)$ is of bounded *cutwidth*.

The cutwidth of an undirected graph G is the minimum $k \in \mathbb{N}$ such that for some linear ordering of the vertices of G along a horizontal axis, every vertical cut intersects at most k edges. Using the cutwidth is advantageous in our work, as vertices of graphs of history already represent a timeline, which is a linear ordering. To rigouroulsy define the cutwidth of a graph, it is necessary to introduce the notion of *cut* of a graph. Let $G = (V, E)$ be a graph with n vertices $v_1, \ldots, v_n$, and σ a permutation[11] of $\{1, \ldots, n\}$, and $\ell \in \{1, \ldots n\}$.

$$Cut_\ell(\sigma, G) \overset{\text{def}}{=} (\{v_{\sigma(1)}, ..., v_{\sigma(\ell)}\}, \{v_{\sigma(\ell+1)}, ..., v_{\sigma(n)}\})$$

defines a *cut* of G. An edge (u, v) crosses a cut $Cut_\ell(\sigma, G) = (L, R)$, if either $(u, v) \in L \times R$ or $(u, v) \in R \times L$. For $G = (V, E)$ a graph, let $\mathsf{Perm}(V)$ denote the set of all possible permutations of the vertices of G.

$$cutwidth(G) \overset{\text{def}}{=} \min_{\sigma \in \mathsf{Perm}(V)} \max_{1 \leq \ell \leq n} \left|\{ (u, v) \mid (u, v) \text{ crosses } Cut_\ell(\sigma, G) \}\right|.$$

In the remainder, we first construct the generator graph G of a given history, then we bound its cutwidth. As explained above, we will bound its cutwidth through a bound on $\max_{1 \leq \ell \leq n} \left|\{ (u, v) \mid (u, v) \text{ crosses } Cut_\ell(\sigma, G) \}\right|$ for the linear ordering $\sigma = ord(H)$ defined by the timestamps of the operations:

$$ord(H) \overset{\text{def}}{=} (a_1, \ldots, a_n) \qquad \text{such that for all } i < j, a_i.stime < a_j.stime.$$

5.2   Constructive Definition of the Subgraph

We now define the relation $\rightarrow$ using an algorithm that iteratively adds new edges to an edge set E. We write $a \twoheadrightarrow b$ to mean that there exists a path from a to b in the graph $G = (V, E)$. Remember that we aim at $\xrightarrow{rb}$ being the transitive closure of $\rightarrow$.

---

[11] in other words, a linear ordering/an enumeration of the vertices of G.

The set of all direct successors of a, written as $\mathsf{succs}(a)$, is defined as $\mathsf{succs}(a) = \{b \mid b \in H \wedge a \xrightarrow{rb} b\} \subset H$ (see Definition 2). Observe that for all $a \in H$, we have $|\mathsf{succs}(a)| \leq |\mathbb{P}|$ because any operation has at most one direct successor on each process. The algorithm operates as follows. It takes as input $ord(H)$, where $H \in \mathcal{H}^*(\mathbb{P}, \mathbb{T}, \mathbb{O}, \mathbb{V})$, and traverses $ord(H)$ in reverse, starting from the last element and proceeding to the first. For each operation, its direct successors are extracted, sorted according to ord, and then processed one by one. If a path to a given successor already exists in the graph, no action is taken; otherwise, a direct edge to that successor is added. This procedure ensures that the number of edges is minimized. The algorithm is formalized as follows.

Algorithm Building a graph of finite history

Require: $H \in \mathcal{H}^*(\mathbb{P}, \mathbb{T}, \mathbb{O}, \mathbb{V})$ with $ord(H) = (a_1, ..., a_n)$, $n \in \mathbb{N}$

Ensure: $G = (H, \rightarrow)$

```
 1: i ← n − 1
 2: E ← ∅
 3: G ← (H, E)
 4: while i > 0 do
 5:     S ← (b₁, ..., bₘ) = ord(succs(aᵢ))
 6:     for j ∈ {1, ..., m} do
 7:         if ¬(aᵢ ↠ bₘ) then
 8:             E ← E ∪ {(aᵢ, bₘ)}
 9:             G ← (H, E)
10:         end if
11:     end for
12:     i ← i − 1
13: end while
```

Remark 8. When building a directed graph as above, each directed edge can be interpreted as a "jump forward in time" —- that is, traversing an edge corresponds to moving along the timeline of certain operations in the history.

We denote by $Alg(H)$ the graph of the finite history H computed by this algorithm. Let $\mathcal{G}_m^*, m \in \mathbb{N}$ denote the set of all such graphs for histories in $\mathcal{H}^*(\mathbb{P}, \mathbb{T}, \mathbb{O}, \mathbb{V})$ with $|\mathbb{P}| = m$. It is the finite execution graph set; for $m \in \mathbb{N}$,

$$\mathcal{G}_m^* \stackrel{\text{def}}{=} \{ Alg(H) \mid H \in \mathcal{H}^*(\mathbb{P}, \mathbb{T}, \mathbb{O}, \mathbb{V}) \text{ and } |\mathbb{P}| = m \}$$

5.3   Bounding the Cutwidth of Histories

In this section, we prove that $\mathcal{G}^*$ has uniformly bounded cutwidth, which, as a by-product, establishes the correctness of the algorithm.

Preliminary Results. It is worth noting that both $\xrightarrow{rb}$ and $\rightarrow$ are transitive. Indeed, given $a \xrightarrow{rb} b$ and $b \xrightarrow{rb} c$, it follows naturally that $a \xrightarrow{rb} c$. Similarly, for $\rightarrow$, if $d \rightarrow e$ and $e \rightarrow f$, then $d \rightarrow f$.

For a a vertex of a graph, we denote its out-degree as $deg_{out}(a)$, and its in-degree as $deg_{in}(a)$. The *out-degree* of a vertex is the number of edges connected to it that are directed away from the vertex. The *in-degree* is the number of connected edges directed towards the vertex.

Lemma 1. *Let $G = (H, \to) \in \mathcal{G}_m^*$, $m \in \mathbb{N}$. Then, for all $a \in H$, $deg_{out}(a) \leq m$.*

Proposition 1. *Let $H \in \mathcal{H}^*(\mathbb{P}, \mathbb{T}, \mathbb{O}, \mathbb{V})$ be a history. For $a, b \in H$,*

$$a \xrightarrow{rb} b \Leftrightarrow \text{there exists a tuple } (h_1, ..., h_q), \ h_i \in H, q \in \mathbb{N} \text{ such that}$$
$$a \xrightarrow{rb}_p h_1 \xrightarrow{rb}_p ... \xrightarrow{rb}_p h_q \xrightarrow{rb}_p b \text{ with } p := b.proc.$$

Proposition 2. *Let $(H, \to) \in \mathcal{G}_m^*$, $m \in \mathbb{N}$. For $a, b \in H$, $a \xrightarrow{rb} b \Leftrightarrow a \twoheadrightarrow b$.*

We have established that for a history $H \in \mathcal{H}^*(\mathbb{P}, \mathbb{T}, \mathbb{O}, \mathbb{V})$, each vertex of $G = Alg(H)$ has at most $m = |\mathbb{P}|$ outgoing edges. We now turn to the complementary property: showing that each vertex has at most m incoming edges.

Lemma 2. *Let $G = (H, \to) \in \mathcal{G}_m^*$, $m \in \mathbb{N}$. Then, for all $a \in H$, $deg_{in}(a) \leq m$.*

Main Proof. To prove cutwidth boundedness of a graph G, we need to define two specific sets of nodes based on the definition of *cut*. These sets are as follows: the set containing the last operations launched on each process before the cut ℓ is denoted by $\Gamma_\ell(G)$, and the set containing the first operations launched on each process after the cut ℓ is denoted by $\Lambda_\ell(G)$.

Let $H \in \mathcal{H}^*(\mathbb{P}, \mathbb{T}, \mathbb{O}, \mathbb{V})$ be a history. For a set $O \subseteq H$, and a process p, we write $\gamma_p(O)$ to denote the singleton containing the last operation of O to be launched on process p, and $\lambda_p(O)$ to denote the singleton containing the first operation of O to be launched on process p. Formally,

$$\gamma_p(O) \overset{\text{def}}{=} \{a \in O \mid a.proc = p \text{ and } \forall b \in O.\ b \approx_{ss} a \Rightarrow b.stime < a.stime\}$$
$$\lambda_p(O) \overset{\text{def}}{=} \{a \in O \mid a.proc = p \text{ and } \forall b \in O.\ b \approx_{ss} a \Rightarrow a.stime < b.stime\}$$

Let us fix $1 \leq \ell \leq n$ and let $(L, R) = Cut_\ell(ord, G)$. The sets $\Gamma_\ell(G)$ and $\Lambda_\ell(G)$ are now defined as[12]

$$\Gamma_\ell(G) := \bigcup_{p \in \mathbb{P}} \gamma_p(L) \quad \text{and} \quad \Lambda_\ell(G) := \bigcup_{p \in \mathbb{P}} \lambda_p(R)$$

By definition $|\Gamma_\ell(G)|$, $|\Lambda_\ell(G)| \leq |\mathbb{P}|$. We now introduce notation for the sets of remaining nodes not included in Γ_ℓ or Λ_ℓ: $L_\ell := L \setminus \Gamma_\ell$ and $R_\ell := R \setminus \Lambda_\ell$.

Lemma 3. *Let a history $H \in \mathcal{H}^*(\mathbb{P}, \mathbb{T}, \mathbb{O}, \mathbb{V})$ and $G = (H, \to) \in Alg(H)$. For a cut $(L, R) = Cut_\ell(ord, G)$, with $1 \leq \ell \leq |H|$, there is no edge that crosses the cut ℓ from R to L: $\nexists a, b \in H : a \to b \land a \in R \land b \in L$.*

Let $G \in \mathcal{G}_m^*$, $m \in \mathbb{N}$, and let $(L, R) = Cut_\ell(ord, G)$ be a cut of G. By Lemma 3 no edge originating from $R = \Lambda_\ell \cup R_\ell$ can cross the cut. Edges in $L_\ell \times R_\ell$ cannot cross the cut either. However, edges in $L_\ell \times \Lambda_\ell$, $\Gamma_\ell \times \Lambda_\ell$ and $\Gamma_\ell \times R_\ell$ can cross the cut ℓ.

We now aim to prove that no edge in $L_\ell \times R_\ell$ crosses the cut ℓ.

---

[12] Observe that it is possible to have $\gamma_p(L) = \emptyset$ and/or $\lambda_p(R) = \emptyset$.

Lemma 4. *Let a history $H \in \mathcal{H}^*(\mathbb{P}, \mathbb{T}, \mathbb{O}, \mathbb{V})$ and $G = (H, \to) \in Alg(H)$. For a cut $(L, R) = Cut_\ell(ord, G)$, with $1 \leq \ell \leq |H|$, there is no edge that crosses the cut ℓ from $L_\ell(G)$ to $R_\ell(G)$: $\nexists\, a, b \in H : a \to b \,\wedge\, a \in L_\ell(G) \,\wedge\, b \in R_\ell(G)$.*

Theorem 3. *Let $G \in \mathcal{G}_m^*, m \in \mathbb{N}$. Then, $cutwidth(G) \leq 2m^2$.*

Proof. Let a cut $(L, R) = Cut_\ell(ord, G)$, with $1 \leq \ell \leq |H|$. Let $\Gamma_\ell \overset{\text{def}}{=} \Gamma_\ell(G)$, $\Lambda_\ell \overset{\text{def}}{=} \Lambda_\ell(G)$, $L_\ell \overset{\text{def}}{=} L_\ell(G)$, $R_\ell \overset{\text{def}}{=} R_\ell(G)$. Cutwidth is traditionally defined for undirected graphs. However, by Lemma 3, only edges originating in L can cross the cut at level ℓ. Intuitively, this means that edges cross the cut only "from left to right". For this reason, we retain the directed nature of the graph to maintain clarity throughout the proof. Thus, the core idea of the proof is to bound the number of edges that can "land" on the right-hand side of the cut; that is, the number of edges originating from $L_\ell \cup \Gamma_\ell$ and landing in $\Lambda_\ell \cup R_\ell$. We have $|\Lambda_\ell| \leq m$, and by Lemma 2 each element of Λ_ℓ has at most m incoming edges. Therefore there are at most m^2 edges "landing" in Λ_ℓ. By Lemma 4, there are no edges in $L_\ell \times R_\ell$, which implies that each edge crossing the cut ℓ and landing in R_ℓ must originate from Γ_ℓ. Since $|\Gamma_\ell| \leq m$ and Lemma 1 states that each element of Γ_ℓ has at most m outgoing edges, the number of edges in $\Gamma_\ell \times R_\ell$ is also bounded by m^2. This implies that at most m^2 edges cross the cut and land in R_ℓ. Adding the two bounds, we obtain a total of at most $m^2 + m^2 = 2m^2$ crossing edges, which establishes the result.

6   Conclusion and Future Work

We introduced HistMSO, a monadic second order logic over histories and abstract executions, the prominent execution model for replicated data systems. We showed that the logic can express 39 out of 42 consistency models inventoried by Viotti and Vukolic [24]. We proposed a translation of HistMSO to MSO over words, leveraging MONA as a tool for automated reasoning on consistency models. We established the soundness and completeness of this translation for all finite and ω-infinite histories, assuming that all the meta-parameters (sets of processes, of values, and of replicated objects) were finite. We extended this translation to abstract executions under two assumptions: real-time arbitration, and k-transient visibility. From this translation, we derive the decidability of HistMSO on finite (respectively ω-infinite) histories and on real-time, k-transient abstract executions. As a direct application, we could fully automate the verification of the hierarchy of consistency models proposed by Viotti and Vukolic. We also established a bound on the cutwidth complexity of the interval graph associated with a given history, grounding connections with previous work on bounded the tree width of some communication models under bounded asynchrony [13].

We believe that the main strength of our framework is to support reasoning about a broad class of consistency properties within a unified logical setting. The other strength of our work is to introduce an encoding of execution traces suitable for consistency verification using finite state automata under minimal assumptions about the structure of these traces. Beyond automated reasoning (i.e. deciding satisfiability of a HistMSO theory), our framework also allows to monitor [15] an execution trace of an instrumented replicated data system, and possibly catch consistency violations of a system. This monitoring is however *offline* (the log trace must first be generated by the instrumented system, then model-checked), and *centralised* (the model-checker needs to access the whole trace, not just the one of each process). An interesting question, that has been successfully addressed in other automata-based framework, is whether online/runtime, and/or distributed monitoring would also be possible. We leave this question for future work, and for more immediate future work, we aim at benchmarking our approach with a tool implementation.

Acknowledgments. This work was supported by a grant from the French government under the "Investissements d'Avenir" program managed by the National Research Agency (ANR), reference ANR-17-EURE-0004, and by the project UCA DS4H.

Disclosure of Interests. The authors have no competing interests to declare that are relevant to the content of this article.

References

1. Alur, R., Dill, D.L.: A theory of timed automata. Theoret. Comput. Sci. **126**(2), 183–235 (1994)
2. Attiya, H., Enea, C., Román-Calvo, E.: Arbitration-free consistency is available (and vice versa). CoRR abs/2510.21304 (2025). https://doi.org/10.48550/ARXIV.2510.21304
3. Basin, D., Klarlund, N.: Automata based symbolic reasoning in hardware verification. Formal Methods Syst. Design **13**, 255–288 (1998), extended version of: Hardware verification using monadic second-order logic. CAV '95, LNCS 939
4. Bengtsson, J., Larsen, K., Larsson, F., Pettersson, P., Yi, W.: Uppaal–a tool suite for automatic verification of real-time systems. In: International Hybrid Systems Workshop, pp. 232–243. Springer (1995)
5. Bozga, M., Daws, C., Maler, O., Olivero, A., Tripakis, S., Yovine, S.: Kronos: a model-checking tool for real-time systems. In: International Conference on Computer Aided Verification, pp. 546–550. Springer (1998)
6. Burckhardt, S.: Principles of eventual consistency. https://www.microsoft.com/en-us/research/wp-content/uploads/2016/02/final-printversion-10-5-14.pdf (2014)
7. Chevrou, F., Hurault, A., Nakajima, S., Quéinnec, P.: A map of asynchronous communication models. In: et al, E.S. (ed.) Formal Methods. FM 2019 International Workshops - Porto, Portugal, 7–11 October 2019, Revised Selected Papers, Part II. Lecture Notes in Computer Science, vol. 12233, pp. 307–322. Springer (2019). https://doi.org/10.1007/978-3-030-54997-8_20
8. Coget, I., Lozes, E.: Histmso: a logic for reasoning about consistency models with MONA (2026). https://arxiv.org/abs/2604.03085
9. Courcelle, B.: Special tree-width and the verification of monadic second-order graph properties. In: FSTTCS. LIPIcs, vol. 8, pp. 13–29. Schloss Dagstuhl - Leibniz-Zentrum für Informatik, Chennai, India (2010)

10. Damgaard, N., Klarlund, N., Schwartzbach, M.I.: YakYak: parsing with logical side constraints. In: Proceedings of DLT'99 (1999)
11. De Moura, L., Bjørner, N.: Z3: an efficient SMT solver. In: International Conference on Tools and Algorithms for the Construction and Analysis of Systems, pp. 337–340. Springer (2008)
12. Demri, S., Nowak, D.: Reasoning about transfinite sequences. In: Peled, D.A., Tsay, Y.K. (eds.) Automated Technology for Verification and Analysis, pp. 248–262. Springer, Berlin, Heidelberg (2005)
13. Di Giusto, C., Ferré, D., Laversa, L., Lozes, É.: A partial order view of message-passing communication models. Proc. ACM Program. Lang. **7**(POPL), 1601–1627 (2023). https://doi.org/10.1145/3571248
14. Engels, A., Mauw, S., Reniers, M.: A hierarchy of communication models for message sequence charts. Sci. Comput. Program. **44**(3), 253–292 (2002). https://doi.org/10.1016/S0167-6423(02)00022-9
15. Havelund, K., Roşu, G.: Runtime verification-17 years later. In: International Conference on Runtime Verification, pp. 3–17. Springer (2018)
16. Herlihy, M., Wing, J.M.: Linearizability: a correctness condition for concurrent objects. ACM Trans. Program. Langu. Syst. (TOPLAS) **12**(3), 463–492 (1990). https://doi.org/10.1145/78969.78972
17. Holzmann, G.J., Bosnacki, D.: The design of a multicore extension of the spin model checker. IEEE Trans. Softw. Eng. **33**(10), 659–674 (2007)
18. Jensen, J.L., Joergensen, M.E., Klarlund, N., Schwartzbach, M.I.: Automatic verification of pointer programs using monadic second-order logic. In: PLDI '97 (1997)
19. Klarlund, N., Nielsen, M., Sunesen, K.: A case study in automated verification based on trace abstractions. In: Broy, M., Merz, S., Spies, K. (eds.) Formal System Specification, The RPC-Memory Specification Case Study. LNCS, vol. 1169, pp. 341–374. Springer Verlag (1996)
20. Klarlund, N., Møller, A.: Mona version 1.4 user manual (2001). https://www.brics.dk/mona/mona14.pdf
21. Kovács, L., Voronkov, A.: First-order theorem proving and vampire. In: International Conference on Computer Aided Verification, pp. 1–35. Springer (2013)
22. Burckhardt, S., Gotsman, A., H.Y.: Understanding eventual consistency. Technical Report MSR-TR-2013-39 (2013)
23. Singla, A., Ramachandran, U., Hodgins, J.K.: Temporal notions of synchronization and consistency in beehive. In: Proceedings of the Ninth Annual ACM Symposium on Parallel Algorithms and Architectures, SPAA 1997, Santa Barbara, California, USA, 23–25 July 1997, pp. 211–220. ACM (1997). https://doi.org/10.1145/258492.258513
24. Viotti, P., Vukolic, M.: Consistency in non-transactional distributed storage systems. http://vukolic.com/consistency-survey.pdf (2016)
25. Weidenbach, C., Dimova, D., Fietzke, A., Kumar, R., Suda, M., Wischnewski, P.: Spass version 3.5. In: International Conference on Automated Deduction, pp. 140–145. Springer (2009)
26. Yu, Y., Manolios, P., Lamport, L.: Model checking tla+ specifications. In: Advanced Research Working Conference on Correct Hardware Design and Verification Methods, pp. 54–66. Springer (1999)

Motif Refinement for the Hierarchical Control of Structured CPSs

Simon Bliudze[1] ⓘ, Sophie Cerf[2] ⓘ, and Olga Kouchnarenko[3](✉) ⓘ

[1] Univ. Lille, Inria, CNRS, Centrale Lille, UMR 9189 CRIStAL, 59000 Lille, France
Simon.Bliudze@inria.fr
[2] Univ. Grenoble Alpes, Inria, CNRS, Grenoble INP, LIG, 38000 Grenoble, France
Sophie.Cerf@inria.fr
[3] Université Marie et Louis Pasteur, CNRS, UMR 6174 FEMTO-ST, 25000 Besançon, France
Olga.Kouchnarenko@femto-st.fr

Abstract. Guaranteeing cyber-physical systems (CPSs) correct and proper behaviour is an essential and challenging issue, as they are widely used in many application domains. This paper aims to contribute to the flexible design and development of *structured* CPSs, composed of similar elements and capable of (self-)adaptation to satisfy evolving internal and external constraints, e.g. using control theory. To this end, based on a model of a hierarchical motif for modeling both systems' elements and controllers, we introduce a control-compatible notion of a motif refinement, and then we show that the stability of control can be preserved regarding a refinement-based development. Motivations and contributions are illustrated by the smart building example.

1 Introduction

Cyber-physical systems (CPSs), which are widely used in many application domains, include interacting networks of physical and computational components [1]. Ensuring CPSs correct and proper behaviour is an essential and challenging issue [15]. In addition, managing (self-)adaptation is crucial for CPSs functional and non-functional requirements, e.g., performance, power consumption, or reliability.

Among various approaches to (self-)adaptation, the well-known MAPE loop [30] has been intensively studied, as well as its extension to knowledge management, MAPE-K. One of the recent waves [41] to self-adaptation has brought feedback control theory (CT) as a suitable adaptation methodology [25,27,36]. Even if the systems considered are CPSs or software, *continuous* control is an adequate technique for self-adaptation [39]. Also, a *linear* control formulation has provided significant results when used for complex and potentially non-linear software systems.

Institute of Engineering Université Grenoble Alpes

This work was partially supported by the ANR grant ANR-23-CE25-0004 (ADAPT).

O. Kouchnarenko was supported by the EIPHI Graduate School (grant number ANR-17-EURE-0002). This work was partially carried out during her research leave at Inria Lille.

R. Casadei and F. Ghassemi (Eds.): COORDINATION 2026, LNCS 16590, pp. 47–69, 2026.
https://doi.org/10.1007/978-3-032-28358-0_3

More precisely, CT aims to stabilize and configure systems that evolve over time, in line with the MAPE-K formulation. To control a system, the general methodology consists in identifying a plant, e.g. the model of the system to be controlled, and designing its associated controller. A feedback control loop is displayed in Fig. 1: the plant captures the impact of changes in the values of the knobs on the values of measures, while the controller sets the value of the knobs based on the values of measures and their reference values (e.g. objective value). Knobs and measures are signals that evolve with time, taking continuous (possibly quantified) values. There can also be disturbances, modeled by external and uncontrolled signals that impact systems' behavior.

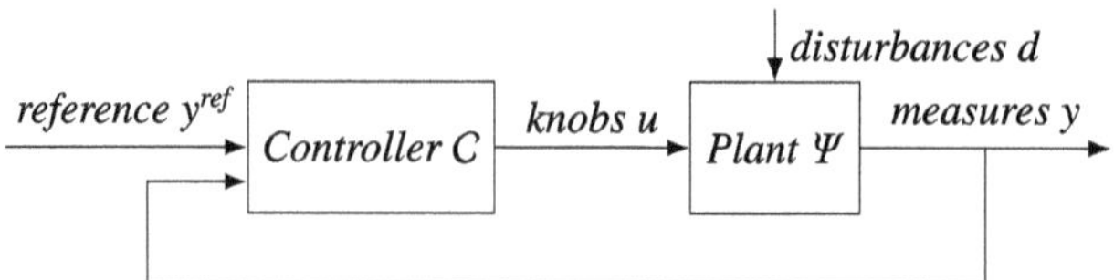

Fig. 1. Schema of a control feedback loop

However, the MAPE-K approach has shown to favor monolithic controllers, such as in Fig. 1, rather than structured controllers—global together with local ones exploiting system's structure—that are more appropriate for (self-)adaptive CPSs [18]. In this context, a modeling approach with hierarchical motifs has been introduced in [12] for both the system and its control, with the aim of allowing *structured* CPSs to be adaptive. Structured CPSs are meant to be composed of similar elements organized in motifs, which are assemblies of sub-systems responsible for carrying out some common functionalities. Structured CPSs may have their implicit software regulators and explicit controllers interwoven, whereas, in general, controller design is too strongly decoupled from the system under control. This is why designing and implementing more flexible controllers is challenging.

In order to allow modular and incremental design of structured CPSs and of their controllers, this paper introduces a notion of motif refinement. Refinement-based modeling and development approaches help users specify and implement complex software and hardware systems [23,33]. Refinement is an important concept in model-driven engineering, which has been thoroughly studied within e.g. ASM, B and Event-B, TLA+, VDM, and Z frameworks. The main advantage of refinement-based approaches is that in general it is easier to establish a property, e.g., safety or some liveness properties, on a high level model than on more detailed models or the code. In addition, such a property, or its more detailed version, can be ensured through refinement, provided that the specific sufficient conditions are verified by refinement steps [11,28]. Moreover, for structured CPSs with components, it is important to associate design by refinement with design by composition [17]. This paper aims to ensure the preservation of stability properties in the presence of control, through the use of refinement of hierarchical motifs. This raises the following research questions:

RQ1 How to define the refinement of the sub-systems of structured CPSs?

RQ2 Is control stability preserved by refinement-based design of such CPSs?

To answer these questions, this paper's contribution consists in defining motif refinement and particularly focuses on two types of refinement–interface or structure refinements–to prove that control-theoretic stability properties can be preserved through refinement.

The remainder of the paper is organized as follows. Section 3 provides an overview of hierarchical motifs, their syntax, and semantics. Section 4 presents the background of the control theory.Section 5 introduces two refinement notions dedicated to hierarchical motifs (RQ1). Afterward, the control stability through refinement is studied (RQ2) in Sect. 6. Related work is presented in Sect. 7, and Sect. 8 concludes the paper.

2   Motivating Example: Temperature Control in a Smart Building

To illustrate controlled CPSs with flexible and hierarchical structure, consider a smart building composed of rooms and hallways equipped with controllable heating systems (see Fig. 2a). Some rooms are modular with folding walls to form larger spaces. The target temperature for a room can vary depending on its type (e.g. office, corridor, server room) and occupation status (vacant or with people inside). Time or weather constraints (e.g. open/closed building, winter/summer) can also modify temperature objectives.

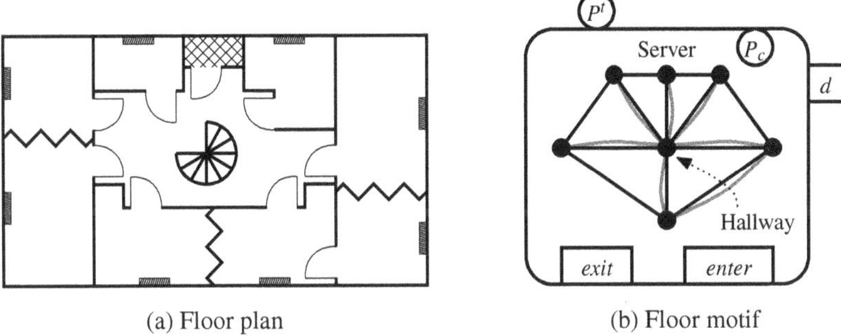

(a) Floor plan   (b) Floor motif

Fig. 2. One floor of the building (In (a), zigzag lines indicate foldable partition walls, the server room is shaded. In (b), outer nodes clockwise from `Server` are `Room`, three `Modular Rooms` and another `Room`; double edges are for visual clarity only—they represent predicates on the underlying graph.)

The heating control is hierarchically structured, with (i) the lower level regulating the temperature in a single room, with one radiator each, (ii) the middle level consisting of sets of modular rooms that can merge or split, (iii) and the higher level setting temperature targets for the different rooms of a floor.

As the configuration of a room evolves, it changes room structure inside its set. The temperature regulation of such a smart building illustrates the control of flexible and hierarchically structured systems.

3   Background: Hierarchical Motifs

In [12], we have introduced the notion of *motifs* with the purpose of allowing for flexible design, hierarchical composition, and the control of structured Cyber-Physical Systems (CPSs). We now present a summary of the relevant definitions, referring the reader to [12] for a step-by-step presentation with detailed examples.

3.1   Motifs: Basic Definitions

Motifs represent organised assemblies of sub-systems, specifying how measures, control commands, and disturbances are propagated through the system hierarchy. They are defined based on *maps*, which are directed graphs with predicates used to convey additional information on the types of nodes and edges.

To be assembled hierarchically, motifs expose *interfaces*, which can be *external* (towards higher levels of the hierarchy) or *internal* (towards the sub-systems located in the nodes of the motif's map). An external interface provides an abstract view of the state space of the sub-tree of the hierarchical assembly rooted in the motif w.r.t. both coordination (i.e. the set of *possible* discrete actions) and control (i.e. the set of *possible* measured values, and the sets of *acceptable* knob positions and disturbances). Dually, an internal interface specifies the sets of *acceptable* actions and measure values, and the sets of *possible* knob positions and disturbances for the sub-tree rooted in a given node of the motif. We assume a universe of actions Act given. Furthermore, we assume Act to be a bounded lattice with the usual lattice operations $\vee$ (join) and $\wedge$ (meet), and bounds $\bot$ (bottom) and $\top$ (top).

Definition 1 (Motif interface). *A motif interface is a tuple $M \stackrel{def}{=} (\mu, (I^n)_{n\in\mu}, I^{ext})$, where*

- *$\mu = (N, E, \mathcal{P})$ is a map, with N the set of nodes, $E \subseteq N \times N$ the set of edges, and $\mathcal{P}$ the set of predicates on nodes and edges,[1]*
- *$I^n = (A^n, S^n_Y, S^n_U, S^n_D, Y^n, U^n, D^n)$, for each $n \in \mu$, are node interfaces, with discrete actions $A^n \subseteq Act$, for all $n \in \mu$, and the measure, knob and disturbance domains represented by the corresponding vector spaces S^n_* and ranges $Y^n \subseteq S^n_Y$, $U^n \subseteq S^n_U$, $D^n \subseteq S^n_D$,[2]*
- *$I^{ext} = (A^{ext}, S^{ext}_Y, S^{ext}_U, S^{ext}_D, Y^{ext}, U^{ext}, D^{ext})$ is an external interface, such that every external action $a \in A^{ext} \subseteq Act$ is a join of internal ones, i.e. there exists $N' \subseteq N$ and $a_n \in A^n$, for each $n \in N'$, such that $a = \bigvee_{n \in N'} a_n$.*

We denote $I^{int} \stackrel{def}{=} \prod_{n\in\mu} I^n$ the internal interface of the motif. Here, the product of interfaces is defined component-wise using disjoint set union for sets of descrete actions and Cartesian product for all other components. It is associative and up-to-isomorphism commutative. We also denote $A^M \stackrel{def}{=} A^{int} \cup A^{ext}$ the set of all actions of a motif.

Note 1. When ambiguity may arise between elements of coinciding interfaces, we will distinguish them by writing, e.g., $a@n$ (for node interfaces) or $a@^{ext}$ (for external interfaces), as appropriate.

---

[1] By abuse of notaton, we write $n \in \mu$ and $(n_1, n_2) \in \mu$, meaning, resp., $n \in N$ and $(n_1, n_2) \in E$.

[2] Throughout the paper, we follow the control theoretic convention and use Y, U, and D when referring, resp., to measures, knobs and disturbances.

Note 2. Internal measures Y^{int}, external knobs U^{ext}, and external disturbances D^{ext} can be construed as inputs of a motif. Dually, external measures Y^{ext}, internal knobs U^{int}, and internal disturbances D^{int} can be construed as its outputs.

Example 1 (Floor motif[3]). Figure 2b shows elements of the interface of a motif representing one floor of a smart building (cf. Fig. 2a). The map has one node for the hallway and the server room, and one for each (modular) room. The edges of the map representing their physical adjacency are shown in black. The node types are distinguished by the corresponding predicates: `Hallway`, `Server`, and `Room` (not shown). The edge predicate shown in blue models the possibility for people to move between the corresponding spaces.

Internal interfaces associated with map nodes are not shown. The boxes inside the motif show the provided external actions, $A^{ext} = \{exit, enter\}$. The external measurement P_c (circled, inside the motif) provided by the motif is the total power consumed by the heating system of the floor. The external knob P^t (circled, outside the motif) is the target value for this power. Finally, disturbance d (boxed, outside the motif) represents the temperature of the room floor T_f, the walls T_w, the outdoor air T_o and the ground T_g, the solar radiation on the walls and windows $\mathcal{R}_s$. $\qquad\qquad\square$

Given a map $\mu = (N, E, \mathcal{P})$, and associated node and external interfaces $(I^n)_{n\in\mu}$ and I^{ext}, resp., coordination of the sub-system actions is specified using a first order *interaction logic* $\mathcal{L}(\Sigma)$ with a signature Σ sufficient to associate external actions to combinations of internal ones under constraints on the inputs of the motif.

Definition 2 (Motif). *A motif is a tuple $M \overset{def}{=} (\mu, (I^n)_{n\in\mu}, I^{ext}, \mathcal{A}, \Phi, \Delta, \varphi)$, where*

- *$(\mu, (I^n)_{n\in\mu}, I^{ext})$, is a motif interface as in Definition 1,*
- *$\mathcal{A} : 2^{A^{int}} \times S_Y^{int} \times S_D^{ext} \to S_Y^{ext}$, such that $\mathcal{A}(2^{A^{int}} \times Y^{int} \times D^{ext}) \subseteq Y^{ext}$, is a measure aggregation specifying how the measures provided by the nodes are aggregated—in view of the current perturbations—to be exposed at the external interface,*
- *$\Phi : 2^{A^{int}} \times S_Y^{int} \times S_U^{int} \times S_U^{ext} \times S_D^{ext} \to S_U^{int}$, such that $\Phi(2^{A^{int}} \times Y^{int} \times U^{int} \times U^{ext} \times D^{ext}) \subseteq U^{int}$, is a control profile, specifying how the knobs are set at each node given the state of the motif and the current disturbance values.*
- *$\Delta : 2^{A^{int}} \times S_Y^{int} \times S_D^{ext} \to S_D^{int}$, such that $\Delta(2^{A^{int}} \times Y^{int} \times D^{ext}) \subseteq D^{int}$, is a disturbance profile, specifying how external disturbances of the motif translate to corresponding disturbances at the nodes,*
- *$\varphi \in \mathcal{L}(\Sigma)$, is an interaction constraint.*

Example 2 (Modular Room motif[6]). Figure 3a shows the map and the external interface of the Modular Room motif. The map has two nodes representing rooms composing the modular room and one node representing a logical component that keeps track of the state of the modular room (split or merged). The node interface at the latter node (not shown) has two actions, *isMerged* and *isSplit*, used to signal the state of the modular room. The node interfaces at the two former nodes (not shown) are the same as the

---

[3] See [12] for a detailed presentation.

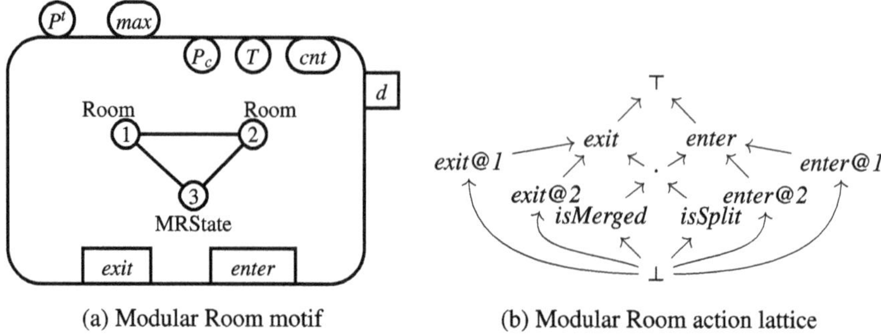

(a) Modular Room motif   (b) Modular Room action lattice

Fig. 3. Modular Room motif and the corresponding action lattice.

external interface of the motif. The association of the *exit* and *enter* actions at these nodes with the corresponding external actions are established through the action lattice (Fig. 3b) and the interaction constraint. For example, the interaction constraint can be written as a conjunction of "local" constraints, e.g.

$$\ldots \wedge \Big(isMerged \wedge \exists n(\text{Room}(n)) : exit@n \implies \forall n(\text{Room}(n)), exit@n \Big)$$
$$\wedge \Big(isSplit \wedge \exists n(\text{Room}(n)) : exit@n \implies \exists! n(\text{Room}(n)) : exit@n \Big) \wedge \ldots$$

$\square$

We model structured CPSs as trees with motifs at all internal nodes and atomic components defining the system behaviour at the leaves. The children of each internal node correspond to the nodes of the map of the motif. See [12] for a detailed example.

As usual, the operational semantics of such assemblies is given in terms of Labelled Transition Systems (LTSs) materialised by the same kind of objects for both atomic components and composed systems, allowing hierarchical composition. Below, we reproduce the definition of object from [12]. Operational semantics is straightforward: measures, knob values and disturbances are plugged in as input-output pairs and transformed within motifs by aggregations and profiles; component actions are synchronised within each motif in accordance with the interaction constraint. Sets of actions that satisfy the interaction constraint—and can therefore be synchronised—are called *interactions*.[4] Formal definition presented in [12] is limited to *closed instantiations*, where an object is plugged into every node of a motif. However, a straightforward conservative extension allows one to define the semantics in the general case, including *open instantiations*, where some nodes do not have objects plugged in.

Definition 3 (Object). *An object O implementing the interface* $(A, S_Y, S_U, S_D, Y, U, D)$ *is an entity that can be given an operational semantics in the form of an LTS* $|O| = (2^A \times Y \times U, A \times U \times D, \rightarrow)$, *such that*

---

[4] Every interaction consists of one external action and a set of corresponding internal ones.

- *for any* $(A^{en}, y, u) \xrightarrow{a, \widetilde{u}, d} (A^{en\prime}, y', u')$, *we have* $a \in A^{en}$ *and* $u' = \widetilde{u}$,
- *for any* (A^{en}, y, u), $u' \in U$, *and* $d \in D$, *there exists* $(A^{en}, y, u) \xrightarrow{\perp, u', d} (A^{en\prime}, y', u')$.

The state of an object is thus defined by the set of *enabled actions* and the current measurements and knob positions. The conditions imposed on the transition relation mean that (*i*) only enabled actions can be fired, ((*ii*) the knob positions can only be set externally and are not affected by the behaviour of the object, and (*iii*) the bottom action is always enabled.

The precise definition of the operational semantics of objects is intentionally left open to be able to accommodate objects of different natures: standard discrete automata, timed automata, hybrid automata, etc..

3.2   Control Motifs

Based on Fig. 1, we consider the basic control signals: measures y, reference values for these measures y^{ref}, and knobs u, a tunable signal that allows leveraging the measure signal. In addition, one may consider an external disturbance d.

Consider an object that implements the interface $(A, S_Y, S_U, S_D, Y, U, D)$. Its control is realized by a *control function* $c : 2^A \times S_Y \times S_U \times S_Y \times S_D \to S_U$. Given the current set of enabled actions $A^{en} \subseteq A$ and the current measure $y \in Y$, the knob position $u \in U$, a reference value $y^{ref} \in Y$, and , the disturbance $d \in D$, the control function defines the new value of the knob $u' = c(A^{en}, y, u, y^{ref}, d) \in U$ of the object.

We define *control motifs*, which are a special case of motifs in Definitions 1 and 2 characterised by such control functions. We put $M_c = (\{\bullet\}, I^{int}, I^{ext}, id_{\mathcal{A}}, c, id_{\Delta}, \varphi^{1:1})$, where (*i*) $\{\bullet\}$ is a singleton map (one node, no edges, no predicates), (*ii*) $I_c^{int} = (A, S_Y, S_U, S_D, Y, U, D)$, (*iii*) $I_c^{ext} = (A, S_Y, S_Y, S_D, Y, Y, D)$, (*iv*) $id_{\mathcal{A}} : 2^A \times S_Y \to S_Y$ and $id_{\Delta} : 2^A \times S_Y \times S_D \to S_D$ are projections on the corresponding last components of their arguments, (*v*) the control function c plays the role of the profile, and (*vi*) $\varphi^{1:1} = \bigwedge_{a \in A}(a@^{ext} \Leftrightarrow a@\bullet)$.

In the external interface of a control motif, the knob is replaced by the reference values of the measures. We do not impose any constraints on the nature of the control function. However, in this paper, we do limit ourselves to *linear* controllers.

4   Control of Structured Motifs

In this section, the definition of motifs and the linear control formulation are linked. Then, the focus is made on hierarchical systems, specifying the plant formulation for motifs whose map is a tree. We illustrate these elements with the example of smart building detailed in [12].

Beforehand, we introduce *transfer functions*, which are the necessary background on the control theory formulation. Indeed, both the plant Ψ and the controller C are represented using transfer functions. A transfer function represents the transformation of signals, e.g. how the knob signal u affects the measure signal y. Thus, this can be written as $y = \Psi u$, where a simple linear relation describes the system behaviour. The notions of plant, controller, and their transfer function can now be linked to the motifs defined in Sect. 3.

4.1 Linking Control Formulation and Motifs

Let us first consider a motif M in the most general case. The *plant* transfer function Ψ captures the impact of the changes of knobs u on measures y. This mathematical model links elements in motif's external interface I^{ext}, with $u \in U^{ext}$ and $y \in Y^{ext}$. The impact of disturbances d on measurements is also taken into account in the model, e.g. by artificially increasing the measurement vector y with disturbances.

The plant Ψ is thus a partial view of a motif, only concerned with the evolution of the external interface signals. Its dependence on internal elements can be explored in the case where the map is specified, as presented in the next subsection.

We now consider a *control motif* M_c. The *controller* C captures the impact of the references and the measures (often through their difference, i.e. the reference tracking error) and the disturbances d on the knobs signal: $u = C(y^{ref}, y, d)$. Thus, the controller C models the link between the elements of the internal and external interfaces of the control motif M_c.

Example 3. (Room temperature control in a Smart Building) The room **plant** Ψ_{Room} models the impact of the knob (here the heating power $u_{\text{Room}} = P_{\text{Room}}$) on the measure (here the room temperature $y_{\text{Room}} = T_{\text{Room}}$), under disturbances d_{Room} (neighboring temperatures, radiations, etc.). We define x as the set of all relevant measures and disturbances: $x \overset{\text{def}}{=} \begin{pmatrix} y_{\text{Room}} \\ d_{\text{Room}} \end{pmatrix}$. The indoor temperatures evolution is modeled as:

$$\begin{cases} x' = Ax + Bu_{\text{Room}}, \\ y_{\text{Room}} = Cx \end{cases} \tag{1}$$

where x' denotes either the derivative of x in the continuous-time case, or its value at the next time-step in the discrete-time case. A and B are matrices taking into account the convection, thermal resistances, and capacity of the various elements around the room. The matrix C selects the room temperature among the disturbances.

The transfer function Ψ_{Room} is then computed using the model matrices: $\Psi_{\text{Room}}(s) = C(sI - A)^{-1} B$, with I the identity matrix of adequate size and s the complex variable.

The room **controller** C_{Room} computes the heat power knob value u_{Room} based on the target temperature y^{ref}_{Room}, the room measured temperature y_{Room} and all the disturbances. For the linear time-invariant system that we consider, the optimal controller can be computed as a state feedback, with precompensation for the reference tracking:

$$C_{\text{Room}}(y^{ref}_{\text{Room}}, y_{\text{Room}}, d_{\text{Room}}) = -K \begin{pmatrix} y_{\text{Room}} \\ d_{\text{Room}} \end{pmatrix} + G y^{ref}_{\text{Room}}, \tag{2}$$

where K is the state feedback gain; and G is the precompensation gain, both being vectors of appropriate sizes. The computation of the controller gains is detailed in [12]. □

4.2 Hierarchical Control

We consider CPSs with a hierarchical structure, in which there is at least one controller. At a given level, the motif map and interfaces are instantiated, and we fix an order on the nodes of the map. Note that here the disturbances are not explicitly written in the following formulations to simplify, as they can be considered as part of the measurement vector y extended with disturbances.

The plant Ψ modeling the knobs-to-measures behaviour of the motif M, can be expressed using the profile function Φ, the aggregation function $\mathcal{A}$, and recursively over the lower level motifs. At a given level, the measure $y \in Y^{ext}$ is the *aggregation* of the measures y_i of the lower levels: $y = \mathcal{A}\mathbf{y}$, with $\mathbf{y} = (y_1, \cdots, y_i, \cdots, y_n)^T \in Y^{int}$ (internal interfaces).

The controller C computes the knob $u \in U^{ext}$ (external interfaces), that is distributed among the lower levels as u_i by the *profile* function Φ: $\mathbf{u} = \Phi u$, with $\mathbf{u} = (u_1, \cdots, u_i, \cdots, u_n)^T \in U^{int}$ (internal interfaces). The measure at a lower level can be derived from the value of the knob that was enforced, and is modelled by P_i, the *subsystem* transfer function $y_i = P_i u_i$.

The hierarchical control consists then in designing C to regulate the *plant* Ψ, recursively formulated as $\Psi = \mathcal{A}\mathbf{P}\Phi$, with $\mathbf{P} \overset{def}{=} (P_1, \cdots, P_i, \cdots, P_n) \times \mathbf{I}_n$.

Example 4. Following Example 3, consider a floor composed of n rooms. The floor model Ψ_{Floor} based on the room models $\Psi_{\text{Room},i}$ and the floor aggregation and profile matrices. At the lower level, each room is controlled by a feedback controller, their equivalent closed-loop transfer function is thus:

$$P_{\text{Room},i} = \frac{C_{\text{Room},i}\Psi_{\text{Room},i}}{1 + C_{\text{Room},i}\Psi_{\text{Room},i}}.$$

The floor power is computed as the sum of all the power used in the rooms. The aggregation $\mathcal{A}_{\text{Floor}}$ is then: $\mathcal{A}_{\text{Floor}} = (1 \cdots 1)^T$.

The profile Φ_{Floor} distributes the temperature references between the rooms: $\Phi_{\text{Floor}} = (\alpha_1 \cdots \alpha_n)$, where α_i is a scaling factor depending on the room usage. It is equal to 1 if the room is occupied, 0.8 if the room is empty or a hallway, and 0.7 in the server room. Overall, the floor plant is then $\Psi_{\text{Floor}} = \mathcal{A}_{\text{Floor}}\mathbf{P}_{\text{Room}}\Phi_{\text{Floor}}$, with $\mathbf{P}_{\text{Room}} = (P_{\text{Room},1} \cdots P_{\text{Room},n}) \times \mathbf{I}_n$. $\qquad\square$

5 Motif Refinement

This section aims to address RQ1. Based on the motif model, we introduce a control-compatible notion of a motif refinement and state its basic properties. More precisely, we propose two kinds of motif refinement: (*i*) refinement of interfaces, potentially introducing new nodes, and (*ii*) refinement of the map by replicating existing nodes. These can be combined arbitrarily to obtain more complex motif refinements.

5.1 Motif Refinement Definitions

Refinement of Interfaces This kind of refinement follows the classical schema for interface and contract refinement: covariant expansion on the inputs and contravariant expansion on the outputs. Although every control-related element of an interface is viewed as an input or an output of a motif, these roles change depending on whether the corresponding interface is internal or external (see Note 2). Furthermore, the particularity of the proposed refinement notions is that we allow expanding the dimensions of the corresponding vector spaces. For example, the refining motif can provide entirely new measures not present in the refined one so long as the range of values does not grow for the existing measures. The ensuing necessity to simultaneously address the dual (co- and contravariant) expansion and the projection of the underlying vector spaces leads us to define separate notions of refinement for internal and for external interfaces.

Definition 4 (Map containment). *A map μ_1 is contained in another map μ_2, denoted $\mu_1 \subseteq \mu_2$, if (i) $N_1 \subseteq N_2$, (ii) $E_1 = E_2 \cap N_1^2$, i.e. there are no "new" edges between the "old" nodes, (iii) $\mathcal{P}_1 \subseteq \mathcal{P}_2$, and (iv) for any $P \in \mathcal{P}_1$, we have $\mu_1.P = \mu_2.P \downarrow_{N_1 \cup E_1}$, i.e. the meaning of the predicates does not change.*

Definition 5 (Interface refinement). *Let $I_i = (A_i, S_{Y,i}, S_{U,i}, S_{D,i}, Y_i, U_i, D_i)$ (with $i = 1, 2$) be two interfaces, such that (i) $A_1 \subseteq A_2$ and (ii) $S_{Y,1}$, $S_{U,1}$, and $S_{D,1}$ are subspaces of $S_{Y,2}$, $S_{U,2}$, and $S_{D,2}$, resp. Denote $\downarrow_{S_{*,1}} \colon S_{*,2} \to S_{*,1}$, for $* \in \{Y, U, D\}$, the corresponding vector space projections. Whenever unambiguously determined by the context, we will write $\downarrow$ without the index indicating the target space.*

Interface I_1 is externally refined by I_2, denoted $I_1 \sqsubseteq^{ext} I_2$, if $Y_2 \downarrow \subseteq Y_1$, $U_1 \subseteq U_2 \downarrow$, and $D_1 \subseteq D_2 \downarrow$. It is refined internally, denoted $I_1 \sqsubseteq^{int} I_2$, if $Y_1 \subseteq Y_2 \downarrow$, $U_2 \downarrow \subseteq U_1$, and $D_2 \downarrow \subseteq D_1$.

Denote $\uparrow^{S_{*,2}}$ (for $* \in \{Y, U, D\}$) the lifting corresponding to the projection $\downarrow_{S_{*,1}}$, that is, for $X \subseteq S_{*,1}$, we have $X \uparrow^{S_{*,2}} \stackrel{def}{=} \{x \in S_{*,2} \mid x \downarrow_{S_{*,1}} \in X\}$. As for projection, we will omit the exponent whenever unambiguously determined by the context.

Definition 6 (Refinement of motif interfaces). *Let $M_i = (\mu_i, (I_i^n)_{n \in \mu}, I_i^{ext}, \mathcal{A}_i, \Phi_i, \Delta_i, \varphi_i)$ (with $i = 1, 2$) be two motifs. Motif M_1 is interface-refined by M_2, denoted $M_1 \sqsubseteq^i M_2$, if hold (i) $\mu_1 \subseteq \mu_2$, (ii) $I_1^{ext} \sqsubseteq^{ext} I_2^{ext}$, (iii) for every node $n \in \mu$, $I_1^n \sqsubseteq^{int} I_2^n$, (iv) $\varphi_1 \Rightarrow \exists_{A^{M_2} \setminus A^{M_1}} \varphi_2$, i.e. for any interaction $\bar{a}_1 \subseteq A^{M_1}$ allowed in M_1, there exists an interaction $\bar{a}_2 \subseteq A^{M_2}$ allowed in M_2, such that $\bar{a}_1 \subseteq \bar{a}_2$ and $\bar{a}_2 \setminus \bar{a}_1 \subseteq A^{M_2} \setminus A^{M_1}$ and (v) all three of the aggregation, control and disturbance profiles commute with the corresponding projections, i.e.*

- *$\mathcal{A}_1(A^{en} \cap A_1^{int}, y\downarrow) = \mathcal{A}_2(A^{en}, y)\downarrow$, for all $A^{en} \subseteq A_2^{int}$ and $y \in Y_1^{int}\uparrow$,*
- *$\Phi_1(A^{en} \cap A_1^{int}, y\downarrow, u\downarrow, u'\downarrow, d\downarrow) = \Phi_2(A^{en}, u, u', d)\downarrow$, for all $A^{en} \subseteq A_2^{int}$, $y \in Y_1^{int}\uparrow$, $u \in U_2^{int}$, $u' \in U_1^{ext}\uparrow$ and $d \in D_1^{ext}\uparrow$,*
- *$\Delta_1(A^{en} \cap A_1^{int}, y\downarrow, d\downarrow) = \Delta_2(A^{en}, y, d)\downarrow$, for all $A^{en} \subseteq A_2^{int}$, $y \in Y_1^{int}\uparrow$, and $d \in D_1^{ext}\uparrow$.*

Notice that the refinement notion in Definition 6 allows new nodes to be added to the refining motif. The internal interface associated with the new nodes would contribute new dimensions to the internal interface of the refining motif. However, according to Definition 5 we still have $I_1^{int} \sqsubseteq^{int} I_2^{int}$ (with I_1^{int}, I_2^{int} as in Definition 1).

Example 5. Straightforward examples of refinement of motif interfaces are (*i*) refining a motif by introducing new nodes without modifying the existing ones, (*ii*) adding new measures, knobs or disturbances to existing nodes, and (*iii*) improving the "quality" of the aggregation, or control or disturbance profiles. $\square$

Node replication A map μ_2 refines another map μ_1 if μ_1 can be obtained from μ_2 by contracting some of the edges. To define this formally, we need the notion of node lifting. Let $\mu_i = (N_i, E_i)$, for $i = 1, 2$.

Definition 7 (Node lifting). *Let $r : N_2 \to N_1$ be a subjective mapping. The* lifting of a node $n \in N_1$ along r *is the sub-graph* $(r^{-1}(n), r^{-1}(n)^2 \cap E_2)$ *of* μ_2.

Definition 8 (Map refinement). *A map μ_1 is refined by μ_2, denoted $\mu_1 \sqsubseteq \mu_2$, if there exists a subjective mapping $r : N_2 \to N_1$, such that (i) the lifting of each node $n \in N_1$ along r is a connected graph, (ii) two nodes in N_1 are connected iff so are their liftings along r, i.e. $E_1 = \{(n_1, n_1') \mid \exists n_2 \in r^{-1}(n_1), n_2' \in r^{-1}(n_1') : (n_2, n_2') \in E_2\}$, (iii) $\mathcal{P}_1 \subseteq \mathcal{P}_2$, (iv) the lifting of a node satisfies the same predicates as the lifted node, i.e., for all $n \in N_2$ and $P \in \mathcal{P}_1$, holds $P(n) = P(r(n))$, and (v) similarly for the edges, i.e., for all $(n, n') \in E_2$ and $P \in \mathcal{P}_1$, either $r(n) = r(n')$ or $P(n, n') = P(r(n), r(n'))$.*

We call r the witness mapping *of the refinement.*

For the remainder of this section, let us fix two motifs $M_i = (\mu_i, (I_i^n)_{n \in \mu_i}, I^{ext}, \mathcal{A}_i, \Phi_i, \Delta_i, \varphi_i)$ (with $i = 1, 2$) with the same external profile, and such that $\mu_1 \sqsubseteq \mu_2$ with a witness mapping $r : N_2 \to N_1$. Assume that, for every $n_1 \in N_1$ and every $n_2 \in r^{-1}(n_1)$, we have $I_2^{n_2} = I_1^{n_1}$. (Hence, for $n \in \mu_1$, we can skip the index on the interface I^n and its components.) As for Definition 6, it follows immediately from Definition 5 that $I_1^{int} \sqsubseteq^{int} I_2^{int}$.

Aggregation $\mathcal{A}_2$ refines $\mathcal{A}_1$ if the measures in I_2^{int} can be "pre-aggregated" so that the aggregated measures coincide with those obtained by $\mathcal{A}_2$.

Definition 9 (Aggregation refinement). *An aggregation $\mathcal{A}_1$ is refined by $\mathcal{A}_2$, denoted $\mathcal{A}_1 \sqsubseteq \mathcal{A}_2$, if there exists a family of* pre-aggregation *mappings $f = (f_n)_{n \in \mu_1}$ with $f_n : (S_Y^n)^{|r^{-1}(n)|} \to S_Y^n$, such that $\mathcal{A}_2 = \mathcal{A}_1 \circ (f, \downarrow)$, i.e.*

$$\mathcal{A}_2(A^{en}, y, d) = \mathcal{A}_1(A^{en} \cap A_1^{int}, f(y), d\downarrow),$$

for all $A^{en} \subseteq A_2^{int}$, $y \in S_{Y,2}^{int}$ and $d \in S_{D,2}^{ext}$.

Control profile refinement is defined similarly to the aggregation one. Recall that, in addition to the set of enabled actions, a profile takes four parameters to compute the updated positions of the internal knobs: the current internal values of the measures, the current positions of the internal knobs, the position of the external knob, and the external disturbance. Thus, profile Φ_2 refines Φ_1 if, similarly to Definition 9, the current internal values of the measures and the current positions of the internal knobs can be "pre-aggregated" before the application of Φ_1. Conversely, for each node $n \in \mu_1$, the result of this application must be further redistributed to the nodes in $r^{-1}(n)$.

Definition 10 (Control profile refinement). *Control profile Φ_1 is refined by Φ_2, denoted $\Phi_1 \sqsubseteq \Phi_2$, if there exist three families of mappings:*

- *measure pre-aggregation $f = (f_n)_{n \in \mu_1}$ as in Definition 9,*
- *knob pre-aggregation $g = (g_n)_{n \in \mu_1}$ with $g_n : (S_U^n)^{|r^{-1}(n)|} \to S_U^n$,*
- *knob re-distribution $h = (h_n)_{n \in \mu_1}$ with $h_n : (S_Y^n)^{|r^{-1}(n)|} \times (S_U^n)^{|r^{-1}(n)|} \times S_U^n \to (S_U^n)^{|r^{-1}(n)|}$,*

such that $g_n \circ h_n = \downarrow$, i.e., for all $n \in \mu_{M_1}$, $y \in \prod_{n' \in r^{-1}(n)} S^{n'}_{Y,2}$, $u \in \prod_{n' \in r^{-1}(n)} S^{n'}_{U,2}$ and $u_n \in S^n_{U,1}$, we have $g_n(h_n(y, u, u_n)) = u_n$ and also $\Phi_2 = h \circ \Phi_1 \circ (f, g, \downarrow, \downarrow)$, i.e.

$$\Phi_2(A^{en}, y, u, u^{ext}, d) = h\Big(y, u, \Phi_1(A^{en} \cap A^{int}_1, f(y), g(u), u^{ext}\downarrow, d\downarrow)\Big), \tag{3}$$

for all $A^{en} \subseteq A^{int}_2$, $y \in S^{int}_{Y,2}$, $u \in S^{int}_{U,2}$, $u^{ext} \in S^{ext}_{U,2}$ and $d \in S^{ext}_{D,2}$.

Disturbance profile refinement is defined similarly to that of the control profile.

Definition 11 (Disturbance profile refinement). *Disturbance profile Δ_1 is refined by Δ_2, denoted $\Delta_1 \sqsubseteq \Delta_2$, if there exist two families of mappings:*

- *measure pre-aggregation $f = (f_n)_{n \in \mu_1}$ as in Definition 9,*
- *disturbance re-distribution $t = (t_n)_{n \in \mu_1}$ with $t_n : (S^n_Y)^{|r^{-1}(n)|} \times S^n_D \to (S^n_D)^{|r^{-1}(n)|}$,*

such that $\Delta_2 = t \circ \Delta_1 \circ (f, \downarrow)$, i.e. $\Delta_2(A^{en}, y, d) = t\big(y, \Delta_1(A^{en} \cap A^{int}_1, f(y), d\downarrow)\big)$, for all $A^{en} \subseteq A^{int}_2$, $y \in S^{int}_{Y,2}$ and $d \in S^{ext}_{D,2}$.

To define the interaction constraint refinement, we have to explain how individual actions of every interface I^n_1 are realised in terms of actions of the interfaces $(I^{n'}_2)_{n' \in r^{-1}(n)}$.

Definition 12 (Interaction constraint refinement). *Interaction constraint φ_1 is refined by φ_2, denoted $\varphi_1 \sqsubseteq \varphi_2$ if, there exists a family of constraints $(\varphi_a)_{a \in I^{int}_1}$, such that (i) each constraint φ_a (for $a \in A^n$) refers precisely to the actions $a@n'$ with $n' \in r^{-1}(n)$, and (ii) $\varphi_2 = \varphi_1 \wedge \bigwedge_{n \in \mu_1} \bigwedge_{a \in A^n} (a@n \Leftrightarrow \varphi_a)$.*

Definition 13 (Refinement of motif maps). *Let M_1 and M_2 be two motifs with $I^{ext}_1 = I^{ext}_2$. Motif M_1 is map-refined by M_2, denoted $M_1 \sqsubseteq^m M_2$, if there exist witness, pre-aggregation and re-distribution mappings r, f, g, h, t resp., such that (i) $\mu_1 \sqsubseteq \mu_2$, (ii) for every node $n_1 \in N_1$ and every node $n_2 \in r^{-1}(n_1)$, we have $I^{n_2}_2 = I^{n_1}_1$, (iii) $\mathcal{A}_1 \sqsubseteq \mathcal{A}_2$, $\Phi_1 \sqsubseteq \Phi_2$, $\Delta_1 \sqsubseteq \Delta_2$ and $\varphi_1 \sqsubseteq \varphi_2$.*

Example 6. Refinement of motif maps allows replicating existing nodes. For instance, the Room nodes of the Floor motif (adjacent to the server room in the floor plan in Fig. 2) could each be replaced by several nodes representing smaller rooms.   □

5.2   Motif Instantiation

We now define what it means to instantiate a node of a motif with an object (which could, in turn be a hierarchically composed system). We generalise the definitions in [12] by relaxing the constraints that objects implement precisely the node interfaces and by allowing open instantiations.

Definition 14 (Instantiation). *A motif instantiation, denoted $M(\{O_n/n \mid n \in N\})$, where M is a motif, $N \subseteq \mu_M$ is a set of nodes, and, for each node $n \in N$, O_n an object implementing an interface I, such that $I^n \sqsubseteq^{ext} I$ of M. An instantiation is closed if N is the set of all nodes of μ_M. Otherwise, it is open.*

The semantics of $M(\{O_n/n\,|\,n \in N\})$ is defined by the following rule, where the changes from the rule in [12] are highlighted in red (premises 7 and 8).

$$
\frac{
\begin{array}{c}
a \in A^{en} \qquad a = \bigvee_{n\in\mu} a_n \qquad u' \in U^{ext} \qquad (a, (a_n)_{n\in\mu}, (y_n)_{n\in\mu}, u) \models \varphi \\[2ex]
(u'_n)_{n\in\mu} = \Phi\!\left(\bigcup_{n\in\mu} A_n^{en}, (y_n)_{n\in\mu}, (u_n)_{n\in\mu}, u'\right) \qquad (d_n)_{n\in\mu} = \Delta\!\left(\bigcup_{n\in\mu} A_n^{en}, (y_n)_{n\in\mu}, d\right) \\[2ex]
\forall n \in N,\ (A_n^{en}, y_n, u_n) \xrightarrow{a_n, u'_n, d_n} (A_n^{en\prime}, y'_n, u'_n) \qquad \forall n \notin N,\ y'_n \in Y_n \\[2ex]
A^{en\prime} = \left\{ a' = \bigvee_{n\in\mu} a'_n \in A^{ext} \;\middle|\; a'_n \in A_n^{en\prime} \wedge (a', (a'_n)_{n\in\mu}, (y'_n)_{n\in\mu}, u') \models \varphi \right\} \\[2ex]
y = \mathcal{A}\!\left(\bigcup_{n\in\mu} A_n^{en}, (y_n)_{n\in\mu}\right) \qquad y' = \mathcal{A}\!\left(\bigcup_{n\in\mu} A_n^{en\prime}, (y'_n)_{n\in\mu}\right)
\end{array}
}{
(A^{en}, y, u) \xrightarrow{a, u', d} (A^{en\prime}, y', u')
} \tag{4}
$$

The generalisation is conservative: the semanitcs of closed instantiations remains the same as in [12]. For open instantiations, the actions associated to the interfaces of non-instantiated nodes are considered to be always enabled; the measures provided can be arbitrary within the corresponding domain.

Proposition 1. $M(\{O_n/n\,|\,n \in N\})$ *is an object in the sense of Definition 3.*

5.3 Properties of Motif Refinement

We provide two basic results about the impact of motif refinement on the behaviour of the coordinated system. We rely on the following notion of object refinement. These results correspond to ideal cases, where the input behaviours match exactly and we do not need control-theoretic results to establish the correspondence. More general results, based on the control-theoretic methodology are presented in Sect. 6.

Definition 15 (Object refinement). *Let O_1, O_2 be two objects implementing, resp., interfaces I_1, I_2, with $I_1 \sqsubseteq^{ext} I_2$. We say that O_2 refines O_1, denoted $O_1 \sqsubseteq O_2$, if for any* $(A_1^{en}, y_1, u_1) \xrightarrow{a_1, u'_1, d_1} (A_1^{en\prime}, y'_1, u'_1)$ *in $|O_1|$ and any (A_2^{en}, y_2, u_2), such that $A_1^{en} = A_2^{en} \cap A_1$, $y_1 = y_2{\downarrow}$, and $u_1 = u_2{\downarrow}$, there exists $(A_2^{en}, y_2, u_2) \xrightarrow{a_2, u'_2, d_2} (A_2^{en\prime}, y'_2, u'_2)$ in $|O_2|$, such that $A_1^{en\prime} = A_2^{en\prime} \cap A_1$, $a_1 = a_2 \cap A_1$, $u'_1 = u'_2{\downarrow}$, $d_1 = d_2{\downarrow}$, and*

$$
\left\{ y'_2{\downarrow} \;\middle|\; (A_2^{en}, y_2, u_2) \xrightarrow{a_2, u'_2, d_2} (A_2^{en\prime}, y'_2, u'_2) \right\} \subseteq \left\{ y'_1 \;\middle|\; (A_1^{en}, y_1, u_1) \xrightarrow{a_1, u'_1, d_1} (A_1^{en\prime}, y'_1, u'_1) \right\}.
$$

Since object refinement is also a preorder, we formulate the two propositions below for one object plugged into one node of a motif. By transitivity, both results can be extended to sets of objects implementing the interfaces of several nodes.

The following proposition states that the result of applying an interface-refined motif to essentially the same object refines the initial assembly. In general, a refined motif cannot be applied to the same object, since the vector spaces in the interface implemented by the object must comprise the corresponding vector spaces in the node interface. Hence, we refine the object to match the required interface. Although it is fairly straightforward to construct such an object with minimal necessary adjustments, we opt for a more general, non-constructive result. Indeed, we claim that any object that refines the initial one while implementing an appropriate interface, achieves the objective.

Proposition 2. *Let O be an object implementing an interface I, such that $I_1^n \sqsubseteq^{ext} I$, for some node n of a motif M_1. Then $M_1 \sqsubseteq^i M_2$ implies $M_1(O/n) \sqsupseteq M_2(O'/n)$, for any O' implementing an interface I', such that $I_2^n \sqsubseteq^{ext} I'$ and $O \sqsupseteq O'$.*

For the refinement by node replication, the intuition is that we split the "work" among the new nodes. For example, instead of requiring one radiator to provide a certain amount of heat, we require two radiators to each provide half of that amount. The difficulty lies in the fact that the control of the nodes is indirect. For the radiators, e.g., we set the power knobs to half the initial value each and expect the produced heat to behave accordingly. Since the domains of the knobs and of the measures of a motif do not necessarily coincide, it is not possible to make this connection directly in full generality. However, this can be done for control motifs, which establish a connection between target values for the measures and the knobs of the controlled objects.

Consider an assembly $M_c(O/\bullet)$, with M_c a control motif. We say that this assembly is *ideally controlled* if, for any $(A^{en}, y, y^{ref}) \xrightarrow{a, y^{ref'}, d} (A^{en'}, y', y^{ref'})$, holds $y' = y^{ref'}$. Recall that control motifs have the same external measure and knob domains.

Proposition 3. *Consider $M_1(M_c(O/\bullet)/n)$, where the ideally controlled assembly $M_c(O/\bullet)$ instantiates a node $n \in N_1$. Let $M_1 \sqsubseteq^m M_2$ with a witness mapping r, and such that measure pre-aggregation f coincides with knob pre-aggregation g. Then $M_1(M_c(O/\bullet)/n) \sqsupseteq M_2(\{M_c(O/\bullet)/n' \mid n' \in r^{-1}(n)\})$, with $|r^{-1}(n)|$ copies of $M_c(O)$.*

6   Refinement and Control Stability

This section addresses RQ2. We explore the stability of the controlled system for several motif refinement cases. Focusing on continuous control, we assume that no discrete transitions occur and disregard the underlying actions. We consider a control motif that controls a refined motif (viewed as the plant).[5] Thus, while the plant or signals are changed (i.e. refined), the stability is evaluated with the *same* original controller. This problem is different from a new controller design. Indeed, if one allows designing a new controller, ensuring the stability of the overall system becomes trivial—in such a case, the controllability property ensures the possibility to design a stable controller [25,43].

Beforehand, we introduce the notion of stability that we consider.

Stability The stability of a controlled system (i.e. a controller C applied to a plant) is ensured by the design of the controller (e.g. choice of the algorithm and its parameters), and set with a tunable stability margin γ [3,4,43]. This formulation ensures that noises

---

[5] Recall that a control motif has only one node.

and disturbances that may affect the measurements are dampened so that knobs and measures do not diverge. The stability margin γ is computed from the sensitivity function S. The sensitivity function is the transfer function modeling the impact of additive noise or disturbances on the measurements: $S \stackrel{def}{=} (1 + \Psi C)^{-1}$. Limiting the magnitude of the sensitivity function ensures that the amplification of disturbances is avoided, reducing their impact. Our metric of stability γ is thus computed based on the norm of S. Formally, the stability margin is defined as the inverse of the ∞-norm of the sensitivity function S: $\gamma \stackrel{def}{=} (\|S\|_\infty)^{-1} = \|1 + \Psi C\|_\infty$.

The larger the stability margin γ, the more robust the controlled system is to variations and disturbances. While other metrics can be used to quantify stability, the *stability margin* is the most common one [22]. Note that the stability margin can be computed in a motif by exploiting the map and interfaces once they are instantiated.

In the following, several types of refinement are considered. For each, we provide a proposition that constrains the refinement to ensure stability preservation. We omit the proofs due to the lack of space. Examples are given in the context of a Smart Building.

6.1   Refinement with Dimensions Increase (Interface Refinement)

In this section, we are interested in studying the stability of a controlled system in case of interface refinement that can be expressed as a dimension increase of the knobs, measures, or disturbance signal. It can be the case, for instance, when a local controller is added to tackle a subsystem independent of the original one, for instance, when adding lightning control at a level where only the temperature was considered.

We aim at proving that there exists a dimension increase, for which the stability of the refined system is preserved even without any controller update.

Proposition 4. *Let be a motif M_1, its aggregation $\mathcal{A}_1$, profile Φ_1, and subsystem P_1, interface-refined by M_2, that is $M_1 \sqsubseteq^i M_2$. If the refined profile, aggregation, and subplants extend the original ones as $\Phi_2 = \begin{pmatrix} \Phi_1 \\ \Phi_{2,1} \end{pmatrix}$, $\mathcal{A}_2 = \begin{pmatrix} \mathcal{A}_1 & \mathcal{A}_{1,2} \end{pmatrix}$, $P_2 = \begin{pmatrix} P_1 & P_{1,2} \\ P_{2,1} & P_{2,2} \end{pmatrix}$, and ensure that*

$$\mathcal{A}_{1,2}P_{2,1}\Phi_1 + \mathcal{A}_1 P_{1,2}\Phi_{2,1} + \mathcal{A}_{1,2}P_{2,2}\Phi_{2,1} = 0, \tag{5}$$

then the refined motif is stable and $\gamma_2 = \gamma_1$.

Proposition 4 provides a condition on the interface-refined motif that ensures that the added measures and knobs have only a local impact and are transparent at a higher level. It is the case, for instance, when adding a subplant and local controller to manage phenomena at a lower level that are independent from the considered interfaces of the original motif. Such an example is given below.

Example 7. For a room presented in Example 3, we now consider its refinement by providing the room with an additional luminosity control. In this case, both knobs and measures interfaces are refined. The measures are extended with data from a sensor of the outside luminosity: $y_2 = \begin{pmatrix} y_1 & y_{\texttt{Light}} \end{pmatrix}^T$. The knobs are extended with an additional dimension allowing to tune the room lighting: $u_2 = \begin{pmatrix} u_1 & u_{\texttt{Light}} \end{pmatrix}^T$. A subplant $P_{\texttt{Light}}$ is added to control the luminosity: Data from the refined outside luminosity sensor and occupation counter are used to set the knob of room luminosity: $\mathbf{P_2} = \begin{pmatrix} \mathbf{P_1} & 0 \\ 0 & \mathbf{P}_{\texttt{Light}} \end{pmatrix}$. Note that the diagonals are 0 here as the subsystems of lighting control and temperature control are independent: there is no impact of one subsystem on the other.

In this example, the refined interface does not impact the original plant. Given the definition of the refined measures and knobs, we have the following profile $\Phi_2 = \left(\Phi_1\ 0 \right)^T$ and aggregation $\mathcal{A}_2 = \left(\mathcal{A}_1\ 0 \right)$. Equation (5) is satisfied, ensuring that the stability is preserved after refinement. $\qquad\square$

6.2 Duplicating Subsystems in a Hierarchical Setup (Map Refinement)

The refinement of a motif map can happen when subsystems are replicated at a given level of a hierarchical control system. For example, in a Smart Building setup, a room with two radiators can be refined by a room with four radiators, following the installation of additional heaters.

Proposition 5 (Stability preservation in case of map refinement). *If M_1 is map-refined by M_2, that is $M_1 \sqsubseteq^m M_2$ in the sense of Definition 13, where* (i) *both plant transfer functions $\Psi_1 = \mathcal{A}_1\mathbf{P_1}\Phi_1$ and $\Psi_2 = \mathcal{A}_2\mathbf{P_2}\Phi_2$ (corresponding respectively to M_1 and M_2) are controlled by the same controller C, and* (ii) *given that the subsystems transfer functions and mappings ensure that for all frequencies $\forall\omega, |\mathbf{P_1}(j\omega)| \leq |F\mathbf{P_2}(j\omega)H|$, where j is the imaginary unit, F and H are the transfer functions corresponding to mappings f and h from Definition 10, then the stability of M_2 is preserved and $\gamma_2 \geq \gamma_1$.*

Proposition 5 shows that, in the case of a refinement by node replication, the addition of subsystems is ensured to be stable if the refined aggregation and profile are correctly mapped to the original ones. The norm inequality ensures that for all frequencies, the refined plant has a similar or lower amplification of the control signal, thus no divergence can happen under the same controller and the stability margin is preserved or even improved. This property contributes to proving that some control properties can be preserved by refinement.

Example 8. We consider the example of the addition of new heaters in a room, for instance to better distribute the heat sources. This can be expressed as the refinement of a room with 2 radiator (M_1) by a room with 4 radiator (M_2).

Let us consider the room plant $\Psi_1 = \mathcal{A}_1\mathbf{P_1}\Phi_1$ [6] where the subplants are the two radiators $\mathbf{P_1} = \begin{pmatrix} \Psi_{\texttt{Radiator}} & 0 \\ 0 & \Psi_{\texttt{Radiator}} \end{pmatrix}$, the value of the power knob is equally distributed among the radiators $\Phi_1 = \left(\frac{1}{2}\ \frac{1}{2} \right)^T$, and the mean temperature is measured $\mathcal{A}_1 = \left(\frac{1}{2}\ \frac{1}{2} \right)$.

Let the refined room plant be composed of subplants with 4 radiators

$$\mathbf{P_2} = \begin{pmatrix} \Psi_{\texttt{Radiator}} & 0 & 0 & 0 \\ 0 & \Psi_{\texttt{Radiator}} & 0 & 0 \\ 0 & 0 & \Psi_{\texttt{Radiator}} & 0 \\ 0 & 0 & 0 & \Psi_{\texttt{Radiator}} \end{pmatrix},$$ for which the power knob is dis-

tributed as $\Phi_2 = \left(\frac{1}{2}\ \frac{1}{2}\ \frac{1}{2}\ \frac{1}{2} \right)^T$, and the mean temperature is measured $\mathcal{A}_2 = \left(\frac{1}{4}\ \frac{1}{4}\ \frac{1}{4}\ \frac{1}{4} \right)$.

---

[6] Subscripts associated with the Room level are not recalled for better readability.

The refinement pre-aggregation F, defined as $\mathcal{A}_2 = \mathcal{A}_1 F$, is $F = \begin{pmatrix} \frac{1}{2} & \frac{1}{2} & 0 & 0 \\ 0 & 0 & \frac{1}{2} & \frac{1}{2} \end{pmatrix}$. The re-distribution H, defined as $\Phi_2 = H\Phi_1$, is $H = \begin{pmatrix} 1 & 1 & 0 & 0 \\ 0 & 0 & 1 & 1 \end{pmatrix}^T$.

In this case, we have $F\mathbf{P_2}H = \begin{pmatrix} \Psi_{\mathtt{Radiator}} & 0 \\ 0 & \Psi_{\mathtt{Radiator}} \end{pmatrix} = \mathbf{P_1}$, thus the conditions of Prop. 5 are met and the stability of the refined plant is ensured. $\qquad\square$

6.3 Refinement of the Plant

Let us now consider the case in which some modifications happen to the plant, resulting in a change of its behavior and thus to its model as a transfer function. If the modifications are for instance a change of the model parameters related to the disturbances impact, it can be translated as a change in the range of variation of the disturbance signal: such refinement corresponds to an interface refinement.

Let us study whether a plant Ψ_1, controlled by a controller C, refined by Ψ_2, equally controlled by C (i.e. without re-computing the controller), is still stable. Intuitively, stability can be preserved if the plant change is small (in some adequate metric sense) compared to the refined system stability margin. Note that the plant dimensions are supposed to remain the same, while allowing a different number of subplants. Let us first define a distance metric between two transfer functions.

Definition 16 (*v*-**gap metric**). *Given two transfer functions Ψ_1 and Ψ_2 with the same dimension, their v-gap metric is computed according to Vinnicombe's definition [40]:*

$$\delta(\Psi_1, \Psi_2) = \sup_{\omega} \frac{|\Psi_1(j\omega) - \Psi_2(j\omega)|}{\sqrt{(1 + |\Psi_1(j\omega)|^2)(1 + |\Psi_2(j\omega)|^2)}}. \tag{6}$$

Proposition 6 (Stability preservation with plant refinement). *If M_2 refines M_1, $M_1 \sqsubseteq M_2$,[7] both controlled by the same controller C, and with Ψ_1 and Ψ_2, the corresponding plants of same dimension, such that* (i) *their v-gap metric, as defined in Definition 16, is bounded :* $\delta(\Psi_1, \Psi_2) \leq \beta$ *and* (ii) *this bound is smaller than the initial stability margin :* $\beta \leq \gamma_1$, *then the controller C stabilizes the plant Ψ_2.*

Proposition 6 shows that, while the refinement modifies the plant under some constraints, the refined motif is ensured to be stable. It can be seen as an example of a *robust* design, e.g. H_∞ methods [43]: the set of models for which the controller is robust in the refined case is included in the original set, which guarantees stability and could even allow for improved stability margin – for certain plants Ψ_2, e.g. with smaller gain.

Although based on previous CT results, Prop. 6 allows us to draw a link between hierarchical motif refinement and control theory, by specifying which notions of stability and metrics, among the diversity that exists in the control literature, fit our formulation.

Notice that Prop. 6 applies to each refined plant Ψ_2 that guarantees $\delta(\Psi_1, \Psi_2) \leq \beta$. That is, the stability guarantee holds if the refinement is of any nature: change of model

---

[7] We denote $\sqsubseteq$ the transitive closure of $\sqsubseteq^i \cup \sqsubseteq^m$.

parameters, addition of dynamics, reduction of uncertainties in an uncertain modeling, modification of the behavior by a local coordinator that constrains plant's behaviour etc..

Example 9. For the Smart Building example, such a refinement can result from a change in the thermal resistance or capacity of some elements in a room (installation of carpets, window replacement, addition of sunshades etc..). In this case, the change impacts the parameters of the room plant Ψ_{Room} (matrix A_1 in Eq. (1) updated in A_2). Ensuring stability translates into ensuring that A_2 guarantees $\delta(\Psi_1, \Psi_2) \leq \gamma_1$.

If furniture is placed close to the radiator, the refinement could also change the knob impact on the room temperature. In this case, it is the B matrix of the model that is modified. More significant changes of plants can be considered, e.g. the addition of a new dynamics, if, for instance, the room is equipped with ceiling fans, introducing convection elements in the plant model, or with actionable sunshades that would modify the dynamics of the solar radiation impact. $\square$

7 Related Work

The interested reader can find related work on component-based models with layered architectures in [12]. In summary, in our work only generic concepts of component-based systems (CBSs) are considered to allow applying the proposals on hierarchical motifs to various component-based models, cf. the survey [17] for a list of component-based models. Even though there are many approaches to support hierarchical style, cf. e.g. [7,9,10,13,16,20], the model of hierarchical motifs for both system's entities and their control contributes to a flexible controllers design for systems with layered architectures. In [14] the control manager is defined as a synchronized product of specific LTSs built over a control data family, context, and adaptation objectives of a managed LTS. Unlike our proposal, the approach in [14] has limitations to deal with "towers" of managed elements in systems with layered architectures.

Our use of motifs was inspired by Dynamic Reconfigurable BIP (DR-BIP) [7]. The results of this paper serve as a proof of concept aiming to implement a (DR-)BIP extension integrating hierarchical control motifs. Some of the above mentioned frameworks support run-time property monitoring and verification. However, the refinement of hierarchical motifs that integrate control and may usefully impact systems' architecture development and bring new verification results is an original contribution.

As mentioned in Sect. 1, control theory is a promising methodology for computing systems' (self-)adaptation [25,27]. An overview of discrete-time control approaches for self-adaptive systems can be found in [19]. In [36], a feedback control for both continuous- and discrete-time cases has been related to the well-known MAPE-K loop in the framework of autonomic computing [30]. In [42], it is considered that MAPE addresses the adaptation of software rather than physical properties or resources, whereas control theory (CT) loops are powerful in keeping some variables either at prescribed set points or within ranges, in the face of disturbances. In model predictive control (MPC), the upper layer commands are fed to the lower levels, adapting its behaviour when the conditions require such an action. Our work contributes to a conjecture in [42] by illustrating that in adaptive software the CT and MPC control scheme can be re-used, where the upper layer may be realized using MAPE. Finally, with relation to [31] focusing on brownout as opposed to blackout, the novelty of our approach consists in considering distributed or hierarchical control, and in handling different functionalities, i.e., in enabling a multi-variable control.

Using formal methods for designing and validating system' controllers with the aim of guaranteeing their desired properties, e.g. safety properties, is not new. However, according to [24], it is difficult to verify the properties of such feedback control systems. In this context, used formal models are often focused on discrete time control part while abstracting continuous-time dynamics, at least partially; See, for example, [2,6]. Unlike these approaches, we integrate the dynamics of plants together with disturbances into the motif notion in order to control and adapt hierarchical systems.

Verification of the representations of data-driven systems controlled with feedback techniques is described in [24], where neural networks (NN) are used for their modeling with the aim of enforcing properties such as reachability, safety and stability of the feedback laws. This data-driven approach is promising; however, in [24], systems with a layered control structure are not addressed.

In [34] the authors aim to establish a common language to unify the study of architecture at different spatio-temporal scales. The proposed language for layered control architectures (LCAs) allows for a form of a hierarchy of control loops. Feedback control, however, is only considered at the lowest level, while other layers use other decision making techniques. Unlike this work, our approach allows modeling of structured systems with controllers potentially available at each level. For LCA systems, [29] introduces a new multiclock logic (MCL) to express assume-guarantee contracts, in order to prove global stability properties of a system using the stability properties of its components. Unlike [29], we use automata-based models of components and their compositions. Our logic is used to express FOL interaction constraints among hierarchical motifs, including control motifs, whereas MCL uses variables and clocks for assume-guaranty contracts at system-level and component-level verification.

In [38], the authors aim to verify the properties of a broad class of continuous-time systems composed of interconnected components. The approach defines weak and strong semantics of assume-guarantee contracts for compositional reasoning, where the week semantics is sufficient to deal with acyclic interconnections, and the strong one is required to reason on cyclic interconnections. In our framework, we aim to extend the class of the systems beyond those described by differential inclusions and invariance assume-guarantee contracts, where this strong-week semantics relationship applies.

In [8], the authors address the control synthesis problem in the ASM framework supporting refinement and show that the resolvable case coincides with a special case of complete ASM refinement. We are interested in guaranteeing control stability through motif refinement, which is a different research problem for structured CPSs. Indeed, for structured CPSs with components, according to the recent survey [17], it is important to associate design by refinement with design by composition.

In [37] the authors advocate contract-based design. Design requirements are implemented in a refinement process using available components. Contracts then formalize the conditions for correctness of component integration (horizontal contracts) for lower level of abstraction to be consistent with the higher ones, and for abstractions of available components to be faithful representations of the actual parts (vertical contracts). A similar approach is presented in [21,32], where vertical refinement expressed by a simulation relation and a horizontal component substitution are combined.

Focusing on CPSs, [5] aims to avoid the impact of problems in the software part on the physical part. A safety controller is generated that ensures a certain restricted class of LTL properties. A decision module can substitute the entire system unverified controller by that controller, by sandboxing, to avoid violations of safety properties. This extension of the system with the safety controller is automatically generated using the reachability methods for hybrid systems. Hardware failures are not considered. The finite state abstractions used for synthesizing controllers are simulations of the original system in the classical sense.

The approximate simulation relations introduced in [26] allow simulating system trajectory to stay within a cylinder around the simulated one. This is achieved by using a controller built by combining a controller for the simulated one and a controller interface derived from the simulation function. In our case, such a controller interface is obtained from the refinement, and approximate simulations should account for noise and redundancy. In [35], the authors strengthen the simulation and bisimulation relations between hybrid systems with uniform continuity constraints, which preserve stability properties with respect to input of hybrid systems. We intend to use them for an upcoming behavioural refinement of hierarchical control motifs.

8 Conclusion

This paper provided theoretical underpinnings to modeling both the system and its control by using hierarchical motifs with the aim to allow structured CPSs to be adaptive. More precisely, hierarchical motifs have been introduced in a control-compatible manner. A new refinement relation among the motifs has allowed an analysis of the control stability through some specific refinements, thus addressing RQ1 and RQ2. Our approach to motif refinement leverages results from control theory to guarantee the stability through refinement, which can be seen as a safety guarantee. The proposed methodology for modeling and analysis using motifs and their refinement is general enough to be applied to various component-based models as well as to different control architectures, a centralized control, as well as distributed hierarchical control.

The paper paves the way for the larger challenge of preserving other control properties through various refinements such as convergence speed, transient response etc.. The theory of control for hybrid systems would be necessary to study the behaviour and preservation of properties such as stability in systems with discrete state changes.

Finally, in future work, we intend to generalise the current tree structure of the hierarchical models to directed acyclic graphs by adding a conflict resolution layer in front of the motif's profile. Such a generalisation would allow modeling dynamically reconfigurable systems, where an object has to be redeployed from one node to another in a non-atomic manner. While already addressed in G-Kells and DR-BIP, such a dynamicity in hierarchical motifs integrating control is a future work direction with a promising motif refinement as introduced in this paper.

Acknowledgements. We are deeply grateful to the anonymous reviewers for their constructive comments whereof we have implemented the majority as space permitted.

References

1. National Institute of Standards and Technology (NIST, USA): framework for cyber-physical systems (special publication 1500-201) (2017)
2. Aréchiga, N., Loos, S.M., Platzer, A., Krogh, B.H.: Using theorem provers to guarantee closed-loop system properties. In: 2012 American Control Conference (ACC), pp. 3573–3580 (2012). ISSN: 2378-5861
3. Astrom, K.J.: PID controllers: theory, design, and tuning. Int. Soc. Measur. Control (1995)
4. Åström, K.J.: Model uncertainty and robust control. In: Lecture Notes on Iterative Identification and Control Design, pp. 63–100 (2000)
5. Bak, S., Manamcheri, K., Mitra, S., Caccamo, M.: Sandboxing controllers for cyber-physical systems. In: 2011 IEEE/ACM International Conference on Cyber-Physical Systems, pp. 3–12 (2011)
6. Balakrishnan, G., Sankaranarayanan, S., Ivančić, F., Gupta, A.: Refining the control structure of loops using static analysis. In: Proceedings of the ACM International Conference on Embedded Software, EMSOFT '09, pp. 49–58 (2009)
7. El Ballouli, R., Bensalem, S., Bozga, M., Sifakis, J.: Programming dynamic reconfigurable systems. In: Bae, K., Ölveczky, P.C. (eds.) FACS 2018. LNCS, vol. 11222, pp. 118–136. Springer, Cham (2018). https://doi.org/10.1007/978-3-030-02146-7_6
8. Banach, R., Zhu, H., Su, W., Wu, X.: ASM, controller synthesis, and complete refinement. Sci. Comput. Program. **94**, 109–129 (2014)
9. Basu, A., et al.: Rigorous component-based system design using the BIP framework. IEEE Softw. **28**(3), 41–48 (2011)
10. Baude, F., et al.: GCM: a grid extension to fractal for autonomous distributed components. Ann. des Télécommun. **64**(1–2), 5–24 (2009)
11. Bellegarde, F., Darlot, C., Julliand, J., Kouchnarenko, O.: Reformulation: a way to combine dynamic properties and *B* refinement. In: Oliveira, J.N., Zave, P. (eds.) FME 2001. LNCS, vol. 2021, pp. 2–19. Springer, Heidelberg (2001). https://doi.org/10.1007/3-540-45251-6_2
12. Bliudze, S., Cerf, S., Kouchnarenko, O.: A hybrid modelling approach for hierarchical control of structured CPSs. In: Mezzina, C.A., Schmitt, A., eds., Components Operationally: Reversibility and System Engineering: Essays Dedicated to Jean-Bernard Stefani on the Occasion of His 65th Birthday, volume 16065 of LNCS, pp. 175–196. Springer Nature Switzerland, Cham (2026). https://doi.org/10.1007/978-3-031-99717-4_10
13. Bruneton, E., Coupaye, T., Leclercq, M., Quéma, V., Stefani, J.-B.: The Fractal component model and its support in Java: experiences with auto-adaptive and reconfigurable systems. Softw. Pract. Exper. **36**(11–12), 1257–1284 (2006)
14. Bruni, R., Corradini, A., Gadducci, F., Lluch Lafuente, A., Vandin, A.: A conceptual framework for adaptation. In: de Lara, J., Zisman, A. (eds.) FASE 2012. LNCS, vol. 7212, pp. 240–254. Springer, Heidelberg (2012). https://doi.org/10.1007/978-3-642-28872-2_17
15. Bures, T., Calinescu, R., Weyns, D.: Special issue on software engineering for trustworthy cyber-physical systems. J. Syst. Softw. **178**, 110972 (2021)
16. Bures, T., Hnetynka, P., Plášil, F.: SOFA 2.0: balancing advanced features in a hierarchical component model. In: Proceedings of the Internatinal Conference (SERA 2006), pp. 40–48. IEEE Computer Society (2006)
17. Coullon, H., Henrio, L., Loulergue, F., Robillard, S.: Component-based distributed software reconfiguration: a verification-oriented survey. ACM Comput. Surv. **56**(1), 2:1–2:37 (2024)

18. de Lemos, R.: Software self-adaptation and industry: Blame MAPE-K. In: Proceedings of the International Symposium. SEAMS 2023, pp. 88–89. IEEE (2023)
19. de Lemos, R., et al.: Software engineering for self-adaptive systems: research challenges in the provision of assurances. In: Software Engineering for Self-Adaptive Systems III. Assurances, volume 9640 of LNCS, pp. 3–30. Springer, Cham (2013). https://doi.org/10.1007/978-3-319-74183-3_1
20. Ding, Z., Chen, Z., Liu, J.: A rigorous model of service component architecture. In: Pu, G., Stolz, V., eds., Proceedings of the International Workshop TTSS 2007, volume 207 of ENTCS, pp. 33–48. Elsevier (2007)
21. Dormoy, J., Kouchnarenko, O., Lanoix, A.: When structural refinement of components keeps temporal properties over reconfigurations. In: Giannakopoulou, D., Méry, D. (eds.) FM 2012. LNCS, vol. 7436, pp. 171–186. Springer, Heidelberg (2012). https://doi.org/10.1007/978-3-642-32759-9_16
22. Doyle, J.C., Francis, B.A., Tannenbaum, A.R.: Feedback control theory. Courier Corporation (2013)
23. Dupont, G., Ameur, Y.A., Singh, N.K., Pantel, M.: Event-B hybridation: a proof and refinement-based framework for modelling hybrid systems. ACM Trans. Embed. Comput. Syst. **20**(4), 35:1–35:37 (2021)
24. Dutta, S., Jha, S., Sankaranarayanan, S., Tiwari, A.: Learning and verification of feedback control systems using feedforward neural networks. IFAC-PapersOnLine **51**(16), 151–156 (2018)
25. Filieri, A., et al.: Software engineering meets control theory. In: Proceedings of the IEEE/ACM International Symposium on Software Engineering for Adaptive and Self-Managing Systems, pp. 71–82. IEEE (2015)
26. Girard, A., Pappas, G.J.: Hierarchical control using approximate simulation relations. In: Proceedings of the IEEE Conference on Decision and Control, pp. 264–269 (2006)
27. Hellerstein, J.L., Diao, Y., Parekh, Y., Tilbury, D.M.: Feedback Control of Computing Systems. John Wiley & Sons (2004)
28. Hoang, S., Schneider, S.A., Treharne, H., Williams, D.M.: Foundations for using linear temporal logic in Event-B refinement. Formal Aspects Comput. **28**, 909–935 (2016)
29. Incer, I., Csomay-Shanklin, N., Ames, A.D., Murray, R.M.: Layered control systems operating on multiple clocks. IEEE Control Syst. Lett. **8**, 1211–1216 (2024)
30. Kephart, J.O., Chess, D.M.: The vision of autonomic computing. Computer **36**(1), 41–50 (2003)
31. Klein, C., Maggio, M., Årzén, K.-E., Hernández-Rodriguez, F.: Brownout: building more robust cloud applications. In: Jalote, P., Briand, L.C., van der Hoek, A., eds., Proceedings of the International Conference ICSE'14, pp. 700–711. ACM (2014)
32. Lanoix, A., Kouchnarenko, O.: Component substitution through dynamic reconfigurations. In: Buhnova, B., Happe, L., Kofron, J., eds. Proceedings of the International Workshop FESCA 2014, vol. 147 of EPTCS, pp. 32–46 (2014)
33. Lecomte, T., Deharbe, D., Prun, E., Mottin, E.: Applying a formal method in industry: a 25-year trajectory. In: Cavalheiro, S., Fiadeiro, J. (eds.) SBMF 2017. LNCS, vol. 10623, pp. 70–87. Springer, Cham (2017). https://doi.org/10.1007/978-3-319-70848-5_6
34. Matni, N., Ames, A.D., Doyle, J.C.: A quantitative framework for layered multirate control: Toward a theory of control architecture. IEEE Control Syst. Mag. **44**(3), 52–94 (2024)
35. Prabhakar, P., Liu, J., Murray, R.M.: Simulations and bisimulations for analysis of stability with respect to inputs of hybrid systems. Discrete Event Dyn. Syst. **28**(3), 349–374 (2018)
36. Rutten, É., Marchand, N., Simon, D.: Feedback control as MAPE-K loop in autonomic computing. In: de Lemos, R., Garlan, D., Ghezzi, C., Giese, H., eds., Software Engineering for Self-Adaptive Systems III. Assurances, vol. 9640 of LNCS, pp. 349–373. Springer, Cham (2013). https://doi.org/10.1007/978-3-319-74183-3_12

37. Sangiovanni-Vincentelli, A., Damm, W., Passerone, R.: Taming Dr. Frankenstein: contract-based design for cyber-physical systems. Eur. J. Control **18**(3), 217–238 (2012)
38. Saoud, A., Girard, A., Fribourg, L.: Assume-guarantee contracts for continuous-time systems. Automatica **134**, 109910 (2021)
39. Shevtsov, S., Berekmeri, M., Weyns, D., Maggio, M.: Control-theoretical software adaptation: a systematic literature review. IEEE Trans. Software Eng. **44**(8), 784–810 (2018)
40. Vinnicombe, G.: Uncertainty and Feedback. World Scientific, H Loop-shaping and the V-gap Metric (2000)
41. Weyns, D.: Software engineering of self-adaptive systems. In: Handbook of Software Engineering, pp. 399–443. Springer, Cham (2019). https://doi.org/10.1007/978-3-030-00262-6_11
42. Weyns, D., et al.: Towards better adaptive systems by combining MAPE, control theory, and machine learning. In: Proceedings of the International Symposium SEAMS@ICSE 2021, pp. 217–223. IEEE (2021)
43. Zhou, K., Doyle, J.C.: Essentials of Robust Control, vol. 104. Prentice Hall (1998)

Distributed Algorithms for Collective Adaptive Systems

Aggregate Indoor Localisation

Giorgio Audrito(✉), Leonardo Bertolino, Ferruccio Damiani,
and Gianluca Torta

Department of Computer Science, University of Turin, Torino, Italy
{giorgio.audrito,ferruccio.damiani,gianluca.torta}@unito.it,
leonardo.bertolino@edu.unito.it

Abstract. Accurate indoor localisation is a key enabling technology for many distributed systems, including collective robotics, smart environments, and user wearable devices. In these settings, localisation must often be achieved without central coordination, under limited sensing capabilities, and in the presence of dynamic environmental changes. Collective indoor localisation algorithms address these challenges by exploiting local interactions among devices to collectively infer positions. However, many existing approaches implicitly assume relatively stable conditions and offer limited guarantees on adaptability and resilience.

In this paper, we investigate cooperative indoor localisation from a self-adaptive perspective. We reformulate two established localisation algorithms within the aggregate programming framework, and propose novel variants of them to improve their performance. We evaluate our proposals through extensive simulation, analysing error and communication cost across a wide range of scenarios, including recovery from disruptive events. Our results uncover the trade-offs between accuracy, resiliency and efficiency, shedding light on the design space of what we call aggregate indoor localisation algorithms.

Keywords: Aggregate programming · Cooperative indoor localisation · Self-stabilisation

1 Introduction

Localization is a fundamental enabling functionality for numerous distributed systems operating in indoor environments, including collective robotics, sensor networks, cyber-physical systems, and smart environments. In such scenarios, knowledge of spatial position enables coordination, motion planning, and efficient resource management. Unlike outdoor scenarios, where satellite systems such as GPS provide a consolidated global infrastructure for positioning, indoor environments render such a solution impractical or highly unreliable [9]. Satellite signals are significantly attenuated by building structures, are subject to reflections and interference that degrade accuracy, and, in many cases, are not received at all in the absence of direct visibility of the satellites. Moreover, even

© IFIP International Federation for Leomation Processing 2026
Published by Springer Nature Switzerland AG 2026
R. Casadei and F. Ghassemi (Eds.): COORDINATION 2026, LNCS 16590, pp. 73–92, 2026.
https://doi.org/10.1007/978-3-032-28358-0_4

when the signal is available, the accuracy provided is generally not sufficient for applications requiring metric or sub-metric precision in complex enclosed spaces.

Consequently, indoor localization cannot rely on a pre-existing global infrastructure, but must instead be achieved through distributed mechanisms based on local information. This requirement is particularly relevant in systems composed of autonomous and potentially mobile devices, which communicate predominantly with physically nearby nodes and operate asynchronously [13]. In such contexts, position must be estimated through cooperative processes in which spatial information is progressively propagated across the network through multi-hop interactions. Despite the extensive literature on cooperative localization, many existing algorithms assume relatively stable conditions, such as reliable connectivity, largely static network topologies, and the absence of significant perturbations. In real scenarios, however, distributed indoor systems are inherently dynamic: devices may join or leave the network, experience temporary failures or variations in measurement quality, and the communication topology may evolve over time. Under these conditions, traditional algorithms can be slow to converge, unstable, or unable to automatically adapt to changes.

The problem we address, therefore, is how to design cooperative localization algorithms that are not only accurate, but also resilient and capable of self-adapting to network dynamics and environmental perturbations without requiring external intervention. In particular, we are interested in solutions that are fit for decentralised, asynchronous systems with proximity-based interactions. We revisit two well-known algorithms from the literature: *distance vector–based positioning* and *non-Bayesian cooperative localisation* [9,17], expressing them within the *aggregate programming* [6] framework, which is designed to support decentralised coordination in mutable environments. This translation enables the algorithms to naturally react to changes and *self-stabilise* towards consistent results without external intervention. We then introduce improved variants of the two algorithms above, working both with and without inter-node distance estimates, and aimed at improving localisation accuracy and communication efficiency.

We evaluate the proposed algorithms through an extensive selection of simulations in dynamic multi-hop scenarios, varying the communication radius, device speed, and measurement noise level. The analysis considers both the localization accuracy and the computational and communication cost, in a scenario which comprises nodes failing and joining to assess resilience. The results highlight an improved trade-off between precision, capacity for self-adaptation, and efficiency of the proposed variants with respect to the original versions of the algorithms. Overall, the evaluation provides a comprehensive guide for choosing the best algorithm for any given scenario at hand.

This paper makes the following contributions:

- **Formalisation in aggregate programming.** We reformulate two established indoor localisation algorithms (distance vector–based positioning and non-Bayesian cooperative localisation) within the aggregate programming paradigm, providing an elegant and compositional specification in the eXchange Calculus (XC) [2] for both of them.

- **Stabilisation guarantees.** We prove that the aggregate reformulation induces (self-)stabilising behaviour, endowing the algorithms with formal convergence guarantees that were not directly available in their original decentralised formulations, particularly for distance vector–based approaches.
- **Algorithmic variants and trade-off analysis.** We design several variants, operating both with and without inter-node distance estimates, and systematically evaluate their behaviour under noise and network disruptions, including recovery from transient perturbations. We provide a comparative study of localisation error and communication cost, highlighting the trade-offs among accuracy, message size, computational cost, and recovery performance in dynamic multi-hop settings.

The remainder of the paper is structured as follows. Section 2 states the problem of cooperative indoor localisation in decentralized multi-hop networks, introducing the system model, the role of anchor nodes, and the self-stabilisation requirement adopted. Section 3 presents the necessary background on the Aggregate Programming paradigm and on the main multi-hop geometric algorithms for indoor localisation. Section 4 describes our aggregate reformulation of the two selected algorithms, illustrating their operation with pseudocode and introducing the proposed variants to improve convergence and robustness. Section 5 presents the experimental evaluation, analysing the results in terms of accuracy, communication cost, and adaptability in dynamic scenarios. Section 6 concludes with final remarks and directions for future work.

2   Problem Statement

We consider the problem of cooperative indoor localisation in decentralised distributed systems composed of multiple devices interacting through proximity-based communication. The system is modelled as a multi-hop network, where each node can exchange information only with neighbours within communication range, and no central coordination entity is assumed. A subset of nodes, called *anchors*, have a fixed and known position in a common reference frame. All other nodes aim to estimate their own position by exploiting local interactions with neighbours. Depending on sensing capabilities, nodes may or may not have access to (noisy) estimates of the distance to their neighbours. The network and the environment are assumed to be mutable: nodes (including anchors) may move, join or leave the network, and communication may fail.

A first, obvious requirement for any proposed solution is that it is *stabilising*, i.e., that after a finite amount of time every node in the network reaches a stable value. However, to address the mutability of the network, localisation algorithms should ideally not only provide accurate position estimates under stable conditions, but also be able to adapt to changes as the ones previously mentioned without requiring explicit reinitialisation or external control. It is then highly desirable that the solutions are also *self-stabilising*, a stronger property than mere stabilisation. Informally, a self-stabilising algorithm is one that, starting from an arbitrary internal state (that may be influenced by e.g. a recent input change), provided that its input data and environment stay constant for enough time, is guaranteed to converge to the correct outcome for its input and environment, independently of the algorithm state before stabilisation.

3 Related Work and Background

3.1 Aggregate Programming

The Internet of Things (IoT) is leading to an exponential growth in the number of connected devices, such as smartphones, drones, sensors, and embedded systems, which primarily rely on proximity-based local communications. Programming approaches centered on individual devices are becoming burdensome for developers, who are forced to directly manage communication, coordination, and behavioral composition, resulting in issues of modularity and reusability.

To address these challenges, Aggregate Programming (AP) emerged as a paradigm for programming the collective behavior of sets of distributed devices. Such devices operate autonomously and asynchronously, do not share memory, and typically communicate only with physically neighboring nodes. The entire computational environment is viewed as a single entity–more precisely, a region–within which the technical details of individual devices are abstracted away. Rather than reasoning about individual devices, programmers reason about the space those devices occupy, using data constructs that span across space and time in the region [6].

Despite this global abstraction, the program is executed locally by the individual devices, which implicitly coordinate to ensure robustness and resilience, even in the presence of failures or dynamic changes in the system. Local execution on each device follows a cyclical round-based schedule, also known as *sense-compute-send-sleep*. In each cycle, the device initially acquires information from local sensors and messages received from neighboring nodes in the previous cycle (*sense*). Based on this data, local computation is then performed (*compute*), at the end of which messages may be produced for adjacent devices (*send*). Once execution is complete, the device remains inactive until the start of the next cycle (*sleep*).

For AP, the reference languages are the Field Calculus (FC) [16] and its recent evolution, XC [2]. The latter is essentially a typed lambda calculus with a fundamental `exchange` operator to provide implicit communication between nearby devices. Within XC, communication between nearby devices does not occur via direct messages but through a special kind of data called *nvalue* (for neighboring value). The nvalue is a map that associates device identifiers with literal values and has a *default* value that is assigned to all other devices, including those that are not known as neighbours by the sender. Neighbouring values are used to represent both values received from directly connected devices, and to represent values that need to be sent back to them. The `exchange` primitive has the following form:

$$\texttt{exchange}(\mathbf{e}_i, \ (\mathbf{n}) \ \texttt{=> return } \mathbf{e}_r \ \texttt{send } \mathbf{e}_s))$$

A device evaluates the expression $\mathbf{e}_i$ to obtain an initial literal value ℓ_i. Then, it substitutes the lambda argument $\mathbf{n}$ with an nvalue that has ℓ_i as *default*, and associates neighbours to the messages received from them for this exchange expression. The expression returns a value $\mathbf{e}_r$ to be used on the device, and simultaneously generates the nvalue $\mathbf{e}_s$ to be sent to neighbors, which will use it in their next round to produce their argument $\mathbf{n}$. In the pseudo-code in the following sections, we will use some convenient specializations of exchange:

```
def share(init, update) {
   exchange(init, (n) => val v = update(n); return v send v)
}

def nbr(init, value) {
   exchange(init, (n) => return n send value)
}

def rep(init, update) {
   exchange(init, (n) => val v = update(self(n)); return v send v)
}
```

The **share** specialization derives a single local value (i.e., an nvalue with only the default and no special values for neighbours) by applying an **update** function to $\mathbf{n}$, then returns it and sends it to all the neighbours. The **nbr** specialization returns the received nvalue, and sends a local value received as parameter to all the neighbours. Finally, the **rep** specialization returns and sends to itself an **update** of the value **self(n)** for the current device in $\mathbf{n}$ (i.e., it propagates local status between rounds).

In a program, there may be multiple exchange calls in the same round, and it is necessary that each such call receives the correct values from neighbours. A mechanism called *alignment* is used to ensure that each exchange receives the correct neighbouring values corresponding to the same exchange expression in neighbours' rounds (both as position in source code syntax tree, and as position in the current stack trace of function calls). This ensures that there are no conflicts between multiple exchanges in the same program. This important feature enables *compositionality*, i.e., an XC program can reuse (one or several) functions that contain exchange, that will just work as expected.

In addition to the fundamental exchange construct and its specializations (**share**, **nbr**, **rep**), XC also provides a higher-level mechanism for managing dynamic spatial computations, called spawn [3,7], which forms the basis of the *aggregate processes* model. The function $\texttt{spawn}(\mathbf{e}_b, \mathbf{e}_k, \mathbf{e}_i)$ allows the initiation and management of sets of distributed processes indexed by keys. The expression $\mathbf{e}_b$ models the process behaviour and is a function that, given an identifying key and an input, returns a pair composed of an output value and a Boolean indicating whether the process should propagate to neighbours or terminate in the current node. The expression $\mathbf{e}_k$ defines the set of process keys for which new processes should be spawned on the current device, while $\mathbf{e}_i$ represents an additional input provided to the process behaviour. The result of spawn is a map that associates each key of an executed process with its corresponding output value.

From a semantic point of view, depending on whether each device decides to keep a process instance active, that instance is automatically propagated to neighbouring devices or not, giving rise to a distributed computation that extends through space and evolves dynamically over time. Furthermore, processes influence the alignment mechanism: an exchange operation executed within a process can only be aligned with corresponding operations belonging to the same process (with the same key) on neighbouring devices. This ensures isolation between parallel computations and allows multiple independent processes to execute simultaneously, preserving modularity and composability.

3.2   Multi-hop Indoor Localisation

The localization of devices (hereafter also referred to as *nodes*) in indoor environments represents a significant challenge, as knowledge of their positions plays a central role in many network applications and functionalities, such as the need to associate collected measurements with a spatial context. The use of GPS is not applicable indoors, due to the attenuation (or complete blocking) of the signal caused by walls and roofs. Even in outdoor scenarios, however, GPS is not always a suitable solution, because, e.g., of costs, power consumption, inaccuracy [9], or simply in GPS-denied areas. Thus, most of the techniques considered here can also be relevant to outdoor settings.

To allow localization without relying on GPS (or similar systems), algorithms based on geometric methods have been introduced, enabling the estimation of node positions relying on other information. Among the most widely used geometric methods are trilateration, and its variant named multilateration. Trilateration [14] is a geometric technique that allows the position of a node to be determined by knowing its distances from three reference nodes (anchors) with known positions. The node position corresponds to the intersection of three spheres, each centered at a reference node and with a radius equal to the measured distance from the unknown node. The determination of the distance between two nodes is itself an interesting problem that is typically addressed with wireless technologies, such as BLE, WiFi, or UWB. Among these technologies, UWB has been reported to achieve positioning accuracy with an error bound of approximately $10cm$ [10]. Explicitly considering the techniques for distance estimation is out of the scope of the present paper. However, we will introduce controlled random estimation errors in the experiments to make them more realistic.

Position estimation through multilateration [1] is formulated as an optimization problem, in which the position of the unknown node is determined by minimizing the Root Mean Square Error (RMSE) between the distances measured from *anchor* nodes and the distances corresponding to the estimated position. This approach makes it possible to achieve robust localization even in the presence of noisy distance measurements, by combining multiple measurements and, if necessary, assigning them appropriate weights. The numerical solution of this least-squares problem can be obtained using the Levenberg–Marquardt method [5]. When at least two anchors are present, the function enters an iterative loop: at each iteration, it computes the total position error by comparing the estimated distances with the actual ones. It then determines the direction in which to move, taking into account both the gradient and the direction in which the error increases. Based on this information (and the *step size*), a new position estimate is computed, for which the error is evaluated again. If the error increases, the new estimate is rejected and the step size is reduced; conversely, if the error decreases, the estimate is accepted and the step size is increased. This adaptation mechanism guarantees the stability and convergence of the algorithm toward a solution that minimizes the error.

Several studies have addressed *multi-hop* localization, that is, localization in networks where nodes can share information with their neighbours to support the localization task where the availability of anchor nodes is limited. Among these, [11] proposes a combined multi-hop localization and time synchronization approach (the latter is necessary for correctly estimating the distances between nodes) using a single anchor node, highlighting the challenges and strategies for localization under resource-limited conditions. Yet, when three or more anchor nodes are available, it is possible to exploit the geometric methods discussed previously. A classic algorithm known as *DV-Hop* [9] (where DV stands for Distance Vector) is structured into three main phases. First, nodes exchange information with their neighbors to determine the distance in hops from the anchors. Second, the anchors, knowing their mutual Euclidean distances, calculate a correction factor to estimate the average hop length. Finally, nodes use this information to perform multilateration and estimate their own position. Note that DV-hop is considered to be a *sequential* algorithm [18], due to unidirectional share of information in the first two phases, followed by local position estimation in the third phase. Another classic approach is *NB-Coop* (which stands for Non-Bayesian Cooperative) [17], in which nodes iteratively update their own position by comparing the estimated distances from neighbors with those calculated from their current estimated positions. It is similar to the multilateration method described above, but with notable differences that will be explained later. One key difference is that a node's neighbors are generally not all anchors. The approach is defined as non-Bayesian because it treats node positions as unknown input parameters, rather than random variables with given probability distributions.

Finally, there is a vast literature on more complex multi-hop geometric algorithms, ranging from Bayesian cooperative message passing [17] to distributed convex optimization [12]. In this paper we will focus on the AP implementation and optimization of the DV-hop and NB-Coop classic algorithms mentioned above. We remark that, to the best of our knowledge, no investigation has been performed in literature on the usage of these algorithms in mutable environments, and in particular on self-stabilisation. Instead, works in literature assume a single execution until convergence on a fixed topology. The convergence proof for the classic NB-Coop algorithm to (local or) global minima can be re-interpreted as a (self-)stabilisation proof for the algorithm. However, classic

Non-Bayesian Cooperative Localisation

Input: *initPos, isAnchor, nbrDist*
  1: **share starting from** *pos* ← *initPos* **update**
  2:     *anchorInfo* ← {(pos_i, $nbrDist_i$) for each neighbour i}
  3:     **if** *isAnchor* **then**
  4:         **return** *pos* ← known position
  5:     **else**
  6:         **return** *pos* ← *gradientDescent* given *anchorInfo* and *pos*
  7:     **end if**
  8: **end share**

```
def nbcoop(initPos, isAnchor, nbrDist) {
  share(initPos, (pos) =>
    val anchorInfo = nfold(cons, tuple(pos, nbrDist), nil);
    if (isAnchor) { knownPos } else {
      gradientDescent(anchorInfo, self(pos))
    }
  )
}
```

Fig. 1. Non-bayesian cooperative localisation algorithm (above) and corresponding XC code (below).

formulations of DV-hop algorithm do not self-stabilise, since these do not include a mechanism to remove knowledge about anchors that exited the network.

4   Aggregate Indoor Localisation Algorithms

4.1 Non-Bayesian Cooperative Localisation

The Non-Bayesian cooperative localisation algorithm [17] proceeds by iterative refinement of a working estimated position. We consider a uniformly random position in the monitored area as the initial estimate *initPos*. As the iterations proceed, the estimate is progressively refined thanks to the exchange of information with neighbours. This strategy of progressive refinement can be naturally expressed as an aggregate algorithm in XC, given in Fig. 1. For presentation purposes, we also include a pseudo-code representation of the algorithm, which we discuss in the following, leaving the interpretation of the XC code to the interested reader.

At each round, each node receives from its neighbours their estimated position *pos* (through the **share** function[1] in line 1) and the measured distance *nbrDist* (algorithm input) that separates the current device from them, both as neighbouring values. If the node is an anchor (line 3), no calculation is needed

---

[1] While in the pseudo-code **share** has a slightly different syntax than as presented in Sect. 3.1, its *init* value and *update* can be easily recognized. A similar observation applies to **rep** and **spawn** in pseudo-code given later.

since its position is already known (line 4). For non-anchor nodes, this information is processed by the *gradientDescent* function (line 6), which is the technical heart of the algorithm. This routine compares measured distances $nbrDist_i$ with the geometric distances of position estimates pos_i, and updates the current position estimate *pos* accordingly, moving it closer to or farther from the neighbours in linear proportion to the discrepancies detected.[2] This procedure corresponds to a gradient descent of the linearised least-squares error (hence the name of the function), which is an approximation of the actual least-squares error that is simpler to optimise.

A key role in this algorithm is played by the anchor nodes, which provide the absolute spatial references necessary to constrain the localization process. In the absence of anchors, the algorithm still converges, but only to a relative solution, which may differ from reality by any global translation or rotation. At least three anchors are needed to remove all ambiguity, and an adequate distribution of more anchors helps to speed up the iterative process and reduce errors.

In order to improve convergence speed and accuracy, we also consider a variant of the algorithm which uses a *multilateration* function instead of *gradientDescent* to update the position of the nodes, substituting line 6 as follows:

6:        **return** *pos* ← *multilateration* given *anchorInfo* and *pos*

This variant differs in the strategy adopted for updating the position of non-anchor nodes. In the standard version based on *gradientDescent*, the node's position is updated incrementally, following the direction reducing the linearised least-squares error between the estimated and measured distances. By contrast, in this *multilateration*-based variant, we directly compute the position minimising the actual least-squares error with the Levenberg–Marquardt method. This approach requires more computation per each round, but may allow for more precise estimates (as we do not resort to the linearised approximation). Further, since we directly compute the optimal position, this method can allow for faster convergence time. However, in general faster convergence may also increase instability in case of noisy or fast-changing input, so the practical effectiveness of the approach has to be evaluated through simulation. We remark that in both variants, the update is iterative and local: at each step, the node modifies its position based on the current state and the information received from neighbours, progressively integrating the contributions of all available measurements. Furthermore, both variants can be shown to be stabilising.

Theorem 1. *Algorithm 1 is stabilising in both the* gradient descent *and* multilateration *variants.*

Proof. Define the total error of the network as the sum of the square of the differences between all measured distances $nbrDist_i$ and the corresponding distances of the estimated positions $\|pos_i - pos\|$. During each round, the algorithm

---

[2] This can be physically interpreted as the overall nudge that would result in a movable point at the estimated position *pos*, that is connected with elastic springs to fixed points at the estimated positions of neighbours pos_i, where the length at rest of the springs is given by the measured distances $nbrDist_i$.

Distance Vector-Based Positioning

Input: *initPos, isAnchor, nbrDist*
 1: **rep starting from** $pos \leftarrow initPos$ and $corr \leftarrow 1$ **update**
 2:     $\{dist_a, pos_a, corr_a$ for each close anchor $a\} \leftarrow anchorsDPC$ algorithm
 3:     **if** *isAnchor* **then**
 4:         $totApxDist \leftarrow$ sum of $dist_a$ if $dist_a$ finite
 5:         $totTrueDist \leftarrow$ sum of $\|pos - pos_a\|$ if $dist_a$ finite
 6:         **return** $pos \leftarrow$ known position, $corr \leftarrow totTrueDist/totApxDist$
 7:     **else**
 8:         $anchorInfo \leftarrow \{(pos_a, dist_a \cdot corr_a)$ for each close anchor $a\}$
 9:         **return** $pos \leftarrow multilateration$ given $anchorInfo$ and $pos, corr \leftarrow 1$
10:     **end if**
11: **end rep**

```
def dv(initPos, isAnchor, nbrDist) {
  rep(tuple(initPos, 1), (old) =>
    val [pos,corr] = old;
    val [D,P,C] = anchorsDPC(pos, corr, isAnchor, nbrDist, param);
    if (isAnchor) {
      val totApxDist = nfold(+, mux(D < ∞, D, 0));
      val totTrueDist = nfold(+, mux(D < ∞, norm(pos - P), 0));
      tuple(knownPos, totTrueDist / totApxDist)
    } else {
      val anchorInfo = tuple(P, D*C);
      tuple(multilateration(anchorInfo, pos), 1)
} ) }
\midskip
```

Fig. 2. Distance Vector-based positioning algorithm (above) and corresponding XC code.

can only (weakly) decrease the error of the current device, thus reducing also the overall error of the whole network. Since the total error is a positive number represented in finite precision, it cannot decrease forever, and a minimum (possibly larger than 0) will be eventually reached. Once that happens, the algorithm will have stabilised.

However, neither of the variants is necessarily *self-stabilising*, that is, so that the stabilisation result does not depend on the initial conditions. In fact, the literature shows [8] that the optimisation may get stuck on local minima, never reaching the global minima, depending on the initial conditions. Special variations have been developed to ensure a single minimum [8], often at the expense of convergence time. In our simulations, however, we never encountered such local minima, proving experimentally that they are unlikely for randomised graphs. Thus, we decided not to consider those variations in this paper.

R-Close Anchors DPC

Input: *pos, corr, isAnchor, nbrDist, R*

1: **spawn for each** anchor *a* **doing**
2:      $dist_a \leftarrow distance$ from *a* using *nbrDist*
3:      $pos_a, corr_a \leftarrow broadcast$ of *pos, corr* from *a* using $dist_a$
4:      **exit process if** $dist_a \geq R$ **else**
5:      **return** $dist_a, pos_a, corr_a$
6: **end spawn**
7: **return** $\{dist_a, pos_a, corr_a$ for each close anchor $a\}$

```
def anchorsDPC(pos, corr, isAnchor, nbrDist, R) {
  spawn((a) => {
    val dist = distance(uid() == a, nbrDist);
    val [pos,corr] = broadcast(dist, tuple(pos,corr));
    tuple(tuple(dist,pos,corr), dist < R)
  }, if (isAnchor) {cons(nil,uid())} else {nil})
}
```

Fig. 3. R-close anchors DPC algorithm (above) and the corresponding XC code (below).

4.2   Distance Vector-Based Positioning

In the DV-Hop algorithm [9], each node progressively builds an estimate of its own position based on information received from anchor nodes. In particular, each node maintains a list of known anchors and their respective estimated distances, which are iteratively updated through the propagation of information across the network. This process of progressive dissemination and update can be naturally expressed as an aggregate algorithm in XC (see Fig. 2), as shown also in the simplified pseudo-code.

At each round, every node internally maintains a copy of the state values *pos* (position) and *corr* (correction factor), through the **rep** function in line 1. Here, *pos* represents the node's current estimate of its spatial position, and *corr* is a scaling factor computed by anchor nodes to rescale estimated distances to more closely match Euclidean distances. The initial values are *pos = initPos* (which may be a fixed or random position in the deployment area) and *corr = 1* (no rescaling). At each round, these values are recomputed from the information received from anchors and stored as persistent state for the next round, keeping track of current estimates during the algorithm execution.

At line 2, we collect *DPC* information (where DPC stands for estimated relative Distance, absolute euclidean Position, Correction factor) from anchors. We accomplish this according to two main variants. In the first, closer to [9], which we call *R-Close Anchors* (Fig. 3), each node considers all anchors whose estimated distance does not exceed a predefined threshold R, stopping the propagation of information beyond this range. In the second variant, called *K-Closest Anchors* (Fig. 4), each node maintains an updated list of reachable anchors, and, if the total number exceeds a maximum value K, it selects only the K closest

K-Closest Anchors DPC

Input: $pos, corr, isAnchor, nbrDist, K$
 1: **share starting from** $dpc \leftarrow \{UID \mapsto (0, pos, corr)\}$ if $isAnchor$ else $\{\}$ **update**
 2:    **for each** neighbour i **and** anchor a in dpc_i **do**
 3:       increase $dist_i(a)$ by $nbrDist_i$ in $dpc_i(a) = (dist_i(a), pos_i(a), corr_i(a))$
 4:    **end for**
 5:    $dpc \leftarrow$ merge of dpc_i for each neighbour i, preferring shorter distances
 6:    **if** size of dpc is larger than K **then**
 7:       $dpc \leftarrow$ select K elements of dpc with smallest distance
 8:    **end if**
 9:    **return** dpc
10: **end share**
11: **return** $dist_a, pos_a, corr_a = dpc(a)$ for each anchor a in dpc

```
def anchorsDPC(pos, corr, isAnchor, nbrDist, K) {
  val init = if (isAnchor) {map(uid(), tuple(0,pos,corr))} else {map()};
  share(init, (ndpc) => {
    val mdpc = nmap(map_inc, ndpc, nbrDist);
    val dpc = nfold(map_join, mdpc, init);
    map_trunc(dpc, K)
  })
}
```

Fig. 4. K-closest anchors DPC algorithm (above) and the corresponding XC code (below). Functions `map_inc`, `map_join` and `map_trunc` respectively increase the first component of tuples in a map, merge maps preferring smaller values for the first component, and select the K values in the map with the smallest first component.

anchors in terms of estimated distance. Regardless of the variant chosen, the DPC information collected from the anchors is then used to update pos and $corr$, as shown in the following lines of the algorithm. If the node is an anchor (lines 4–6), the position is known and no calculation is needed to update pos. Instead, $corr$ is set to the ratio between the sum of Euclidean distances and the sum of estimated distances to the other anchors, providing the needed scaling factor from estimated to Euclidean. For non-anchor nodes, there is no associated correction factor, and $corr$ is hence just set to 1. Instead, pos is updated through multilateration (lines 9), where the distances to anchors are obtained by multiplying estimated distances and correction factors (line 8).

In the R-Close Anchors variant (Fig. 3), a **spawn** of a new aggregate process is performed for each anchor (line 1) to handle data collection concurrently. Each process checks the estimated distance to the anchor using distance estimates to neighbours $nbrDist$ (line 2) and performs a broadcast of the anchor's position and correction factor (line 3). If the distance exceeds the predefined threshold R, the current node exits the aggregate process (line 4), ensuring that only "close enough" anchors are considered. This is crucial to ensure self-stabilisation: if a node stops being an anchor, distance estimates from it will start increasing until when its process is fully terminated. The algorithm terminates (line 7) returning a collection of distance, position and correction values for each anchor whose process was active in the current device (thus, only those within a distance of R).

In the K-Closest Anchors variant (Fig. 4), the node maintains a distributed table of anchor information using the **share** construct (line 1). For each neighbour i and anchor a in the table received from that neighbour (line 2), the node updates the distance estimates in that table by adding the distance estimate to the neighbour $nbrDist$ (line 3). All tables received are then merged, preferring shorter distances if the same anchor appears in multiple tables (line 5). If the total number of anchors in the resulting table dpc exceeds the maximum value K (lines 6–7), only the K closest anchors in it are retained. Finally, the selected anchors are shared with neighbours (line 9), and returned to be used in the subsequent multilateration step (line 11).

In both variants, distances between nodes and anchors are expressed according to a given metric $nbrDist$, which may take very different forms: for instance, it may only represent the number of hops (if $nbrDist$ is equal to 1 for each neighbour) or on noisy estimated distances (for instance, calculated with power ratio RSSI or message round-trip time measurements). The correction factor is crucial to ensure that any such metric can be used to estimate distances, leveraging the exact positional knowledge of anchors to compensate for systematic errors or even totally different scales, such as when distances are measured in hops. Furthermore, both variants can be shown to be self-stabilising.

Theorem 2. *Algorithm 2 is self-stabilising with either sub-routines in Algorithm 3 or Algorithm 4.*

Proof. Algorithm 3 is self-stabilising since it is a `spawn` on a fixed (thus stable) set of keys, whose process body consists of the *distance* and *broadcast* algorithms together with local-only computations, which are all known from literature to be self-stabilising [15].

Algorithm 4 is also self-stabilising, since it is an instance of the minimising pattern presented in [15]. In this pattern, a **share** repeatedly updates partially ordered values by first *increasing* with an increasing function all values received by neighbours, and then returning their *join* (maximum lower bound). This is exactly the structure of Algorithm 4, where:

- values are maps of at most K elements or the form $UID \mapsto (dist, pos, corr)$;
- values are partially ordered by $m \leq m'$ iff for each $\delta \in \mathbf{dom}(m) \cap \mathbf{dom}(m')$ we have that $m(\delta)_1 \leq m'(\delta)_1$ and $m(\delta)_1 = m'(\delta)_1 \Rightarrow m(\delta) = m'(\delta)$ (for devices appearing in both maps, the distances in m are not larger than those in m', and if they are the same so are the position and correction values), and for each $\delta' \in \mathbf{dom}(m') \setminus \mathbf{dom}(m)$ we have that $m'(\delta')_1 \geq m(\delta)_1$ for all $\delta \in \mathbf{dom}(m)$ (the distances in m' for devices that do not appear in m are larger than all distances in m);
- notice that this partial order induces a *join* operation (maximum lower bound) that is exactly the K elements with smallest distance among both maps after removing duplicates by favoring shorter distances (which is what Algorithm 4 calculates in dpc);

- the increasing function is the one updating distances in a map m by adding them the values $nbrDist_i$, which is indeed increasing with respect to the partial order above.

Thus, Algorithm 2 obtains its *dpc* values from a self-stabilising algorithm, whose inputs are the positions *pos* of anchors (which is an algorithm input, so stable by hypothesis) and corrections of anchors *corr*, which are computed by the algorithm itself, so we have to prove that they are also self-stabilising. First, notice that both Algorithms 3 and 4 do not use the correction values to calculate distances and positions. It follows that even if corrections are not stable, those algorithms already self-stabilise for their computation of distances and positions in finite time. After distances and positions are stable, the correction factors of anchors as computed in Algorithm 2 also stabilise. At this point all inputs of Algorithms 3 and 4 are stable, so in additional finite time also the correction factors computed by those algorithms will be stable. Since the position computed by Algorithm 2 is a local function of those values, this concludes the self-stabilisation proof.

5   Evaluation

We evaluated the algorithms presented in this paper in the following variations. For *distance vector-based positioning*, we considered:

- multilateration with R-close anchors using aggregate processes, where R is sufficiently large to include all anchors in the area (in the following, we will call it `dv all`);
- multilateration with the six closest anchors (`dv 6close`).

For each of them we considered both a `hop` version (where distance measures to neighbours are not available, and hop-counts are used instead), and the `real` version (using noisy distance measures with neighbours). For *non-bayesian cooperative localisation*, we considered both the version from literature based on gradient descent (`nbcoop`) and our variation based on multilateration (`mlcoop`). These algorithms assume the availability of distance measures, so do not have a `hop` version. The algorithms and simulation setup were implemented in the FCPP library [4].

We considered three simulation parameters: *radius* (r), *speed* (v) and *variance* (d). The *radius* parameter, from 50m to 300m, determined the distance at which communication between devices becomes impossible, and indirectly affected the overall size of the network in hops (larger radius, fewer hops) and the average number of anchors in neighbourhoods (larger neighbourhoods contain more anchors). The *speed* parameter, from $0\,\mathrm{m/s}$ to $5\,\mathrm{m/s}$, determined the speed of long-range movement for the devices. The *variance* parameter, from 0% to 50%, determined the relative standard error of the three sources of noise that we considered: *(i)* error in round timing; *(ii)* error in distance measures; *(iii)* variance in communication success rate (more details below). We considered the speed parameter only in isolation, using zero speed when varying the

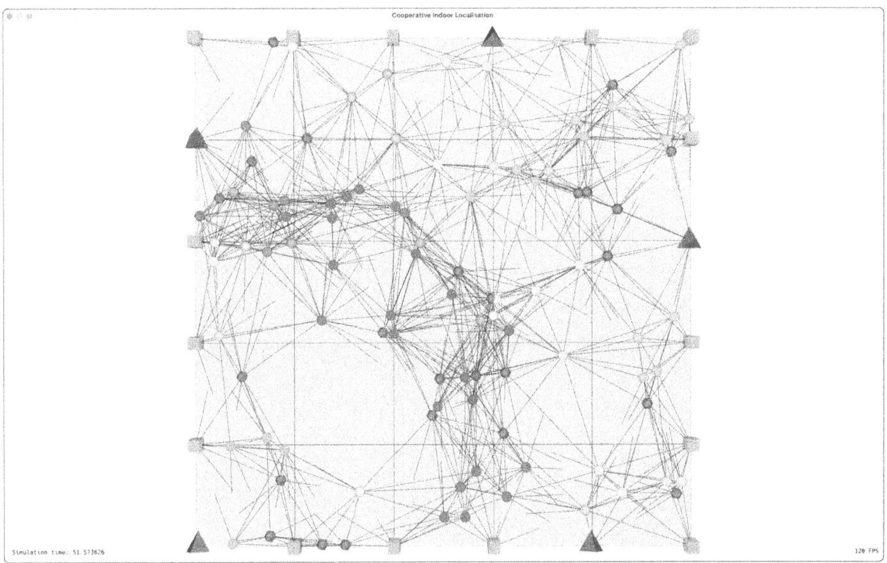

Fig. 5. Screenshot of the simulation with parameters $r = 150\,\mathrm{m}$, $v = 0\,\mathrm{m/s}$ and $d = 20\%$ at about $51\,\mathrm{s}$ after the start. Crashed anchors and nodes are coloured in gray, with tetrahedron and icosahedron shapes respectively. The other anchors and nodes, with cubic and spherical shape respectively, are coloured according to the current error of the position estimated by the `nbcoop real` algorithm (hues changing continuously from green to yellow, red, purple with increasing error). Lines between nodes represent communication links (half lines represent asymmetric communication). (Color figure online)

other parameters, since that allowed for trends to be observed more clearly in the plots.

We simulated a rectangular area of $500\,\mathrm{m} \times 500\,\mathrm{m}$, with 20 stationary anchors uniformly positioned along the border, and 100 devices positioned inside the area uniformly at random, which moved across randomly-generated checkpoints at a constant speed v. Devices performed rounds every second on average, with standard error d. Distance measures where computed by multiplying exact distances with a Weibull distribution of mean 1 and standard deviation d. We used a probabilistic model for connectivity based on real-world data, tuned to have an about 100% delivery success at 0m distance, about 0% delivery success beyond *radius* distance, and 50% delivery success at distance $r \cdot (1 - d)$. This entails that with $d = 0$, messages always succeed within r and fail above it; and as d increases more devices get an higher chance of communication failure.

In order to test the resiliency of the proposed algorithms, we simulated that $1/4$ of the devices and anchors crash after $50\,\mathrm{s}$ of simulated time, and are replaced (or fixed) after $100\,\mathrm{s}$ of simulated time, until simulation ends at $150\,\mathrm{s}$. We run simulations for 26 values of *radius*, 21 values of *speed*, 26 values of *variance*, and 100 different random seeds for each scenario, for a total of 7100 simulations.

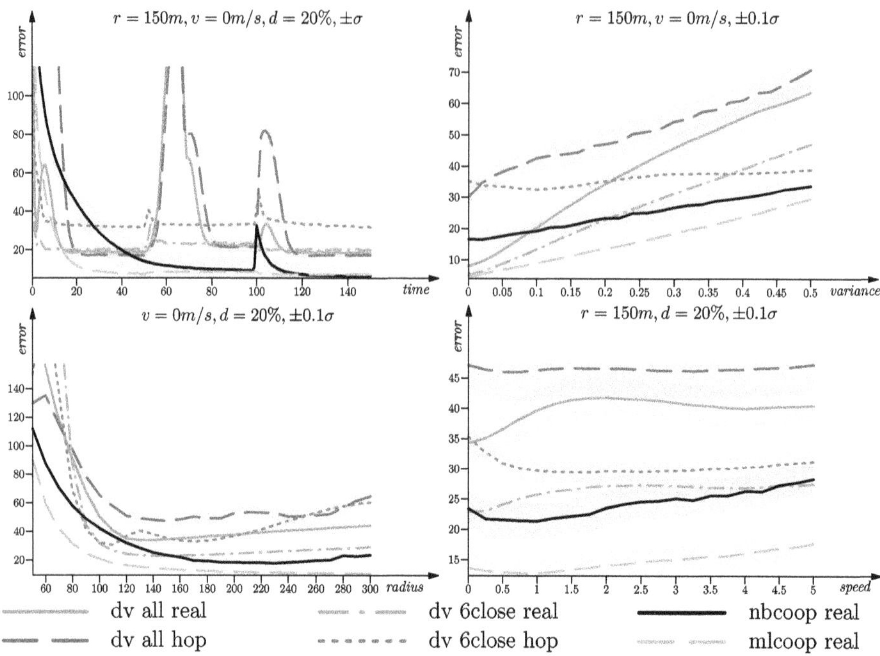

Fig. 6. Average localisation error over time (top-left, in seconds), variance (top-right, a dimensionless value from 0% to 50%), radius (bottom-left, in meters), and speed (bottom-right, in m/s). Lightly coloured bands represent the standard deviation of the results for the time plot, or 0.1 the standard deviation for the other plots (which have an higher deviation, since the average is calculated also over varying time points). (Color figure online)

The experiments were run on a MacBook Pro 2019 with a 2.4 GHz i9 8-core CPU and 32 GB 2667 MHz DDR4 RAM and required about 8 h to complete. The experiment source code is publicly available online on Zenodo,[3] and can run both graphical simulations (see Fig. 5) and plots from batch simulations (see Fig. 6).

First, we inspected the size of messages exchanged for the various algorithms. The results had an average for `dv all` at 1889 bytes, `dv 6close` at 321 bytes, and both `coop` algorithms at 32 bytes, with almost zero variance across time and different scenarios so we do not include a plot for them (as it would just consist of horizontal lines). By profiling, we also inspected the time spent on the different algorithms during a simulation, obtaining about 4.6s for `dv all`, 1.1s for `dv 6close` and 0.3s for `coop` algorithms. Hop versions were a bit more efficient than their real counterparts, and `nbcoop` was a bit more efficient than `mlcoop`, but with a difference below 10%.

---

[3] https://doi.org/10.5281/zenodo.19443874.

Then, we inspected the mean *error* (distance in meters between the estimated position and true position) among all devices, both as time passes in a default scenario (with $r = 150\,\text{m}, v = 0\,\text{m/s}, d = 20\%$) and as one of the parameters r, v or d vary (with other parameters at the default), averaged across all simulated time (see the four plots in Fig. 6). The times when devices and anchors crash and then get replaced induce spikes in error that are then recovered (top-left graph). The `dv all` algorithms have significantly worst spikes, that are much lower for the other algorithms. Furthermore, both cooperative algorithms to not produce a spike in error when anchors are removed, while `mlcoop` and `dv 6close real` do not produce a spike when anchors are reintroduced. Generally, increasing *variance* (top-right plot) degrades performance as expected, but not by the same amount for each algorithm: `dv 6close hop` is the least affected as it is almost constant, probably partially because it doesn't rely on the increasingly noisier distance estimates. Reducing *radius* (bottom-left plot) also tends to degrade performance, as the network becomes increasingly disconnected: with smaller values, more and more devices resort to totally random estimates of their position, as they are not connected to any anchor. More unexpectedly, also a larger *radius* tends to degrade performance: this is probably due to the fact that an increased *radius* also reduces the hop-diameter of the network to a few units, so that `hop` algorithms have an hard time getting reasonable estimates. However, this also affects `real` algorithms (except for `mlcoop`), although by a smaller extent, for unclear reasons. Finally, increasing *speed* (bottom-right plot) also tends to degrade performance, although not significantly nor uniformily, proving the resilience in mutable environments of all algorithms we tested.

Summarizing the information across all plots, the `real` versions consistently outperform their `hops` counterparts, except for `dv 6close` when *variance* is very high (above 38%). Thus, using distance estimates proves to be useful whenever they are available, except when they are so noisy that they become effectively more inaccurate than just estimating hops.

Furthermore, `dv 6close` outperforms `dv all` almost always: the only exception is when *radius* is below $80m$ (so that the network is almost disconnected), or for the `hop` variants when *variance* is below 2%. Thus, considering only the closest anchors tends to improve performance, which can be justified since the distances to the farthest anchors are the least accurate. Given that `dv all` also requires much larger message sizes, its use is basically never advised.

Overall, the `mlcoop` algorithm is a clear winner in basically every scenario. This algorithm not only achieves the best steady-state values (together with `nbcoop`), but also provides the faster convergence time on simulation startup, while being almost unaffected by both the removal and addition of new devices. Also `nbcoop` performs quite well and is unaffected by device removal, but gets penalised by its slow initial convergence and by the error spike when new devices are added. Although it is still the second best algorithm in most conditions, it is outperformed by `dv 6close real` for small *variance* and for *radius* between about $90m$ and $150m$. On the other hand, we remark that both `coop` algorithms are stabilising but not necessarily self-stabilising, since they may converge to a local minimum [8]. In summary, the best algorithms depending on the setting are:

- if distance estimates are not available, or formal self-stabilisation is required and variance is very high, `dv 6close hop`; otherwise
- if formal self-stabilisation is required, `dv 6close real`; otherwise
- if initial convergence is not an issue (long-running system), and computational power is very constrained, `nbcoop` provides the best steady-state values with small messages and few computations per round; otherwise
- `mlcoop` provides the best accuracy and resilience overall with small messages.

6   Conclusion

In this work, we addressed the problem of distributed multi-hop localisation in indoor environments, in which devices must estimate their position through local interactions, in the presence of measurement noise and dynamic network conditions. We reformulated two classical geometric approaches (DV-based positioning and NB-cooperative) within the aggregate computing paradigm, exploiting the exchange and alignment constructs of the XC language to obtain modular, composable, fully distributed and (self-)stabilising implementations. In addition to the versions more directly translated from the literature, we introduced and analysed improved variants: the K-Closest anchor selection strategies for DV-based positioning, and a variant of NB-cooperative based on multilateration instead of gradient descent. Through an extensive experimental set-up conducted within the FCPP framework, which considered different configurations of communication radius, mobility, and noise levels, we evaluated accuracy, convergence time, resilience to node crashes, message size, and computational cost. The results show that selecting only the closest anchors significantly improves the performance of DV-based variants. Furthermore, the multilateration-based cooperative version represents, overall, the solution with the best trade-off between accuracy, convergence speed, and robustness, while maintaining small message sizes and limited computational costs.

Despite the encouraging results, this work presents some limitations that open interesting directions for future research. First, the analysis focused on two representative classical algorithms and related variants, leaving room for the integration of additional cooperative localisation strategies. Among these, a weighted version of the *mlcoop* algorithm appears particularly promising. In such version, each node also maintains an estimate of its own error and uses it as a weight in the multilateration process. This may modulate the contribution of different nodes according to their reliability and potentially improve robustness in scenarios with high variability or highly noisy measurements. Furthermore, the guaranteed self-stabilising version of the *coop* algorithm inspired from [8], albeit with expected slower convergence, should also be evaluated. Second, the evaluations were conducted in a highly synthetic simulated environment, although extensive and parametric. A natural evolution of this work could consist in defining a more realistic case study, modelled on a concrete application scenario and aimed at a future experimental validation in the field. This would make it possible to analyse more deeply aspects such as hardware constraints, energy consumption, radio interference, and real environmental dynamics, further consolidating the practical applicability of the proposed solutions.

Acknowledgments. This publication is part of the project NODES, which has received funding from the MUR – M4C2 1.5 of PNRR funded by the European Union - NextGenerationEU (Grant agreement no. ECS00000036). This study has been supported by the Italian PRIN project "CommonWears" (2020HCWWLP) and was carried out within the Agritech National Research Center and received funding from the European Union Next-GenerationEU (PIANO NAZIONALE DI RIPRESA E RESILIENZA (PNRR) – MISSIONE 4 COMPONENTE 2, INVESTIMENTO 1.4 – D.D. 1032 17/06/2022, CN00000022). This manuscript reflects only the authors' views and opinions, neither the European Union nor the European Commission can be considered responsible for them.

Disclosure of Interests. The authors have no competing interests to declare that are relevant to the content of this article.

References

1. Asmaa, L., Aroussi, H.K., Mouloudi, A.: Localization algorithms research in wireless sensor network based on multilateration and trilateration techniques. In: Mohajir, M.E., Achhab, M.A., Chahhou, M. (eds.) Third IEEE International Colloquium in Information Science and Technology, CIST 2014, Tetouan, Morocco, October 20-22, 2014. pp. 415–419. IEEE (2014). https://doi.org/10.1109/CIST.2014.7016656
2. Audrito, G., Casadei, R., Damiani, F., Salvaneschi, G., Viroli, M.: The exchange calculus (XC): a functional programming language design for distributed collective systems. J. Syst. Softw. **210**, 111976 (2024). https://doi.org/10.1016/J.JSS.2024.111976
3. Audrito, G., Casadei, R., Damiani, F., Torta, G., Viroli, M.: Programming distributed collective processes in the exchange calculus. Log. Methods Comput. Sci. **21**(4) (2025). https://doi.org/10.46298/LMCS-21(4:3)2025
4. Audrito, G., Torta, G.: FCPP to aggregate them all. Sci. Comput. Program. **231**, 103026 (2024). https://doi.org/10.1016/J.SCICO.2023.103026
5. Basterrech, S., Mohamed, S., Rubino, G., Soliman, M.A.: Levenberg - marquardt training algorithms for random neural networks. Comput. J. **54**(1), 125–135 (2011). https://doi.org/10.1093/COMJNL/BXP101
6. Beal, J., Pianini, D., Viroli, M.: Aggregate programming for the Internet of Things. IEEE Comput. **48**(9) (2015). https://doi.org/10.1109/MC.2015.261
7. Casadei, R., Viroli, M., Audrito, G., Pianini, D., Damiani, F.: Engineering collective intelligence at the edge with aggregate processes. Eng. Appl. Artif. Intell. **97**, 104081 (2021). https://doi.org/10.1016/j.engappai.2020.104081
8. Morano, G., Hrovat, A., Švigelj, A., Velkaverh, J., Žnidaršič, P., Javornik, T.: Experimental performance evaluation of cooperative localization in indoor environment. IEEE Sens. J. **25**(23), 43426–43445 (2025). https://doi.org/10.1109/JSEN.2025.3620118

9. Niculescu, D., Nath, B.: DV based positioning in ad hoc networks. Telecommun. Syst. **22**(1-4), 267–280 (2003). https://doi.org/10.1023/A:1023403323460
10. Qiao, J., Yang, F., Liu, J., Huang, G., Zhang, W., Li, M.: Advancements in indoor precision positioning: A comprehensive survey of UWB and Wi-Fi RTT positioning technologies. Network **4**(4), 545–566 (2024). https://doi.org/10.3390/network4040027, https://www.mdpi.com/2673-8732/4/4/27
11. Shams, R., Otero, P., Aamir, M., Khan, F.H.: Joint algorithm for multi-hop localization and time synchronization in underwater sensors networks using single anchor. IEEE Access **9**, 27945–27958 (2021). https://doi.org/10.1109/ACCESS.2021.3058160
12. Simonetto, A., Leus, G.: Distributed maximum likelihood sensor network localization. IEEE Trans. Signal Process. **62**(6), 1424–1437 (2014). https://doi.org/10.1109/TSP.2014.2302746
13. Testa, L., Audrito, G., Damiani, F., Torta, G.: Aggregate processes as distributed adaptive services for the industrial internet of things. Pervasive Mob. Comput. **85**, 101658 (2022). https://doi.org/10.1016/j.pmcj.2022.101658
14. Thomas, F., Ros, L.: Revisiting trilateration for robot localization. IEEE Trans. Robotics **21**(1), 93–101 (2005). https://doi.org/10.1109/TRO.2004.833793
15. Viroli, M., Audrito, G., Beal, J., Damiani, F., Pianini, D.: Engineering resilient collective adaptive systems by self-stabilisation. ACM Trans. Model. Comput. Simul. **28**(2), 16:1–16:28 (2018). https://doi.org/10.1145/3177774
16. Viroli, M., Beal, J., Damiani, F., Audrito, G., Casadei, R., Pianini, D.: From distributed coordination to field calculus and aggregate computing. J. Log. Algebraic Methods Program. **109** (2019). https://doi.org/10.1016/j.jlamp.2019.100486
17. Wymeersch, H., Lien, J., Win, M.Z.: Cooperative localization in wireless networks. Proc. IEEE **97**(2), 427–450 (2009). https://doi.org/10.1109/JPROC.2008.2008853
18. Xiong, Y., Wu, N., Shen, Y., Win, M.Z.: Cooperative localization in massive networks. IEEE Trans. Inf. Theory **68**(2), 1237–1258 (2022). https://doi.org/10.1109/TIT.2021.3126346

A Self-stabilizing Min-Max Consensus
via Path-Loop Detection

Angela Cortecchia$^{(\boxtimes)}$, Danilo Pianini , and Mirko Viroli

Department of Computer Science and Engineering, Alma Mater
Studiorum—Università di Bologna, Via dell'Università 50, Cesena (FC),
47522 Emilia-Romagna, Italy
{angela.cortecchia,danilo.pianini,mirko.viroli}@unibo.it

Abstract. In large-scale distributed systems, such as the Internet of
Things (IoT), min-max consensus algorithms provide a mechanism for
collective coordination by enabling nodes to converge on a "best" value
produced by one of the participants in the computation. However, min-
max consensus algorithms are monotonic and non-self-stabilizing by
nature: once a value is merged into the aggregate it cannot be retracted,
leading to propagation of stale or incorrect data in the presence of transient faults or topology changes. In this work, we propose a novel self-
stabilizing min-max consensus algorithm ensuring convergence to the
best available value in the network by propagating information along
shortest valid paths. Each gossip message carries a value and path
of nodes that have acknowledged it, enabling loop-freedom and natural pruning of obsolete contributions. We rely on field-based coordination and specifically the Aggregate Computing paradigm to present the
algorithm, prove self-stabilization, and provide an implementation as a
reusable library for the *Collektive* DSL. This work contributes a foundational building block for resilient coordination in pervasive computing
systems, paving the way to more complex, self-stabilizing distributed
applications.

Keywords: Aggregate Computing · Gossip Algorithm ·
Self-Stabilization · Distributed Systems

1 Introduction

Gossip protocols are a widely adopted strategy for coordinating large sets of
nodes in distributed systems. By enabling each node to periodically exchange
and aggregate information with its neighbors, gossip allows the estimation of
collective states in a decentralized, scalable, and fault-tolerant manner. This
makes gossip a valuable coordination primitive for emerging application domains
such as the Internet of Things (IoT), where devices are deployed across physical
space to sense, plan, and act collectively [3, 10, 37].

© IFIP International Federation for Information Processing 2026
Published by Springer Nature Switzerland AG 2026
R. Casadei and F. Ghassemi (Eds.): COORDINATION 2026, LNCS 16590, pp. 93–114, 2026.
https://doi.org/10.1007/978-3-032-28358-0_5

In these scenarios, the ability of the system to adapt to failures, disconnections, and dynamic changes in topology is crucial. Classical gossip algorithms, however, suffer from fundamental limitations that make them ill-suited to dynamic environments. In particular, once a value has been merged into the collective state, it is challenging to retract or correct it, especially when that value becomes obsolete.

Typical solutions in the literature involve strategies such as periodic resets of the gossip state [21, 32], or using of versioning and timestamps to identify and discard stale information [20, 36], to more refined strategies based on running multiple overlapped gossip instances to avoid abrupt information resets [27].

Contribution. In this paper, we propose to address this limitation for a specific class of gossip protocols, known as *min-max consensus* protocols [24], where the goal is to propagate the best value in the network according to a shared condition, such as selecting the minimum or maximum value among those contributed by nodes. We do so by proposing a novel *self-stabilizing* [17] *min-max consensus algorithm* that guarantees convergence to the best value present in the network, even in the face of transient faults. Our solution augments each propagated value with a path of validating nodes, allowing devices to track the flow of information and prevent loops. By enforcing value selection through the shortest valid path, our algorithm maintains correctness, locality, and low overhead, while enabling robust recovery from inconsistent states.

The proposed algorithm does not leverage any central coordination point or global reset mechanism. Instead, it relies solely on local interactions and asynchronous execution, making decisions based on the information received from neighbors over a comparison function which determines whether a value is better than another.

Structure of the Paper. The remainder of this paper is organized as follows.

Section 2 introduces the theoretical and practical context of this work: it revisits classical gossip protocols and their limitations in dynamic environments, recalls the notion of self-stabilization, and related approaches, including epidemic techniques, Conflict-free Replicated Data Type (CRDT) based solutions, and aggregate-computing building blocks. This discussion motivates the need for a fully decentralized and self-stabilizing gossip mechanism.

Section 3 presents the proposed solution. We first describe the intuition behind path-based validation and loop detection, then formalize the local decision process. The Sect. 3.2 also details an implementation in the *Collektive* framework, showing how the algorithm can be realized as a reusable aggregate operator. The formal proof of self-stabilization is provided in Sect. 3.3, where we show that the algorithm conforms to the minimizing-share pattern, thus guaranteeing convergence after transient perturbations under standard assumptions.

Section 4 reports the experimental evaluation carried out in simulation, demonstrating both correctness under dynamic topology changes and behavior in terms of convergence and scalability. Finally, Sect. 5 concludes the paper, summarizing the main contribution and outlining directions for future work.

2   Background and Related Work

2.1   Gossip Protocols

In a generic gossip protocol, each node exchanges values with its neighbors and aggregates them using an operator f, such as minimum, maximum, or set union. This process leads to the emergence of a collective state v from a stream of local inputs x_δ, where δ is a device.

The merge function f is required to be *idempotent* ($f(a, f(a,b)) = f(a,b)$) and *commutative* ($f(a,b) = f(b,a)$), properties which ensure convergence and resilience to message duplication. The resulting protocols are scalable, redundant, and tolerant to individual node failures.

However, these same properties introduce significant limitations: gossip protocols are inherently *asymmetric* and *information-destroying*. Due to the idempotent nature of the merge operation, a value may be merged multiple times without impacting the aggregate result, making it infeasible to track the exact number of occurrences or retract invalid contributions. For instance, with $f = \min(a,b)$, values can decrease but never increase; similarly, $f = \max(a,b)$ only allows increases. This makes it difficult and costly to remove outdated values once they have influenced the aggregate.

This results in a *non-self-stabilizing* protocol, where the system may fail to recover from transient faults or outdated inputs. If a node starts with an incorrect value, or if its value becomes obsolete, it may continue to influence the collective state indefinitely. This leads to inconsistent behavior across nodes, despite local correctness.

These limitations motivate the need for self-stabilizing gossip protocols, which can autonomously recover from inconsistencies and converge to a correct global state. The notion of self-stabilization, first introduced by Dijkstra [17], refers to the ability of a distributed system to reach a legitimate configuration from any initial state within a finite number of steps, and to remain in that configuration unless perturbed by faults. This is particularly relevant in dynamic systems where nodes may join, leave, or change state unpredictably.

Several approaches have been proposed to address these limitations:

-   Identify values for x_δ with a unique identifier of the source or a timestamp, in such a way to update the old values or remove them and keep the newest ones. This approach is used for gossip algorithms that build indexing or routing data structures, e.g., in peer-to-peer systems [20,36]. However, most of the devices know only a fragment of the aggregate value v, or the size of the exchanging data will be too large, since every value has to be tracked individually.
-   Periodically restart the gossip protocol to discard the old values of x_δ and to reset v [21,32]. As an advantage, this approach is very lightweight, but can lead to lagging information in the network before the changes are effectively acknowledged and large transients in v_δ during the restart phase. Moreover, it must be avoided to share old gossip values with the new ones; otherwise there is the risk of contaminating the new gossip with obsolete values, resulting in no benefit from the restart.

– Run multiple overlapping gossip instances, each with a different identifier, to allow a smooth transition between old and new values [27]. This approach can mitigate the issues of periodic restarts at the price of increased complexity and overhead.

Recent advances in Aggregate Computing (AC) [10] have introduced self-stabilizing building blocks [34] to disseminate, collect [6], and elect leaders [26, 28], which can be combined to implement self-stabilizing gossip protocols via the self-organising coordination regions (SCR) pattern [29]. Although these can be composed to implement self-stabilizing gossip protocols, since a leader is required to coordinate the collection and redistribution of information, they need a coordination point to achieve convergence, which may introduce fragility in dynamic networks [7].

2.2 Self-stabilizing Leader Election with Local Agreements

A related line of research concerns self-stabilizing leader election and local agreement protocols, which aim at achieving coordination objectives such as electing a unique leader or reaching agreement on a distinguished value starting from arbitrary initial configurations [18]. These algorithms typically provide strong correctness guarantees, ensuring convergence despite transient faults and asynchronous execution. However, they usually focus on establishing a single global structure, such as a leader or a spanning tree, and often require additional assumptions on the execution model or the maintenance of auxiliary global state.

In contrast, the problem addressed in this work is not to elect or maintain a unique global coordinator, but rather to continuously propagate and update the best available value in the network according to a comparator. Alternative approaches that do not rely on explicit symmetry-breaking phases or global agreement steps preserve the decentralized and local nature of gossip-based interactions.

2.3 Epidemic Protocols, TTL/Ageing and CRDTs

Epidemic and gossip-based dissemination protocols often address stale information by introducing explicit versioning mechanisms, such as timestamps, sequence numbers, or time-to-live (TTL) counters [16]. These techniques limit the persistence of obsolete data and reduce long-term contamination of aggregates, but their correctness typically depends on parameter tuning and does not provide self-stabilization in the presence of arbitrary transient faults. In particular, outdated values may still influence the system for unbounded time intervals if aging parameters are poorly calibrated or network conditions change.

Conflict-Free Replicated Data Types (CRDTs) [23] represent another prominent approach to achieving convergence in distributed systems by relying on commutative, associative, and idempotent merge operations. While CRDTs guarantee eventual consistency of replicated state, they are inherently monotonic and do not support the semantic retraction of previously merged contributions once they become obsolete. In contrast, approaches that explicitly couple value selection with lightweight path-based validation can enable the removal of stale information without relying on global resets or monotonic state growth.

Despite the variety of existing approaches, the closest class of protocols to our setting are selector-based gossip mechanisms, which restrict aggregation to the propagation of a single candidate value.

2.4   Min-Max Consensus

A particular class of gossip protocols, known as *min-max consensus* protocols, employ a comparison function to determine which values to propagate. Provided an arbitrary type X, comparator $f : X^2 \rightarrow \{1, 0, -1\}$ provides a selection strategy for values in X, such that $f(a, b) = 1$ if a is considered better than b according to the selection criterion, $f(a, b) = 0$ if a and b are considered equivalent, and $f(a, b) = -1$ otherwise. These protocols are particularly useful when nodes need to agree on a single value from a set of candidates, such as selecting the minimum or maximum value, or choosing a leader based on specific criteria. However, restricting gossip protocols to the family of min-max consensus protocols does not inherently guarantee self-stabilization: most protocols typically converge only when starting from a legal configuration, and may fail to recover from transient faults or stale information without explicit stabilization mechanisms.

In this work, we present a lightweight and fully asynchronous min-max consensus protocol that combines a comparator-based selection with local path tracking to achieve self-stabilization. Our algorithm ensures loop-freedom and resilience to faults, while maintaining the decentralized nature and minimal state typical of gossip-based solutions.

2.5   Field Calculus and Aggregate Computing

AC [10] is a functional macro-programming paradigm for engineering self-adaptive systems, grounded in the notion of *computational fields* [25], distributed data structures that associate situated devices to values. Building upon this foundation, the Field Calculus (FC) [9] provides higher-order functional abstractions for defining, transforming, and composing such fields, based exclusively on local observations and interactions.

An *AC system* is therefore composed of multiple autonomous agents that interact with their surrounding environment through sensors and actuators, while exchanging information with nearby peers, effectively abstracting away the details of the underlying communication topology. Devices execute a common aggregate program in asynchronous rounds, which repeatedly senses the local environment, computes a new local state based on the current state and the information received from neighbors, and shares the updated state with nearby devices. Within this framework, AC enables the expression of *reusable* self-organizing collective behaviors by means functions.

This modeling approach is suitable for a broad spectrum of application domains, and has been successfully applied to various scenarios, including applications to crowd management [10], disaster detection and response [1], morphogenetic algorithms [15], and swarm behaviors [2].

Practical Aggregate Computing. Multiple aggregate programming languages have been developed to support the practical implementation of AC systems, including Protelis [31] (a stand-alone Domain-Specific Language (DSL)), Scafi [12] (a DSL embedded in Scala), FCPP [8] (a C++ library), and, more recently, *Collektive*[1] [13], a Kotlin-multiplatform DSL. In the remainder of this paper, we will introduce aggregate programming concepts and the proposed gossip algorithm using *Collektive*, although the same principles and patterns can be applied in any of the aforementioned languages.

Evolution in Time and Space. To support the evolution of a computational field over both time and space, AC relies on the `share` construct [4], which models stateful information exchange among neighboring agents. The `share` function takes an initial local value together with an operator that computes over a field of values of the same type, and produces an updated value that is locally returned and propagated to neighbors:

```
1  fun <T> share(intial: T, op: (Field<T>) -> T): T
```

Computing Distances. As a representative example, `share` can be exploited to implement a self-healing variant of the Bellman–Ford algorithm, used to estimate the hop-distance from the nearest device satisfying a given condition [34]:

```
1  import Double.POSITIVE_INFINITY as infinity
2  fun <ID, Type> Aggregate<ID>.bellmanFord(isSource: Boolean): Double =
3    share(infinity) { distances: Field<Double> ->
4      val minDistance = (distances + 1.0).neighbors.values.min ?: infinity
5      if (isSource) 0 else minDistance
6  }
```

Gossiping Values. A non-self-stabilizing version of a gossip algorithm can be realized through a structurally similar pattern:

```
1  fun <ID, T> Aggregate<ID>.gossip<Type>(local: T, combiner: (T, T) -> T) =
2    share(local) { it.all.values.reduce(combiner) }
```

Here, `local` represents the value contributed by each device, while `combine` is an associative and commutative operator used to aggregate values across the field. For instance, assuming that `temp()` returns the current temperature reading of a device, the following expression computes the maximum temperature *ever* observed in the network:

---

[1] https://collektive.github.io/.

```
1  val maxTemp = gossip(temp(), Double::max)
```

Similarly, the identifiers of all devices that *ever* joined the system can be collected as follows:

```
1  val allIds = gossip(setOf(localId), Set::plus)
```

Note that, in both cases, we specified that these algorithms return the maximum temperature and the set of all identifiers *ever* observed in the network; indeed, these simple implementations do not provide any mechanism to remove obsolete values, and the `gossip` construct we obtain this way is inherently *non-self-stabilizing*. This behavior represents a known limitation of classical gossip mechanisms.

Self-stabilizing Building Blocks and SCR-Gossip. AC provides a catalog of fundamental self-stabilizing primitives [34]. These include mechanisms for information dissemination (encompassing adaptive gradient algorithms such as the Bellman–Ford variant discussed above), for information aggregation and for symmetry breaking (commonly adopted for multi-leader election). A key property of these primitives is that their functional composition preserves self-stabilization guarantees.

By relying on these patterns, a self-stabilizing gossip protocol can be implemented by:

1. electing a leader using a self-stabilizing leader election protocol;
2. propagating a distance information from such leader, building a "potential" field with a single minimum at the leader's position;
3. building a minimum spanning tree rooted at the leader by using the potential field as base gradient, and performing collection and aggregation along such tree, so that every device contributes its value exactly once;
4. broadcasting the aggregated value to the entire network with a second gradient-based dissemination, so that every device receives the same value.

These steps resemble an instance of the more general SCR pattern [29], which consists of a symmetry-breaking phase (multi-leader election), followed by the construction of downstream (from the leader) and upstream (to the leader) communication structures.

Although this solution is conceptually straightforward and self-stabilizing by construction, it can be insufficiently responsive in networks with high churn or frequent topology changes, as the leader election and tree construction phases may take a significant amount of time to converge.

3 Self-stabilizing Min-max Consensus with Path Loop Detection

We now introduce a self-stabilizing min-max consensus algorithm, based on the AC paradigm, that allows nodes to converge to a consistent state even in the presence of transient faults.

3.1 Idea and Algorithm

The algorithm is based on the idea of tracking the origin and propagation of the "best" known value in the network (that we denote as X) by annotating it with the path of nodes that have validated it, while discarding values whose path is incoherent (loop detection). The algorithm requires, as input, the local value of the node and a comparison function f as described in Sect. 2.4. Moreover, devices must be uniquely identifiable, and their identifiers must be comparable to break ties. These identifiers can be derived from the hardware (e.g., Medium Access Control (MAC) addresses) or can be software generated (e.g., Universally Unique IDentifiers (UUIDs)). From the algorithm point of view, a change in a device identifier is equivalent to a device being replaced by another one in the network, de-facto increasing the churn. Each device δ propagates a couple (x_δ, P_δ), where x_δ is the best value found so far according to the comparison function, and P_δ is the path (ordered list) of nodes that leads to the closest device where $x_\delta = X$.

At every round, each device δ will receive, for each neighbor $\nu \in \mathcal{N}$, a couple (x_ν, P_ν)—namely, it will operate on a set of such pairs. The algorithm is a filtering and folding process that proceeds as follows:

1. discard any couple (x_ν, P_ν) where $\delta \in P_\nu$ (loop detection);
2. reduce the remaining couples by applying the comparison function f to their x values;
3. in case of a tie, select the couple with the shortest path P;
4. in case of further tie, compare the identifiers in P pairwise between the two candidates, and select the one with the lowest[2] identifier at the first position where they differ;
5. if the resulting best couple in the neighborhood $(x_\mathcal{N}, P_\mathcal{N})$ is better than the local value, propagate $(x_\mathcal{N}, P_\mathcal{N} \cdot \langle \delta \rangle)$ and return $x_\mathcal{N}$; otherwise, propagate $(x_\delta, \langle \delta \rangle)$ and return x_δ.

Figure 1 conveys the idea behind the algorithm graphically by showing colored arcs that represent the path along which the best value (in this case, the minimum identifier) propagates through the network. If the node with the best value (e.g., node 0 in Fig. 1) becomes unreachable, the network automatically adapts: the stale information is pruned by the loop detection mechanism, and the next best value (e.g., node 1) is propagated through the network along the shortest valid path.

In memory, this approach has a worst-case cost that grows linearly with the diameter of the network, as the path P can grow up to the diameter in the worst case. To get an idea of the practical implications of this cost, for a large-scale deployment on an Internet-like network, whose router-level diameter is estimated to be in the order of tens (10–40) [11, 19, 22, 38], using UUIDs as identifiers (16 bytes) would require a maximum of 160–640 bytes, which is easily manageable for most modern networked devices. Of course, smaller identifiers (e.g., 6-byte MAC addresses) can be used to further reduce this overhead.

---

[2] Lowest here is used for simplicity. As long as a total order is defined on the identifiers, any deterministic tie-breaking strategy can be applied.

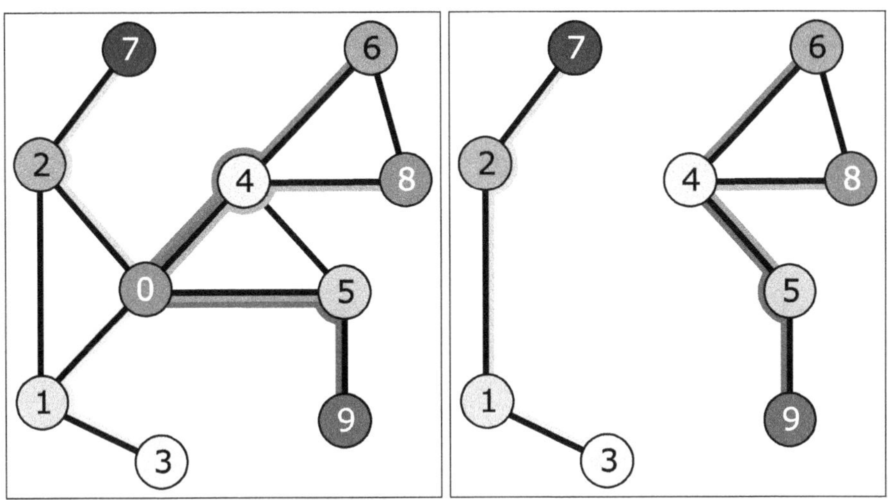

Fig. 1. A graph where nodes represent devices identified by unique IDs, of which we are searching the minimum. Communication links are in black; colored arcs illustrate the shortest valid path used to propagate the best value through the network. The figure on the left shows a stabilized network, while the right one depicts the same network after the failure of the node with the best value (node 0) and the adaptation process.

3.2   Implementation in Collektive

Listing 1.1, shows the implementation of the self-stabilizing min-max consensus algorithm in *Collektive*. The code is structured around a compact message format, GossipValue, and a single share-based state evolution function, findMaxOf.

Message Format. GossipValue (Lines 1–6) encodes the pair (X, P) described in Sect. 3. Property **best** (Line 2) stores the candidate value X. Property **path** (Line 3) stores the validation path P, namely the sequence of device identifiers that propagated the value. Method **addHop** (Line 5) implements the path extension step by appending the current device identifier when forwarding a candidate to neighbors.

State Evolution via share. Function **findMaxOf** (Lines 8–33) is parametric in the local contribution **local** and in a **Comparator**, so that the same implementation can realize arbitrary selections by passing the appropriate comparator. At each round, the device starts from the locally generated candidate **localGossip** (Line 12) and executes a share (Line 13) over the neighborhood field of received GossipValue messages (**gossip**).

The core selection logic is implemented as a fold over neighbors (Line 14), which mirrors the algorithmic steps in Sect. 3. First, loop-freedom is enforced by discarding any candidate whose path already contains the local identifier (Line 16): such a message would imply that the candidate has traversed a cycle

Listing 1.1. Implementation of the proposed self-stabilizing gossip algorithm proposed inside the DSL *Collektive*.

```
1   data class GossipValue<ID : Comparable<ID>, Value>(
2     val best: Value,
3     val path: List<ID> = emptyList(),
4   ) {
5     fun addHop(id: ID) = GossipValue(best, path + id)
6   }
7
8   fun <ID : Comparable<ID>, Value> Aggregate<ID>.findMaxOf(
9     local: Value,
10    comparator: Comparator<in Value>,
11  ): Value {
12    val localGossip = GossipValue<ID, Value>(best = local)
13    return share(localGossip) { gossip ->
14      gossip.neighbors.values.fold(localGossip) { current, neighbor ->
15        when {
16          localId in neighbor.path -> current // Ignore paths that loop back
17          else -> when(comparator.compare(neighbor.best, current.best)) {
18            0 -> when { // If values tie, select based on path
19              neighbor.path.size == current.path.size ->
20                // If paths are of equal length, compare their last element
21                // (they necessarily come from different neighbors)
22                listOf(neighbor, current).minBy { it.path.last() }
23              // Select the shortest path
24              else -> listOf(neighbor, current).minBy { it.path.size }
25            }
26            // Pick the best value according to the comparator
27            in 1..Int.MAX_VALUE -> neighbor
28            else -> current
29          }
30        }
31      }.addHop(localId)
32    }.best
33  }
```

and is therefore considered invalid. Second, candidates whose `best` values tie according to the comparator (Line 18) are ordered by the length of their validation path, preferring the shortest one (Line 24). If the competing paths have equal length (Line 19), a deterministic tie-breaker is applied based on the last element of the path (Line 22), ensuring stable decisions even under symmetry. In this implementation, we do not need to check the entire same-length paths pairwise for tie-breaking, since, by construction, the `gossip` field will contain one entry per neighbor, and in every case the last element of the path will be the neighbor id that forwarded the candidate to the local device. Additionally, no conflicts are possible with the local candidate, since it is initialized with an empty path, and will win by length against any neighbor-derived candidate with a `best` value that ties with it.

When candidates do not tie, the fold selects the one whose `best` is preferred by the comparator (Line 27). After the best neighbor-derived candidate (or the local one) has been selected, the device acknowledges it by appending its own identifier to the path (Line 31), and finally returns the selected value to the caller via `.best` (Line 32).

Operational Implications. The only additional information carried beyond classical min/max gossip is the path list, which is used exclusively for (i) loop detection and (ii) deterministic tie-breaking. As a result, stale candidates that survive because of transient faults or topology changes are naturally pruned when they re-enter a cycle, enabling convergence without global resets or coordinated epochs, while preserving a fully local, asynchronous execution model.

3.3 Proof of Self-stabilization

We prove that the field computed by `findMaxOf` is self-stabilizing under these assumptions: *(i)* each connected component contains a finite set of devices $\mathcal{D}$; *(ii)* each device only considers the last value received from each neighbor (i.e., the neighborhood field contains at most one value per neighbor); *(iii)* device identifiers are totally ordered; and *(iv)* after some time, both local inputs `local` and neighborhood relations stabilize. To make the argument easier to inspect, we separate the proof obligations as follows: *(i)* *loop-freedom*: forwarded candidates cannot be accepted after re-entering a device already appearing in their path; *(ii)* *resilience to stale information*: after the environment stabilizes, unsupported candidates are eventually pruned; *(iii)* *convergence*: the remaining candidates converge to the best value available in each connected component. We then show that the implementation conforms to the minimizing-rep framework of [34, §5.2.2], which gives the self-stabilization result.

Preliminaries. We recall that the minimizing-rep pattern is defined in field-based coordination (as a generalization of the result in [35]) as follows:

$$\text{rep}(e)\{\, x \mapsto f^R\big(\, \text{minHoodLoc}\,\big(f^{MP}(\text{nbr}\{x\}, \bar{s}),\ s\big),\ x,\ \bar{e}\big)\,\} \tag{1}$$

where:

- minHoodLoc(ϕ, s) is a built-in operator returning the minimum of the neighboring field values in ϕ and the local self-stabilizing value s. If the neighborhood is empty, the result is s.
- f^{MP} (the *monotonic-progressive* function) is a stateless function used to "inflate" the neighbors' candidate values before taking the minimum. It must satisfy, w.r.t. a partial order $\leq$:
  1. *Monotonic non-decreasing in the first argument:* if $a_1 \leq a_2$, then $f^{MP}(a_1, \bar{s}) \leq f^{MP}(a_2, \bar{s})$.

2. *Progressive in the first argument:* $f^{MP}(a, \bar{s}) > a$ or $f^{MP}(a, \bar{s}) = \top$ (where $\top$ is the maximum element of the type).

In the minimizing-rep pattern, f^{MP} is applied pointwise to the neighbor field $\mathrm{nbr}\{x\}$, possibly also depending on additional self-stabilizing inputs $\bar{s}$.

- f^R (the *raising* function) combines the selected minimum candidate, the previous local state, and any extra inputs $\bar{e}$, while being constrained so it cannot prevent convergence. It is required to be *raising* w.r.t. two partial orders (typically: $\leq$ for the "minimum" and another noetherian[3] order $\preceq$ controlling how f^R can deviate transiently), namely:

1. $f^R(a, a, \bar{e}) = a$;
2. $f^R(a_1, a_2, \bar{e}) \succeq \min(a_1, a_2)$;
3. either $f^R(a_1, a_2, \bar{e}) \succ a_2$ or $f^R(a_1, a_2, \bar{e}) = a_1$.

Without loss of generality, we introduce the *minimizing share* pattern, which is a variant of the minimizing-rep pattern, where the share construct [5] is used to replace the combination of rep and nbr:

$$\mathrm{share}(e)\{\, \phi_x \mapsto f^R\big(\, \mathrm{minHoodLoc}\,\big(f^{MP}(\phi_x, \bar{s}),\ s\big),\ \mathrm{local}(\phi_x),\ \bar{e}\,\big)\,\} \qquad (2)$$

where ϕ_x is the neighboring field corresponding to $\mathrm{nbr}\{x\}$, and $\mathrm{local}(\phi_x)$ is the local device's previous state x. This modification speeds up the computation by avoiding sharing the previous round information with neighbors, without affecting the program's self-stabilizing semantics [5].

Conformance to the Minimizing-Share Pattern. We now show that our implementation is an instance of Equation (2) (minimizing rep pattern), hence, it is self-stabilizing by the results in [34, §5.2.2].

State Space and Order. Let `cmp` be the comparator passed to `findMaxOf`. Assume `cmp` induces a total preorder $\preceq_V$ on `Value` in the standard way:

$$a \preceq_V b \triangleq \mathsf{cmp}(a, b) \leq 0.$$

Since `findMaxOf` selects the *maximum* according to `Comparator` (Line 27), we define an order where *better values are smaller*:

$$a \leq_V b \triangleq b \preceq_V a \quad \text{equivalently} \quad a \leq_V b \iff \mathsf{cmp}(a, b) \geq 0.$$

Hence, min w.r.t. $\leq_V$ coincides with max w.r.t. the comparator. The algorithm exchanges and computes elements of $\mathsf{GV} \triangleq \{(v, P) \mid v \in Value,\ P \in ID^*\}$ (corresponding to GossipValue). To model loop rejection we extend GV with the greatest element $\top$ (ignored by minimization), obtaining $\mathsf{GV}_\top \triangleq \mathsf{GV} \cup \{\top\}$.

Let $\leq_{ID}$ be the total order on identifiers. We define a total order $\leq_P$ on paths by *shortest-first* and, in case of equal length, by comparison of the last identifiers in the path (i.e., the sender neighbor, which is guaranteed to be different for

---

[3] A *noetherian* order is a partial order that contains no infinite ascending chains.

different candidates, since the neighborhood field contains at most one entry per neighbor):

$$P_1 \leq_P P_2 \;\triangleq\; \big(|P_1| < |P_2|\big) \;\vee\; \big(|P_1| = |P_2| \wedge P_1\,[|P_1|-1] \leq_{ID} P_2\,[|P_2|-1]\big),$$

We now define the order $\leq$ over $\mathsf{GV}_\top$ so that the minimum corresponds to the selection policy:

- $\forall g \in \mathsf{GV},\ g \leq \top$;
- for $g_i = (v_i, P_i) \in \mathsf{GV}$:

$$(v_1, P_1) \leq (v_2, P_2) \;\triangleq\; \big(v_1 <_V v_2\big) \;\vee\; \big(v_1 =_V v_2 \wedge P_1 \leq_P P_2\big).$$

Auxiliary Functions. Fix a device with identifier δ. The sanitizer $\sigma_\delta : \mathsf{GV} \to \mathsf{GV}_\top$ that discards candidates that loop back to δ can be modeled as a function:

$$\sigma_\delta(v, P) \triangleq \begin{cases} \top & \text{if } \delta \in P, \\ (v, P) & \text{otherwise.} \end{cases}$$

Define the inflation function $f_\delta^{MP} : \mathsf{GV}_\top \to \mathsf{GV}_\top$ by:

$$f_\delta^{MP}(g) \triangleq \begin{cases} \top & \text{if } g = \top, \\ (v,\ P + \langle \delta \rangle) & \text{if } g = (v, P). \end{cases}$$

This corresponds to `addHop(localId)` (Line 31).

The intended role of these two functions is already enough to explain the key properties informally. The sanitizer σ_δ enforces *loop-freedom* locally, because any candidate whose path already contains δ is mapped to $\top$ and therefore cannot be selected by δ. The inflation function f_δ^{MP} enforces *progress* by strictly increasing the path whenever a candidate is forwarded. Hence, in a finite stabilized component, a stale candidate that is not regenerated by any local input cannot survive forever: it is either discarded by σ_δ when it closes a loop, or eventually loses to a better/shorter valid candidate.

Minimizing-Share Instance. Consider the following `share` expression that returns a value in $\mathsf{GV}_\top$:

$$\text{share}(e)\{\ \phi \mapsto \text{minHoodLoc}\,\big(f_\delta^{MP}(\sigma_\delta(\phi)),\ s\big)\ \}, \tag{3}$$

where ϕ ranges over the neighbor field entries (i.e., `gossip.neighbors`), $s \triangleq (v_\delta, \langle \delta \rangle)$ is the local self-stabilizing candidate, and e is any initial value. We take f^R to be the identity: $f^R(a, x, \bar{e}) \triangleq a$.

Inside `findMaxOf`, the fold (Line 14) computes the $\leq$-minimum among: *(i)* the local candidate `localGossip` (Line 12) and *(ii)* all neighbor candidates not rejected by the loop guard (Line 16), using the ordering "best first, then shortest path, then smallest sender id" (Lines 18–22). The final `.addHop(localId)`

(Line 31) is exactly f_δ^{MP}. Thus, the value returned by the share body in the implementation is the same as the value computed by Equation (3) up to the convention that the local candidate is compared with empty path and then inflated. This convention can only affect the **path** chosen when the best values tie (p in (v, p)), but never the **best** component (v in (v, p)) for any comparison among GossipValues.

Conditions for Minimizing-Share. Under the order $\leq$ above, the assumptions stated at the beginning of the subsection are used as follows. Finiteness of each connected component is needed to rule out infinite strictly progressive path extensions. Keeping only the last value received from each neighbor ensures that the neighborhood field contains a finite set of candidates with at most one entry per sender, which is exactly the setting used by the fold and by the tie-break on the last hop. The total order on identifiers makes the tie-break deterministic. Finally, stabilization of local inputs and neighborhood relations fixes both the set of locally generated candidates and the graph over which valid shortest paths are compared. Under these assumptions:

- *monotonic*: if $g_1 \leq g_2$ then $f_\delta^{MP}(g_1) \leq f_\delta^{MP}(g_2)$, because best values are unchanged and all paths are extended by the same suffix $\langle \delta \rangle$;
- *progressive*: for any $g \in \mathsf{GV}$, $f_\delta^{MP}(g) > g$ since path length strictly increases while best is unchanged.

The identity raising function $f^R(a, x, \bar{e}) = a$ trivially satisfies the raising constraints [34].

Therefore, Eq. (3) is an instance of the minimizing-share pattern Eq. (2), hence it is self-stabilizing in $\mathsf{GV}_\top$ when the environment stabilizes [5,34]. The function returns the projection $\pi_{\text{best}}(v, P) = v$ (Line 32). Since π_{best} is stateless and the underlying share state is self-stabilizing, the returned field of values is self-stabilizing as well; hence, findMaxOf is self-stabilizing. $\square$

Consequences. The previous argument makes explicit the three properties used in the informal discussion of the algorithm:

1. *loop-freedom* holds because a device never selects a candidate whose path already contains its own identifier.
2. *resilience to stale information* holds because, once local inputs and neighborhood relations stabilize, unsupported candidates are no longer regenerated locally, while progressive path extension cannot continue indefinitely in a finite component without eventually being rejected by the sanitizer.
3. *convergence* holds because the minimizing-share result guarantees stabilization to the $\leq$-minimum candidate, which by construction coincides with the best value according to the comparator, refined by shortest valid path and deterministic identifier-based tie-breaking.

4 Evaluation

We now present an evaluation of the proposed self-stabilizing gossip algorithm via simulation, demonstrating its correctness visually, and measuring its convergence time and communication cost.

4.1 Experimental Setup and Reproducibility

We leverage the Alchemist[4] simulator [30], which we also relied upon during the development of the algorithm to perform preliminary tests and debugging. The experiments have been open sourced with a permissive license and are available on a public GitHub repository[5]. An archival copy [14] is available for future reference and reproduction on Zenodo. Every numeric experiment is repeated 32 times with different random seeds. The data presented is the average of these runs.

4.2 Scenario Description

We configure a bidimensional environment where N_0 devices are deployed randomly in a square area of side L, and communicate within a radius R. Devices are assigned unique identifiers, and run a minimizing operation with a round frequency of $1\,\text{Hz}$, starting asynchronously. We let the system evolve until all devices converge to the same value, and then we perform a sequence of perturbations/topology changes to observe how the network adapts and reconverges to a consistent state.

Metrics. We evaluate the algorithms correctness by measuring the *Root Mean Squared Error (RMSE)* between the expected gossip value and the actual gossip value as provided by an oracle with global system knowledge which can instantly compute the "correct" value for each device in the network regardless of communication delays. In case of network partitioning, we compute the RMSE separately for each subnetwork, considering the expected gossip value, and then we run a weighted sum of the errors, using the inverse subnetwork size as weight. The global RMSE is defined as follows:

$$\text{RMSE} = \sum_{j \in \mathcal{S}} \frac{1}{\|\mathcal{S}_j\|} \sqrt{\sum_{i \in \mathcal{S}_j} (v_i - \hat{v}_i)^2}$$

where $\mathcal{S}$ is the set of network partitions, v_i is the current value of device i, and $\hat{v}_i$ is the true value of device i.

To understand the communication cost, we measure the *data rate* required to sustain the algorithm, defined as the average weighted size of messages exchanged

---

[4] https://alchemistsimulator.github.io.
[5] https://bit.ly/3OnjCQA.

per device per time step. We compute the message size by implementing a custom network component which intercepts the calls the framework performs to run network operations. Every message in *Collektive* is a map from an encoding of the location in the Abstract Syntax Tree (AST) that produced the message to the value being sent. In a typical networked deployment, the AST location is hashed to a short identifier; we decided to consider 4 bytes per entry for the key size (which is reasonable for most deployments), while we serialize the corresponding value using Kryo [33].

Baselines. We compare the proposed algorithm with two baselines: *(i)* a *non-self-stabilizing gossip*, implemented as in Sect. 2.5, that does not include any mechanism for loop detection, and thus is not self-stabilizing; *(ii)* a *time-replicated gossip*, which is a self-stabilizing gossip algorithm that relies on time-based replication of messages to ensure convergence, as proposed in [34]. The latter requires two parameters: the launch period p and the number of replicas k. These are tuned using the relation $p = {4d\tau}/{(k-1)}$, where d is the network diameter in hops, and τ is the device frequency. We estimate the network diameter as $d \approx \sqrt{2L^2}/R \approx 7$. We use three overlapping replicas ($k = 4$) to balance between convergence time and communication cost; considering that devices run at 1 Hz, the resulting launch period is $p = 9$ s.

The Proposed Algorithm at Work. We show the behavior of the algorithm in Fig. 2, in a scenario with $N_0 = 50$, $L = 50$ m, and $R = 10$ m. The min-max consensus is configured to find the minimum identifier in the network, which is 0 in this case. We can observe that the algorithm self-stabilizes after network partitions and reconnections, as we expect from the theoretical analysis in Sect. 3.3.

4.3   Performance Analysis

We analyze the performance of the proposed algorithm in a scenario where $N_0 = 100$, $L = 20$ m, and $R = 4$ m, where we deploy devices with a uniform random distribution (controlled by the random seed).

At the beginning of the simulation, devices compute a random value in $[-1, 1]$, and the algorithms are configured to find the minimum value in the network. After a stabilization period of 50 s, we introduce a network partition by moving all devices on the right side of the arena in a new arena. 50 s after the partition, we add a second perturbation, by generating new random values for all devices in the network, this time in $[-1/2, 1/2]$, and we observe how the different algorithms adapt to the new values in the network. Finally, we move the devices back to the first area, returning to the initial topology, and wait for further 50 s, for a total duration of 200 s.

Results. In Fig. 3, we can observe the Root Mean Square Error (RMSE) over time for the different gossip algorithms after network segmentation, transient

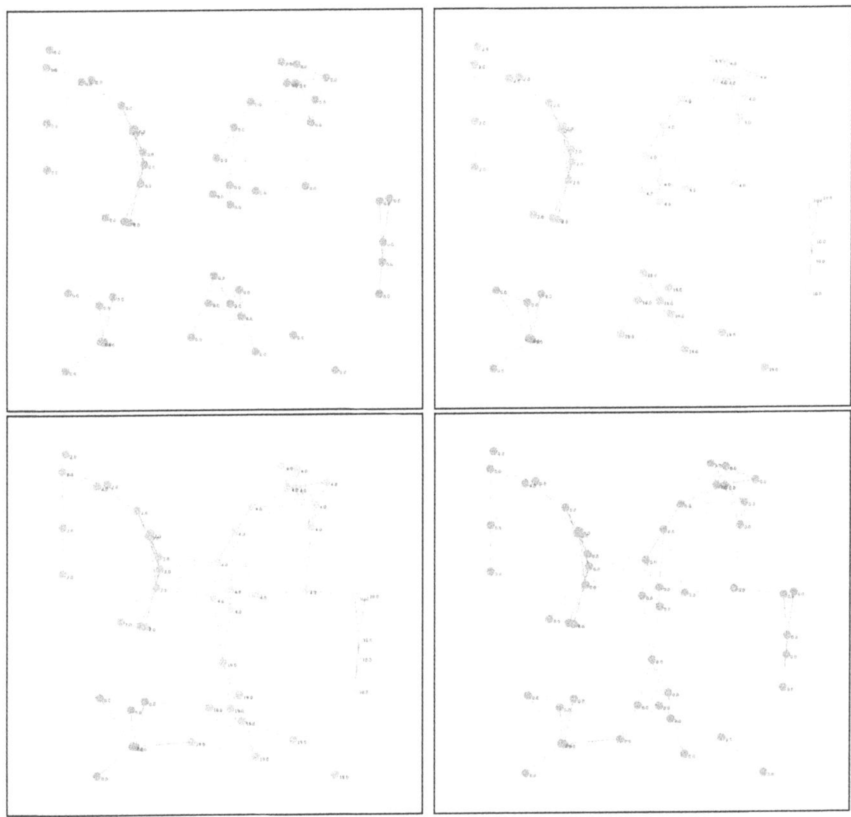

Fig. 2. Self stabilizing nature of the algorithm. Different colors represent different outputs of the min-max consensus algorithm. We partition a stabilized network in five segments (top left). We observe that every segment converges to the best value within the segment (top right). We then reconnect the network (bottom left) and we observe that the whole network returns to the initial best value.

fault injection, and network reconnection. The proposed self-stabilizing gossip algorithm shows a different, smoother convergence pattern compared to time-replicated gossip: convergence starts as soon as the perturbation occurs, while time-replicated gossip shows a delayed convergence pattern, with a sudden drop in RMSE after first replica that captured the new values becomes valid. If we consider the time to reach the correct final values after the perturbation, a well-tuned instance of time-replicated gossip outperforms the proposed approach, as it is pure gossip without the overhead of path tracking and loop detection, while the proposed algorithm needs to progressively prune stale candidates through loop detection. However, if the designer prefers a lower mean error during the transient over the time to reach the correct final values, then the proposed algorithm is a better choice, as it starts converging immediately after the perturbation.

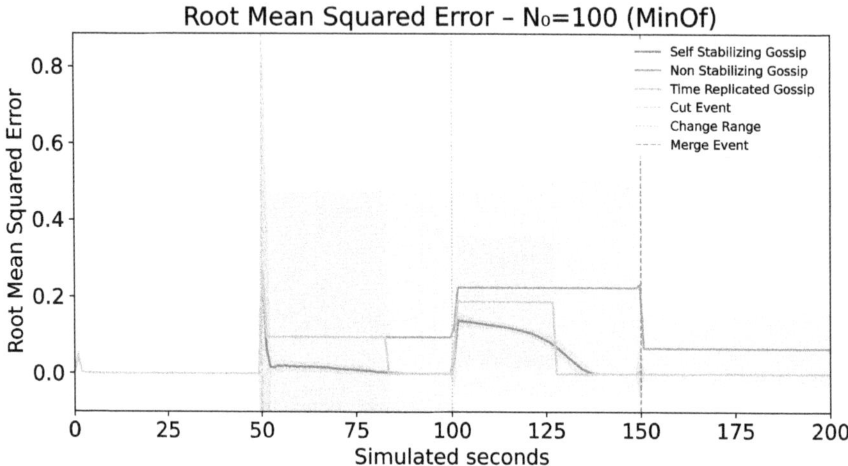

Fig. 3. RMSE over time. Vertical lines show the timing of the disruption events in the scenario, shaded areas show mean $\pm\sigma$ intervals.

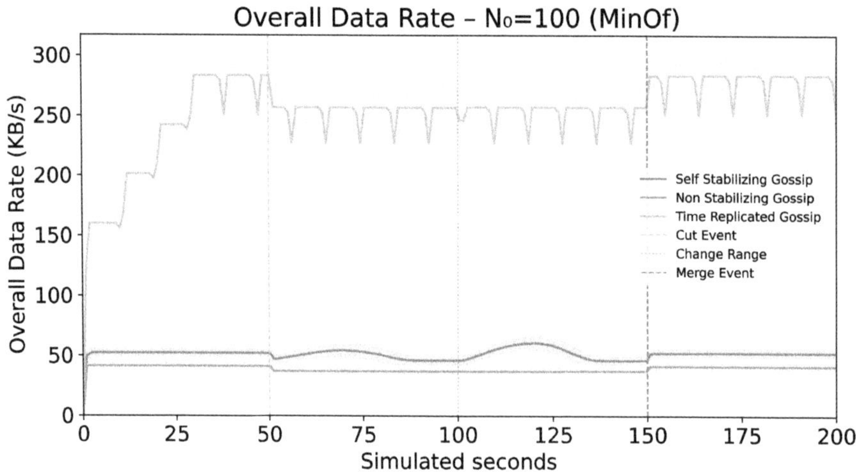

Fig. 4. Communication overhead over time, measured as the overall data rate used by all devices. Vertical lines show the timing of the disruption events in the scenario, shaded areas show mean $\pm\sigma$ intervals.

The other baseline, being non-self-stabilizing, fails to converge after any of the perturbations.

In Fig. 4, we report the data rate over time for the different gossip algorithms under network segmentation, transient fault injection, and subsequent reconnection. The time-replicated gossip algorithm shows a significantly higher data rate than the proposed approach, due to the overhead of maintaining multiple replicas and the associated metadata. We can observe a drop for all the algorithms in the central part of the scenario, when the network is partitioned, as the average neighborhood size decreases. The chart shows the periodic nature of the time-replicated gossip algorithm pretty clearly, with troughs corresponding to the expiration of old replicas, and immediate peaks corresponding to the launch of the new ones. The proposed algorithm requires higher data rate than the non-self-stabilizing gossip algorithm, due to the additional path data, yet the communication overhead is significantly lower than the time-replicated gossip algorithm, whose cost once the algorithms reach regular operation is about four times larger. Upon disruptions, we observe a slow increase in the data rate for the proposed algorithm, as paths grow until they eventually get pruned by loop detection.

5   Conclusion and Future Work

In this work, we introduced a self-stabilizing gossip algorithm in the AC paradigm, designed to address key limitations of traditional gossip in dynamic and fault-prone environments. The approach propagates the best value according to a selector function while explicitly encoding the validation path used for its dissemination. By evaluating candidate values individually and enforcing loop-freedom through path tracking, devices adopt only values supported by coherent propagation paths, allowing stale or inconsistent information to be naturally discarded. This preserves the lightweight and fully decentralized nature of gossip without requiring resets, timestamps, or centralized coordination.

We formally showed that the algorithm conforms to the minimizing-share pattern, thereby inheriting self-stabilization guarantees under standard assumptions of eventual input and topology stability.

An implementation in the *Collektive* DSL demonstrates how the approach can be realized as a reusable aggregate operator, and simulation-based evaluation confirms its ability to recover from perturbations and reconverge after topology changes without relying on global resets or centralized coordination.

Overall, the proposed solution provides a building block for resilient distributed coordination, enabling selector-based gossip processes that remain correct and able to adapt to topology changes and perturbations without requiring global coordination.

Future work will focus on extending the evaluation of the proposed algorithm to a broader range of network topologies, densities, and fault scenarios, in order to more thoroughly characterize its performance and scalability. In particular, we plan to investigate highly dynamic settings in which nodes frequently join and leave the network, as well as environments affected by heterogeneous communication delays and message loss. Such conditions challenge the eventual-stability assumptions underlying self-stabilization, as the path-based loop detection depends on obsolete paths being gradually eliminated after neighborhood relationships settle. For this reason, we plan to analyze how persistent churn affects convergence behavior and to investigate possible refinements that increase robustness when the system operates under continuously changing conditions.

This loop detection mechanism can be further investigated for other algorithmic contexts beyond gossip-based coordination, as it provides a general approach to enforce consistency and prevent the propagation of stale information in distributed systems, such as gradient-based coordination.

References

1. Aguzzi, G., Casadei, R., Pianini, D., Viroli, M.: Dynamic decentralization domains for the internet of things. IEEE Internet Comput. **26**(6), 16–23 (2022). https://doi.org/10.1109/MIC.2022.3216753
2. Aguzzi, G., Casadei, R., Viroli, M.: Macroswarm: a field-based compositional framework for swarm programming. In: Jongmans, S., Lopes, A. (eds.) DisCoTec 2023. LNCS, vol. 13908, pp. 31–51. Springer (2023). https://doi.org/10.1007/978-3-031-35361-1_2
3. Apolloni, B., Aitis, C., Maffetti, M.: Watching by gossip. Internet Things **3-4**, 90–103 (2018). https://doi.org/10.1016/J.IOT.2018.09.008
4. Audrito, G., Beal, J., Damiani, F., Pianini, D., Viroli, M.: The **share** operator for field-based coordination. In: Riis Nielson, H., Tuosto, E. (eds.) COORDINATION 2019. LNCS, vol. 11533, pp. 54–71. Springer, Cham (2019). https://doi.org/10.1007/978-3-030-22397-7_4
5. Audrito, G., Beal, J., Damiani, F., Pianini, D., Viroli, M.: Field-based coordination with the share operator. Log. Methods Comput. Sci. **16**(4) (2020). https://lmcs.episciences.org/6816
6. Audrito, G., Casadei, R., Damiani, F., Pianini, D., Viroli, M.: Optimal resilient distributed data collection in mobile edge environments. Comput. Electr. Eng. **96**(Part), 107580 (2021). https://doi.org/10.1016/J.COMPELECENG.2021.107580
7. Audrito, G., Pianini, D., Damiani, F., Viroli, M.: Aggregate centrality measures for iot-based coordination. Sci. Comput. Program. **203**, 102584 (2021). https://doi.org/10.1016/j.scico.2020.102584
8. Audrito, G., Torta, G.: FCPP to aggregate them all. Sci. Comput. Program. **231**, 103026 (2024). https://doi.org/10.1016/J.SCICO.2023.103026
9. Audrito, G., Viroli, M., Damiani, F., Pianini, D., Beal, J.: A higher-order calculus of computational fields. ACM Trans. Comput. Log. **20**(1), 5:1–5:55 (2019). https://doi.org/10.1145/3285956
10. Beal, J., Pianini, D., Viroli, M.: Aggregate programming for the internet of things. IEEE Comput. **48**(9), 22–30 (2015). https://doi.org/10.1109/MC.2015.261
11. Carisimo, E., Wang, C., Weaver, M., Bustamante, F.E., Barford, P.: A hop away from everywhere: a view of the intercontinental long-haul infrastructure. Proc. ACM Measur. Anal. Comput. Syst. **7**(3), 47:1–47:26 (2023). https://doi.org/10.1145/3626778
12. Casadei, R., Viroli, M., Aguzzi, G., Pianini, D.: Scafi: a scala DSL and toolkit for aggregate programming. SoftwareX **20**, 101248 (2022). https://doi.org/10.1016/j.softx.2022.101248
13. Cortecchia, A.: Multiplatform self-organizing systems through a kotlin-mp implementation of aggregate computing. In: IEEE International Conference on Autonomic Computing and Self-Organizing Systems, ACSOS 2024 - Companion, Aarhus, Denmark, September 16-20, 2024, pp. 155–157. IEEE (2024). https://doi.org/10.1109/ACSOS-C63493.2024.00048

14. Cortecchia, A.: angelacorte/experiments-coordination-self- stabilizing-gossip: 1.1.0, February 2026. https://doi.org/10.5281/zenodo.18942476
15. Cortecchia, A., Ciatto, G., Casadei, R., Pianini, D.: Fieldvmc: an asynchronous model and platform for self-organising morphogenesis of artificial structures. Complex Intell. Syst. **12**(2), 63 (2025). https://doi.org/10.1007/s40747-025-02141-y
16. Demers, A.J., et al.: Epidemic algorithms for replicated database maintenance. In: Schneider, F.B. (ed.) Proceedings of the Sixth Annual ACM Symposium on Principles of Distributed Computing, Vancouver, British Columbia, Canada, August 10-12, 1987. pp. 1–12. ACM (1987). https://doi.org/10.1145/41840.41841
17. Dijkstra, E.W.: Self-stabilizing systems in spite of distributed control. Commun. ACM **17**(11), 643–644 (1974). https://doi.org/10.1145/361179.361202
18. Dolev, S.: Self-Stabilization. MIT Press (2000). http://www.cs.bgu.ac.il/%7Edolev/book/book.html
19. Faloutsos, M., Faloutsos, P., Faloutsos, C.: On power-law relationships of the internet topology. In: Proceedings of the ACM SIGCOMM 1999 Conference on Applications, Technologies, Architectures, and Protocols for Computer Communication, August 30 - September 3, 1999, Cambridge, Massachusetts, USA, pp. 251–262. ACM (1999). https://doi.org/10.1145/316188.316229
20. Gupta, I., Birman, K., Linga, P., Demers, A., van Renesse, R.: Kelips: building an efficient and stable P2P DHT through increased memory and background overhead. In: Kaashoek, M.F., Stoica, I. (eds.) IPTPS 2003. LNCS, vol. 2735, pp. 160–169. Springer, Heidelberg (2003). https://doi.org/10.1007/978-3-540-45172-3_15
21. Jelasity, M., Montresor, A., Babaoglu, Ö.: Gossip-based aggregation in large dynamic networks. ACM Trans. Comput. Syst. **23**(3), 219–252 (2005). https://doi.org/10.1145/1082469.1082470
22. Kirci, E.C., Torsiello, V., Vanbever, L.: What is the next hop to more granular routing models? In: Proceedings of the 23rd ACM Workshop on Hot Topics in Networks, HOTNETS 2024, Irvine, CA, USA, November 18-19, 2024, pp. 343–351. ACM (2024). https://doi.org/10.1145/3696348.3696859
23. Letia, M., Preguiça, N.M., Shapiro, M.: Crdts: consistency without concurrency control. CoRR abs/0907.0929 (2009). http://arxiv.org/abs/0907.0929
24. Li, H., Yang, J., Yin, Z., Zhou, L., Xi, J., Zheng, Y.: Min-max consensus of multiagent systems in random networks. Neurocomputing **600**, 128148 (2024). https://doi.org/10.1016/J.NEUCOM.2024.128148
25. Mamei, M., Zambonelli, F.: Programming pervasive and mobile computing applications: the TOTA approach. ACM Trans. Softw. Eng. Methodol. **18**(4), 15:1–15:56 (2009). https://doi.org/10.1145/1538942.1538945
26. Mo, Y., Audrito, G., Dasgupta, S., Beal, J.: Near-optimal knowledge-free resilient leader election. Autom. **146**, 110583 (2022). https://doi.org/10.1016/J.AUTOMATICA.2022.110583
27. Pianini, D., Beal, J., Viroli, M.: Improving gossip dynamics through overlapping replicates. In: Lluch Lafuente, A., Proença, J. (eds.) COORDINATION 2016. LNCS, vol. 9686, pp. 192–207. Springer, Cham (2016). https://doi.org/10.1007/978-3-319-39519-7_12
28. Pianini, D., Casadei, R., Viroli, M.: Self-stabilising priority-based multi-leader election and network partitioning. In: IEEE International Conference on Autonomic Computing and Self-Organizing Systems, ACSOS 2022, Virtual, CA, USA, September 19-23, 2022, pp. 81–90. IEEE (2022). https://doi.org/10.1109/ACSOS55765.2022.00026

29. Pianini, D., Casadei, R., Viroli, M., Natali, A.: Partitioned integration and coordination via the self-organising coordination regions pattern. Future Gener. Comput. Syst. **114**, 44–68 (2021). https://doi.org/10.1016/j.future.2020.07.032
30. Pianini, D., Montagna, S., Viroli, M.: Chemical-oriented simulation of computational systems with ALCHEMIST. J. Simulation **7**(3), 202–215 (2013). https://doi.org/10.1057/JOS.2012.27
31. Pianini, D., Viroli, M., Beal, J.: Protelis: practical aggregate programming. In: Proceedings of the 30th Annual ACM Symposium on Applied Computing, Salamanca, Spain, April 13-17, 2015, pp. 1846–1853 (2015). https://doi.org/10.1145/2695664.2695913
32. Pruteanu, A., Iyer, V., Dulman, S.: ChurnDetect: a gossip-based churn estimator for large-scale dynamic networks. In: Jeannot, E., Namyst, R., Roman, J. (eds.) Euro-Par 2011. LNCS, vol. 6853, pp. 289–301. Springer, Heidelberg (2011). https://doi.org/10.1007/978-3-642-23397-5_29
33. Taranov, K., Bruno, R., Alonso, G., Hoefler, T.: Naos: serialization-free RDMA networking in java. In: Calciu, I., Kuenning, G. (eds.) Proceedings of the 2021 USENIX Annual Technical Conference, USENIX ATC 2021, July 14-16, 2021, pp. 1–14. USENIX Association (2021). https://www.usenix.org/conference/atc21/presentation/taranov
34. Viroli, M., Audrito, G., Beal, J., Damiani, F., Pianini, D.: Engineering resilient collective adaptive systems by self-stabilisation. ACM Trans. Model. Comput. Simul. **28**(2), 16:1–16:28 (2018). https://doi.org/10.1145/3177774
35. Viroli, M., Damiani, F.: A calculus of self-stabilising computational fields. In: Kühn, E., Pugliese, R. (eds.) COORDINATION 2014. LNCS, vol. 8459, pp. 163–178. Springer, Heidelberg (2014). https://doi.org/10.1007/978-3-662-43376-8_11
36. Voulgaris, S., van Steen, M.: An epidemic protocol for managing routing tables in very large peer-to-peer networks. In: Brunner, M., Keller, A. (eds.) DSOM 2003. LNCS, vol. 2867, pp. 41–54. Springer, Heidelberg (2003). https://doi.org/10.1007/978-3-540-39671-0_5
37. Zambonelli, F.: Toward sociotechnical urban superorganisms. Computer **45**(8), 76–78 (2012). https://doi.org/10.1109/MC.2012.280
38. Zhu, J., Zhang, Y., Wang, Y., Zhang, H., Fang, B.: A method for quantifying global network topology based on a mathematical model. Mathematics **12**(19), 3114 (2024). https://doi.org/10.3390/math12193114

Simulation Tools and Methodologies for Collective Adaptive Systems

SCALATROPY: Multiparty Coordination with Monadic Communication Primitives

Nicolas Farabegoli[(✉)], Luca Tassinari, Gianluca Aguzzi, and Mirko Viroli

University of Bologna, Bologna, Italy
{nicolas.farabegoli,gianluca.aguzzi,mirko.viroli}@unibo.it,
luca.tassinari10@studio.unibo.it

Abstract. Multiparty languages provide a concrete foundation for expressing complex coordination behaviors in a single, coherent specification. Based on this idea, several paradigms have been proposed in the literature over the years. Among them, choreographic programming is a widely adopted paradigm for defining deadlock-free distributed systems, while multitier programming takes a different approach, focusing on partitioning system logic across different execution tiers.

Recognizing that these paradigms share fundamental similarities as multiparty languages, we build on choreographic programming while importing static architectural descriptions and placement types inspired by ScalaLoci. We introduce SCALATROPY, a coordination language that integrates multiple communication schemes to establish both isotropic and anisotropic communication patterns, while incorporating placement types and type-level architecture specification inspired by ScalaLoci, advancing beyond the capabilities of traditional choreographic languages. We provide a Scala implementation leveraging monadic constructs, which cleanly separate the language specification from the underlying monadic effects that drive coordination mechanisms. Finally, we present an empirical evaluation demonstrating the language's expressiveness and an analysis of communication overhead.

Keywords: Multiparty languages · Tagless final · Choreographic Programming · Multitier programming

1 Introduction

Choreographic programming [1,21] and *multitier programming* [29] are two prominent paradigms in the landscape of multiparty languages [17]. They address the challenge of coordinating modern distributed systems—from microservice architectures to IoT networks—by providing high-level abstractions to define complex collective behaviors in a single, coherent codebase, abstracting away low-level details such as message passing and synchronization protocols.

Choreographic programming focuses on defining the interactions between multiple parties in a distributed system from a global perspective. It allows

© IFIP International Federation for Information Processing 2026
Published by Springer Nature Switzerland AG 2026
R. Casadei and F. Ghassemi (Eds.): COORDINATION 2026, LNCS 16590, pp. 117–137, 2026.
https://doi.org/10.1007/978-3-032-28358-0_6

developers to describe the overall system as a "third-person narrative", specifying how each party should behave and interact with others. Typically, choreographic languages provide high-level abstractions for defining which peer executes which part of the code, and for specifying communication patterns between peers, as well as specifying which peers are involved in the system. Over the years, a strong theoretical foundation has been built around choreographic programming [2], with formal models and verification techniques ensuring properties such as deadlock-freedom and communication safety [4,14]. These foundations have influenced a rich ecosystem of practical frameworks, from the Jolie service-oriented language [22] to choreographic tools ensuring correctness properties such as AIOCJ [12], and have been comprehensively systematized in [15].

A related approach is taken by multitier programming, which focuses on partitioning the system logic across different execution tiers. Differently from choreographic programming, multitier programming describes the distributed system as a relation between different tiers, without involving explicit communication primitives, but rather the communication is inferred from the placement of code across tiers. A common feature in multitier languages is the definition of an architecture, i.e., a set of peers and their relationships, which allows preventing unintended communications between peers not allowed by the architecture specification [27].

While both paradigms have proven effective in their respective domains, opportunities remain to enhance their communication models to address emerging practical requirements. On the one hand, choreographic languages typically focus on point-to-point communication patterns, with selective multicast communication to subsets of participants sometimes requiring additional constructs or workarounds, such as broadcast-style primitives combined with conditional filtering or defining restricted scopes like conclaves. For instance, in a distributed auction system, selectively sending updates only to bidders interested in a specific item may require broadcasting to all participants followed by filtering, which can introduce additional network traffic. On the other hand, multitier programming languages leverage implicit communication through shared placements: while this is an elegant approach for tier-crossing data flow, it can make explicit selective communication patterns less straightforward to express.

Recognizing that choreographic programming can benefit from richer architectural information, we extend choreographic programming with static architectural descriptions and placement types inspired by ScalaLoci, aimed at enriching overall expressiveness. To this end, this paper introduces SCALATROPY, a choreographic coordination language that integrates type-level architecture encoding via placement types (Sect. 3.1) with choreographic global specification (Sect. 3.3), and extends choreographic programming with differentiated communication primitives that support both isotropic (broadcast-style) and anisotropic (selective) communication patterns.

This paper provides the following key contributions:

- **Unified multiparty language design**: we present the coordination language SCALATROPY, which integrates choreographic global specification with

ScalaLoci-inspired architectural constraints, enabling developers to express complex multiparty patterns while maintaining architectural discipline.

- **Differentiated communication schemes**: we introduce a communication model supporting both isotropic (broadcast-style) and anisotropic (selective) communication patterns, allowing developers to optimize information flow based on application requirements.
- **Type-level architecture enforcement**: inspired by ScalaLoci [28], we provide a programming interface to encode architectural constraints at the type level, preventing invalid communications between peers at compile time and ensuring adherence to the specified architecture.
- **Monadic implementation framework**: we provide a Scala implementation of SCALATROPY as a monad, using so-called "tagless final encoding" [6], which cleanly separates language semantics from execution effects, facilitating extensibility and integration with other effects.

We validate SCALATROPY through empirical evaluation by implementing representative use cases drawn from the choreographic and ScalaLoci literature, showing that in certain contexts our approach can reduce communication overhead and improve code maintainability compared to existing approaches. Additionally, we demonstrate that SCALATROPY's type system catches common distributed programming errors at compile time that would otherwise manifest as runtime failures. The full code of the framework along with the case studies presented in the paper are released as open source with a permissive license[1], and permanently archived on Zenodo [13].

The rest of the paper is structured as follows. Section 2 motivates the need for differentiated communication patterns in multiparty languages. Section 3 presents the design and features of SCALATROPY, while Sect. 4 and Sect. 5 describe its Scala implementation and empirical evaluation, respectively. Section 6 discusses related work in the field of multiparty languages. Finally, Sect. 7 concludes the paper and outlines future research directions.

2 Communication Patterns in Multiparty Languages

Before introducing the SCALATROPY language, we motivate the need for differentiated communication patterns in multiparty languages.

To establish a fair comparison, we evaluate our approach against frameworks that are similarly implemented as internal domain-specific languages (DSLs), matching the design of SCALATROPY. While more mature and feature-rich implementations of both paradigms exist [16], focusing on internal DSLs ensures a consistent baseline for analysis.

Since our goal is to enrich choreographic programming with explicit architectural descriptions, to make a fair comparison, we selected *HasChor* [26] as a representative choreographic language and *ScalaLoci* [28] as the source of the architectural typing discipline adopted in SCALATROPY. The former is a Haskell

---

[1] https://github.com/nicolasfara/scalatropy.

embedded DSL that leverages monadic constructs to express choreographies, sharing similarities with our (monadic) approach. The latter is a Scala embedded DSL that introduces type-level architecture specification, which we also adopt in SCALATROPY. ScalaLoci is one of the most mature and popular multitier programming languages, providing strong static guarantees, and as it is implemented in Scala, it shares similarities with our Scala-based implementation of SCALATROPY.

Let us formally characterize the communication patterns supported by multiparty languages. Before defining the communication patterns, we introduce some notation inspired by the formalism used in [28].

With P we denote a peer type, which represents a class of devices in the distributed system. We define $\mathcal{A}$ as the architecture specification of the distributed system, composed of a set of peer types P and a set of tie relationships $P_1 \mapsto P_2$ between peers.

$$\mathcal{A} ::= \{P\} \mid \mathcal{A} \cup \mathcal{A} \mid P_1 \mapsto^1 P_2 \mid P_3 \mapsto^* P_4$$

With $P_1 \mapsto^1 P_2$ we denote a tie relationship where peer type P_1 is tied to a single instance of peer type P_2, and with $P_3 \mapsto^* P_4$ we denote a tie relationship where peer type P_3 is tied to multiple instances of peer type P_4.

We further define as Ω the runtime peer configuration, composed of a set of peer instances π_n^P, where n is a unique identifier for the peer instance and P is the peer type of the instance, and a set of communication links $\pi_n^{P_1} \to \pi_m^{P_2}$ between peer instances. We omit the subscript of the peer instance when it is not relevant for the discussion.

Definition 1 (Architecture satisfaction). *A runtime peer configuration Ω satisfies an architecture specification $\mathcal{A}$, written as $\Omega \models \mathcal{A}$, when:*

- *For every peer type $P \in \mathcal{A}$, there exists at least one peer instance $\pi_n^P \in \Omega$.*
- *For every tie relationship $P_1 \mapsto^1 P_2 \in \mathcal{A}$, there exists a single $\pi_n^{P_1} \to \pi_m^{P_2} \in \Omega$.*
- *For every tie relationship $P_3 \mapsto^* P_4 \in \mathcal{A}$, for every peer instance $\pi_n^{P_3} \in \Omega$, there exists at least one communication link $\pi_n^{P_3} \to \pi_m^{P_4} \in \Omega$.*

Definition 2 (Point-to-Point Communication). *Given $\Omega \models \mathcal{A}$ and peer instances $\pi^{P_s}, \pi^{P_r} \in \Omega$ with $\pi^{P_s} \to \pi^{P_r} \in \Omega$, a point-to-point communication transmits a message m from the sender instance π^{P_s} to the receiver instance π^{P_r}:*

$$\pi^{P_s} \xrightarrow{m} \pi^{P_r}$$

This is the most basic form of communication in multiparty languages (Fig. 1a).

Definition 3 (Isotropic Communication). *Given $\Omega \models \mathcal{A}$ and peer instances $\pi^{P_s}, \{\pi_1^{P_r}, \ldots, \pi_n^{P_r}\} \subseteq \Omega$ with $\pi^{P_s} \to \pi_i^{P_r} \in \Omega$, an isotropic communication transmits the same message m from the sender instance π^{P_s} to every receiver instance $\pi_i^{P_r}$:*

$$\pi^{P_s} \xrightarrow{m} \{\pi_1^{P_r}, \ldots, \pi_n^{P_r}\}$$

Isotropic communication (Fig. 1b) models broadcast-style dissemination where every receiver obtains an identical copy of the payload, such as a leader broadcasting a configuration update to all replicas.

Definition 4 (Anisotropic Communication). *Given $\Omega \models \mathcal{A}$ and peer instances $\pi^{P_s}, \{\pi_1^{P_r}, \ldots, \pi_n^{P_r}\} \subseteq \Omega$ with $\pi^{P_s} \to \pi_i^{P_r} \in \Omega$, an anisotropic communication transmits a potentially different message m_i from the sender instance π^{P_s} to each receiver instance $\pi_i^{P_r}$:*

$$\pi^{P_s} \xrightarrow{\ m_i\ } \{\pi_1^{P_r}, \ldots, \pi_n^{P_r}\}$$

Anisotropic communication (Fig. 1c) generalises the isotropic case by allowing the sender to tailor each message to its recipient, for example when a coordinator assigns distinct tasks to individual workers.

Definition 5 (Co-anisotropic Communication). *Given $\Omega \models \mathcal{A}$ and peer instances $\{\pi_1^{P_s}, \ldots, \pi_n^{P_s}\}, \pi^{P_r} \subseteq \Omega$ with $\pi_i^{P_s} \to \pi^{P_r} \in \Omega$, a co-anisotropic communication transmits a potentially different message m_i from each sender instance $\pi_i^{P_s}$ to the receiver instance π^{P_r}:*

$$\{\pi_1^{P_s}, \ldots, \pi_n^{P_s}\} \xrightarrow{\ m_i\ } \pi^{P_r}$$

Co-anisotropic communication (Fig. 1d) captures fan-in scenarios, such as multiple sensors reporting their readings to a single aggregator.

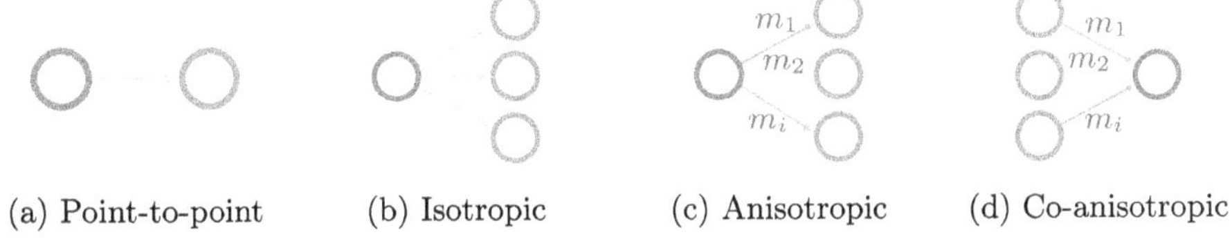

(a) Point-to-point   (b) Isotropic   (c) Anisotropic   (d) Co-anisotropic

Fig. 1. Communication patterns in multiparty languages.

These communication patterns provide a comprehensive set of primitives for expressing various communication scenarios in multiparty languages.

2.1 Communication Operations in Other Languages

To provide an overview of the communication operations supported by the selected DSLs, Table 1 summarizes the primitives provided by HasChor, Cloud-Chor, ScalaLoci, and SCALATROPY. We also include CloudChor [19] as an internal DSL which, unlike the basic point-to-point interactions in HasChor, provides support for differentiated communication patterns.

From the table, we can see that HasChor only supports point-to-point communication, meaning that if we want to support, for instance, isotropic communication, we need to manually provide the logic to send the same message

Table 1. Communication operations supported by multiparty languages.

Comm. Types	HasChor	CloudChor	ScalaLoci	SCALATROPY
Point-to-point	~>	~>	asLocal*	**comm**
Isotropic	-	~>*	asLocalFromAllSeq*	**isotropicComm**
Anisotropic	-	~>.	V per P **on** R **	**anisotropicComm**
Co-anisotropic	-	*~>	V per R **on** P **	**coAnisotropicComm**

* We considered the functions that trigger the communication.
** Differentiated communications are expressed at the type level.

to multiple receivers, e.g., by invoking multiple point-to-point communications. ScalaLoci, on the other hand, supports both point-to-point and isotropic communication, allowing the receiver to extract the messages from all senders. It also supports anisotropic and co-anisotropic communication, however it requires boilerplate code to express these communication patterns, as can be seen in the following example.

```
val deployTask: Signal[Task] per Worker on Master =
  { worker: Remote[Worker] => Signal { assocs().get(worker) }}
```

To express anisotropic communication in ScalaLoci, developers must define a signal parameterized by the remote peer (`worker: Remote[Worker]`) and manually extract the appropriate message from an association map (`assocs().get(worker)`). While flexible, this approach requires boilerplate code and lacks the clarity of a dedicated communication primitive. In contrast, SCALATROPY provides native support for all communication patterns from Sect. 2 through dedicated primitives, simplifying multiparty coordination without sacrificing expressiveness.

3   The SCALATROPY DSL

Before introducing the characteristics of SCALATROPY, we present the main *choreographic* and *multitier* concepts that inspired our work.

3.1   Type-Level Architecture Definition

Having a clear and type-safe definition of the architecture of a distributed system is a fundamental aspect of SCALATROPY. While several multiparty languages describe participants and communication structure in different ways, our work adopts the explicit type-level architecture description introduced by ScalaLoci [28], where developers declare peer families together with their admissible communication ties. In SCALATROPY, we import this ScalaLoci-inspired architectural layer into a choreographic setting, allowing developers to define a set of peers and their communication relationships. Inspired by ScalaLoci, we defined an architecture with three peers: `Client`, `Server`, and `Database`, where the `Client` can communicate with the `Server`, and the `Server` can communicate with the `Database`.

```scala
// Clients (peer) can communicate with a single Server (tie relationship)
type Client <: { type Tie <: Single[Server] }
// Servers can communicate with a single Database and multiple Clients
type Server <: { type Tie <: Single[Database] & Multiple[Client] }
// Database can communicate with one Server
type Database <: { type Tie <: Single[Server] }
```

The architecture above specifies which *class* of devices (i.e., peer types) are involved in the distributed system. To declare *instances* of these peers, we use the **type** Client syntax as defined in the architecture. To define *connections* (i.e., which peer can communicate with which other peer), we refine the peer definition specifying the Client to be a subtype (the <: in Scala refers to subtyping) of a structural type, i.e., an anonymous type with members defined inline, enclosed in curly braces. Such structural type defines a type member Tie, which specifies the communication relationships of the peer with other peers. In the case of Client, the Tie type member is defined as **Single**[Server], indicating that the Client can communicate with a single instance of Server. When defining ties, we can use the *intersection type* operator & to specify multiple communication relationships, as shown in the definition of Server.

Ties Relationships. Leveraging the high flexibility of Scala's type system, we can define the "structural signature" of a peer as **type** Peer = { **type** Tie }. Such a definition specifies a type alias to a structural type with a type member Tie. However, as such, the Tie type member is unconstrained, meaning that it can be defined arbitrarily. Therefore, to impose constraints on the Tie type member, we introduce two type constructors:

```scala
enum Quantifier[-P <: Peer]:
  case Single()
  case Multiple()
```

The **Quantifier** enum (i.e., an algebraic data type) introduces two type constructors: **Single** to denote a tie $P_1 \mapsto^1 P_2$ where a peer is tied to a single instance of another peer, and **Multiple** to denote a tie $P_1 \mapsto^* P_2$ where a peer is tied to multiple instances of another peer. However, with this definition we are only describing the *quantifier* of the tie relationship, but we are not actually specifying which peer types are involved in the tie.

To overcome this limitation, we introduced two types:

```scala
type TiedSingle[P <: Peer] = { type Tie <: Single[P] }
type TiedMultiple[P <: Peer] = { type Tie <: Multiple[P] }
```

The first one models a peer that is tied with a single instance of peer type P, while the second one models a peer that is tied with multiple instances of peer type P. Such types are useful to express constraints on communication patterns between peers, as we will see in the next sections.

3.2   Placement Types

Both *choreographic* and *multitier* programming use the concept of "values that live in the context of certain peer(s)"; in the former, it is often referred to as *located values* while in the latter, they are called *placed values*. Specifically, at the type level, we refine the value type with a notion of *placement*, indicating where the value is located in the distributed system.

In SCALATROPY, we reuse the syntax from ScalaLoci to define placement types. In Scala, we can define a value of type `Int` that is placed at the `Client` peer as `Int` **on** `Client`. The **on** type is an infix type which takes two type parameters: the first is the base type (here, `Int`), and the second is the peer where the value is placed (here, `Client`).

Intuitively, a value of type `V` **on** `P` should be read as "a value of type `V` owned by peer `P`". When a multiparty program executes **on[P]**, only peers of type `P` actually evaluate the computation and materialize the value locally; all other peers only keep a typed reference to that placed value. As a consequence, the value can be inspected with **take** only from within an **on[P]** context, while communication primitives are the mechanism that makes the value available at other placements.

Placement types are crucial in SCALATROPY, as they allow us to express where computations and data reside in the distributed system, effectively encoding the peer instances π_n^P of the runtime peer configuration Ω (Definition 1) at the type level. In conjunction with the architecture definition, they enable the type system to enforce communication constraints between peers. This means that any attempt to communicate between peers not allowed by the architecture will result in a compile-time error, thus preventing potential runtime failures due to invalid communications.

3.3   Language Primitives

SCALATROPY provides two categories of operations: **placed computations** for defining peer-specific computations and extracting local values, and **communication primitives** for peer-to-peer communication with differentiated schemes, all enforcing architecture constraints at the type level. These operations are defined in a single language trait, **MultiParty[F[_]:** Monad**]**, which abstracts over the effect type `F[_]`. This trait requires a `Monad` constraint (via context bound syntax in Scala, namely : `Monad`) to support monadic composition and allow for various execution strategies, as detailed in Sect. 4. We now introduce the main primitives in detail.

Place and Extract Values. To define computations that execute on specific peers, we need a mechanism to specify the execution context (the peer) and a mechanism to access values placed at that context. In SCALATROPY, these capabilities are provided by the following primitives:

```scala
trait MultiParty[F[_]: Monad]:
  def on[L <: Peer, V](body: Label[L] ?=> F[V]): F[V on L]
  def take[L <: Peer](using Label[L])[V](placed: V on L): F[V]
  /* ... other primitives ... */
```

Specifically, the **on** function executes computations only at peer instances of type L. Its body parameter is a context function with an implicit `Label[L]` parameter, enabling peer-specific operations like **take**. The result is a placement type V **on** L wrapped in the effect F[_].

The **take** function extracts values placed at peer type L, requiring an implicit `Label[L]` parameter available only within on[L] contexts. This ensures that only locally placed values can be extracted; attempting to extract remote values results in a compile-time error.

The following example demonstrates **on** and **take** together.

```scala
def example[F[_]: Monad](using MultiParty[F]): F[Int on Client] = for
  placedValue: String on Client <- on[Client] { "Hello, from Client!" }
  stringLength: Int on Client <- on[Client] { take(placedValue).map(_.length) }
yield stringLength
```

The <- operator acts as variable assignment in a monadic composition—namely, it is internally turned into a `flatMap` method call, namely, the bind monadic operation. First, we place a string at Client producing String **on** Client. Then, we extract it using **take**, compute its length, and place the result back at Client.

Point-to-Point Communication. Following Definition 2, where a message m is transmitted from a single sender π^{P_s} to a single receiver π^{P_r}, the **comm** function transmits values from source peer S to destination peer R.

```scala
trait MultiParty[F[_]: Monad]:
  /* ... other primitives ... */
  def comm[S <: TiedSingle[R], R <: TiedSingle[S], V](value: V on S): F[V on R]
```

The transmission is reflected in the type signature: the input is a value placed at the sender V **on** S, and the result is a value placed at the receiver V **on** R—this type-level encoding is also used for the other communication primitives. Crucially, this primitive enforces architectural compliance by constraining S and R to be mutually tied to a single instance via `TiedSingle`. This primitive definition is similar to the one found in Choral [16] and HasChor/CloudChor [26].

To illustrate point-to-point communication, consider a simple message exchange between two peers, Alice and Bob. We assume these peers are defined in the architecture with a mutual single-instance tie relationship, allowing them to exchange messages directly:

```scala
def pointToPointExample[F[_]: Monad](using MultiParty[F]): F[Unit] = for
  messageFromAlice <- on[Alice] { "Hello, Bob!" }
  messageAtBob <- comm[Alice, Bob](messageFromAlice)
  _ <- on[Bob]:
    take(messageAtBob).map(msg => println(s"Bob received: $msg"))
yield ()
```

Isotropic Communication. Recalling Definition 3, isotropic communication sends the same message m from one sender π^{P_s} to all receiver instances $\{\pi_1^{P_r}, \ldots, \pi_n^{P_r}\}$—

a selective multicast to a specific peer class, distinct from indiscriminate broadcast.

```scala
trait MultiParty[F[_]: Monad]:
  /* ... other primitives ... */
  def isotropicComm[S <: TiedMultiple[R], R <: TiedSingle[S], V](v: V on S):
      F[V on R]
```

The function requires S tied to multiple R instances, and R tied to a single S instance.

The following example shows the Server communicating with multiple Clients. The **isotropicComm** function (line 3) shares updateFromServer from Server to all Client instances. Then, each value is extracted in each client's context through **take** (line 5).

```scala
def isotropicExample[F[_]: Monad](using MultiParty[F]): F[Unit] = for
  updateFromServer <- on[Server] { "Update available." }
  updateAtClients <- isotropicComm[Server, Client](updateFromServer)
  _ <- on[Client]:
    take(updateAtClients).map(update => println(s"Client received: $update"))
yield ()
```

Anisotropic Communication. Corresponding to the pattern defined in Definition 4, anisotropic communication allows sending potentially different messages m_i from a single sender π^{P_s} to each receiver $\pi_i^{P_r}$, enabling per-receiver customization and reducing unnecessary communication overhead.

```scala
trait MultiParty[F[_]: Monad]:
  type Remote[P <: Peer]
  type Anisotropic[P <: Peer, V]
  /* ... other primitives ... */
  def anisotropicMessage[S <: TiedMultiple[R], R <: TiedSingle[S], V](
    using Label[S]
  )(value: Map[Remote[R], V], default: V): F[Anisotropic[R, V]]
  def anisotropicComm[S <: TiedMultiple[R], R <: TiedSingle[S], V](
    value: Anisotropic[R, V] on S
  ): F[V on R]
  def reachablePeers[R <: Peer]: F[NonEmptyList[Remote[R]]]
```

This pattern requires two functions: **anisotropicMessage** creates an **Anisotropic**[R, V] value mapping remote instances to messages (with a default), and **anisotropicComm** transmits it. The **reachablePeers** function returns all reachable instances of a given peer type. Together with the statically declared ties, this lets a choreography tailor messages to the concrete peer instances that are currently reachable and architecturally admissible.

The following example shows Server sending different updates to Clients.

```scala
def anisotropicExample[F[_]: Monad](using MultiParty[F]): F[Unit] = for
  updates: Anisotropic[Client, String] on Server <- on[Server]:
    anisotropicMessage[Server, Client, String](
      reachablePeers[Client].map(client -> s"Update for $client").toMap,
      "No Updates"
    )
  updateAtClients <- anisotropicComm[Server, Client](updates)
  _ <- on[Client]:
```

```
    take(updateAtClients).map(update => println(s"Client received: $update"))
  yield ()
```

We create an anisotropic message mapping each `Client` to a custom update, then transmit it via **anisotropicComm**. Each `Client` extracts its specific update using **take**.

Co-anisotropic Communication. Dual to the anisotropic case (cf. Definition 5), co-anisotropic communication captures the fan-in scenario where multiple senders $\{\pi_1^{P_s}, \ldots, \pi_n^{P_s}\}$ transmit potentially different messages m_i to a single receiver π^{P_r}.

```
trait MultiParty[F[_]: Monad]:
  /* ... other primitives ... */
  def coAnisotropicComm[S <: TiedSingle[R], R <: TiedMultiple[S], V](
    value: V on S
  ): F[Anisotropic[S, V] on R]
  def takeAll[L <: Peer, R <: Peer](using Label[L])[V](
    placed: Anisotropic[R, V] on L
  ): F[Map[Remote[R], V]]
```

The **coAnisotropicComm** function collects messages from multiple S senders to a single R receiver, producing **Anisotropic[S, V] on** R. The **takeAll** function extracts individual messages as a map. The following example shows multiple `Client`s sending to a single `Server`.

```
def coAnisotropicExample[F[_]: Monad](using MultiParty[F]): F[Unit] = for
  messageFromClient <- on[Client] { "Hello, Server!" }
  messagesAtServer <- coAnisotropicComm[Client, Server](
    messageFromClient
  )
  allMessages <- on[Server] { takeAll(messagesAtServer) }
  _ <- on[Server]:
    allMessages.foreach { case (client, msg) =>
      println(s"Server received from $client: $msg")
    }
  yield ()
```

Each `Client` sends via **coAnisotropicComm**, and `Server` aggregates all messages using **takeAll**.

4 Implementation

SCALATROPY is implemented as an embedded DSL in Scala, leveraging Scala's powerful type system and monadic abstractions to define the language semantics and execution model. Its type system allows us to encode the architectural constraints and communication patterns at the type level, ensuring that any architectural violation is caught at compile time, while keeping the syntax clean and lightweight.

4.1 Monadic Implementation

Distributed systems inherently involve various computational effects: network communication, asynchronous operations, error handling, and state management. To ensure modularity and composability, we adopt a monadic approach combined with the *tagless final* [6] encoding style. Programs are parameterized by an abstract effect type `F[_]`, with semantics defined purely through operations on this abstraction, thereby decoupling language specification from concrete execution strategies.

This is particularly effective in multiparty scenarios where coordination primitives must compose seamlessly regardless of whether they execute locally, communicate over the network, or involve other side effects. In ScalaTropy, this translates to the **MultiParty**`[F[_]]` trait, whose primitives (e.g., **on**, **comm**, **isotropicComm**) are defined against the abstract effect `F[_]`. The bound Monad on `F[_]` ensures that we can compose these operations in a monadic style, facilitating sequencing and error handling. A production interpreter may instantiate `F` with `IO` backed by a real MQTT network, while a test interpreter may substitute a pure, in-memory effect, reusing the same program definition in both cases without modification. Compared to free monads, tagless final avoids the overhead of re-defining the language semantics for each interpreter, reducing error-prone boilerplate and improving maintainability. This design still ensures good testability—by allowing effect substitution for testing purposes—and maintainability, as the language semantics is defined in a single place, independent of the execution strategy.

In practice, the **MultiParty** effect is implemented by composing two lower-level effects: **Network**, which abstracts the underlying communication layer, and **Environment**, which encapsulates the peer's local execution context. The **MultiParty** interpreter accepts these effect handlers as dependencies, delegating network operations and context queries to them while orchestrating the high-level coordination logic.

4.2 Placement Types

The placement type implementation in ScalaTropy is rather straightforward, as it is expressed as an infix type constructor **on** that takes a base type and a peer type as parameters. Under the hood, the **on** type is implemented as an *algebraic data type* (ADT) with two type constructors: `Local` which contains a unique identifier for the value placed, and the value itself; and Remote which contains only the unique identifier of the value placed. Notably, the unique identifier is a deterministic value that is used to reference the placed value in the distributed system.

A placement type is created out of a placed computation through the **on**`[P]` function. At runtime, when the **on**`[P]` function is evaluated, the `P` peer is compared to the current peer type: if they match, the lambda body of the **on**`[P]` function is executed and the resulting value is wrapped in a `Local` constructor; otherwise, the **on**`[P]` skips the execution of the lambda body and returns a Remote indicating that the value is not available locally.

Any operation that deals with a placement type checks whether the value is local or remote, and acts accordingly. For instance, the **comm** function sends the value via network to the destination peer type `R` only if the value is local, otherwise it interacts with the network to retrieve the value from the remote peer type S. The general principle is very close to the one provided in [3], where the *end-point-projection* (EPP) is performed at runtime.

4.3   Network Layer

The network layer is a dependency of the **MultiParty** interpreter, abstracting the underlying communication mechanism and providing a uniform interface for sending and receiving messages between peers. Its interface defines two main operations: (i) a `send` primitive that takes a message, its reference, and the destination peer type as parameters, and sends the message to the destination peer type; (ii) a `receive` primitive that takes a message reference and the source peer type as parameters, and waits for a message to be received from the source peer type with the given reference. To complete the network layer, we also need a primitive to retrieve the list of reachable peer instances of a given peer type, and the local peer instance identifier.

```scala
trait Network[F[_], LP <: Peer]:
  type Address[P <: Peer]

  val localAddress: Address[LP]
  def send[V, To <: Peer](value: V, ref: Reference, to: Address[To]): F[Unit]
  def receive[V, From <: Peer](ref: Reference, from: Address[From]): F[V]
  def alivePeersOf[RP <: Peer: PeerTag]: F[NonEmptyList[Address[RP]]]
```

The network layer is intended as a (monadic) capability, allowing a seamless integration with the **MultiParty** language—via the tagless final encoding—enabling multiple implementations of the network layer for different communication protocols like MQTT, HTTP, and gRPC.

Despite its simplicity, the network layer ensures high flexibility and extensibility, as we can implement `send` and `receive` primitives with different semantics (e.g., reliable vs unreliable, ordered vs unordered, etc.) and different underlying communication protocols, providing specific guarantees to the layer above (i.e., the **MultiParty** interpreter). The only constraint is imposed by the `alivePeersOf` primitive, which must return a non-empty list of peer instances, as the communication primitives in SCALATROPY assume that there is at least one reachable peer instance of the destination peer type. This deals well with dynamic network topologies, where peers can join and leave the network at runtime, as the `alivePeersOf` primitive is implemented to reflect the current state of the network. In this way, the static architecture fixes which peer families may communicate, while runtime peer discovery determines which concrete instances participate in each communication.

5   A Taste of SCALATROPY

To assess the practical utility of SCALATROPY, we evaluate it across two dimensions: expressiveness, and communication overhead.

5.1   Case Studies

To showcase the expressiveness of SCALATROPY on patterns studied in both the ScalaLoci and choreographic programming literature, we consider two representative examples: a Master-Worker application [28] and a Replicated Key-Value Store [26].

Master-Worker Application. We consider a Master-Worker application in which a Master peer dispatches tasks to multiple Worker peers, and then aggregates the results to produce a final result (see Fig. 2).

```
object MasterWorker:
  type Master <: { type Tie <: Multiple[Worker] }
  type Worker <: { type Tie <: Single[Master] }

  case class Task(x: Int) { def compute: Int = x * x }

  def masterWorkerProgram[F[_]: MonadThrow](using MultiParty[F]): F[Unit] = for
    tasks <- on[Master]:
      for
        peers <- reachablePeers[Worker]
        allocation = peers.map(_ -> Task(Random.nextInt(100))).toList.toMap
        message <- anisotropicMessage[Master, Worker](allocation, Task(0))
      yield message
    taskOnWorker <- anisotropicComm[Master, Worker](tasks)
    partialResult <- on[Worker]:
      for
        t <- take(taskOnWorker)
        res <- t.compute.pure[F]
      yield res
    allResults <- coAnisotropicComm[Worker, Master](partialResult)
    result <- on[Master] { takeAll(allResults).map(_.values.sum) }
  yield ()
```

Fig. 2. Master-Worker implementation in SCALATROPY.

From an architectural perspective, the Master peer is tied to multiple Worker peers, while each Worker peer is tied to a single Master. The application logic is implemented in the masterWorkerProgram function, parameterized by an effect type F[_] constrained by MonadThrow to handle potential errors gracefully, and a **MultiParty**[F] instance to access the language primitives.

Initially (lines 10–15), on the Master peer, the reachable Worker peers are discovered; a task is allocated to each, preparing an *anisotropic message* for transmission. Transmission is delegated to the **anisotropicComm** primitive, which sends the corresponding task from the Master to each Worker, ensuring each Worker receives only its allocated task. Next (lines 17–22), on the Worker side, the task is extracted, computed locally, and the partial result is sent back to the Master using **coAnisotropicComm**, which collects the partial results into an anisotropic message placed on the Master. By its semantics, **coAnisotropicComm** implements a barrier synchronization, blocking until all reachable Worker peers have computed and returned their results. Finally (lines 24–26), the Master extracts all partial results and reduces them to produce the final result.

This program can be instantiated on a concrete peer instance, provided a network implementation and a coherent effect type as presented hereafter.

```scala
object MasterNode extends IOApp.Simple:
  override def run: IO[Unit] =
    val mqttNetwork = MqttNetwork
      .localBroker[IO, Master](Config(appId = "masterworker"))
    ScalaTropy(masterWorkerProgram[IO]).projectedOn[Master](using mqttNetwork)
```

Replicated Key-Value Store. The second example we considered is a Key-Value client-server application, where multiple clients interact with a remote key-value store, maintained by a server, supporting put (store) and get (retrieve) operations. To ensure fault tolerance, the data store is replicated across multiple server instances, following a primary-backup replication scheme. In this setup, clients communicate with a primary server instance for their operations, while the primary server is responsible for forwarding put operations to the backup server nodes to maintain data consistency across replicas.

The architecture of this system therefore consists of three peer types: Client, Primary, and Backup. Each Client is tied to a single Primary server instance to which it sends its requests, while the Primary server is tied to multiple Backup server instances and multiple Client peers. Backup nodes are tied to a single Primary server instance from which they receive updates. Responses and requests are encoded as ADTs as shown in the following code snippet.

```scala
object KeyValueStoreChoreo:
  type Client  <: { type Tie <: Single[Primary] }
  type Primary <: { type Tie <: Multiple[Backup] & Multiple[Client] }
  type Backup  <: { type Tie <: Single[Primary] }

  enum Request:
    case Get(key: String)
    case Put(key: String, value: String)
    case Empty

  enum Response:
    case Value(value: Option[String])
    case Ack
    case Empty
```

The code snippet in Fig. 3 shows a synchronous implementation of the Key-Value client-server application: the Primary server applies writing operations, gathers acknowledgments from the Backup nodes, and then sends responses back to the clients.

First, at line 5, Client peers wait for a request (coming from user's input or other sources). Next, at line 6, each Client sends its request to the Primary server instance it is connected to, leveraging the **coAnisotropicComm** primitive. Server-side, once all requests are received, they are unpacked, processed by the Primary server's local storage, and the corresponding responses are prepared for anisotropic communication back to the Client peers (lines 8–14). Before sending, on the Primary server, all Put requests are extracted and forwarded to the Backup server instances using isotropic communication (lines 16–20). This ensures each Backup node receives and consistently applies the client operations to its replica

```scala
def kvs[F[_]: {Sync, Console}](
  primaryStorage: KeyValueStore[F, String, String] on Primary,
  backupStorage: KeyValueStore[F, String, String] on Backup,
)(using MultiParty[F]): F[Unit] = for
  requestOnClient <- on[Client](waitForRequest)
  requestsOnPrimary <- coAnisotropicComm[Client, Primary](requestOnClient)
  responsesOnPrimary <- on[Primary]:
    for
      store <- take(primaryStorage)
      requests <- takeAll(requestsOnPrimary)
      responses <- store processAll requests
      message <- anisotropicMessage[Primary, Client](responses, Empty)
    yield message
  putRequests <- on[Primary]:
    takeAll(requestsOnPrimary).map(_.values.collect { case r: Put => r })
  requestsOnBackups <- isotropicComm[Primary, Backup](putRequests)
  ack <- on[Backup]:
    for
      store <- take(backupStorage)
      requests <- take(requestsOnBackups)
      _ = requests.foreach(request => store process request)
    yield Ack
  _ <- coAnisotropicComm[Backup, Primary](ack)
  responseOnClient <- anisotropicComm[Primary, Client](responsesOnPrimary)
  _ <- on[Client]:
    take(responseOnClient) flatMap (response => F.println(s"> $response"))
  _ <- kvs(primaryStorage, backupStorage)
yield ()
```

Fig. 3. Key-Value Store implementation in SCALATROPY.

storage. Finally, when all the Backup nodes have acknowledged the updates, the Primary server sends each response back to the corresponding Client using the **anisotropicComm** primitive (lines 22–24). Computation continues recursively, allowing the system to process multiple requests over time.

By adopting an architectural definition, together with architecture-aware communication primitives, the above implementation is guaranteed to work correctly with any number of backup replica servers. In contrast, traditional choreographic implementations require the number of backup instances to be known in advance, and the communication logic to be explicitly defined for each instance.

5.2 Selective Communication Advantages

SCALATROPY's support for selective communication primitives serves three main purposes: (i) reducing unnecessary communication overhead, (ii) enhancing security by preventing information leakage to unintended recipients, and (iii) providing richer expressiveness.

Communication Efficiency. Selective communication primitives enable the sender to transmit to each peer only the information that they require to accomplish their tasks. This avoids the overhead associated with broadcasting messages to all participants and then filtering them at the receiver side, proving to be particularly beneficial in scenarios where the number of peers is large or when the total message size is significant.

To quantify the benefits of this approach, we consider a variant of the Master-Worker application discussed in Sect. 5, for computing the matrix-vector product over large inputs. This represents a canonical data-parallel workload, where the Master partitions the matrix row-wise and distributes distinct row blocks to each Worker, enabling independent computation of the corresponding partial results. By introducing a dedicated primitive for anisotropic communication, SCALATROPY avoids suboptimal communication patterns, such as broadcasting the entire matrix to all Workers, which would then filter out their relevant rows. This prevents significant communication overhead as the matrix size and number of Workers grow. Figure 4 presents this communication overhead for a 50×50 representative matrix, plotting the total data transmitted by the Master (or, equivalently, the cumulated data received by the Workers) for the broadcast and the anisotropic communication approaches, as the number of Workers increases. Both were implemented in SCALATROPY, where the broadcast variant simply replaces `anisotropicComm` with `isotropicComm`, making them directly comparable within the same framework. Data transmitted is measured in kilobytes (KB) at the network level; the results are independent of the underlying network protocol or deployment setup. As expected, while the broadcast approach incurs a linear increase in communication overhead with the number of Workers, the selective communication approach maintains almost constant overhead, with only a marginal increase due to per-Worker metadata and the distribution of the vector to be multiplied.

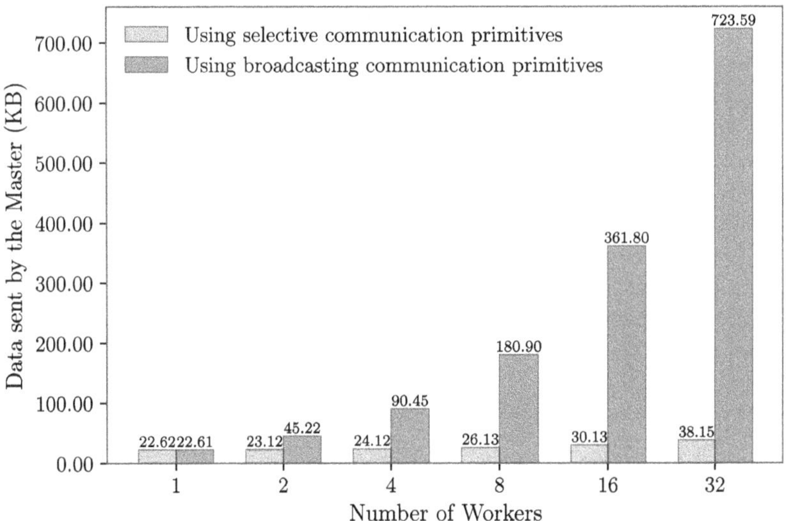

Fig. 4. Communication overhead comparison between broadcast and selective communication in a matrix-vector product application.

Security. Beyond efficiency, selective communication primitives contribute to data confidentiality at the communication level: by construction, each peer receives only the information necessary to perform its task, reducing the risk of unintended information disclosure compared to broadcast-based approaches.

Expressiveness. Lastly, first-class support for selective communication patterns allows developers to express their intent more clearly in the code, avoiding the opaque communication mechanisms required by existing multitier languages, such as the ScalaLoci pattern discussed in Sect. 2.

6   Related Work

This work sits at the intersection of choreographic programming and multitier programming, two paradigms that share the common goal of simplifying distributed system development through high-level abstractions. Although session types represent a relevant line of research for multiparty communication, with several notable implementations such as Scribble [18], Ferrite [7], we do not discuss them in detail here, as our approach focuses on the integration of choreographic and multitier paradigms rather than on session-typed communication channels.

Choreographic Programming. Choreographic programming formalizes distributed coordination through global specifications [4]. On the practical side, the Jolie language [22] pioneered service-oriented coordination and influenced choreographic frameworks such as AIOCJ [12], which supports safe runtime adaptation. More recent implementations target specific host languages: Choral [16] is a Java-based external DSL; HasChor [26] embeds choreographies in Haskell using monadic constructs; and ChoRus [20] brings choreographic programming to Rust. These approaches primarily use point-to-point or broadcast communication, which can introduce overhead for selective multicast patterns. Procedural Choreographies [11] formalizes this setting through a connection graph, while also supporting unbounded process creation and name mobility. In [10], real-world computational algorithms are showcased using this language model. CloudChor [19] extends HasChor with multicast primitives for selective dissemination but lacks architectural constraints. Like HasChor and CloudChor, SCALA-TROPY uses monadic semantics for effect integration, but additionally enforces architectural constraints at the type level.

Multitier Programming. The Multi-Tier Calculus [23] formalizes tier-crossing computations but provides no concrete implementation. Practical languages include Ur/Web [8], Links [9], and Hop [25], which unify client and server code but rely on implicit communication through shared placements. ScalaLoci [28] provides type-level architecture specification and enforcement, ensuring communications respect the declared architecture at compile time. However, selective communication patterns in ScalaLoci require composition of lower-level primitives, which can increase syntactic overhead compared to dedicated first-class constructs. SCALATROPY imports ScalaLoci's type-level architectural descriptions into a choreographic language with explicit selective communication primitives.

7   Conclusion

We presented SCALATROPY, a choreographic language for multiparty coordination that integrates ScalaLoci-inspired architectural descriptions in a single, coherent framework. We introduced explicit communication primitives for point-to-point, isotropic, anisotropic, and co-anisotropic communication patterns, enabling developers to express their intent clearly and efficiently while ensuring architectural compliance through type-level constraints. The monadic implementation of SCALATROPY allows for flexible execution strategies and seamless integration of effects, while the placement type system ensures that values are accessed only in their intended contexts.

We evaluated SCALATROPY through representative case studies, demonstrating its expressiveness and efficiency in implementing common distributed coordination patterns. Moreover, we analyzed the communication overhead of selective communication primitives, showing their advantages over traditional broadcast approaches in terms of efficiency and security.

Future work includes formalizing the semantics of SCALATROPY and proving properties such as type safety and deadlock freedom, as typical in the choreographic programming literature, and architectural compliance and communication correctness for the ScalaLoci-inspired architectural layer adopted by the language. Another direction is to investigate how existing choreographic languages such as Choral and HasChor could benefit from similar architectural descriptions and runtime role-instance information.

References

1. Ancona, D., et al.: Behavioral types in programming languages. Found. Trends Program. Lang. **3**(2-3), 95–230 (2016). https://doi.org/10.1561/2500000031
2. Barbanera, F., Lanese, I., Tuosto, E.: A theory of formal choreographic languages. Log. Methods Comput. Sci. **19**(3) (2023). https://doi.org/10.46298/LMCS-19(3: 9)2023
3. Bates, M., Kashiwa, S., Jafri, S., Shen, G., Kuper, L., Near, J.P.: Efficient, portable, census-polymorphic choreographic programming. Proc. ACM Program. Lang. **9**(PLDI) (2025). https://doi.org/10.1145/3729296
4. Carbone, M., Montesi, F.: Deadlock-freedom-by-design: multiparty asynchronous global programming. SIGPLAN Not. **48**(1), 263274 (2013). https://doi.org/10.1145/2480359.2429101
5. Carbone, M., Montesi, F.: Deadlock-freedom-by-design: multiparty asynchronous global programming. In: Giacobazzi, R., Cousot, R. (eds.) The 40th Annual ACM SIGPLAN-SIGACT Symposium on Principles of Programming Languages, POPL 2013, Rome, Italy - 23–25 January 2013, pp. 263–274. ACM (2013). https://doi.org/10.1145/2429069.2429101

6. Carette, J., Kiselyov, O., Shan, C.: Finally tagless, partially evaluated: tagless staged interpreters for simpler typed languages. J. Funct. Program. **19**(5), 509–543 (2009). https://doi.org/10.1017/S0956796809007205

7. Chen, R.F., Balzer, S., Toninho, B.: Ferrite: a judgmental embedding of session types in rust. In: Ali, K., Vitek, J. (eds.) 36th European Conference on Object-Oriented Programming (ECOOP 2022). Leibniz International Proceedings in Informatics (LIPIcs), vol. 222, pp. 22:1–22:28. Schloss Dagstuhl – Leibniz-Zentrum für Informatik, Dagstuhl, Germany (2022). https://doi.org/10.4230/LIPIcs.ECOOP.2022.22. https://drops.dagstuhl.de/entities/document/10.4230/LIPIcs.ECOOP.2022.22

8. Chlipala, A.: Ur/web: a simple model for programming the web. SIGPLAN Not. **50**(1), 153–165 (2015). https://doi.org/10.1145/2775051.2677004

9. Cooper, E., Lindley, S., Wadler, P., Yallop, J.: Links: web programming without tiers. In: de Boer, F.S., Bonsangue, M.M., Graf, S., de Roever, W.-P. (eds.) FMCO 2006. LNCS, vol. 4709, pp. 266–296. Springer, Heidelberg (2007). https://doi.org/10.1007/978-3-540-74792-5_12

10. Cruz-Filipe, L., Montesi, F.: Choreographies in practice. In: Albert, E., Lanese, I. (eds.) FORTE 2016. LNCS, vol. 9688, pp. 114–123. Springer, Cham (2016). https://doi.org/10.1007/978-3-319-39570-8_8

11. Cruz-Filipe, L., Montesi, F.: Procedural choreographic programming. In: Bouajjani, A., Silva, A. (eds.) FORTE 2017. LNCS, vol. 10321, pp. 92–107. Springer, Cham (2017). https://doi.org/10.1007/978-3-319-60225-7_7

12. Dalla Preda, M., Gabbrielli, M., Giallorenzo, S., Lanese, I., Mauro, J.: Dynamic choreographies: theory and implementation. Log. Methods Comput. Sci. **13** (2017)

13. Farabegoli, N., Tassinari, L., Aguzzi, G.: nicolasfara/scalatropy: release v1.1.4 (2026). https://doi.org/10.5281/zenodo.19407062

14. Ghilezan, S., Jaksic, S., Pantovic, J., Scalas, A., Yoshida, N.: Precise subtyping for synchronous multiparty sessions. J. Log. Algebraic Methods Program. **104**, 127–173 (2019). https://doi.org/10.1016/J.JLAMP.2018.12.002

15. Giallorenzo, S., Montesi, F., Gabbrielli, M.: Applied choreographies. In: International Conference on Formal Techniques for Distributed Objects, Components, and Systems, pp. 21–40. Springer (2018)

16. Giallorenzo, S., Montesi, F., Peressotti, M.: Choral: object-oriented choreographic programming. ACM Trans. Program. Lang. Syst. **46**(1) (2024). https://doi.org/10.1145/3632398

17. Giallorenzo, S., Montesi, F., Peressotti, M., Richter, D., Salvaneschi, G., Weisenburger, P.: Multiparty languages: the choreographic and multitier cases (pearl). In: Møller, A., Sridharan, M. (eds.) 35th European Conference on Object-Oriented Programming, ECOOP 2021, Aarhus, Denmark (Virtual Conference), 11–17 July 2021. LIPIcs, vol. 194, pp. 22:1–22:27. Schloss Dagstuhl - Leibniz-Zentrum für Informatik (2021). https://doi.org/10.4230/LIPICS.ECOOP.2021.22

18. Honda, K., Mukhamedov, A., Brown, G., Chen, T.-C., Yoshida, N.: Scribbling interactions with a formal foundation. In: Natarajan, R., Ojo, A. (eds.) ICDCIT 2011. LNCS, vol. 6536, pp. 55–75. Springer, Heidelberg (2011). https://doi.org/10.1007/978-3-642-19056-8_4

19. Ionescu, A., Russo, A.: Towards lightweight and efficient choreographic cloud services. In: Kameyama, Y., Xie, N. (eds.) Proceedings of the 2026 ACM SIGPLAN International Workshop on Partial Evaluation and Program Manipulation, PEPM 2026, Rennes, France, 11–17 January 2026, pp. 45–60. ACM (2026). https://doi.org/10.1145/3779209.3779537

20. Kashiwa, S., Kuper, L.: Chorus: library-level choreographic programming in rust. Choreographic Programming (CP) (2024). https://users.soe.ucsc.edu/~lkuper/papers/chorus-cp24.pdf
21. Montesi, F.: Choreographic programming (2014)
22. Montesi, F., Guidi, C., Zavattaro, G.: Service-oriented programming with jolie. In: Bouguettaya, A., Sheng, Q.Z., Daniel, F. (eds.) Web Services Foundations, pp. 81–107. Springer (2014). https://doi.org/10.1007/978-1-4614-7518-7_4
23. Neubauer, M., Thiemann, P.: From sequential programs to multi-tier applications by program transformation. In: Proceedings of the 32nd ACM SIGPLAN-SIGACT Symposium on Principles of Programming Languages, POPL 2005, pp. 221–232. Association for Computing Machinery, New York, NY, USA (2005). https://doi.org/10.1145/1040305.1040324
24. Neubauer, M., Thiemann, P.: From sequential programs to multi-tier applications by program transformation. SIGPLAN Not. **40**(1), 221–232 (2005). https://doi.org/10.1145/1047659.1040324
25. Serrano, M., Gallesio, E., Loitsch, F.: Hop: a language for programming the web 2.0. In: Tarr, P.L., Cook, W.R. (eds.) Companion to the 21th Annual ACM SIGPLAN Conference on Object-Oriented Programming, Systems, Languages, and Applications, OOPSLA 2006, 22–26 October 2006, Portland, Oregon, USA, pp. 975–985. ACM (2006). https://doi.org/10.1145/1176617.1176756
26. Shen, G., Kashiwa, S., Kuper, L.: Haschor: functional choreographic programming for all (functional pearl). Proc. ACM Program. Lang. **7**(ICFP) (2023). https://doi.org/10.1145/3607849
27. Weisenburger, P., Salvaneschi, G.: Implementing a language for distributed systems: choices and experiences with type level and macro programming in scala. Art Sci. Eng. Program. **4**, 17 (2020). https://doi.org/10.22152/programming-journal.org/2020/4/17
28. Weisenburger, P., Köhler, M., Salvaneschi, G.: Distributed system development with scalaloci. Proc. ACM Program. Lang. **2**(OOPSLA), 129:1–129:30 (2018). https://doi.org/10.1145/3276499
29. Weisenburger, P., Wirth, J., Salvaneschi, G.: A survey of multitier programming. ACM Comput. Surv. **53**(4), 81:1–81:35 (2021). https://doi.org/10.1145/3397495

Bach4Popper: Towards Federated Inductive Logic Programming Using Coordination

Yasmine Akaichi[1]([✉]) , Manel Barkallah[1] , Jean-Marie Jacquet[1] ,
Isabelle Linden[2] , and Wim Vanhoof[1]

[1] Nadi Research Institute, Faculty of Computer Science, University of Namur, Rue
Grandgagnage 21, 5000 Namur, Belgium
{yasmine.akaichi,manel.barkallah,jean-marie.jacquet,wim.vanhoof}@unamur.be
[2] Nadi Research Institute, EMCP Faculty, University of Namur, Rempart de la
Vierge 8, 5000 Namur, Belgium
isabelle.linden@unamur.be

Abstract. Although it is ubiquitous, machine learning still faces two major challenges: explainability and privacy. To address the first challenge, this paper focuses on Inductive Logic Programming (ILP), a framework for learning declarative, symbolic, and interpretable models from multi-relational data. However, existing ILP systems are fundamentally centralized, an assumption that conflicts with privacy requirements and with many real-world scenarios in which data are inherently distributed and cannot be shared. To overcome this limitation and address the second challenge, we introduce Bach4Popper, a federated ILP framework that combines Popper, an ILP learning system, with Bach, a coordination language developed by the authors. We show, both theoretically and empirically, that Bach4Popper is correct with respect to the corresponding centralized version of Popper. Experimental results further demonstrate that computational performance is preserved when moving from a centralized to a federated setting.

Keywords: Coordination · Federated Learning · Machine Learning · Inductive Logic Programming

1 Introduction

Driven by the availability of large datasets and powerful computational resources, machine learning has become ubiquitous across a wide range of domains, including healthcare, finance, autonomous systems, and scientific discovery. Despite its success, machine learning faces two major and persistent challenges: explainability and privacy. Modern models, particularly deep neural networks, often operate as black boxes, making their decisions difficult to interpret or justify, which limits trust, accountability, and adoption in high-stakes

© IFIP International Federation for Information Processing 2026
Published by Springer Nature Switzerland AG 2026
R. Casadei and F. Ghassemi (Eds.): COORDINATION 2026, LNCS 16590, pp. 138–158, 2026.
https://doi.org/10.1007/978-3-032-28358-0_7

applications. This lack of transparency has motivated a growing body of work on explainable and interpretable machine learning. At the same time, machine learning systems are increasingly trained on sensitive personal or proprietary data, raising serious privacy concerns. Moreover, centralized data collection and training can expose individuals and organizations to risks such as data leakage, membership inference, and model inversion attacks, and may violate regulatory constraints such as data protection laws. Addressing explainability and privacy is therefore essential for the responsible and sustainable deployment of machine learning systems.

Being rooted in logic programming, which deals with symbolic programs of a declarative nature, inductive logic programming [11,24] provides an interesting solution to the explainability issue in machine learning. Indeed, inductive logic programming learns hypotheses expressed as sets of logical rules and thus makes explicit the relational structure and reasoning steps underlying predictions. As a result, this declarative and symbolic representation allows learned models to be directly inspected, validated, and reasoned about by domain experts.

However, inductive logic programming (ILP) is often formulated as a centralized learning task: it requires access to all data and assumes that the required knowledge, examples and background knowledge, is available on a single machine. This restricts its applicability in privacy-sensitive or multi-institutional settings where data must remain distributed, precisely in scenarios in which explainability offered by ILP would be most beneficial. Federated learning [23] has been designed precisely to that end. In fact, it provides a decentralized architecture in which a central server orchestrates training while data remain strictly local. However, most existing research on federated learning relies on sub-symbolic models, most often on neural networks, that offer limited explainability. Hence the question naturally arises whether inductive logic programming can be reformulated in a federated setting thereby offering a machine learning framework both explainable and respecting privacy and distributed issues.

The aim of this paper is to establish that data-driven coordination languages constitute a good means to combine federated learning and inductive logic programming. However, our work should be understood as a first step towards exploring the use of coordination languages for federated inductive logic programming. Rather than aiming for an exhaustive comparison of distributed computing paradigms, we focus on Bach, a Linda-like coordination language, as a representative and well-understood model that enables us to explicitly capture and analyze the coordination mechanisms underlying distributed hypothesis evaluation.

Nevertheless, in contrast to standard federated learning approaches, which typically rely on aggregating numerical model updates, our coordination-based approach enables the explicit orchestration of symbolic interactions, where only abstract evaluation outcomes are exchanged instead of data or model parameters.

On the learning side, we consider Popper [9], a recent ILP system that is particularly appealing due to its ability to learn from failures and to find globally optimal hypotheses. Bach [10], grounded in logic programming principles, provides the coordination layer through which distributed evaluation is orchestrated. The resulting combination, named Bach4Popper, is shown to be correct with respect to Popper, in the sense that it computes equivalent models. This is established both theoretically and experimentally, and we further show that computational performance is preserved when moving from a centralized to a federated setting.

The rest of the paper is organized as follows. The two following sections introduce the background knowledge in the two domains connected by our contribution. First, Sect. 2 introduces the basic notions on which *logic programming* relies and explains *inductive logic programming* with a particular focus on Popper. Then, Sect. 3 presents the main features of *the Bach coordination language* and details a socket-based implementation in Python, named BLPy. Using that background, Sect. 4 presents our main contributions: it introduces *the Bach4Popper framework* and *proves that it is correct* with respect to Popper. These theoretical concerns are completed with experimental ones in Sect. 5. It shows that these results are confirmed on experiments and demonstrates that computational performance is preserved when moving from a centralized to a federated setting. Section 6 compares our work to related work and Sect. 7 draws our conclusions.

2   Inductive Logic Programming

Inductive Logic Programming lies at the intersection of machine learning and logic programming. In brief, it aims to learn logical rules from positive and negative examples, as well as from background knowledge. All of these elements, rules, examples, and background knowledge are expressed within the framework of logic programming.

2.1   Logic Programming

A full introduction to the concepts underlying logic programming is outside the scope of the current paper. We assume the reader is familiar with these concepts, in particular with the notions of term and predicate, and refer him to [21] for a comprehensive overview. In this section, we will just mention that programs we shall consider consist of implications (or Horn clauses) of the form $\forall X_1 \cdots \forall X_n\ H \Leftarrow B_1 \wedge \cdots \vee B_m$ and that two semantics are given to them.

On the one hand, the declarative semantics of logic programs defines their meaning purely in logical terms without any reference to an execution model. Central to this semantics is the notion of logical consequence, which is defined by stating that a goal G is a logical consequence of a set of Horn clauses S iff every model of S is also a model of G. This is subsequently denoted as $S \models G$.

A major result of model theory in the case of Horn clauses is that the set M_P of logical consequences of a set of Horn clauses P can be determined as the intersection of all its so-called Herbrand models and may be further characterized as the least fixed point of the immediate consequence operator T_P. Obviously, by construction, one has $T_P(M_P) = M_P$. It turns out that this result can be generalized for Horn clauses extended with negative literals in their body. We refer the reader to [3] for more explanations. For this introduction, it is sufficient to say that, under some conditions, the stable semantics developed by M. Gelfond and V. Lifschitz has allowed to identify stable models in the sense that they are fixed points of (suitable extensions) of the T_P operator dealing with negation. This has led to the development of so called answer set programming [20], which is a framework in which one computes stable models for logic programs, potentially extended to include constraints and optimization.

On the other hand, the operational semantics defines the semantics of Horn clauses through the successive derivation of a goal, each derivation producing a computed answer substitution, i.e. a single substitution summarizing the values given to the variables along the derivation path. In case the computation is successful, we shall use the notation $P \vdash G\,[\sigma]$ denote the existence of this successful derivation of the goal G yielding σ as a computed answer substitution.

The two semantics are established equivalent. See for instance [21] for a proof.

2.2 Inductive Logic Programming

Inductive Logic Programming (ILP for short) [25] aims to learn a hypothesis H describing a predicate as a logic program, using positive examples E^+ of this predicate, negative examples E^- of this predicate, and a background knowledge B_k, and this in a way such that $H \cup B_k$ entails all positive examples and none of the negative ones. ILP is typically applied in a centralized setting in which all examples are available on a single machine.

Several concepts need to be introduced to further characterize ILP. The background knowledge B_k is used to provide a context for learning. It contains a set B of facts and rules that describe relationships already understood about the domain. It also includes a so-called declaration bias D, which aims at restricting the hypotheses that can be constructed. Examples include predicate declarations, which specify which predicate names can appear in the head of clauses, in particular the form of the arguments, as well as body declarations, which do the same for predicates appearing in the body of clauses. It is assumed that no predicate symbol in the body of a clause in B_k appears in a head declaration of D. In other words, we assume that B_k does not depend on any hypothesis.

It is worth noting that predicate declarations can be expressed as constraints at the level of a meta-language. This is one of the core properties of the language Popper [9] we shall use. Assuming such a meta-language $\mathcal{L}$, a hypothesis constraint is a constraint expressed in $\mathcal{L}$. For instance, the atom `head_literal(Clause,Pred,Arity,Vars)` is used in Popper to denote that the clause `Clause` has a head literal with the predicate symbol `Pred`, is of arity `Arity`, and has the arguments `Vars`. As a further use

```
:- head_literal(_,p,2,_).
```

states that a predicate symbol `p` of arity 2 cannot appear in the head of any clause in a hypothesis.

The input of the inductive learning problem can then be formulated as composed of the following ingredients.

Definition 1. *The ILP problem input is a tuple* (B, D, C, E^+, E^-) *where*

- *B is a Horn program denoting background knowledge*
- *D is a declaration bias*
- *C is a set of hypothesis constraints*
- *E^+ is a set of ground atoms denoting positive examples of the predicate to be learnt*
- *E^- is a set of ground atoms denoting negative examples of the predicate to be learnt.*

We now define what constitutes a valid hypothesis for an ILP problem.

Definition 2. *Let* (B, D, C, E^+, E^-) *be an ILP problem input and H be a hypothesis. Then H is:*

- *complete when $B \cup H \models e^+$ for any $e^+ \in E^+$*
- *consistent when $B \cup H \not\models e^-$ for any $e^- \in E^-$*

A hypothesis is a solution when it is both complete and consistent.

Example 1. The *Zendo* dataset [5] is one of the benchmarks used ILP. The target predicate is `zendo/1`, whose argument is a state. The background knowledge B encodes properties and relations between objects. A fragment of B includes typically facts such as:

$$B = \{\&\texttt{piece(s1,p1)},\ \texttt{piece(s1,p2)}, \texttt{size(p1,1)},\ \texttt{small(1)},\ \texttt{red(p2)}\ \}$$

The declaration bias D constrains the hypothesis space by specifying admissible predicates and structural limits on candidate clauses. A simplified example of such a bias is:

$$D = \{\texttt{head\_pred(zendo,1)},\ \texttt{body\_pred(piece,2)}, \texttt{max\_clauses(4)}\}$$

Positive and negative examples are given as ground atoms over states:

$$E^+ = \{\texttt{zendo(s1)},\ \texttt{zendo(s7)}\}\quad E^- = \{\texttt{zendo(s2)},\ \texttt{zendo(s6)}\}$$

The constraint set C is progressively refined during the learning process to prune the hypothesis space. For example, it may contain auxiliary rules and hard constraints such as:

```
included_clause(h,Cl) :- head_literal(Cl,zendo,1,(A)),
    body_literal(Cl,piece,2,(A,D)).

:- included_clause(h,C0), body_size(C0,5), C0 >= 0.
```

Here, `Cl` denotes a clause identifier used internally by Popper to represent candidate hypotheses. The auxiliary predicate `included_clause(h,Cl)` identifies clauses matching a given syntactic pattern, while the hard constraint excludes clauses of this form from the search space. This illustrates how C is refined to eliminate unpromising hypotheses.

An example of an explainable and human-readable hypothesis H learned on the *Zendo* dataset is:

$$H = \{\texttt{zendo(A):-piece(A,B),contact(B,D),size(D,C),small(C),red(B). }\}$$

This rule states that a state A satisfies the target concept `zendo/1` if it contains a piece B that is in contact with another piece D whose size is small, and where B is red.

In practice there can be many solutions to an inductive learning problem input. One is thus naturally interested by optimal solutions, which are typically defined by minimizing the number of literals used.

Definition 3. *The size of a hypothesis H, denoted $size(H)$, is the total number of literals employed in H. Given an inductive learning problem input, an optimal solution is defined as a solution H such that any other solution H' verifies $size(H) \leq size(H')$.*

It is not always possible to find a complete and consistent hypothesis. In that case, one tries to get the best hypothesis in the sense that it entails the largest number of positive examples and the smallest number of negative examples. This leads to the notions of confusion matrix and score.

Definition 4. *Let (B, D, C, E^+, E^-) be an input tuple and H be a hypothesis. Then the confusion matrix for H, denoted $conf\_matrix(H)$, is the tuple (TP, FN, TN, FP) whose components are defined as follows:*

- *TP is the number of positive examples correctly entailed by $B \cup H$ (true positives)*
- *FN is the number of positive examples not entailed by $B \cup H$ (false negatives)*
- *TN is the number of negative examples not entailed by $B \cup H$ (true negatives)*
- *FP is the number of negative examples incorrectly entailed by $B \cup H$ (false positives)*

The score of H, denoted $score(H)$, is defined as $TP + TN$.

In the past thirty years, many inductive logic systems have been introduced. The reader is referred to [7] for a detailed description. Pioneer languages, such as Progol and Metagol, have explored subsumption lattices, amounting to trees of rules. In contrast, Popper has taken a meta-language approach which allows generating hypotheses by using Answer Set Programming (ASP) and which allows to learn from failures. It is generally considered as very appealing since it allows to find globally optimal hypotheses whereas Progol and Metagol may produce only locally optimal hypotheses. We shall turn in this paper to Popper. Its main algorithm is described in Algorithm 1 as a Python function inspired by the one presented in [9]. The function takes as arguments the sets E^+, E^-, D, C described in Definition 1. Three other arguments are added to limit the search space: the maximum number of variables, literals and clauses in a hypothesis. The Python function returns a hypothesis: either a solution, if there is one, or an hypothesis that maximizes the score function otherwise. The algorithm mainly consists of two loops. The outer one (starting on line 9 of Algorithm 1) is responsible for searching hypotheses which increasingly add literals. For a fixed number of literals, the inner loop (starting on line 12) embodies the Popper generate-test-constraint loop. Given a current set CC of constraints, the call to the generate function (line 13) generates a hypothesis. This is obtained through Answer Set Programming acting over the constraints CC of a meta-language. The produced solution, if there is one, is a hypothesis meeting the constraints of CC. In case there is no solution then the variable c_solvable is set to false (line 15) which leads to finish the inner loop. Otherwise the solution is tested against the positive and negative examples by additionally using the background knowledge of B. This is operated by the call to the function test (line 17). This results in a confusion matrix as specified in Definition 4. Two outputs are computed therefrom: an outcome and a score (lines 18 and 19). The outcome summarizes how many positive and negative examples are covered. For the positive examples, either all of them are covered (which is denoted as "all"), or some are covered (which is denoted by "some") or none are covered (which is denoted by "none"). For the negative examples, either some are covered (which is denoted by "some", this including the case where all are covered) or none are covered (which is denoted by "none"). Obviously a solution is found in case (all, none) is produced. In the other cases, the article [9] explains which constraints are to be added to the CC constraints. Note that this is operated so as to exclude answer sets in the ASP resolution, which makes the algorithm converge. Technically in the algorithm this is achieved by the call to the function learn_constraints (line 26). The important point for our work is that the added constraints can be determined in view of the outcome and do not need the knowledge of positive nor negative examples. It is also worth noting that, having computed its score, the new hypothesis is retained as the best one if its score is better than the one memorized in variable best_hyp (line 25).

3   The BLPy Coordination Language

3.1   The Bach Coordination Language

Bach is a Linda-like coordination language developed at the University of Namur [15]. It has been conceived in a constraint logic programming flavor. As a result, Linda tuples are replaced by ground logic programming terms, also called si-terms, the shared space is referenced as the store, and Linda primitives are reformulated as the following primitives: $tell(t)$ to place an occurrence

---

Algorithm 1. Popper (inspired by [9])

```
1 def popper(E+, E−, B, D, C, max_vars, max_literals,
     max_clauses):
2
3    best_score = 0
4    best_hyp = { }
5    end_popper = false
6    num_literals = 0
7    CC = C
8
9    while not end_popper and num_literals <= max_literals:
10      c_solvable = true
11      num_literals += 1
12      while not end_popper and c_solvable:
13          hyp = generate(D, CC, max_vars, num_literals,
                                          max_clauses)
14          if not hyp:
15              c_solvable = false
16          else:
17              conf_matrix = test(E+, E−, B, hyp)
18              outcome = compute_outcome(conf_matrix)
19              score = compute_score(conf_matrix)
20              if outcome == ('all', 'none'):
21                  best_hyp = hyp
22                  end_popper = true
23              else:
24                  if best_score < score:
25                      best_hyp = hyp
26                  CC += learn_constraints(hyp, outcome)
27
28    return best_hyp
```

---

of t on the store, $ask(t)$ to verify that t is present on the store, $get(t)$ to proceed similarly but by consuming one occurrence of t, and $nask(t)$ to check that t is absent from the store. Note that the last three primitives suspend until their associated condition is met.

Matching is operated in Bach as syntactic equality. We shall soften it in this paper by allowing a partially specified si-term to match a more complete si-term. This will be very useful later to get values from non specified arguments. The precise definition is as follows.

Definition 5. *Let $t = f(t_1, \cdots, t_m)$ and $u = g(u_1, \cdots, u_n)$ be two si-terms. Then t matches u iff, on the one hand, their functors are the same i.e. $f = g$ and, on the other hand, the list $[t_1, \cdots, t_m]$ of arguments of t is a prefix of the list $[u_1, \cdots, u_n]$ of arguments of u. This is subsequently denoted by $t \lhd u$. On the point of terminology, in that case, it is also said that u is matched by t.*

Primitives are composed in Bach to form more complex instructions, called agents, by using traditional composition operators from concurrency theory: sequential composition, parallel composition and non-deterministic choice. It is worth noting, however, that we shall only use the two first subsequently.

3.2   The BLPy Implementation

For the purpose of exploiting federated inductive logic programming using Bach, an implementation has been developed in Python. It is based on sockets and organized around, on the one hand, a server, managing the store and the actions of primitives, and, on the other hand, clients interacting with the store. The core part is threefold: it consists in defining a grammar to parse the messages, in implementing the store, and in designing an interpreter. As regards the grammar, our work is based on the `parsimonious` module, which provides fast arbitrary-lookahead parsers written in pure Python. The store is implemented using three data structures:

- a dictionary, named `theStore`, which represents the real contents of the store. For each functor it contains as a key it associates a dictionary mapping si-terms formed with this functor to integers, denoting the numbers of occurrences of the considered si-terms currently on the store;
- a dictionary, named `theWaitingList`, that registers process identifiers waiting for the presence of si-terms. Technically, it associates with a functor name a list of triples, composed of a process identifier, the si-term on which the process is suspended and the destructive nature of the operation (according to the fact that the process is suspended on a ask or a get request);
- a dictionary, named `theNWaitingList`, that registers process identifiers waiting for the absence of si-terms. Its structure is similar to that of `theWaitingList` except that processes are there waiting for the absence of the corresponding si-terms and that no destructive feature is recorded.

That being said, the implementation of the primitives is as follows:

- the execution of $tell(t)$ consists in checking whether the functor of t, say f, is registered in `theStore`. If this is the case and if t already appears as a key of `theStore[f]` then the number of associated occurrences is increased by one. If f is a key of `theStore` but t is not a key of `theStore[f]` then a new entry is added for t with 1 as associated integer. If f is not a key of `theStore` then it is introduced in `theStore` keys with a mapping from t to 1 as associated value. In all the cases, the processes of `theWaitingList` are looked at to see whether processes can be waken up.
- the execution of $ask(t)$ is dual. It succeeds in case the functor f of t is a key of `theStore` and if there is a si-term matching t in `theStore[f]`. If this is not the case then the identifier of the process running $ask(t)$ together with t is added to `theWaitingList`.

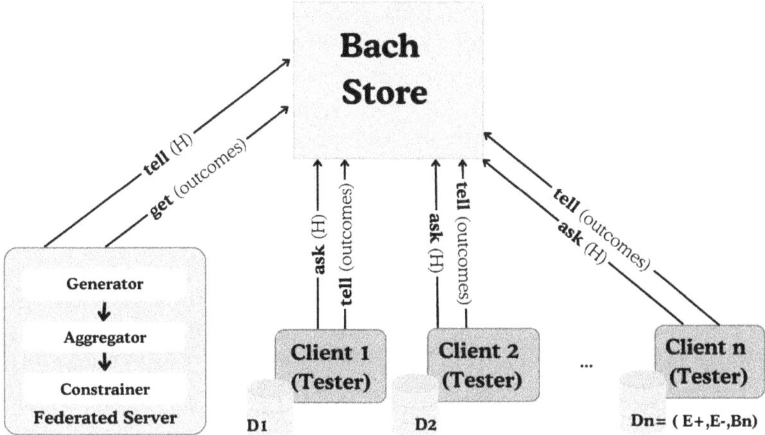

Fig. 1. Architecture of Bach4Popper illustrating the coordination mechanism underlying federated ILP. The federated server generates candidate hypotheses (Generator), aggregates client evaluations (Aggregator), and refines the hypothesis space through constraints (Constrainer). Hypotheses are communicated to clients via the shared Bach store using `tell`, while clients retrieve them using `ask`, evaluate them on local datasets, and return outcomes. This interaction implements a distributed version of the generate–test–constrain loop of Popper, where hypothesis evaluation is performed locally and coordination is handled through the shared store.

– the execution of $get(t)$ is similar but consists of removing an occurrence of a matching u is case such a si-term is present. In a dual perspective as $tell(t)$ processes of `theNWaitingList` are inspected to determine whether they can be waken up.
– finally the execution of $nask(t)$ is dual to that of $ask(t)$, asking for the absence of si-terms u matched by t and resulting in the process identifier being added to `theNWaitingList` together with t in case of suspension.

Sequential and parallel compositions are not implemented directly, but rather are handled at the Python level.

As a proof of concept, a Python package, named BLPy, has been developed. It can be downloaded at the address mentioned in [4].

4   The Bach4Popper Framework

4.1   The Framework

We are now in a position to explain how to implement federated inductive logic programming using Popper and BLPy. As illustrated in Fig. 1, given the store made available by BLPy, the basic idea is to have a BLPy server process, named `bbpopper`, handling the store, and two types of BLPy client processes communicating through it. One of them, referred to as `srvpopper`, is deployed in a unique instance. It is responsible for the generate and constraint parts of Algorithm 1. The other types of clients, named `clipopper`, are deployed in as many instances as data entities available. They are responsible for the test part of Algorithm 1 on their local data. The two types of clients communicate via the store. It is assumed that the number of `clipopper` clients is known in advance, that `clipopper` clients are identified by numbers ranging from 1 to this number, and that no intruder modifies the content of the store.

Basically, from a coordination perspective, the `srvpopper` process iteratively publishes the current hypothesis to the shared store (through a tell primitive) and queries (by means of get primitives) the local evaluation feedback produced by the `clipopper` clients. Each client evaluates the hypothesis locally and returns the symbolic feedback derived from its confusion matrix. The `srvpopper` process aggregates these feedbacks, computes new logical constraints, and uses them to refine the hypothesis.

Algorithm 2 details the server-side learning procedure. It is directly derived from Algorithm 1. It uses the `srvpopper` function as the main function. The prototype is the same as the one of function `popper` in Algorithm 1 except that the argument B providing the background knowledge is omitted. This omission reflects the fact that background knowledge is locally available on the distributed `clipopper` processes. The initialization phase follows the same structure as in centralized Popper, with the addition of an integer variable `r` that tracks the current federated round in the generate–test–constrain cycle. The two loops in Algorithm 1 are also essentially repeated, with the following differences. Instead of calling the `test` function to determine the confusion matrix, the current hypothesis (in case it exists) is told via the execution of the `tell(hypsi(r,hyp))` primitive (see line 18). Then the `srvpopper` process waits for the confusion matrices computed by the `clipopper` processes by means of the execution of the `ask(fedcmtuple(r,i))`, the result being stored in an array `fedcm` (see line 20). Each element of this array reflects the result of a local computation, which is then aggregated by the `aggregate_outcome` and `aggregate_score` functions (see lines 21 and 22). The end of the execution is then similar to the one of function `popper`, with as two differences that the end of the execution is reported by telling an empty hypothesis by the primitive `tell(hypsi(r,end_hyp))` (see line 26) and that each iteration ends by updating the `r` counter (see line 31). The precise definitions of the `aggregate_outcome` and `aggregate_score` functions are given in Definition 9 when theoretical results will make clear what they should be.

A `clipopper` client, say identified by i, executes dually. Basically it iterates by asking for the current hypothesis, tests it on its local data E_i^+, E_i^-, B_i, computes the confusion matrix and tells it. This is operated by function `clipopper` of Algorithm 3.

4.2   Theoretical Results

As a summary of the previous subsection, by identifying the processes with their main function and by keeping the maximum number of variables, literals and

---

Algorithm 2. Srvpopper client

```
1 def srvpopper(N, D, C, max_vars, max_literals, max_clauses):
2
3       best_score = 0
4       best_hyp = { }
5       end_popper = false
6       num_literals = 0
7       CC = C
8       r = 1
9
10      while not end_popper and num_literals <= max_literals:
11          c_solvable = true
12          num_literals += 1
13          while not end_popper and c_solvable:
14              hyp = generate(D, CC, max_vars, num_literals,
                                max_clauses)
15              if not hyp:
16                  c_solvable = false
17              else:
18                  tell(hypsi(r,hyp))
19                  for i in range(1,N+1):
20                      fedcm[i] = ask(fedcmtuple(r,i))
21                  outcome = aggregate_outcome(fedcm)
22                  score = aggregate_score(fedcm)
23                  if outcome == ('all', 'none'):
24                      best_hyp = hyp
25                      end_popper = true
26                      tell(hypsi(r,nil_hyp))
27                  else:
28                      if best_score < score:
29                          best_hyp = hyp
30                          CC += learn_constraints(hyp, outcome)
31              r = r+1
32
33      return best_hyp
```

---

clauses as local data of the Popper server, the federated computation consists in executing the following parallel agent:

$$FedPopper(N) = bbpopper || srvpopper(N, D, C) || \tag{1}$$
$$clipopper(1, E_1^+, E_1^-, B_1) || ... || clipopper(N, E_N^+, E_N^-, B_N)$$

We now have to establish that the final hypothesis computed by this execution is the same as the one computed by function **popper** of Algorithm 1. This is obviously only possible if a relation is identified between positive and negative examples, on the one hand, and the background knowledge, on the other hand. This is precisely the aim of the following definitions.

Algorithm 3. Clipopper client

```
1   def clipopper(i, Ei+, Ei-, Bi):
2
3           end_popper = false
4           r = 1
5
6           while not end_popper:
7               hyp_asked = ask(hypsi(r))
8               if (hyp_asked = hyp(r,end_hyp):
9                   end_popper = true
10              else:
11                  conf_matrix = test(Ei+, Ei-, Bi, hyp_asked)
12                  tell(fedcmtuple(r,Id,conf_matrix)
13              r = r+1
```

Definition 6. *Let E be a set of ground atoms. The set $U(E)$ is defined as the set of ground terms formed from constants and functions appearing in the arguments of atoms of E. By extension, if E^+ and E^- are sets of positive and negative examples on a predicate p, the set $U(E^+, E^-)$ is defined as $U(E^+) \cup U(E^-)$.*

Definition 7. *A Horn clause program B is said to be well-structured if it can be partitioned into a set SF of facts and a set SH of definite Horn clauses whose literal arguments are variables and whose head does not involve predicate of SF. Such a partition is unique by construction. The two sets are respectively referred to as $sf(B)$ and $sh(B)$, respectively.*

Intuitively the federated learning we are thinking about involves background knowledge that is shared among distributed clients and data that is distinct on each client. Technically, this leads in the subsequent definition to define a partition as having the sets $sf(B_1), \ldots, sf(B_n)$ form a partition of $sf(B)$ in the mathematical sense while the sets $sh(B_1), \ldots, sh(B_n)$ and $sh(B)$ are identical.

Definition 8. *Let $E^+, E_1^+, \cdots, E_n^+$ and $E^-, E_1^-, \cdots, E_n^-$ be respectively sets of positive and negative examples on a predicate p. Let $B, B_1, \cdots, B_n$ be well-structured Horn clause programs. The set $\{(B_1, E_1^+, E_1^-), \cdots, (B_n, E_n^+, E_n^-)\}$ is a federated partition of (B, E^+, E^-) iff the following conditions hold:*

- *$U(sf(B_i)) \subseteq U(E_i^+, E_i^-)$, for any $i = 1, \cdots, n$*
- *$sf(B_1) \cdots, sf(B_n)$ form a partition of $sf(B)$*
- *the sets $U(E_i^+, E_i^-)$ and $U(E_j^+, E_j^-)$ are disjoint, for any $i, j = 1, \cdots, n$ with $i \neq j$*
- *one has $sh(B_1) = \cdots = sh(B_n) = sh(B)$*
- *$E_1^+, \cdots, E_n^+$ form a partition of E^+*
- *$E_1^-, \cdots, E_n^-$ form a partition of E^-*

Proposition 1. *Let $\{(B_1, E_1^+, E_1^-), \cdots, (B_n, E_n^+, E_n^-)\}$ be a federated partition of (B, E^+, E^-) with positive and negative examples over the predicate p. Let H be a Horn clause program. Then for any $e^+ \in E^+$, one has $B \cup H \vdash e^+ [\theta]$ iff $B_i \cup H \vdash e^+ [\theta]$ for some $i = 1, \cdots, n$.*

Proof. Assume first that $B \cup H \vdash e^+ [\theta]$. Then there exists a derivation $Deriv$ from e^+ using clauses of $B \cup H$ ending with the empty clause and producing θ as computed answer substitution. This derivation uses clauses of H, $sh(B)$ and facts from $sf(B)$. As $E_1^+, \cdots, E_n^+$ form a partition of E^+ there exists one and only one i such that $e^+ \in E_i^+$. In view of the federated partition assumption, the set of the facts used in $Deriv$ are then included in $sf(B_i)$. As the Horn clauses of $sh(B_i)$ are those of $sh(B)$, it follows that the derivation $Deriv$ is also a derivation establishing that $B_i \cup H \vdash e^+ [\theta]$.

Assume now $B_i \cup H \vdash e^+ [\theta]$, for some i. There is thus a derivation from e^+ using clauses of $B_i \cup H$ ending with the empty clause and producing θ as computed answer substitution. As $sh(B_i) = sh(B)$ and $sf(B_i) \subseteq sf(B)$, this derivation is also a derivation using clauses of $B \cup H$. It follows that $B \cup H \vdash e^+ [\theta]$.

As a direct consequence, any $e^- \in E^-$ is not derivable from $B \cup H$ if it is not derivable from $B_i \cup H$ for any i. However, the federated partition property allows to go one step further.

Proposition 2. *Let $\{(B_1, E_1^+, E_1^-), \cdots, (B_n, E_n^+, E_n^-)\}$ be a federated partition of (B, E^+, E^-) with positive and negative examples over the predicate p. Let H be a Horn clause program. Let e^- be a negative example of E^-. It is thus a negative example of some E_j^-. Then e^- is not derivable from $B \cup H$ iff it is not derivable from $B_j \cup H$.*

Proof. Indeed, in view of the federated partition assumption, $U(sf(B_j)) \subseteq U(E_j^+, E_j^-)$ and the sets $U(E_k^+, E_k^-)$ are disjoint. Therefore checking whether $B \cup H \vdash e^+ [\theta]$ holds amount to checking whether $B_j \cup H \vdash e^+ [\theta]$ hold.

It follows from Propositions 1 and 2 that the confusion matrix computed (centrally) on (B, E^+, E^-) consists of the component-based sum of the confusion matrices computed (locally) for the (B_i, E_i^+, E_i^-).

Proposition 3. *Let $\{(B_1, E_1^+, E_1^-), \cdots, (B_n, E_n^+, E_n^-)\}$ be a federated partition of (B, E^+, E^-) with positive and negative examples over the predicate p. Let H be a Horn clause program. Let (TP, FN, TN, FP) be the confusion matrix for H determined with respect to (B, E^+, E^-). For any $i = 1, \cdots, n$, let (TP_i, FN_i, TN_i, FP_i) be the confusion matrix for H determined with respect to (B_i, E_i^+, E_i^-). Then*

$$TP = \sum_{i=1}^{n} TP_i \qquad TN = \sum_{i=1}^{n} TN_i$$
$$FP = \sum_{i=1}^{n} FP_i \qquad FN = \sum_{i=1}^{n} FN_i$$

Proof. Direct consequence of Propositions 1 and 2

This result allows for a direct aggregation of confusion matrices. However as the confusion matrix is not used as such but through the outcome and score only, it is possible to go one step further. Before that, let us define an aggregation of outcomes and scores as follows.

Definition 9. *Define*
$\oplus : \{all, some, none\} \times \{all, some, none\} \to \{all, some, none\}$ *as follows:*

$$o_1 \oplus o_2 = \begin{cases} all & \text{if } o_1 = o_2 = all \\ none & \text{if } o_1 = o_2 = none \\ some & \text{otherwise} \end{cases}$$

It is easy to verify that the operator $\oplus$ is commutative and associative. This allows to state the following proposition.

Proposition 4. *Let $\{(B_1, E_1^+, E_1^-), \cdots, (B_n, E_n^+, E_n^-)\}$ be a federated partition of (B, E^+, E^-) with positive and negative examples over the predicate p. Let H be a Horn clause program. Let (po, no) and s be respectively the outcome and score computed for H with respect to (B, E^+, E^-). Moreover, for any $i = 1, \cdots, n$, let (po_i, no_i) and s_i be respectively the outcome and score computed for H with respect to (B_i, E_i^+, E_i^-). Then*

$$po = po_1 \oplus \cdots \oplus po_n$$
$$no = no_1 \oplus \cdots \oplus no_n$$
$$s = s_1 + \cdots + s_n$$

Proof. The proposition directly follows from Proposition 3.

The correctness of the federated computation embodied in Eq. 1 and Algorithms 2 and 3 with respect to the central computation embodied in Algorithm 1 then comes from the fact that hypotheses *hyp* successively computed by Algorithm 1 (see line 12) are those that are successively told in Algorithm 2 (see line 14). This is easily established by induction, as thanks to Proposition 4, the outcome and score computed in a distributed manner are exactly the same as those computed centrally and therefore induce identical constraints for the generation phase.

5   Experiments

In this section, we evaluate `Bach4Popper` from two complementary perspectives[1]:

- *P1 (Correctness).* Does `Bach4Popper` compute hypotheses that are equivalent to those learned by (centralized) Popper despite strict data locality constraints and the absence of shared examples?
- *P2 (Performance and Coordination Cost).* How does coordination-based federated execution impact the symbolic search process in terms of execution time compared to (centralized) Popper?

Table 1. Datasets and corresponding Popper configuration used in the experiments.

Dataset	Target Pred.	#Pos	#Neg	MaxClauses	MaxVars	MaxBody
Trains	f/1	5	5	3	5	6
Zendo1	zendo/1	20	20	4	5	7
iggp-rps	next_score/1	108	356	4	5	7

The evaluation is conducted on standard ILP benchmark datasets obtained from the official Popper implementation [6]. These benchmarks are widely used to assess symbolic hypothesis search under controlled bias settings. Table 1 summarizes the datasets along with their corresponding configurations. Note that, as we do not have access to data really distributed, we shall partition these datasets in order to fulfill the hypotheses of Definition 8. Each client thus only accesses its own examples, while coordination is handled through a central server.

We consider three representative benchmarks covering different levels of relational complexity:

- *Trains.* The Trains dataset [17] is a classical ILP benchmark where the goal is to distinguish between eastbound and westbound trains. Although relatively small, it requires structured relational reasoning over background knowledge and is commonly used to validate the correctness of ILP systems.
- *Zendo.* The Zendo dataset [5] consists of structured configurations from which a hidden concept must be inferred. Inspired by a rule-discovery game, it features a richer hypothesis space than *Trains* and is therefore suitable for evaluating symbolic generalization.
- *IGGP-RPS.* The IGGP-RPS dataset originates from Inductive General Game Playing [8] and involves learning rules that describe state transitions in a game environment. This benchmark is more challenging due to both the size of the example set and the complexity of the relational background knowledge.

We consider a cross-silo federated learning setting composed of three clients and a central server. To simulate this setting, each dataset is partitioned into three client-specific subsets, each containing a balanced distribution of positive and negative examples. Each client evaluates candidate hypotheses using only its local data, while coordination is performed by the server. No examples, background knowledge, or intermediate evaluation results are shared between clients or with the server. The server has access only to the bias.

5.1   Correctness

Unlike statistical learning, Popper seeks a hypothesis that is logically complete and consistent with the specification. Thus, accuracy and recall here indicate

---

[1] To allow the interested reader to reproduce the experiments, the code of Bach4Popper is available at the address mentioned in [1].

Table 2. Convergence of Bach4Popper towards centralized Popper in terms of descriptive performance.

Setting	Trains		Zendo		IGGP-RPS	
	Accuracy	Recall	Accuracy	Recall	Accuracy	Recall
Centralized	1.00	1.00	1.00	1.00	1.00	1.00
Bach4Popper	1.00	1.00	1.00	1.00	1.00	1.00

logical satisfaction rather than predictive generalization: a value of 1.00 means that all positive examples are entailed and all negative examples are rejected.

We first evaluate whether Bach4Popper preserves the models computed by centralized Popper. To that end, we consider a hybrid evaluation protocol combining federated learning with centralized testing. Algorithm 2 is enriched with access to the full dataset: lines 16–18 of Algorithm 1 are inserted before line 18 of Algorithm 2, after which outcomes and scores obtained in the federated and centralized settings are compared.

As shown in Table 2, the coordinated learning process consistently converges to hypotheses that are complete and consistent on the full dataset, confirming that federation preserves the correctness guarantees, thereby addressing *P1 (Correctness)*. This provides an empirical validation of Propositions 1–4 established in Sect. 4, showing that federated evaluation preserves the logical correctness of the learned hypotheses.

5.2   Performance and Symbolic Cost

We now evaluate the execution cost induced by distributing the testing phase of Popper. Unlike statistical federated learning, Bach4Popper does not distribute model optimization but preserves the symbolic generate-test-constrain loop of Popper while delegating hypothesis evaluation to multiple clients. To analyze this cost, we measure the following:

- *tCentralPopper*: time spent inside the symbolic ILP engine (generation of hypotheses, constraint construction, grounding, and solver update);
- *tFedPopper*: time spent performing federated coordination, i.e., transmitting hypotheses, waiting for client evaluations, and aggregating outcomes;
- *global_time*: total execution time from the first generated hypothesis until termination.

Two timing modes are used. On the one hand, by using Python `process_time()`, we measure only CPU time and ignore waiting periods. This shows the pure computation cost of the algorithm. On the other hand, by using Python `perf_counter()`, we measure real elapsed time, including communication and synchronization between clients. In other words, the first mode shows how much computation federation adds, while the second shows the actual runtime in a distributed setting.

Table 3. Execution time decomposition of Bach4Popper. "With Suspension" uses `perf_counter()` (including communication delays), while "Without Suspension" uses `process_time()` (CPU time only). CENT denotes the Popper symbolic core and FED the federated coordination cost.

Dataset	With Suspension			Without Suspension		
	CENT (s)	FED (s)	Glob (s)	CENT (s)	FED (s)	Glob (s)
Trains	0.1437	26.9676	27.2257	0.0415	0.0073	0.0790
Zendo	0.1682	5.3198	5.7002	0.2087	0.0260	0.5039
IGGP-RPS	268.77	100.91	600.04	275.83	2.7582	483.15

This distinction is clearly reflected in Table 3. For all datasets, the federated cost (FED) drops significantly when suspension is removed. For instance, on the *Trains* dataset, FED decreases from 26.96 s to 0.0073 s, and on *Zendo*, from 5.31 s to 0.026 s. Even for the more complex *IGGP-RPS* dataset, FED drops from 100.91 s to only 2.75 s.

This behavior is also influenced by the complexity of the learning task. For simpler datasets such as *Trains* and *Zendo*, the search converges in fewer iterations, and the execution time is therefore largely dominated by coordination latency. In contrast, for more complex datasets such as *IGGP-RPS*, a higher number of iterations is required, which leads to both increased computational cost and an accumulation of coordination delays.

This consistent behavior across datasets shows that the overhead introduced by federation is primarily due to coordination latency, i.e., communication, synchronization, and waiting between components, rather than actual computation. In particular, the very low FED cost in the CPU-only setting indicates that the distributed evaluation itself is computationally lightweight.

Overall, Bach4Popper preserves the computational behavior of Popper, and the additional cost of federation mainly originates from distributed execution rather than increased algorithmic complexity. These results address point *P2* above.

Although execution time is influenced by the size and complexity of the datasets, the results show that this factor alone does not account for the observed overhead. The discrepancy between CPU time and wall-clock time demonstrates that coordination introduces additional latency that is independent of the underlying ILP computation. This confirms that the cost of federation arises not only from larger problem instances, but also from the coordination mechanisms required to distribute the evaluation process.

6   Related Work

Federated learning has emerged as a powerful paradigm for collaborative model training without centralizing data, addressing privacy, regulatory, and data-silo constraints [18,30]. However, most approaches rely on sub-symbolic models such as deep neural networks, whose decision processes are inherently opaque. While numerous explainability techniques have been proposed, they are predominantly post-hoc, providing approximate explanations that are not guaranteed to faithfully reflect the underlying model behavior [22]. Our work contrasts by adopting from the outset the interpretable setting of inductive logic programming. This has allowed us to establish theoretical properties which have no counterpart in these pieces of work.

Beyond neural networks, several works have explored interpretable or symbolic models in federated settings, including decision trees [13,19,28] and fuzzy logic models [14,16,26,27,29]. These approaches demonstrate that interpretability can be integrated into federated learning, but they typically focus on aggregating model structures or parameters. In contrast to our work, they are not designed to support relational hypothesis induction under explicit background knowledge, as required in Inductive Logic Programming, and do not emphasize the logical semantics and soundness guarantees central to logic programming systems.

As regards coordination, to the best of our knowledge, the article [12] is the only other coordination-based approach that has coped with federated learning. However, the approach is quite different from ours. First, the authors have used aggregate-based computing whereas we have employed a classical Linda-like approach. Moreover, as their goal is to tackle heterogeneity in data distribution, they have proposed Field-Based Federated Learning to allow the construction of several personalized model zones, each with its own model tailored to its local data, instead of a single global model shared across all data entities. We adopt an opposite perspective in our work by addressing data entities of a similar nature and showing that a model that would have been classically learned in a centralized way can actually be learned in a distributed manner.

Finally, our work is a continuation of a first approach in federated learning in which we explored the aggregation of locally learned hypotheses through majority voting [2]. However, in contrast to this work, our approach operates at the level of complete hypotheses and does not federate the internal learning process itself.

7   Conclusion

In the aim of addressing two main concerns in current machine learning techniques – explainability and privacy – this paper has introduced a new framework for federated learning based on the Bach coordination language and the inductive logic programming system Popper. This framework, named Bach4Popper, consequently relies on coordination primitives to learn Horn clauses from failures in a distributed manner while preserving data locality and thus without sharing examples.

Technically, the core contribution of this work lies in the federation of Popper's internal generate-test-constrain loop. Hypothesis generation and constraint induction are performed centrally, while hypothesis evaluation is delegated to distributed clients that operate exclusively on local data. Through symbolic aggregation of local outcomes and scores, the global learning process remains logically equivalent to centralized Popper.

We formally proved that, under well-defined federated partitioning assumptions, the symbolic outcomes and scores computed locally by distributed clients can be exactly aggregated to recover their centralized counterparts. As a result, Bach4Popper is correct with respect to centralized Popper in the sense that the same models are computed. Experimental results on standard ILP benchmarks confirm this analysis. Across all datasets, Bach4Popper converges to hypotheses that are descriptively equivalent to those learned centrally in terms of accuracy and recall. Moreover, experiments show that the computational performance of the federated setting is reasonably close to that of a centralized computation.

Future work will focus on exploring larger relational domains, studying heterogeneous and noisy data distributions, and extending the theoretical results of Sect. 5 to other forms of partitioning.

Acknowledgment. The authors thank the University of Namur for its support. They also thank the Walloon Region for partial support through the Ariac project (convention 210235) and the CyberExcellence project (convention 2110186).

References

1. Akaichi, Y., Jacquet, J.M.: The Bach4Popper Framework. https://doi.org/10.5281/zenodo.18981901
2. Akaichi, Y., Jacquet, J.M., Linden, I., Vanhoof, W.: Federated inductive logic programming for explainable artificial intelligence. In: Proceedings of the Second Workshop on Explainable Artificial Intelligence for the medical domain-25-30 October (2025)
3. Apt, K.R., Bol, R.N.: Logic programming and negation: a survey. J. Log. Program. **19**(20), 9–71 (1994)
4. Barkallah, M., Jacquet, J.M.: The BLPy Framework. https://doi.org/10.5281/zenodo.18672845
5. Bramley, N.R., Rothe, A., Tenenbaum, J.B., Xu, F., Gureckis, T.M.: Grounding compositional hypothesis generation in specific instances. In: Proceedings of the Annual Meeting of the Cognitive Science Society, vol. 40 (2018)
6. Cropper, A.: Popper: An Inductive Logic Programming System (2020). https://github.com/logic-and-learning-lab/Popper
7. Cropper, A., Dumančić, S.: Inductive logic programming at 30: a new introduction. J. Artif. Intell. Res. **74**, 765–850 (2022)
8. Cropper, A., Evans, R., Law, M.: Inductive general game playing. Mach. Learn. **109**(7), 1393–1434 (2020)
9. Cropper, A., Morel, R.: Learning programs by learning from failures. Mach. Learn. **110**(4), 801–856 (2021)
10. Darquennes, D., Jacquet, J.M., Linden, I.: On multiplicities in tuple-based coordination languages: the bach family of languages and its expressiveness study. Lecture Notes in Computer Science, vol. 10852, pp. 81–109 (2018)
11. De Raedt, L.: Logical and Relational Learning. Springer (2008)

12. Domini, D., Aguzzi, G., Esterle, L., Viroli, M.: Field-based coordination for federated learning. In: Castellani, I., Tiezzi, F. (eds.) Proceedings of the 26th International Conference on Coordination Models and Languages. Lecture Notes in Computer Science, vol. 14676, pp. 56–74. Springer (2024)
13. Dong, T., Li, S., Qiu, H., Lu, J.: An Interpretable Federated Learning-based Network Intrusion Detection Framework. arXiv preprint arXiv:2201.03134 (2022)
14. Ducange, P., Marcelloni, F., Renda, A., Ruffini, F.: Federated learning of XAI models in healthcare: a case study on Parkinson's disease. Cogn. Comput. **16**(6), 3051–3076 (2024)
15. Jacquet, J.M., Linden, I.: Coordinating context-aware applications in mobile ad hoc networks. In: Proceedings of the First ERCIM Workshop on eMobility, pp. 107–118 (2007)
16. Jiang, W., et al.: Fuzzy ensemble-based federated learning for EEG-based emotion recognition in internet of medical things. J. Ind. Inf. Integr. **44**, 100789 (2025)
17. Larson, J., Michalski, R.S.: Inductive inference of VL decision rules. ACM SIGART Bull. **1**(63), 38–44 (1977)
18. Li, Q., et al.: A survey on federated learning systems: vision, hype and reality for data privacy and protection. IEEE Trans. Knowl. Data Eng. **35**(4), 3347–3366 (2021)
19. Li, Q., et al.: Fedtree: a federated learning system for trees. Proc. Mach. Learn. Syst. **5** (2023)
20. Lifschitz, V.: Answer set programming and plan generation. Artif. Intell. **138**(1–2), 39–54 (2002)
21. Lloyd, J.W.: Foundations of Logic Programming, 2nd edn. Springer (1987)
22. Lopez-Ramos, L.M., et al.: Interplay between Federated Learning and Explainable Artificial Intelligence: a Scoping Review. arXiv preprint arXiv:2411.05874 (2024)
23. McMahan, B., Moore, E., Ramage, D., Hampson, S., y Arcas, B.A.: Communication-efficient learning of deep networks from decentralized data. In: Artificial Intelligence and Statistics, pp. 1273–1282. PMLR (2017)
24. Muggleton, S.: Inductive logic programming. New Gener. Comput. **8**(4), 295–318 (1991)
25. Muggleton, S.: Inverse entailment and progol. N. Gener. Comput. **13**(3), 245–286 (1995)
26. Połap, D.: Fuzzy consensus with federated learning method in medical systems. IEEE Access **9**, 150383–150392 (2021)
27. Srivastava, V., et al.: An IoT-based framework employing fuzzy logic and federated learning for decentralized decision-making. Int. J. Inf. Technol. 1–7 (2025)
28. Truex, S., et al.: A hybrid approach to privacy-preserving federated learning. In: Proceedings of the 12th ACM Workshop on Artificial Intelligence and Security, pp. 1–11 (2019)
29. Wilbik, A., Grefen, P.: Towards a federated fuzzy learning system. In: 2021 IEEE International Conference on Fuzzy Systems (FUZZ-IEEE), pp. 1–6. IEEE (2021)
30. Yang, Q., Liu, Y., Chen, T., Tong, Y.: Federated machine learning: concept and applications. ACM Trans. Intell. Syst. Technol. (TIST) **10**(2), 1–19 (2019)

Runtime Adaptation as a Programming Pattern in Service Composition

Carlos G. Lopez Pombo[1(✉)] , Pablo Montepagano[2], and Emilio Tuosto[3]

[1] Centro Interdisciplinario de Telecomunicaciones, Electrónica, Computación y Ciencia Aplicada, Universidad Nacional de Río Negro - Sede Andina and CONICET, Viedma, Argentina
`cglopezpombo@unrn.edu.ar`
[2] Departamento de Computación, Facultad de Ciencias Exactas y Naturales, Universidad de Buenos Aires, Buenos Aires, Argentina
[3] Gran Sasso Science Institute, L'Aquila, Italy

Abstract. We propose a programming pattern for runtime architectural adaptation of service-oriented applications. Our approach enables transparent reconfiguration of distributed services at runtime leveraging on the key features for dynamic discovery binding of services supported developed in an existing platform. More precisely, in this paper we equip the platform with monitoring capabilities supporting the transparent reconfiguration of the architecture of service-oriented applications triggered by changes in the execution context. We demonstrate the effectiveness of the approach on the adaptable TeaStore benchmark.

1 Introduction

Adaptability can be intuitively understood as the property of a system respond appropriately to changes in its execution environment. Often, adaptation impacts on the behaviour of the system without necessarily affecting its architecture. For instance, fault-tolerance can be tackled by replicating components without affecting the overall architecture. If we embrace the view that for cloud applications this is not necessarily the case, raises the problem of devising adaptation mechanisms of architectures. Arguably, the problem boils down to adopting suitable programming features allowing developers to implement countermeasures against changes in the execution context. Let us introduce a running example that we use here to illustrate this point and we will appeal to in order to demonstrate our approach throughout the paper. Our example elaborates on the adaptable TeaStore benchmark[1] proposed in [3] to evaluate adaptation mechanisms.

C. G. Lopez Pombo—On leave from Instituto de Ciencias de la computación CONICET–UBA and Departamento de Computación, Facultad de Ciencias Exactas y Naturales, Universidad de Buenos Aires.

[1] These scenarios are based on the TeaStore use case [10] originally proposed to benchmark micro-services.

R. Casadei and F. Ghassemi (Eds.): COORDINATION 2026, LNCS 16590, pp. 159–175, 2026.
https://doi.org/10.1007/978-3-032-28358-0_8

More precisely, this benchmark is designed to treat adaptability as a first-class design concern in service-oriented architectures. In particular, the benchmark classifies services as mandatory and optional and as external or local, envisages multiple versions of components (featuring e.g., different functionalities) in order to specify and evaluate reconfiguration policies across diverse operational scenarios.

Our running example involves a web user-interface, an image provider service, and a locally hosted database service. The web user-interface, say WebUI, is the entry point to the application for users; in particular it displays images of products generated by an image provider, say Image provider. According to the specification in [10],
- image providers manipulate images (e.g., applying filters, resizing, etc.);
- WebUI connects to an image provider service in order to generate webpages to display products to users.

A local storage service, say Local DB, manages a database of images that WebUI can resort to when e.g., the quality of images elaborated by Image provider is sub-optimal. The application can resort to locally stored default images if necessary.

Back to the application-dependent aspects of architectural adaptation, let us consider a few possible ways to realize the reconfiguration required when the TeaStore application needs to resort to the use of a default image. A first possibility is that service WebUI might trigger the search for another image provider until the connection with the original provider becomes acceptable. Alternatively, WebUI may resort to querying the service Local DB. Or else, if the service Local DB performance is compromised by CPU overload, the WebUI might simply access a predefined file in the local drive, so avoiding further interactions with other services. Obviously, which is the most reasonable options depends on the application.

It is also worth remarking that, depending on the choice of how to realize the adaptation, also the conditions triggering the reconfiguration of the components in charge of the countermeasures to adopt are application-dependent. For instance, the second alternative could depend on the responsiveness of Local DB when the adaptation is required.

Although the actual tasks to execute when a reconfiguration is required are application-dependent, there are activities that are common to all cases. In particular, the detection of anomalous situations that require adaptation and the decision of which countermeasures to take can be cast in the pattern presented in this paper. Indeed, we explore the possibility of reusing known mechanisms borrowed from the *service-oriented computing* (SOC) paradigm.[2] Our exploration hinges on a platform, dubbed SEArch (after Service Execution Architecture) [14], for the discovery and binding of distributed services featuring

---

[2] Although the terminology has evolved, SOC is still widely used and, we believe, still applies to variants such as cloud computing, fog and edge computing, or the many forms of distributed computing associated with what is known as the *Internet of (Every)Things*.

(non-)functional and behavioural compliance of services. We showcase how our platform can support architectural reconfigurations dictated by changes in the underlying *execution context*. More precisely, in this paper we disregard adaptation that dependents on application-level conditions and focus on reconfigurations due to variations at lower levels such as network speed, CPU load, memory consumption, etc. As we will see, on the one hand this yields a simplified programming pattern for adaptation and, on the other hand, is a limitation of our approach.

Structure of the Paper. Section 2 illustrates the key features of our platform necessary to appreciate our programming pattern; more precisely, we survey the behavioural contracts, and the searching and binding mechanism featured by our platform.

Section 3 introduces our programming pattern and how it is cast in the architecture of our platform. We give the architecture of our adaptation framework in Sect. 3.1; the elements of the programming pattern are key to the design of the control loop that decides how to reconfigure an application at run-time. This decision procedure is detailed in Sect. 3.2 together with the specification of the adaptation contracts of our running example which concern control data of the execution environment.

Section 4 describes the adaptation of our running example. We give the behavioural contracts in terms of CFSMs for some scenarios borrowed from the adaptable TeaStore benchmark [3]. Here, we also spell out how the adaptation process is triggered by the control loop given in Sect. 3.2.

Finally, we draw some conclusions and discuss further work in Sect. 5.

2   An Overview of SEArch

The key role in our platform is played by *service brokers* that are used by *service providers* to register their services, and by *service clients* to dynamically *discover* and *bind* to services satisfying their requirements. These roles are typically advocated in SOAs; the originality of our platform however is the use of *behavioural contracts* to support *semantic-based* composition of services. More precisely, the composition mechanism realised by service brokers of SEArch relies on a notion of behavioural compliance of contracts which we briefly review here.

To support SOC, our platform offers a mechanism for populating service repositories and composing service-based applications. The registration of a service (see Fig. 1a) is conceptually simple: the service provider sends the contract and the unique resource identifier of the provided service, to broker, through its local SEArch middleware. The execution process is significantly more complex since its underlying computational model are *Asynchronous Relational Networks* (ARNs) [9]. This theory envisages *processes* and *communication channels* exposing *ports* with behavioural contracts: processes' ports, called *provides-points*, can be dynamically "coalesed" with ports of communication channels, called *requires-points*, provided that the behavioural contracts associated with

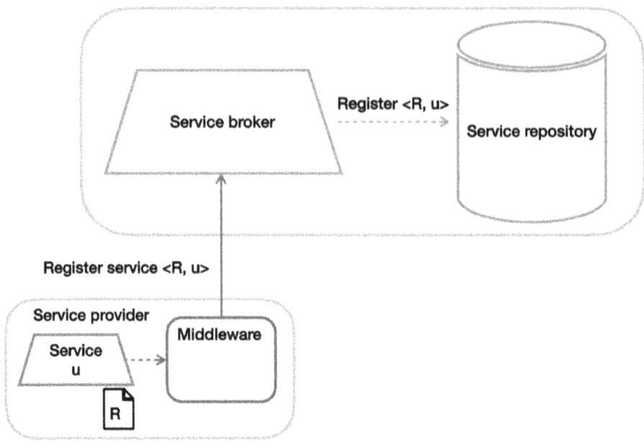

(a) Service registration procedure

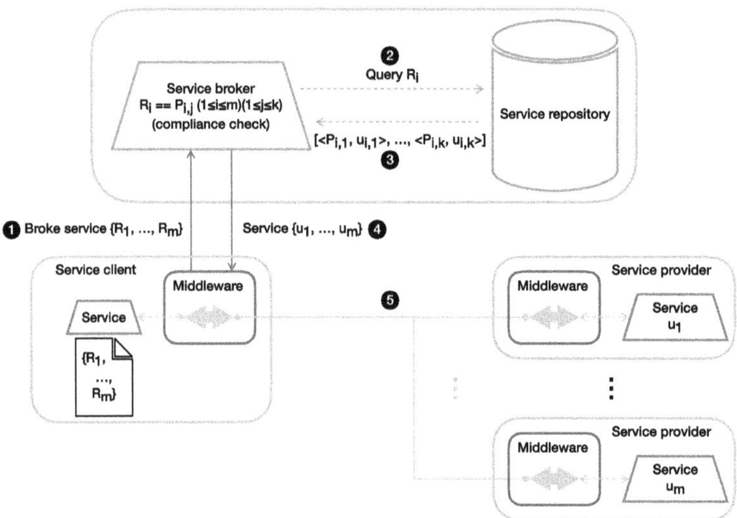

(b) Service brokering procedure

Fig. 1. Service management procedures in SEArch.

merged ports are "semantically compliant". The notion of compliance adopted is defined in terms of contracts formalised in terms of a bisimilarity relation between *extended Communicating Finite State Machines* (extended CFSM for short) [11], a variant of *communicating finite-state machines* [4] enabling the specification of functional and non-functional behaviour. We now describe our execution process.

When launched on a SEArch node, a service registers the extended CFSMs of its exposed requirement contracts on the local *middleware*, which will mediate the communication with other services. Basically, the middleware, intercepts the communications a local service attempts over a communication channel, establishes a communication session for that channel (in case the session does not yet exists), and triggers the dynamic reconfiguration sketched in Fig. 1 which we now describe:

❶ the middleware sends the service broker the contract $\{R_1, \ldots, R_m\}$ of the communication channel, consisting of one extended CFSM for each participant required by the service client;

❷ for each extended CFSM R_i in the contract, the service broker queries the service repository for candidates;

❸ the service repository returns a set of candidates[3] $\{\langle P_{i,1}, u_{i,1}\rangle, \ldots, \langle P_{i,k_i}, u_{i,k_i}\rangle\}$ where, for all $1 \leq j \leq k_i$, $P_{i,j}$ is an extended CFSM and $u_{i,j}$ is the URI of the service;

❹ the broker checks whether there is a provision contract $\langle P_{i,j}, u_{i,j}\rangle$, with $1 \leq j \leq k$, compatible with the requirement contract R_i, for all $1 \leq i \leq m$; this is done by resorting to a bisimilarity check; once the service broker has found services satisfying all the requirement contracts, it returns the set of URIs $\{u_1, \ldots, u_m\}$ to the middleware;

❺ finally, the middleware opens a communication with the middleware of each service returned by the provider requiring the execution of the corresponding service.

Once the composition is achieved, the middleware interacts with the middlewares of the partner services; and the execution process proceeds. Notice that during the execution new requirements might crop up; for instance, because some brokered services need further services.[4] This will initiate a new brokerage phase to discover the newly required services.

The schematic view discussed before establishes several requisites over the implementation of the middleware and the service broker which are omitted as inessential here; interested readers are referred to [14] for details.

3   Adaptability as a Programming Pattern

In a quest for a notion of adaptation, the authors of [5] advocate a conceptual framework grounded on a neat separation of concerns. Starting from the observation that the behaviour of a component is determined by a program defining *control* and manipulating *data*, adaptation requires to consider, and possibly, modify specific computational or physical resources. The conceptual framework in [5] envisages *adaptation* as the possibility of a component to manipulate and

---

[3] The query is resolved by filtering the extended CFSMs in the repository according to heuristics based on structure of R_i.

[4] This implies that a service may have one or more required-points associated to communication channels of its own.

take decisions according to a well-identified set of *control data*. For instance, an adaptive behaviour may need to account for memory usage, network traffic, or environmental physical conditions like e.g., temperature.

We render the conceptual framework in our platform as detailed in Sects. 3.1 and 3.2.

3.1   An Architecture for Runtime Adaptation

Embracing the conceptual framework introduced in [5] allows one to define adaptation as the property of a component of controlling and possibly modifying at run-time its behaviour based on a specific set of control data.

This acceptation implicitly requires a *monitor* that can collect and make available the control data necessary for enforcing adaptive behaviour. Noteworthy, the nature of control data impacts on the complexity of the monitoring activities. When control data are *exogenous*, namely they originate outside the application (e.g., from sensors, operating system, etc.), their usage in the adaption process can be simply attained by requesting the information to the monitor (e.g., with a request-response interaction). Otherwise, for *endogenous* control data, namely data produced by some components of the application, monitor and application are more coupled and their interactions can require the definition of specific application-level protocols.

Leveraging the API of SEArch, we propose a programming pattern to support the conceptual framework proposed in [5]. We focus on exogenous control data, leaving adaptation endogenous control data for future work.

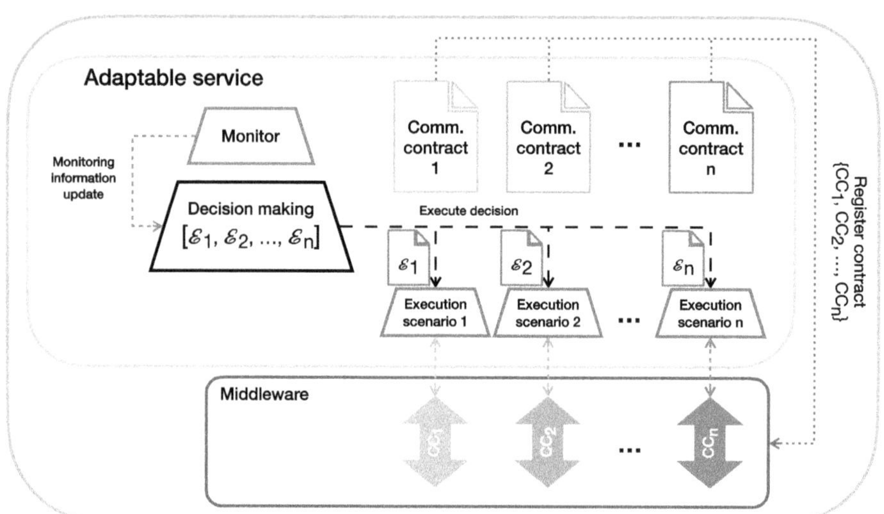

Fig. 2. Architectural view of our programming pattern for adaptation.

Figure 2 provides a high-level architectural view of an adaptable agent implemented over our platform; the two main elements of the architecture are the *adaptable service* itself and the local *middleware* (dark blue box) that sets up the communication infrastructure necessary for the dynamic composition of services. As shown, the adaptable service runs behind the middleware, which mediates the interactions of the services/applications in execution on a node with every other component in the network, including other middlewares and the service broker. The mediation basically connects (via the channels $CC_1, \cdots, CC_n$) the required ports of the adaptable service with the provided ports of brokered external components.

The structure of an adaptable service is rather complex and consists of:

- a collection of contracts (specified as extended CFSMs) corresponding to each of the execution scenarios ($\{$Communication contract i$\}_{1 \leq i \leq n}$ in the topmost part of the orange box, so that each Communication contract i corresponds to the middleware's channel CC_i; we also emphasise this correspondence with colours),
- a collection of implementations corresponding to each of the execution scenarios $\{$Execution scenario i$\}_{1 \leq i \leq n}$, each equipped with an *adaptation contract* $\mathcal{E}_i$ formalising the environmental conditions under which the execution scenario should be run (bottom-most part of the inner orange box), and
- a decision procedure that runs a control loop, which uses the control data received from the monitor to determine an appropriate execution scenario to run (leftmost part of the orange box).

We remark that each channel CC_i is used by the middleware to trigger the adaptation scenarios according to the Communication contract i. The details of the control loop and of the adaptation contracts of the execution scenarios are given in Sect. 3.2.

3.2   An Implementation of the Control Loop

As discussed above, taking inspiration from [5], we understand adaptability as the capacity of an agent to respond to changes in the environment. Thus, a significant aspect of our approach relies on the exogenous control data received from the monitor, and how the decision making process uses it to determine an appropriate execution scenario at runtime.

Our programming pattern relies on a fixed set $\mathcal{A}$ of (*quantitative*) *attributes* (ranged over by a) which store the exogenous control data.

Example 1. For the sake of our running example, we make the following assumptions:

- Local DB and WebUI run on the same node while the image provider Image provider runs on a different node (cf. Figure 4 and Fig. 5 in Sect. 4);
- adaptations are triggered depending on some constraints involving the attributes L (network latency), R (responsiveness of Image provider), and C (CPU load at the node of WebUI).

The adaptation contracts of our running examples will be constraints on these attributes. ◇

The programming pattern proposed here essentially hinges on SEArch features to instantiate communication channels used in the control loop to manage adaptation. More precisely,

- the invocation of a service triggers the registration of the n alternative communication channels in the middleware of the local node of the service,
- the control loop managing the runtime adaptations consists of iterating the following steps:
  a. acquire from the most recent control data from the monitor (cf. [5]) as an assignment of values to the attributes in $\mathcal{A}$;
  b. select a suitable execution scenario according to the control data provided by the monitor;
  c. trigger the execution of the code implementing the selected scenario;
  d. stop the running execution scenario if the updated control data determine that the current execution scenario is no longer admissible (i.e., the contract of the running scenario is invalidated by newly acquired control data) and repeat from step b.

The control loop sketched above is designed to select one of the possible execution scenarios according to the control data provided by the monitor. More precisely, the identification of a suitable scenario depends on the control data returned by the monitor, which we render as mappings $m : \mathcal{A} \to \mathfrak{R}$ that assign a real value to each attribute in $\mathcal{A}$. This design decision is supported by the framework introduced in [12,13] which guaranties the existence of a decision procedure for determining satisfiability of a class of constraints expressed in a first-order logic with equality whose formulae predicate on real values.[5] Hence, this framework enables the use of *Satisfiability Modulo Theories solvers* [2] (SMT solvers for short) such as Z3 [7], Yices [8], or CVC5 [1]. In fact, we formalise adaptation contracts as constraints on real values.

Example 2. We set the following conditions[6] on L, R, and C:

$$\mathcal{E}_1 = L < 5ms \quad \wedge \quad R < 1\,s$$
$$\mathcal{E}_2 = \neg\mathcal{E}_1 \quad \wedge \quad 0 \leq C \leq .9$$
$$\mathcal{E}_3 = \neg\mathcal{E}_1 \quad \wedge \quad C > .9$$

---

[5] The framework is based on *real closed fields* [15], a decidable first-order theory of the real numbers [15, Theorem 37]) to specify contracts on quantitative aspects of software artefacts. For the sake of this paper, it is enough to assume that contracts consist of decidable constraints; the interested reader is referred to [12,13] and references therein for details.

[6] The adaptation contracts in our running example are pretty basic, for simplicity. We remark that our platform can handle non-trivial constraints expressed as formulae of the decidable first-order logic over real closed fields.

The intuition behind these conditions is that the interaction between W and P is satisfactory when $\mathcal{E}_1$ holds otherwise an adaptation should take place. We conceive two adaptations when the remote interaction degrades; W retrieves the images through S when the local CPU is not overloaded ($\mathcal{E}_2$), otherwise a default image is displayed ($\mathcal{E}_3$). ◇

The dynamic selection of execution scenarios appeals to the use of SMT solvers to decide the satisfiability of the adaptation contracts associated to the execution scenarios. To tackle this issue, we equip our platform with the procedure expressed in Pythonic pseudo-code in Listing 1.1 which relies on threads and on the following assumptions on the execution scenarios (cf. lines 1-2 of Listing 1.1):

scenarios the functions implementing each execution scenario are collected in a module called ExcScenarios which also exports the list ES of such functions; for simplicity, we assume that these functions do not take parameters;

coordination the module ExcScenarios also exports a boolean variable done, shared with the control loop, and used to determine when the scenario has completed its execution;

termination each execution scenario is guaranteed to atomically set[7] done to True before returning and to terminate.

The control loop starts by setting[8] the done flag to False and entering the loop on line 6 which, until the done flag is not set:

a. chooses a scenario to run if none is running (lines 6–17) and
b. keeps checking if a running scenario should be stopped or it gracefully finished (lines 19–26).

To select the execution scenario, the control loop iterates over the list of function ES and stops as soon as it finds a function whose adaptation contract is true. This is checked by querying an SMT solver whether the negation of $\mathcal{E}_i[a \mapsto \mathsf{m}(a)]_{a \in \mathcal{A}}$ is satisfiable or not;[9]

– gets the control data from the monitor (line 11; assume that monitor_update takes care of communicating with the monitor and returning the mapping to the control loop),
– if the adaptation contract $\mathcal{E}_i$ is violated (namely its negation is satisfiable) under the returned control data, then the scenario cannot be chosen,
– otherwise, the scenario is chosen and a thread running the associated implementation is started (lines 14–15) and the execution continues on line 19.
– the loop on lines 19–26 keeps checking that the adaptation contract of the running scenario is still valid; if the contract gets violated, the scenario is terminated (line 26).

---

[7] We use the syntax $\langle \ldots \rangle$ to mark critical sections.

[8] Notice that there is no need to make an atomic assignment since the control loop has not spawned any other thread yet.

[9] As usual, $\mathcal{E}[a \mapsto v_a]_{a \in \mathcal{A}}$ denotes the application to the formula $\mathcal{E}$ of the substitution $[a \mapsto v_a]_{a \in \mathcal{A}}$ which maps each attribute $a \in \mathcal{A}$ to a value v_a.

```python
from  threading  import  Thread
from  ExcScenarios  import  ES,  done

done = False

while ⟨ not done ⟩ :                                  # atomic access
   stop,  scenario = False,  None
   i = 0
   while scenario == None:
      # get monitored data
      m = monitor_update()
      if not SMT(not $\mathcal{E}_i[a \mapsto m(a)]_{a \in \mathcal{A}}$) == SAT:
         # spawn the chosen scenario ES[i]
         scenario = Thread(target = ES[i])
         scenario.start()
      else:
         i = (i + 1) mod len(ES)

   while not (done or stop):
      old_m = m
      # get monitored data
      m = monitor_update()
      if not old_m == m:
         stop = SMT(not $\mathcal{E}_i[a \mapsto m(a)]_{a \in \mathcal{A}}$) == SAT
      if stop:
         scenario.terminate()
```

Listing 1.1. Pythonic pseudo-code implementing the control loop.

For simplicity, the thread running the execution scenario is terminated; we indeed opted for a lighter presentation instead of devising a more general mechanism to coordinate the thread and the control loop for a graceful termination (where e.g., the thread restores some application-dependent invariants before terminating) at the cost of complicating the presentation.

4   The Adaptable TeaStore in SEArch

We now apply the programming pattern presented in Sect. 3 to our running example and detail how the control loop of Listing 1.1 manages the reconfigurations specified by the policies established with the adaptation contracts in Example 2.

4.1   Deploying Our Running Example

Our control loop can be thought as a scheme for a "combinator" that allows to build adaptable services from other services. One such a combinator is provided, the execution of an adaptable service would be as follows:

1. the communication with the local middleware is established and the communication contracts are registered in the middleware;
2. the service is connected to the communication channels created by the middleware for its execution scenarios and the decision making procedure executing our control loop is spawned;
3. the decisions making procedure requests the monitor for an update on the adaptation data and chooses the first adaptation contract satisfied by it (lines 6–17 of Listing 1.1).

While the selected execution scenario runs, the control loop continues by checking if an update of the control data violates the adaptation contract of the running execution scenario. If such a violation occurs, the running execution scenario is terminated and the decision making procedure repeats step 3 above in order to adapt the runtime behaviour of the adaptable service to the new environmental conditions.

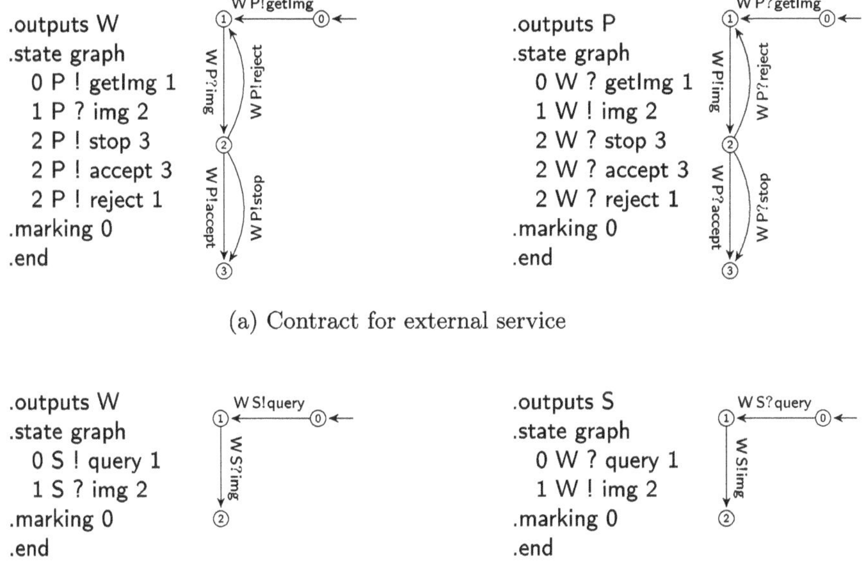

(a) Contract for external service

(b) Contract for the fallback scenario with the storage service

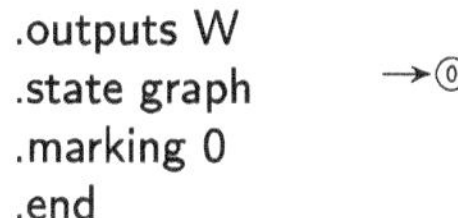

(c) Contract for the use of default locally stored images

Fig. 3. Contracts for the scenario-based adaptable TeaStore.

We instantiate the procedure above to deploy an adaptable service WebUI of our running example using the communication contracts in Fig. 3, which yields both the textual format of CFSMs (which SEArch borrows from [6]) and their usual graphical notation where initial states are marked by an incoming arrow with no source state and transitions are labelled with send or receive actions (e.g., W S!query represents the sending of message query done by W to S and W S?query is the dual receive action).

We start by observing that the communication contract corresponding to $\mathcal{E}_3$ in Fig. 3c consists just of a CFSM with a single state and no transitions since the adaptation does not involve any interactions (e.g., the default image can be read from a file on a local hard drive). The contract involving the persistent service (Fig. 3b) consists of the CFSM S used to query the broker for a storage service that can respond to a query from WebUI by sending an image. The CFSM W in (Fig. 3b) specifies the behaviour of WebUI in this scenario. Likewise, the CFSM W in Fig. 3a specifies how WebUI interacts with an external image provider queried to the broker using the CFSM P which features a more complex protocol to allow WebUI to repeatedly ask for images when those provided by the external service are not suitable, or to stop the interaction with P.

The architectural view of the scenario involving the external image provider is depicted in Fig. 4.

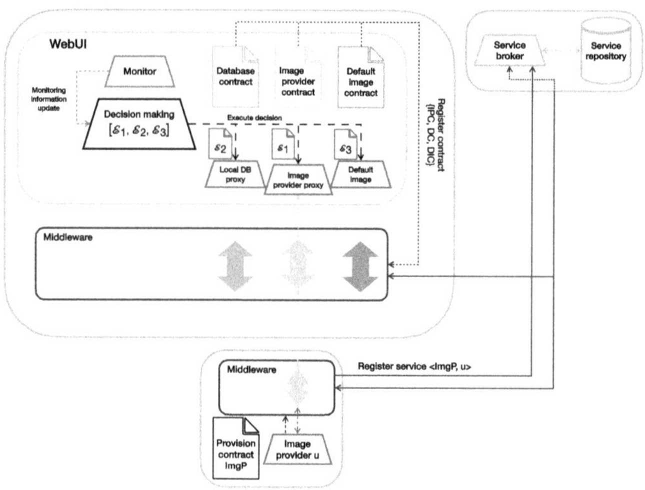

Fig. 4. Architectural view for the external service scenario.

This view casts the architecture in Fig. 2 for the running example. More precisely, the :

1. registers the , used by the local process Image provider proxy to communicate with an external image provider service (see Fig. 3a), the Database contract, used by the local process Local DB proxy to communicate with a locally hosted database service (see Fig. 3b), and Default image contract, used by the local process Default image[10] (see Fig. 3c), in the Middleware
2. initiates the execution of the Monitor, and
3. spawns the decision making procedure executing the control loop, which asks the monitor for the first update and chooses one of the execution scenarios accordingly.

Let us now consider how the architecture can possibly evolve at runtime when control data changes.

4.2   No Degradation of the Interaction with the Image Provider

As long as runtime changes of control data do not invalidate the adaptation contract $\mathcal{E}_1$, the architecture stays as in Fig. 4; in fact,

Step 1 the Monitor responds to monitor_update() with $\{L \mapsto 4.7, R \mapsto 0.6, C \mapsto 0.54\}$ (line 11);

Step 2 not $\mathcal{E}_1[L \mapsto 4.7, R \mapsto 0.6, C \mapsto 0.54]$ is not SAT (i.e., UNSAT) thus, the control loop creates a thread for executing the local process Image provider proxy, connected to its associated communication channel generated from the contract (lines 12–15), yielding the architecture in Fig. 4;

Step 3 in this thread, the local process Image provider proxy implements the communication pattern of the CFSM W in the contract of Fig. 3a; in particular, it starts by sending the message getImg thus triggering the brokering process in the Service broker (see Fig. 1b and the corresponding reference)

Step 4 the external service (executing the process Image provider) is bound to the application and, since it implements a communication pattern compliant to the CFSM P in Fig. 3a, it receives the request and returns an image to the caller by sending a message img;

Step 5 as the thread executing the local process Image provider proxy has not set the shared variable done and there is no instruction to stop the execution through the variable stop, the invocation to monitor_update() obtains an update of the control data (line 22) from the Monitor.

---

[10] Recall that this contract yields a communication channel whose behaviour reflects that no communication will take place.

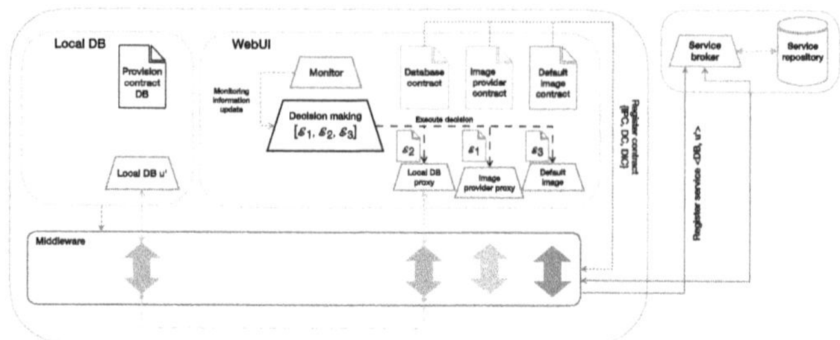

Fig. 5. Reconfiguration according to adaptation contract $\mathcal{E}_2$ upon violation of $\mathcal{E}_1$.

We now consider cases where the environmental conditions violate the adaptation contract $\mathcal{E}_1$ of the running execution scenario.

4.3   Degradation of the Interaction with the Image Provider

In our running example, a degradation of the interaction between WebUI (more specifically, the local process Image provide proxy) and the external service Image provider requires a reconfiguration when the latency (L) or the responsiveness (R) becomes too high. Let us assume that the external image provider service becomes unresponsive, the other case is similar.

Step 6 while the local process Image provide proxy interacts with the service Image provider through the communication channel generated from the Image provider contract, the Monitor responds to monitor_update() with $\{L \mapsto 5.3, R \mapsto 0.7, C \mapsto 0.51\}$ (line 22);

Step 7 the control loop accounts for the change in m and, as not $\mathcal{E}_1[L \mapsto 5.3, R \mapsto 0.7, C \mapsto 0.51]$ now is SAT because $L \geq 5ms$, terminates the thread executing the local process Image provider proxy using terminate() and returns to the code fragment that performs the selection of an appropriate execution scenario (lines 9–17);

Step 8 not $\mathcal{E}_2[L \mapsto 5.3, R \mapsto 0.7, C \mapsto 0.51]$ is not SAT thus, the control loop creates a thread for executing the local process Local DB proxy, connected to its associated communication channel generated from the contract Database contract (lines 12-15), yielding the architecture in Fig. 5;

Step 9 in this thread, the local process Local DB proxy implements the communication pattern of the CFSM W in the contract of Fig. 3b; in particular, it starts by sending the message query thus triggering the brokering process in the Service broker but fixing the local service Local DB as the provider;

Step 10 the service Local DB (executing the process Local DB) is bound to the application and, since it implements a communication pattern compliant to the CFSM S in Fig. 3b, it receives the request and returns an image to the caller by sending a message img.

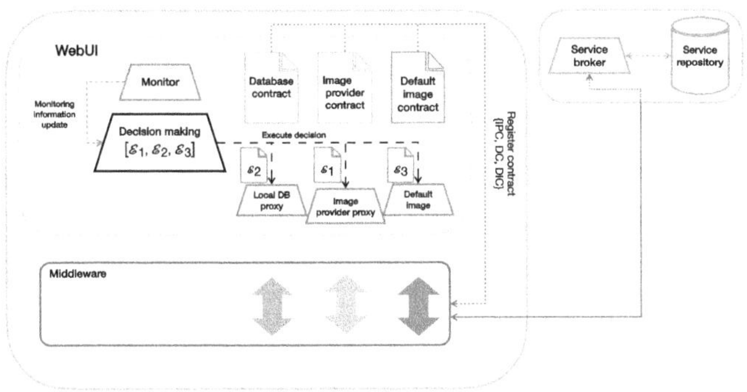

Fig. 6. Reconfiguration according to adaptation contract $\mathcal{E}_3$ upon violation of $\mathcal{E}_2$.

4.4   Local Node Overloaded

According to our adaptation contracts, the execution shown in Sect. 4.3 requires a reconfiguration when the CPU gets overloaded. Our control loop will therefore terminate the thread running the process Local DB proxy.

Step 11 while the local process Local DB proxy interacts with the service through the communication channel generated from the contract Database contract, the Monitor responds to the invocation of monitor_update() with $\{L \mapsto 6.2, R \mapsto 0.4, C \mapsto 0.92\}$ (line 22);

Step 12 the control loop accounts for the change in m and, as not $\mathcal{E}_2[L \mapsto 6.2, R \mapsto 0.4, C \mapsto 0.92]$ now is SAT because $C \geq 0.9$, terminates the thread executing the local process Local DB proxy using terminate() and returns to the code fragment that performs the selection of an appropriate execution scenario (lines 9–17);

Step 13 not $\mathcal{E}_3[L \mapsto 6.2, R \mapsto 0.4, C \mapsto 0.92]$ is not SAT thus, the control loop creates a thread for executing the local process Default image, yielding the architecture in Fig. 6 (lines 12–15);

Step 14 the execution continues according to the behaviour of the local process Default image. This process is implemented satisfying Default image contract so no communication takes place over the generated communication channel, consequently, the task of finding an image is performed resorting only to resources that are locally accessible by the local process Default image.

5   Conclusions

In this paper we advocate a programming pattern for adaptations that possibly reconfigure the architecture of service-oriented applications. Our pattern is supported by SEArch, a platform featuring semantic-based dynamic discovery and binding of services. We identified some reconfigurations policies on the adaptable TeaStore benchmark to demonstrate our approach; in particular, our policies fit with the scenarios in [3, Sections 3.2.3 and 3.2.4]. This benchmark includes other scenarios that we did not consider here; however, we argue that our approach is general enough to express the other scenarios specified in [3] since the architectural reconfigurations they encompass depend only on exogenous control data.

As recalled in Sect. 2, SEArch contracts are formalised in terms of extended CFSMs. This allows us to specify contracts concerning application-level (non-)functional requirements. For instance, the quality of the image hinted in our running example could be modelled as a quantitative attribute, say Q. As mentioned in Sect. 3 we assume that control data are exogenous. This implies that they cannot include application-level information; for instance, Q cannot be used in the control loop to trigger an adaptation when the image provided is sub-optimal (in fact, our solution in Sect. 4 handles this in the application contract of Fig. 3a and not in adaptation contracts). Overcoming this limitation requires the introduction of mechanisms to specify the interactions among the monitor and the execution scenarios. This can be readily supported in SEArch since the monitor can be conceived as a service local to a node whose behaviour is specified by a suitable extended CFSM. Even further, our platform could also support monitors as outsourced services that could be dynamically discovered and used by other services once suitable behavioural contracts are established for their usage. These generalisations are in scope of future work.

Our programming pattern hinges on the control loop presented in Sect. 3 that, liaising with a monitor that observes control data, decides if a run-time architectural reconfiguration is necessary and triggers the application-dependent activities provided by the developer. One could simplify this architecture by embedding the control loop in the monitor. We opted for a solution with two separated components because it yields more flexibility and can be extended more easily. For instance, the generalisation to endogenous control data can be attained more straightforwardly in our solution that in one where control loop and monitor are entangled.

Our control loop can –at an abstract level– be envisaged as "combinator" that composes the application-dependent functions (the adaptation scenarios) necessary for reconfigurations. In this paper, we adopted a rather simplistic mechanism for the composition of these functions. Depending on the nature of the reconfigurations required by an application, it could be necessary to appeal to more sophisticated composition mechanisms. For instance, it could be necessary that the control loop passes some data when invoking the adaptation scenario. This can be supported by our platform at the cost of more complex interactions between the control loop and execution scenarios.

Finally, we recall that, for simplicity, the running adaptation scenario is abruptly terminated when a reconfiguration is triggered (line 26 in Listing 1.1). This may not be desirable; we plan to develop mechanisms for guaranteeing graceful termination in future work.

Acknowledgements. We thank reviewers for their thorough reports and their suggestions that helped us to improve the paper.

References

1. Barbosa, H., et al.: cvc5: a versatile and industrial-strength SMT solver. In: TACAS 2022. LNCS, vol. 13243, pp. 415–442. Springer, Cham (2022). https://doi.org/10.1007/978-3-030-99524-9_24
2. Biere, A., Heule, M., Van Maaren, H., Walsh, T. (eds.): Handbook of Satisfiability: Second Edition, Frontiers in Artificial Intelligence and Applications, vol. 336. IOS Press (2021)
3. Bliudze, S., de Palma, G., Giallorenzo, S., Lanese, I., Zavattaro, G., Ndadji, B.A.Z.: Adaptable TeaStore. On-line (2024). https://arxiv.org/abs/2412.16060
4. Brand, D., Zafiropulo, P.: On communicating finite-state machines. J. ACM **30**(2), 323–342 (1983)
5. Bruni, R., Corradini, A., Gadducci, F., Lluch Lafuente, A., Vandin, A.: A conceptual framework for adaptation. In: de Lara, J., Zisman, A. (eds.) FASE 2012. LNCS, vol. 7212, pp. 240–254. Springer, Heidelberg (2012). https://doi.org/10.1007/978-3-642-28872-2_17
6. Coto, A., Guanciale, R., Lange, J., Tuosto, E.: ChorGram: tool support for choreographic development (2015). https://bitbucket.org/eMgssi/chorgram/src/master/
7. de Moura, L., Bjørner, N.: Z3: an efficient SMT solver. In: Ramakrishnan, C.R., Rehof, J. (eds.) TACAS 2008. LNCS, vol. 4963, pp. 337–340. Springer, Heidelberg (2008). https://doi.org/10.1007/978-3-540-78800-3_24
8. Dutertre, B.: Yices 2.2. In: Biere, A., Bloem, R. (eds.) CAV 2014. LNCS, vol. 8559, pp. 737–744. Springer, Cham (2014). https://doi.org/10.1007/978-3-319-08867-9_49
9. Fiadeiro, J.L., Lopes, A.: An interface theory for service-oriented design. Theoret. Comput. Sci. **503**, 1–30 (2013)
10. von Kistowski, J., Eismann, S., Schmitt, N., Bauer, A., Grohmann, J., Kounev, S.: Teastore: a micro-service reference application for benchmarking, modeling and resource management research. In: 26th IEEE International Symposium on Modeling, Analysis, and Simulation of Computer and Telecommunication Systems (MASCOTS 2018), pp. 223–236. IEEE Computer Society (2018)
11. Lopez Pombo, C.G., Martinez Suñé, A.E., Melgratti, H.C., Senarruzza Anabia, D.N., Tuosto, E.: Behavioural, functional, and non-functional contracts for dynamic selection of services. In: Giusto, C.D., Ravara, A. (eds.) COORDINATION 2025. LNCS, vol. 15731, pp. 153–174. Springer, Cham (2025). https://doi.org/10.1007/978-3-031-95589-1_8
12. Lopez Pombo, C.G., Martinez Suñé, A.E., Tuosto, E.: A dynamic temporal logic for quality of service in choreographic models. In: Ábrahám, E., Dubslaff, C., Tarifa, S.L.T. (eds.) ICTAC 2023. LNCS, vol. 14446, pp. 119–138. Springer, Cham (2023). https://doi.org/10.1007/978-3-031-47963-2_9
13. Lopez Pombo, C.G., Martinez Suñé, A.E., Tuosto, E.: A dynamic temporal logic for quality of service in choreographic models. Theoret. Comput. Sci. **1043**, 115247 (2025)
14. Lopez Pombo, C.G., Montepagano, P., Tuosto, E.: SEArch: an execution infrastructure for service-based software systems. In: Castellani, I., Tiezzi, F. (eds.) COORDINATION 2024. LNCS, vol. 14676, pp. 314–330. Springer, Cham (2024). https://doi.org/10.1007/978-3-031-62697-5_17
15. Tarski, A.: A Decision Method for Elementary Algebra and Geometry. University of California Press (1951)

PHYELDS: A Pythonic Framework for Aggregate Computing

Gianluca Aguzzi, Davide Domini[✉], Nicolas Farabegoli, and Mirko Viroli

University of Bologna, Bologna, Italy
{gianluca.aguzzi,davide.domini,nicolas.farabegoli,
mirko.viroli}@unibo.it

Abstract. Aggregate programming is a field-based coordination paradigm with over a decade of exploration and successful applications across domains including sensor networks, robotics, and IoT, with implementations in various programming languages, such as Protelis, ScaFi (Scala), and FCPP (C++). A recent research direction integrates machine learning with aggregate computing, aiming to support large-scale distributed learning and provide new abstractions for implementing learning algorithms. However, existing implementations do not target data science practitioners, who predominantly work in Python—the de facto language for data science and machine learning, with a rich and mature ecosystem. Python also offers advantages for other use cases, such as education and robotics (e.g., via ROS). To address this gap, we present PHYELDS, a Python library for aggregate programming. PHYELDS offers a fully featured yet lightweight implementation of the field calculus model of computation, featuring a Pythonic API and an architecture designed for seamless integration with Python's machine learning ecosystem. We describe the design and implementation of PHYELDS and illustrate its versatility across domains, from well-known aggregate computing patterns to federated learning coordination and integration with a widely used multi-agent reinforcement learning simulator.

Keywords: Aggregate programming · Distributed machine learning · Field-based coordination

1 Introduction

The proliferation of distributed computing systems—from sensor networks and IoT infrastructures to robotic swarms and edge-cloud continua—has created an urgent need for programming abstractions that can effectively manage collective behavior at scale [12]. Traditional approaches to distributed system development focus on individual devices, requiring programmers to manually orchestrate communication, synchronization, and coordination among potentially thousands of heterogeneous nodes. This device-centric perspective becomes increasingly

© IFIP International Federation for Information Processing 2026
Published by Springer Nature Switzerland AG 2026
R. Casadei and F. Ghassemi (Eds.): COORDINATION 2026, LNCS 16590, pp. 176–193, 2026.
https://doi.org/10.1007/978-3-032-28358-0_9

untenable as systems grow in scale and complexity, motivating the emergence of *macroprogramming* paradigms [13] that shift the focus from individual devices to the collective behavior of the system as a whole.

Among macroprogramming approaches, aggregate programming [10] has gained significant attention due to its principled foundation in the *field calculus* [8]—a minimal functional language that models computation as the manipulation of *computational fields*, where values are distributed across space and evolve over time. Application domains span sensor networks, swarm robotics, smart cities, and IoT systems, where the ability to reason about global behavior while ensuring local execution is paramount.

A promising research direction integrates aggregate programming with machine learning [4]. This synergy is bidirectional: aggregate programming facilitates scalable distributed learning—e.g., in federated learning and multi-agent reinforcement learning [5,19,21]—while machine learning enables data-driven adaptation within aggregate programs [3]. However, realizing this potential faces a significant practical barrier: existing implementations of aggregate programming—such as Protelis [33], ScaFi [15], and FCPP [7]—target languages (Java, Scala, and C++, respectively) that are not commonly used by machine learning practitioners. Python has become the *de facto* standard for data science and machine learning, boasting a rich ecosystem of libraries including TensorFlow [1], PyTorch [30], and scikit-learn [31]. The absence of a Python-based aggregate programming framework thus hinders the adoption of this paradigm in machine learning contexts and limits the potential for cross-pollination between these research communities.

To bridge this gap, we present PHYELDS[1], a lightweight and Pythonic library for aggregate programming. PHYELDS delivers a compact but comprehensive implementation of the field calculus, offering an API that embraces Python's idioms and conventions. Unlike its functional predecessors, PHYELDS adopts an imperative and object-oriented programming style that is more familiar to the majority of Python developers, lowering the barrier to entry for newcomers to aggregate programming. The framework is designed with seamless integration in mind, providing bindings for popular machine learning libraries such as TensorFlow and PyTorch, as well as multi-agent reinforcement learning environments like VMAS [11]. We demonstrate its applicability through well-known aggregate computing patterns, self-organizing federated learning [17,20,21], and multi-agent reinforcement learning via integration with the VMAS simulator [11], where aggregate programming abstractions are leveraged to coordinate collective agent behavior.

Beyond machine learning, bringing aggregate programming into the Python ecosystem opens opportunities in other Python-dominated domains. In **education**, Python's gentle learning curve makes it an ideal vehicle for introducing students to collective programming concepts. In **robotics**, integration with ROS (Robot Operating System) [24] enables the deployment of aggregate programs on physical robot swarms.

---

[1] https://github.com/phyelds/phyelds.

The remainder of this paper is structured as follows. Section 2 provides a brief overview of aggregate programming, covering the system model (Sect. 2.1), the field calculus operators (Sect. 2.2), and the alignment mechanism (Sect. 2.3). Section 3 presents the design and implementation of PHYELDS. Section 4 illustrates the library through concrete examples, including common aggregate computing patterns, self-organizing federated learning, and integration with the VMAS multi-agent reinforcement learning simulator. Finally, Sect. 5 concludes with directions for future work.

2   Aggregate Programming A Brief Overview

Aggregate computing (AC) [10] is a macroprogramming paradigm for the development of distributed systems, where the focus is on the collective behavior of a system of devices, rather than on the individual behavior of each device. Starting from natural inspiration, the computation is expressed as a manipulation over *computational fields*, where the value of a field at a given point in space and time represents the state of the device located there. The field calculus [10] is a minimal functional language that captures the essence of aggregate programming, providing a formal model for reasoning about field computations.

2.1   System Model

Typically, an aggregate computing system consists of a collection of devices, each equipped with local computation capabilities, sensors for perceiving the environment, and communication interfaces for exchanging information with neighboring devices. Each device is connected to a subset of other devices, forming a dynamic and potentially unreliable network topology. The communication model is typically based on message passing, where devices can send and receive messages asynchronously to and from their neighbors.

Each device executes the same aggregate program, which can be conceptually viewed as a function that takes the device's local state and the values received from neighbors as input, and produces an output value that represents the device's contribution to the global computation. Specifically, each device organizes its execution into discrete rounds, where in each round it performs the following steps (Fig. 1):

1. **Sense**: the device collects the neighbors' messages, reads its sensors, and gathers the previous local state;
2. **Compute**: the device executes the aggregate program using the collected information, producing a new local state and an output value;
3. **Interact**: the device sends the output value to its neighbors, and stores the new local state for the next round.

The rounds are not globally synchronized, and they typically proceed asynchronously across devices. This execution model is resilient to topology changes, communication and device failures, relying on an eventual behavior, which is the foundational property of self-stabilization.

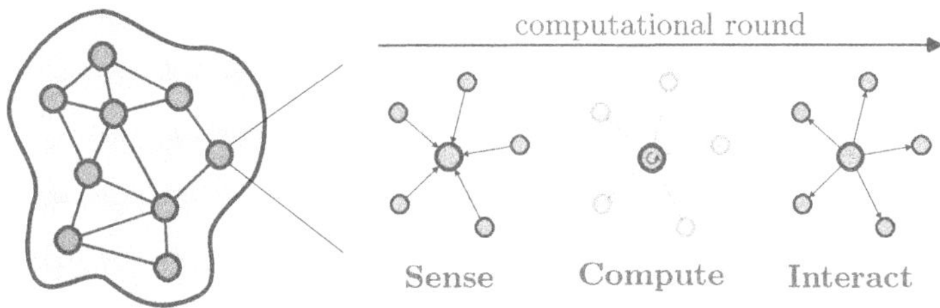

Fig. 1. Graphical representation of the aggregate computing system model.

2.2   Field Calculus Operators

The field calculus provides a small set of core operators that enable the expression of complex distributed computations in a concise and composable manner. In what follows, we briefly describe the main operators of the field calculus.

On top of these core operators, a rich library of higher-level constructs can be built, including gradient computation, information spreading and collection, gossip protocols, and leader election algorithms.

2.3   Alignment Mechanisms

The alignment is a fundamental aspect of aggregate programming, ensuring that devices evaluating the same program are considered (aligned) and can correctly exchange information. We refer to *aligned devices* as those that satisfy the following two conditions: (i) the devices are executing the exact same program; (ii) the produced output (i.e., the value tree) resulting from the execution, reflects the same sequence of function calls and operator applications.

Any violation of these conditions results in *misalignment*, where the devices are not considered part of the same computation.

When an aggregate program is executed, two devices may be aligned for some parts of the program and misaligned for others. Consider a program where an `if` operation is used. Based on the boolean condition evaluated at runtime, some devices may execute the `then` branch, while others execute the `else` branch. This divergence at runtime leads to *intended* misalignment, where on the two branches, only a subset of devices is aligned with each other. Once the execution of the branches is completed, all the devices will realign as they will converge to the same program point again. The reconciliation of the devices is because of the assumption that all the devices execute the same program, and thus they will eventually converge to the same program point again, despite the divergence at runtime.

In practice, the alignment mechanism is implemented by associating a unique identifier to each aggregate operator which requires either a stateful operation (e.g., `rep`), a neighbor interaction (e.g., `nbr`) or a network partitioning (e.g., `if`).

3   The Phyelds Library

PHYELDS was conceived with three key design goals. First, we provide an **API** that is idiomatic to Python, embracing its object-oriented and imperative programming style to lower the barrier to entry for developers. First, existing frameworks are predominantly based on functional languages and adopting an imperative style is crucial to make aggregate programming accessible to the majority of Python users. Second, the library relies on a **lightweight and modular architecture** designed for applicability across diverse contexts, ranging from small-scale simulations and machine learning applications to deployment on physical devices. To support this versatility, users can selectively incorporate only the components relevant to their specific use case. Third, we ensure **integration with the Python ecosystem** by providing a simple execution framework for verifying the behavior of implemented blocks. Additionally, we provide bindings to popular machine learning libraries, multi-agent reinforcement learning environments, and robotics frameworks.

With these goals in mind, the architecture of PHYELDS is structured into distinct modules, each responsible for a specific aspect of the aggregate programming model. Namely, it comprises five principal components (Fig. 2): the VM, the `Data`, the `Calculus`, the `Library`, and the `Simulator` modules.

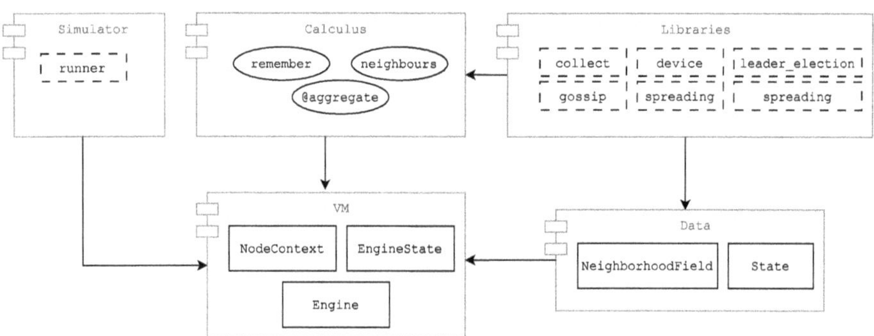

Fig. 2. Architecture of PHYELDS. Modules (components) contain classes (rectangles), submodules (dashed borders), and functions (ovals). Arrows indicate dependencies.

VM Module. The VM module governs the execution of aggregate programs. It provides the low-level APIs required to track device states, manage function calls for the alignment mechanism, and maintain execution contexts. Specifically, this module handles gathering messages from neighbors, persisting device state across rounds, and orchestrating the execution of field calculus operators. The principal classes in this module are **Engine**, **NodeContext**, and **EngineState**. The **Engine** class embodies the core logic of the virtual machine and serves as the interface between the VM and the rest of the library. To use the engine, it must be initialized with messages received from neighbors, the previous state, the device identifier, and the device context (encapsulating time, sensor readings, and other contextual data). Subsequently, the aggregate program is executed, leveraging this information to perform computations and generate a new state alongside messages for neighboring devices. Finally, the engine is reset to prepare for the next round. The typical usage pattern is illustrated in Listing 1.1:

```python
from phyelds import engine
from phyelds.vm import Engine
# 1. Setup: initialize the engine with the current context
engine.get().setup(
    node_context=node_ctx,
    messages=received_messages,
    state=previous_state
)
# 2. Execute the aggregate program
result = my_aggregate_program()
# 3. Cooldown: reset engine and retrieve messages to send
new_state, messages_to_send = engine.get().cooldown()
```

Listing 1.1. Engine usage pattern.

Data Module. The Data module contains the fundamental data structures representing computational fields. The two principal components are the `State` and `NeighborhoodField` classes. The `State` class maintains a device's state across rounds, corresponding to the **rep** construct in traditional field calculus. Implemented as a proxy object, it allows manipulation as a standard Python object. Additionally, the `State` class stores the usage path to ensure the alignment mechanism functions correctly. The `NeighborhoodField` class represents values received from neighboring devices, corresponding to the **nbr** construct. Although internally implemented as a dictionary mapping device identifiers to values, this detail is abstracted from the user, who interacts with it as a standard Python object. The class supports operations such as element addition, arithmetic operations between neighboring fields, and field merging. Instead of exposing an ad-hoc `foldhood` operator, aggregation over neighbors is achieved through standard Python constructs such as list comprehensions and built-in functions like `sum` or `max`.

Calculus Module. The Calculus module provides the primary API for writing aggregate programs, encompassing the core operators and constructs of the field calculus. The central element is the `@aggregate` decorator, which transforms a standard Python function into one executable within an aggregate context. Annotated functions undergo a transformation as illustrated in Listing 1.2:

```python
def aggregate(func):
    def wrapper(*args, **kwargs):
        # Enter the execution context
        engine.get().enter(func.__name__)
        # Apply code transformations if necessary
        result = transform_code(func)(*args, **kwargs)
        # Exit the execution context
        engine.get().exit()
        return result
    return wrapper
```

```
11  # User-defined aggregate program
12  @aggregate
13  def my_program(sensors):
14      return sensors["temperature"] + 1
```

Listing 1.2. Transformation of an `@aggregate` function.

The `transform_code` function is responsible for managing alignment. Under the hood, it parses the function's source code into an Abstract Syntax Tree (AST) and applies a node transformer to intercept `if` statements. To ensure the engine can track and match execution paths across devices, the transformer rewrites the code by wrapping the `if` and `else` bodies within explicit `align_left()` and `align_right()` context managers. Listing1.3 shows an example of how this transformation is applied.

```
1   # Original user code
2   if condition:
3       do_something()
4   else:
5       do_other()
6   # Transformed code executed by the engine
7   if condition:
8       with align_left():
9           do_something()
10  else:
11      with align_right():
12          do_other()
```

Listing 1.3. Example of code transformation for conditionals.

The `engine` object is a globally accessible instance containing the current VM. It is initialized prior to program execution and reset after each round. To support parallel execution (e.g., in simulation contexts), this object is defined as a context variable (Listing 1.4):

```
1   from contextvars import ContextVar
2   from phyelds.vm import Engine
3   engine: ContextVar[Engine] = ContextVar("engine")
```

Listing 1.4. Engine as a context variable.

The other two fundamental operators are `remember` and `neighbors`, which implement the `rep` and `nbr` constructs of the field calculus. The `remember` operator maintains state across rounds. In standard field calculus, `rep` is a functional operator that takes an initial value and an update function:

```
1   rep(0) { (value) => value + 1 }
```

While this style is native to functional languages, it is often less familiar to Python developers. Therefore, inspired by React's state management, calling `remember` returns a tuple containing a setter function and the current value, clearly separating state updates from value access:

```
1   set_value, value = remember(0)
2   set_value(value + 1)   # Imperative state update
```

Listing 1.5. Using the `remember` construct.

The `neighbors` construct facilitates interaction with neighboring devices. It takes a value, transmits it to neighbors, and returns the values received from neighbors as a `NeighborhoodField`:

```
nbr_values = neighbors(my_value)  # Returns NeighborhoodField
```

Listing 1.6. Using the `neighbors` construct.

When the argument of the `neighbors` function is a `State` object, transmission occurs lazily: the `State` value is only sent if it has changed since the previous round, enabling efficient tracking of state updates.

Library Module. The Library module builds upon the Calculus module, providing a collection of higher-level constructs and building blocks for common aggregate programming patterns. These blocks implement well-established algorithms from aggregate programming literature, enabling developers to compose complex distributed behaviors from reusable components.

The module is organized into several sub-modules, each addressing a specific aspect of aggregate computation. The `device` sub-module accesses device-specific information such as the local identifier (`local_id`), spatial coordinates (`local_position`), and sensor readings (`sense`). The `time` sub-module offers temporal primitives including current simulation time, a round counter, and decay functions for time-dependent behaviors. The `distances` sub-module computes inter-device distances using either Euclidean metrics based on positions or hop-count metrics for topology-based reasoning. The `spreading` sub-module implements information dissemination patterns. Its core function, `distance_to`, computes a gradient (potential field) emanating from designated source nodes. This serves as the foundation for higher-level operations such as `broadcast`, which propagates data outward from sources, and `cast_from`, which applies accumulation functions along the propagation path. Complementing spreading, the `collect` sub-module implements convergecast patterns that aggregate information toward source nodes along gradient paths. The `find_parent` function establishes parent-child relationships based on potential values, while `collect_with` enables flexible aggregation using user-defined accumulation functions. Specialized variants include `count_nodes` for counting devices in sub-regions and `sum_values` for numeric aggregation. The `gossip` sub-module provides epidemic-style communication protocols for network-wide information sharing. The generic `gossip` function spreads values across the network using a user-specified combination operator, with convenience functions `gossip_max` and `gossip_min` for computing global extrema. A self-stabilizing variant, `stabilizing_gossip`, bounds propagation by the network diameter to ensure convergence. Finally, the `leader_election` module implements a well-known self-stabilizing algorithm [29] via the `elect_leaders` function, using random identifiers to break symmetry. It ensures that every device is within a specified distance d from exactly one leader, creating a stable Voronoi partition that converges regardless of the initial state. More details on the algorithm can be found in the original paper [29] and in further extensions [27,28].

These building blocks can be composed to implement complex distributed algorithms. For instance, combining leader election with gradient computation and collection enables hierarchical data aggregation systems where elected leaders collect and summarize sensor readings from their respective regions. Detailed usage examples are provided in Sect. 4.

Simulator Module. The Simulator module provides a framework for testing and debugging aggregate programs in a controlled environment. It enables users to create virtual networks of devices, define their communication, and observe program execution over multiple rounds.

The module is built around three core abstractions. The `Node` class represents an individual device characterized by a unique identifier, spatial position, and arbitrary sensor data. The `Environment` class manages the collection of nodes and, crucially, determines the neighborhood topology via a configurable neighborhood function. The `Simulator` class orchestrates execution using a discrete-event model, maintaining an event queue that schedules program execution across nodes. Neighborhood definition is a key aspect of the simulator design. Rather than hard-coding a specific topology, the module provides pluggable neighborhood functions to determine which nodes can communicate. Built-in options include `radius_neighborhood` (nodes within a specified Euclidean distance), `k_nearest_neighbors` (each node connects to its k closest peers), and `full_neighborhood` (fully connected network). Users can also define custom neighborhood functions to model arbitrary communication patterns or dynamic topologies. The module also provides deployment utilities for generating common spatial distributions, including regular grid layouts (`grid_generation`), perturbed lattices (`deformed_lattice`) for more realistic deployments, and random distributions within circular regions (`random_in_circle`). For observability, the simulator supports `Monitor` objects attached to the simulation. Monitors receive callbacks at the start, after each event, and at completion, enabling logging, visualization, or metric collection.

Additionally, the module integrates with the VMAS [11] framework through the `VmasEnvironment` class, enabling aggregate programs to control agents in physics-based multi-agent reinforcement learning scenarios. This integration allows researchers to combine aggregate programming abstractions with learned policies for coordinated robot control.

4 Example of Use

In this section, we provide several examples of use of the PHYELDS library[2], demonstrating how to implement common aggregate programming patterns and how to integrate with machine learning frameworks for coordination-relevant learning scenarios. PHYELDS can be used in a normal Python environment, such

---

[2] https://github.com/domm99/artifact-coordination-2026-phyelds.

as a Jupyter notebook[3], and it also provides a native simulator for testing and debugging aggregate programs.

Common Aggregate Computing Patterns. A common and well-established pattern in AC is the construction of a *channel* between a source device and a target device. This pattern is frequently employed to model information flows, logical routing structures, or spatial constraints within a distributed system.

A channel (Fig. 3a) is defined as the set of devices that lie within a given distance from a minimum path connecting the source and the target. This distance represents the *width* of the channel, allowing the model to range from a single-device path to a wider region surrounding the optimal route. The final desired outcome is a boolean computational field, where devices belonging to the channel evaluate to `True`, while all others evaluate to `False`.

Listing 1.7 shows the PHYELDS code implementing this behavior. The first step consists of computing the computational field containing distances to neighboring devices, which is obtained through the library function `neighbors_distances` (line 3). Based on this field, the distance from the target device is then computed using the `distance_to` operator (line 4), with the source argument given by the ``target'' sensor, which evaluates to `True` exclusively on the target device. To construct the channel, all devices lying on the minimum path between the source and the target are collected (line 5). This is achieved by propagating information from the target distance field while constraining it with the ``source'' sensor, effectively identifying the devices belonging to the shortest path (line 6). Finally, to assign a channel width different from one (i.e., a singlespsdevice path), each device computes its distance from the minimal channel and is included in the final boolean field if this distance is smaller than the specified channel width (line 7).

```
@aggregate
def main():
    distances = neighbors_distances()
    target_distance = distance_to(sense("target"), distances)
    nodes_in_path = collect_or(target_distance, sense("source"))
    distance_from_path = distance_to(nodes_in_path, distances)
    channel = 1.0 if distance_from_path < width else 0.0
    return channel
```

Listing 1.7. Construction of a channel from a source device to a target device.

Listing 1.8 shows how to set up and run the simulation for the channel example (also available in the online Binder notebook). A `Simulator` is first instantiated and configured with a radius-based neighborhood function (lines 1–2). A 20×20 deformed lattice topology is then created with positional noise to model a realistic device deployment (line 3). Each node is initialized with `source` and `target` sensor values set to `False`; the first node in the list is designated as the source and the last as the target (lines 5–10). The aggregate program

---

[3] Please, take a look at the online binder repository at https://mybinder.org/v2/ gh/phyelds/phyelds-examples/HEAD?urlpath=%2Fdoc%2Ftree%2F%2Fbinder %2Fphyelds-example.ipynb.

(i.e., the `main` function) is scheduled on every node with a fixed time step of 0.1 seconds (lines 12–13). Finally, a `RenderMonitor` is attached to visualize the evolving field using colored nodes and drawn edges, saving the result to a video file, and the simulation is run for 10 seconds (lines 15–24).

```python
simulator = Simulator()
simulator.environment.set_neighborhood_function(radius_neighborhood(0.12))
deformed_lattice(simulator, 20, 20, 0.1, 0.01)
# initialise sensor data on each node
for node in simulator.environment.nodes.values():
    node.data = {"source": False, "target": False}
# designate source and target nodes
simulator.environment.node_list()[0].data["source"] = True
target = simulator.environment.node_list()[-1]
target.data["target"] = True
# schedule the aggregate program on every node
for node in simulator.environment.nodes.values():
    simulator.schedule_event(0.0, aggregate_program_runner, simulator, 0.1, node, main)
# configure rendering and run
RenderMonitor(
    simulator,
    RenderConfig(
        effects=[DrawEdges(), DrawNodes(color_from="result")],
        mode=RenderMode.SHOW,
        save_as="channel.mp4",
        dt=0.1
    )
)
simulator.run(10)
```

Listing 1.8. Simulation setup and execution for the channel example.

A second widely used pattern in aggregate computing is known as *Self-Organizing Coordination Regions* (SCR) [14]. This pattern is inspired by classical results in distributed systems [16, 22, 32], where large-scale systems are often partitioned into smaller subcomponents, each governed by a special node—referred to as a *leader*—responsible for coordination tasks. SCR enables the spatial partitioning of devices into disjoint subregions, effectively forming a Voronoi tessellation [9] of the space, and the election of a leader within each region. Once leaders have been established, each of them acts as the coordinator for its own region. In particular, non-leader devices funnel their local information toward the leader through a convergecast process, the leader computes a new result based on the collected data, and subsequently disseminates the updated information back to all devices in the region via a broadcast operation.

Listing 1.9 illustrates an instance of this pattern, where SCR is used to count the number of devices belonging to each region and to propagate the resulting count to all devices within the same region. This is achieved by first electing leaders (line 4), then assigning devices to regions according to minimum-distance potentials(line 5), and finally combining convergecast (line 6) and broadcast operations to aggregate (line 7) and disseminate information.

Although this example focuses on a simple aggregation task, the SCR pattern is general and can be applied in significantly more complex scenarios. For instance, it can be used to coordinate the training of a machine learning model independently within each region, as discussed in the following subsection.

```python
@aggregate
def main():
    distances = neighbors_distances()
    leader = elect_leaders(4, distances)
    potential = distance_to(leader, distances)
    nodes = count_nodes(potential)
    area_value = broadcast(leader, nodes, distances)
    return area_value
```

Listing 1.9. Self-organizing Coordination Regions pattern.

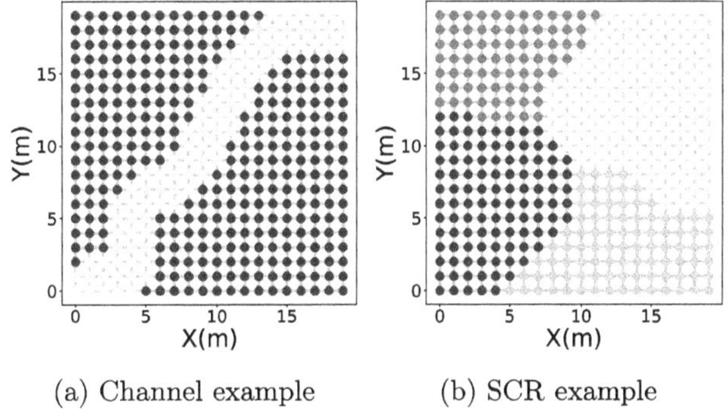

(a) Channel example   (b) SCR example

Fig. 3. Examples of common aggregate programming patterns implemented in PHYELDS. On the left, a channel is constructed between a source device (bottom left) and a target device (top right). The channel color is yellow. On the right, devices are partitioned into coordination regions (different colors).

Self-Organizing Federated Learning. Federated Learning (FL) [25,26] is a distributed learning paradigm in which multiple devices collaboratively train machine learning models while keeping training data local and private. Self-Organizing Federated Learning (SOFL) [17,21] extends this paradigm by removing centralized coordination and enabling devices to autonomously form multiple federations, each learning a specialized model that better reflects local data characteristics. This is achieved by combining clustered federated learning with self-organizing coordination mechanisms, allowing the system to adapt dynamically to spatial deployment and non-Identicaly and independently distributed (non-IID) data, specially when heterogeneity comes from spatial distribution of partecipating devices [18].

Listing 1.10 shows an implementation of a SOFL client using PHYELDS. Each device interleaves local training with self-organizing coordination. The computation starts by maintaining local state through the **remember** construct (line 3), storing the current model parameters and a logical training round counter. Each device then performs a local training step on its private dataset (line 5), producing an updated model and an associated training loss. To enable self-organized federation formation, devices compute a dynamic notion of distance based on model performance similarity. This is achieved through the function `loss_based_distances` (line 6), which derives a computational field reflecting how well neighboring models perform on local validation data. Leaders are then elected using `elect_leaders` (line 7), and a potential field toward each leader is computed via `distance_to` (line 8), implicitly defining coordination regions in a data-driven and adaptive manner. Within each coordination region, model updates are aggregated at the leader using a convergecast operation implemented through `collect_with` (line 9). In the example, local models are combined and averaged to obtain a regional aggregated model (line 10). The leader subsequently disseminates the updated model back to all devices in the region using `broadcast`(line 11), ensuring that federation members are synchronized for the next training iteration (line 12).

```
@aggregate
def client(initial_model_params):
    set_value, value = remember((initial_model_params, 0))
    local_model, tick = value
    evolved_model, train_loss = local_training(local_model, training_data)
    distances = loss_based_distances(evolved_model, validation_data)
    leader = elect_leaders(threshold, distances)
    potential = distance_to(leader, distances)
    models = collect_with(potential, [evolved_model], lambda x, y: x + y)
    aggregated_model = average_weights(models)
    area_model = broadcast(leader, aggregated_model, distances)
    set_value((area_model, tick + 1))
    return potential
```

Listing 1.10. Implementation of SOFL [21] in Phyelds.

Integration with Third-Party Simulators. An additional relevant aspect of PHYELDS is that, although it provides a native simulator, it is designed to seamlessly integrate with external simulation frameworks by supplying appropriate bindings. This design enables PHYELDS to operate in heterogeneous simulation ecosystems without constraining the choice of the underlying simulator.

To demonstrate this capability, we developed an integration with the VMAS simulator [11], 1 which is widely used in the context of multi-agent reinforcement learning (MARL) and swarm robotics. Supporting an external simulator requires the implementation of two core components. The first component is a simulator-specific *runner* (in this case, a VMAS runner). At each simulated time step, the runner retrieves the action computed by each agent, executes these actions within the selected simulator, and then provides the resulting observations or outcomes back to the agents. The second component is an *environment wrapper* for VMAS. This wrapper specifies how agents are initialized and how their state is updated at each simulation step. It is invoked by the runner and acts as an abstraction layer between PHYELDS and the VMAS environment.

To showcase the functionality of the VMAS integration module, we implemented a simple aggregate program that reproduces flocking behavior according to the Vicsek model [34]. Each agent i is characterized by its position $\mathbf{r}_i(t)$ and by the angle $\Theta_i(t)$ defining the direction of its velocity at time t. At each discrete time step Δt, agents align their direction with that of their neighbors within a fixed interaction radius r, up to a noise term:

$$\Theta_i(t + \Delta t) = \langle \Theta_j \rangle_{\|\mathbf{r}_i - \mathbf{r}_j\| < r} + \eta_i(t), \tag{1}$$

where $\langle \Theta_j \rangle_{\|\mathbf{r}_i - \mathbf{r}_j\| < r}$ denotes the average direction of all agents (including i) located within distance r from agent i, and $\eta_i(t)$ represents a stochastic noise term.

After updating its direction, each agent moves at constant speed v according to

$$\mathbf{r}_i(t + \Delta t) = \mathbf{r}_i(t) + v\,\Delta t \begin{pmatrix} \cos \Theta_i(t) \\ \sin \Theta_i(t) \end{pmatrix}. \tag{2}$$

Listing 1.11 reports the aggregate program implementing the Vicsek flocking model within the PHYELDS framework. Figure 4, instead, shows the temporal evolution of the environment as obtained through the native rendering capabilities of VMAS. As time progresses (from left to right), agents progressively align their directions, eventually exhibiting coherent and collective motion.

```python
@aggregate
def action():
    myself = sense('agent')
    vel = myself.state.vel.squeeze()
    neighbors_info = neighbors(vel).exclude_self()
    velocities = [vel for vel in neighbors_info.values()]
    avg_vel = mean_velocity(velocities)
    theta = velocity_to_angle(vel, avg_vel)
    noise = perturbation()
    theta = theta + 0.1 * noise
    next_vel = [torch.cos(theta).item(), torch.sin(theta).item()]
    store("action", next_vel)
```

Listing 1.11. Implementation of the Vicsek Model in Phyelds using VMAS.

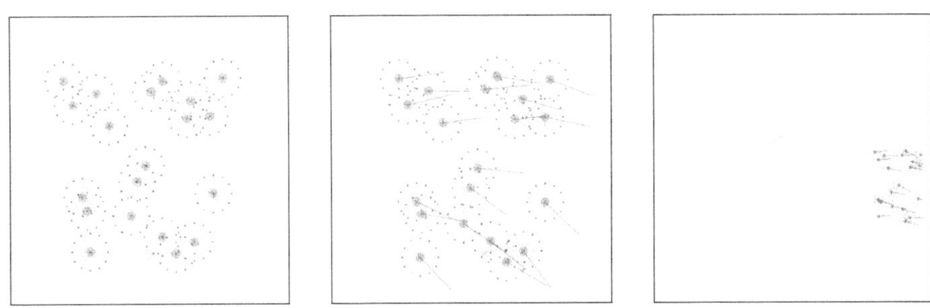

Fig. 4. Vicsek flocking simulation in VMAS using PHYELDS. Agents (circles) align their velocities over time (left to right), exhibiting coherent collective motion.

5   Conclusion

This paper introduces PHYELDS, a Pythonic framework embodying a self-contained implementation of the field calculus within the Python ecosystem. By combining the formal foundations of aggregate programming with an imperative and object-oriented API, PHYELDS lowers the barrier to adoption for data science and machine learning practitioners.

Its modular architecture supports both core field calculus operators and higher-level coordination patterns, while enabling seamless integration with machine learning libraries and external simulators such as VMAS. The presented examples demonstrate the expressiveness of the framework across classical aggregate computing patterns, self-organizing federated learning, and multi-agent coordination scenarios.

Future work will focus on performance and scalability improvements, deeper integration with mainstream ML toolchains, systematic benchmarking against existing frameworks, integration with other third-party simulators (e.g., [23,35]) and deployment in real-world edge and robotic systems (e.g., [2,6]) to further validate the practical potential of Python-based aggregate programming.

References

1. Abadi, M., et al.: TensorFlow: a system for large-scale machine learning. In: Keeton, K., Roscoe, T. (eds.) 12th USENIX Symposium on Operating Systems Design and Implementation, OSDI 2016, Savannah, GA, USA, November 2-4, 2016, pp. 265–283. USENIX Association (2016). https://www.usenix.org/conference/osdi16/technical-sessions/presentation/abadi
2. Aguzzi, G., et al.: A demonstrator for self-organizing robot teams. In: Giusto, C.D., Ravara, A. (eds.) Coordination Models and Languages - 27th IFIP WG 6.1 International Conference, COORDINATION 2025, Held as Part of the 20th International Federated Conference on Distributed Computing Techniques, DisCoTec 2025, Lille, France, June 17-19, 2025, Proceedings. Lecture Notes in Computer Science, vol. 15731, pp. 230–244. Springer (2025). https://doi.org/10.1007/978-3-031-95589-1_12, https://doi.org/10.1007/978-3-031-95589-1_12
3. Aguzzi, G., Casadei, R., Viroli, M.: Addressing collective computations efficiency: towards a platform-level reinforcement learning approach. In: 2022 IEEE International Conference on Autonomic Computing and Self-Organizing Systems (ACSOS), pp. 11–20. IEEE (2022)
4. Aguzzi, G., Casadei, R., Viroli, M.: Machine learning for aggregate computing: a research roadmap. In: 2022 IEEE 42nd International Conference on Distributed Computing Systems Workshops (ICDCSW), pp. 119–124. IEEE (2022)
5. Aguzzi, G., Viroli, M., Esterle, L.: Field-informed reinforcement learning of collective tasks with graph neural networks. In: 2023 IEEE International Conference on Autonomic Computing and Self-Organizing Systems (ACSOS), pp. 37–46. IEEE (2023)
6. Andruccioli, M., et al.: HarmoniKt: a unifying middleware for heterogeneous robot fleets. In: 23rd Consumer Communications & Networking Conference, CCNC 2026, Las Vegas, NV, USA, January 9-12, 2026, pp. 1–6. IEEE (2026). https://doi.org/10.1109/CCNC65079.2026.11366553, https://doi.org/10.1109/CCNC65079.2026.11366553

7. Audrito, G., Torta, G.: FCPP to aggregate them all, p. 103026 (2024). https://doi.org/10.1016/J.SCICO.2023.103026

8. Audrito, G., Viroli, M., Damiani, F., Pianini, D., Beal, J.: A higher-order calculus of computational fields (1), 5:1–5:55 (2019). https://doi.org/10.1145/3285956

9. Aurenhammer, F.: Voronoi diagrams - a survey of a fundamental geometric data structure. ACM Comput. Surv. **23**(3), 345–405 (1991)

10. Beal, J., Pianini, D., Viroli, M.: Aggregate programming for the internet of things (9), 22–30 (2015). https://doi.org/10.1109/MC.2015.261

11. Bettini, M., Kortvelesy, R., Blumenkamp, J., Prorok, A.: VMAS: a vectorized multi-agent simulator for collective robot learning. In: Bourgeois, J., Paik, J., Piranda, B., Werfel, J., Hauert, S., Pierson, A., Hamann, H., Lam, T.L., Matsuno, F., Mehr, N., Makhoul, A. (eds.) Distributed Autonomous Robotic Systems - 16th International Symposium, DARS 2022, Montbéliard, France, 28-30 November 2022. Springer Proceedings in Advanced Robotics, vol. 28, pp. 42–56. Springer (2022). https://doi.org/10.1007/978-3-031-51497-5_4

12. Casadei, R.: Macroprogramming: concepts, state of the art, and opportunities of macroscopic behaviour modelling **55**(13s), 275:1–275:37 (2023). https://doi.org/10.1145/3579353

13. Casadei, R., et al.: Software engineering for collective cyber-physical ecosystems (2025)

14. Casadei, R., Pianini, D., Viroli, M., Natali, A.: Self-organising coordination regions: a pattern for edge computing. In: Nielson, H.R., Tuosto, E. (eds.) Coordination Models and Languages - 21st IFIP WG 6.1 International Conference, COORDINATION 2019, Held as Part of the 14th International Federated Conference on Distributed Computing Techniques, DisCoTec 2019, Kongens Lyngby, Denmark, June 17-21, 2019, Proceedings. Lecture Notes in Computer Science, vol. 11533, pp. 182–199. Springer (2019). https://doi.org/10.1007/978-3-030-22397-7_11

15. Casadei, R., Viroli, M., Aguzzi, G., Pianini, D.: SCAFI: a scala DSL and toolkit for aggregate programming, p. 101248 (2022). https://doi.org/10.1016/J.SOFTX.2022.101248

16. Cortés, J., Martínez, S., Karatas, T., Bullo, F.: Coverage control for mobile sensing networks. IEEE Trans. Robotics Autom. **20**(2), 243–255 (2004)

17. Domini, D., Aguzzi, G., Esterle, L., Viroli, M.: FBFL: A field-based coordination approach for data heterogeneity in federated learning. Logical Meth. Comput. Sci. **22**, 30 (2026). https://doi.org/10.46298/lmcs-22(1:19)2026, https://lmcs.episciences.org/17663

18. Domini, D., Aguzzi, G., Viroli, M.: ProFed: a benchmark for proximity-based non-IID federated learning. J. Open Res. Softw. **14** (2026). https://doi.org/10.5334/jors.624

19. Domini, D., Cavallari, F., Aguzzi, G., Viroli, M.: ScaRLib: towards a hybrid toolchain for aggregate computing and many-agent reinforcement learning. Sci. Comput. Program. **238**, 103176 (2024)

20. Domini, D., et al.: Sparse self-federated learning for energy efficient cooperative intelligence in society 5.0. In: International Joint Conference on Neural Networks, IJCNN 2025, Rome, Italy, June 30 - July 5, 2025, pp. 1–8. IEEE (2025). https://doi.org/10.1109/IJCNN64981.2025.11228400

21. Domini, D., Farabegoli, N., Aguzzi, G., Viroli, M., Esterle, L.: Decentralized proximity-aware clustering for collective self-federated learning. Int. Things **35**, 101841 (2026)

22. Heinzelman, W.R., Chandrakasan, A.P., Balakrishnan, H.: Energy-efficient communication protocol for wireless microsensor networks. In: 33rd Annual Hawaii International Conference on System Sciences (HICSS-33), 4-7 January, 2000, Maui, Hawaii, USA. IEEE Computer Society (2000). https://doi.org/10.1109/HICSS.2000.926982

23. ter Hoeven, E., et al.: Mesa 3: agent-based modeling with python in 2025. J. Open Source Softw. **10**(109), 7668 (2025). https://doi.org/10.21105/JOSS.07668

24. Macenski, S., Foote, T., Gerkey, B.P., Lalancette, C., Woodall, W.: Robot operating system 2: design, architecture, and uses in the wild. Sci. Robotics **7**(66) (2022). https://doi.org/10.1126/SCIROBOTICS.ABM6074

25. McMahan, B., Moore, E., Ramage, D., Hampson, S., y Arcas, B.A.: Communication-efficient learning of deep networks from decentralized data. In: Singh, A., Zhu, X.J. (eds.) Proceedings of the 20th International Conference on Artificial Intelligence and Statistics, AISTATS 2017, 20-22 April 2017, Fort Lauderdale, FL, USA. Proceedings of Machine Learning Research, vol. 54, pp. 1273–1282. PMLR (2017). http://proceedings.mlr.press/v54/mcmahan17a.html

26. McMahan, H.B., Moore, E., Ramage, D., y Arcas, B.A.: Federated learning of deep networks using model averaging. CoRR **abs/1602.05629** (2016). http://arxiv.org/abs/1602.05629

27. Mo, Y., Audrito, G., Dasgupta, S., Beal, J.: A resilient leader election algorithm using aggregate computing blocksâĄŐâĄŐsupported by the defense advanced research projects agency (darpa) under contract no. hr001117c0049. the views, opinions, and/or findings expressed are those of the author(s) and should not be interpreted as representing the official views or policies of the department of defense or the u.s. government. this document does not contain technology or technical data controlled under either u.s. international traffic in arms regulation or U.S. export administration regulations. approved for public release, distribution unlimited (darpa distar case 32200, 10/31/19). mo was also partially supported by the australian research council under grant dp190100887 and dp160104500. IFAC-PapersOnLine **53**(2), 3336–3341 (2020). https://doi.org/10.1016/j.ifacol.2020.12.1497, https://www.sciencedirect.com/science/article/pii/S2405896320319637, 21st IFAC World Congress

28. Mo, Y., Audrito, G., Dasgupta, S., Beal, J.: Near-optimal knowledge-free resilient leader election. Autom. **146**, 110583 (2022)

29. Mo, Y., Beal, J., Dasgupta, S.: An aggregate computing approach to self-stabilizing leader election. In: 2018 IEEE 3rd International Workshops on Foundations and Applications of Self* Systems (FAS*W), pp. 112–117. IEEE (2018). https://doi.org/10.1109/FAS-W.2018.00034

30. Paszke, A., et al: PyTorch: an imperative style, high-performance deep learning library. In: Wallach, H.M., Larochelle, H., Beygelzimer, A., d'Alché-Buc, F., Fox, E.B., Garnett, R. (eds.) Advances in Neural Information Processing Systems 32: Annual Conference on Neural Information Processing Systems 2019, NeurIPS 2019, December 8-14, 2019, Vancouver, BC, Canada, pp. 8024–8035 (2019). https://proceedings.neurips.cc/paper/2019/hash/bdbca288fee7f92f2bfa9f7012727740-Abstract.html

31. Pedregosa, F., et al.: Scikit-learn: machine learning in Python. J. Mach. Learn. Res. **12**, 2825–2830 (2011)

32. Pianini, D., Casadei, R., Viroli, M., Natali, A.: Partitioned integration and coordination via the self-organising coordination regions pattern, pp. 44–68 (2021). https://doi.org/10.1016/J.FUTURE.2020.07.032

33. Pianini, D., Viroli, M., Beal, J.: Protelis: practical aggregate programming, pp. 1846–1853. ACM (2015). https://doi.org/10.1145/2695664.2695913
34. Vicsek, T., Czirók, A., Ben-Jacob, E., Cohen, I., Shochet, O.: Novel type of phase transition in a system of self-driven particles. Phys. Rev. Lett. **75**(6), 1226 (1995)
35. Zinoviev, D.: Discrete event simulation: it's easy with simpy! CoRR **abs/2405.01562** (2024). https://doi.org/10.48550/ARXIV.2405.01562

Coordination Languages, Frameworks, and Patterns

Proof of Delivery: Mechanized Mailbox Types

Edgard Schiebelbein[1]([✉])[iD], Annette Bieniusa[1][iD], and Simon Fowler[2][iD]

[1] RPTU University Kaiserslautern-Landau, Kaiserslautern, Germany
{edgard.schiebelbein,annette.bieniusa}@cs.rptu.de
[2] University of Glasgow, Glasgow, UK
simon.fowler@glasgow.ac.uk

Abstract. Programming languages based on the actor model such as Erlang and Elixir rely on message passing for communication. A core concept of this communication model are mailboxes: all actors are allowed to send messages to a mailbox, but only its owner may retrieve them. A major challenge in such systems is detecting and eliminating protocol violations and deadlocks. Mailbox types are a novel type system that enables static reasoning about the contents of mailboxes, but the metatheory of mailbox type systems is complex and requires extensive reasoning about subtyping. This paper establishes a machine-checked foundation for mailbox types. As a basis for this, we formalize Pat, the first programming language to use mailbox types, in Rocq. With its help, we identified and corrected several oversights in the original definitions. Furthermore, we provide mechanized proofs of several properties of the semantics of mailbox types and the substitution lemma for Pat.

Keywords: Mailbox types · Behavioural type systems · Formal verification · Actor languages

1 Introduction

Programming concurrent and distributed systems is notoriously difficult. Communication-centric programming languages such as Erlang or Elixir, and frameworks like MPI, are based around *message passing* concurrency, where processes send and receive messages to coordinate computation, rather than relying on shared memory. These actor languages have seen much industrial interest due to their suitability for distribution and compatibility with failure recovery idioms such as supervision hierarchies [2]. However, these languages are also susceptible to issues like communication mismatches and deadlocks which pose significant problems at runtime, and are also difficult to detect and fix.

Mailbox types [6,9] are a novel behavioural type system with a focus on mailboxes, as used in actor languages like Erlang and Elixir. Mailboxes are incoming message queues: multiple processes can *write* to a mailbox, but only the process that owns a mailbox can read from it.

R. Casadei and F. Ghassemi (Eds.): COORDINATION 2026, LNCS 16590, pp. 197–217, 2026.
https://doi.org/10.1007/978-3-032-28358-0_10

As an example of mailbox typing, consider the following Erlang implementation of a *future variable* [9], which is a write-once placeholder variable.

```
1   empty_future() →
2      receive
3         {put, X} → full_future(X)
4      end.
5   full_future (X) →
6      receive
7         {get, Pid} → Pid ! {reply, X},
8            full_future (X);
9         {put, _} →
10           erlang: error ("Multiple writes")
11     end.

12  client () →
13     Future = spawn(future, empty_future, []),
14     Future ! {put, 5},
15     Future ! {get, self ()},
16     receive
17        {reply, Result} →
18           io: fwrite ("~w~n", [Result])
19     end.
```

The process empty_future waits to receive a put message containing the value to hold. This is a *selective receive*: other messages may be present in the mailbox but they will not be retrieved. After the put message has been received, the process then calls full_future with the provided value X. In full_future the process waits to receive get messages containing the process ID of the requesting actor, and responds by sending value X to the sender. Since a future variable should only be set once, the process throws an error if more put messages are received. Even in small examples such as this, protocol violations such as unexpected messages, forgotten replies and self-deadlocks may occur. All of these problems can be addressed and statically detected using mailbox typing [6,9].

A mailbox type consists of a *capability* and a *pattern*. The capability indicates whether the type describes messages that must be sent (!) or describe messages to be received from a mailbox (?). A pattern is a commutative regular expression that describes the contents of a mailbox. For the above example, we can define the following mailbox types:

$$\mathsf{EmptyFuture} \triangleq ?(\mathsf{Put}[\mathsf{Int}] \odot \mathsf{Get}[!\mathsf{Reply}[\mathsf{Int}]]^\star) \qquad \mathsf{FullFuture} \triangleq ?\mathsf{Get}[!\mathsf{Reply}[\mathsf{Int}]]^\star$$

Type EmptyFuture describes a mailbox that may contain a single Put message with payload of type Int, and a potentially arbitrary amount of Get messages. Each Get message contains a mailbox reference that expects a Reply message to be sent. Type FullFuture is more restrictive in that it describes a mailbox only containing an arbitrary amount of Reply messages. By using these types, the type system can statically require that exactly one Put message is sent, and can ensure that every Get request receives a Reply message.

Of course, a type system can only guarantee correctness if its own specification is correct. It is therefore crucial to rigorously prove the properties a type system gives. Verifying that these proofs are indeed correct can be challenging in itself. Errors or oversights can remain undetected, resulting in false promises about type checked programs. For example, a mechanization of multiparty session typing [13] uncovered errors nearly a decade later [22].

In this paper, we report on our mechanization of the semantics of mailbox types, and of the *Pat* [9] programming language that incorporates mailbox types. Although Pat includes extensive pen-and-paper proofs of correctness, the proofs

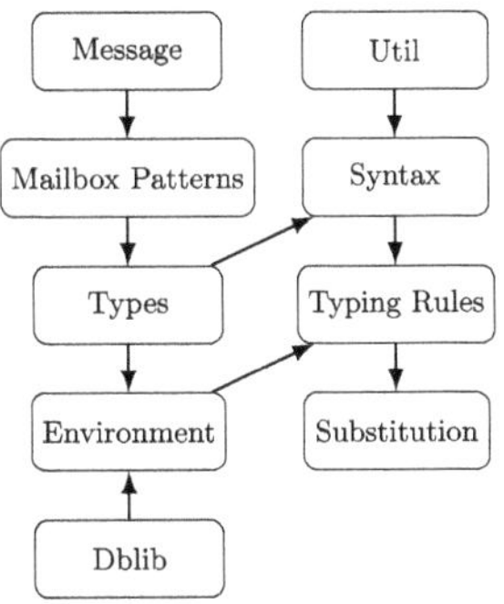

Module	LOC	Definitions	Lemmas
Message	177	7	9
Mailbox Patterns	828	8	44
Types	695	35	30
Environment	3142	16	131
Util	48	6	2
Syntax	180	16	0
Typing Rules	317	4	12
Substitution	1325	2	28
	6712	94	256

Fig. 1. Dependency graph of the modules in the Rocq project. Transitive dependencies are omitted.

have not been mechanized. In particular, we have mechanized numerous properties about mailbox types themselves, and have mechanized the static semantics of Pat. During our mechanization, we discovered several oversights in the original definitions and proofs which have since been fixed.

We use the Rocq [20] proof assistant for our mechanization. Figure 1 summarizes the structure of our Rocq project and shows the lines of code, number of definitions and lemmas for each file. Due to the necessity of *type combination* and *environment subtyping*, the `Environment` module contains, by far, the largest number of lemmas.

Throughout this paper, definitions and lemmas that are accompanied with the -symbol link to the corresponding code in the online documentation. The project can be found at https://github.com/edgardSchi/mailbox-types-rocq.

Methodology. Our mechanization includes both the syntax and type system of Pat, and prove several properties of the language such as the substitution lemma. We limit the scope of this paper to Pat's static semantics, which alone requires a significant mechanization effort; a full account of Pat's operational semantics and preservation theorem would require significant additional work and is left as a future direction. We concentrate on properties that are needed for proving preservation, but also do not require a description of Pat's operational semantics.

We use Rocq due to its maturity and active development: several successful mechanizations have been conducted in Rocq, such as *CompCert* [15], the first fully formally verified real-world compiler, and formalizations of session types [22] and process calculi [1], modelling communication between processes.

Contributions. The main contributions of this paper are as follows:

- The first mechanization of the syntax and semantics of mailbox types (Sect. 2).
- A formalization of the static semantics of Pat, including definitions that are more amenable to mechanization (Sect. 3).

$$\begin{array}{llll}
\text{Mailbox configurations } (\clubsuit) & m & ::= & \langle\rangle \mid \langle \mathsf{m} \rangle \mid m_1 \uplus m_2 \qquad \text{Pattern power } (\clubsuit)\\
\text{Mailbox patterns } (\clubsuit) & E, F & ::= & \mathbb{0} \mid \mathbb{1} \mid \langle\!\langle \mathsf{m} \rangle\!\rangle \mid E \odot F \qquad E^0 \quad := \mathbb{1}\\
& & \mid & E \oplus F \mid E^\star \qquad\qquad\qquad E^{n+1} := E \odot E^n
\end{array}$$

Fig. 2. The syntax of mailbox configurations and patterns.

- Proofs of metatheoretical properties of the static semantics, including the nontrivial substitution lemma (Sect. 3), requiring over 200 auxiliary lemmas.
- We identify missing cases in the original definitions and places where the original proofs could be improved, that have since been fixed (Sect. 2 and Sect. 3).

2   Mailbox Types

We begin by describing mailbox configurations and mailbox patterns, before formalising mailbox types along with the necessary notion of type combination. Due to the potentially infinite representation of mailbox semantics, we require novel definitions that are more amenable to mechanization.

2.1   Mailboxes and Mailbox Patterns

Like Pat but unlike in the original definition of mailbox types [6], we do not include message payloads as part of a mailbox type, but rely only on *message tags* m like Put and Get and associate types with messages when defining the typing rules for Pat (Sect. 3.5).

Mailbox Configurations. A mailbox represents an unordered collection of messages, where a message can be included multiple times. Figure 2 shows the definition of a *mailbox configuration* m. It is either the empty mailbox $\langle\rangle$, a singleton mailbox $\langle \mathsf{m} \rangle$ containing only message m, or the union of two mailboxes $m_1 \uplus m_2$. In Rocq, we model mailbox configurations as lists, where $\uplus$ is implemented as append. To reason about the equality of mailboxes, i.e. mailboxes with the same content, we need to take into account that order does not matter. Mailbox configurations m_1 and m_2 are equal, written $m_1 \approx m_2$, if they are permutations of each other ( ). We then have $\langle \mathsf{m} \rangle \uplus \langle \mathsf{m} \rangle \uplus \langle \mathsf{n} \rangle \approx \langle \mathsf{m} \rangle \uplus \langle \mathsf{n} \rangle \uplus \langle \mathsf{m} \rangle$, but $\langle \mathsf{n} \rangle \uplus \langle \mathsf{n} \rangle \not\approx \langle \mathsf{n} \rangle$.

Mailbox Patterns. The crucial building block of mailbox types are *mailbox patterns*. They can be thought of as a commutative regular expression that describes the content of a mailbox. Figure 2 shows the definition of mailbox patterns. The pattern $\mathbb{0}$ denotes an *unreliable* mailbox, i.e. one that received an unexpected message and which cannot be used for further communication. Pat's type system ensures that it is not possible to create such a mailbox using well-typed terms. Pattern $\mathbb{1}$ represents an *empty* mailbox, containing zero messages. The pattern $\langle\!\langle \mathsf{m} \rangle\!\rangle$ denotes a mailbox containing a *single message* m. Mailbox *composition* is

$$\frac{}{\langle\rangle \in \mathbb{1}} \qquad \frac{}{\langle \mathsf{m} \rangle \in \langle\!\langle \mathsf{m} \rangle\!\rangle} \qquad \frac{m \in E}{m \in E \oplus F} \qquad \frac{m \in F}{m \in E \oplus F} \qquad \frac{\exists n.\; m \in E^n}{m \in E^\star} \qquad \frac{m \approx m_1 \uplus m_2 \quad m_1 \in E \quad m_2 \in F}{m \in E \odot F}$$

Fig. 3. The semantics of mailbox patterns ( ).

described by pattern $E \odot F$, combining both patterns E and F. As an example, pattern $\langle\!\langle \mathsf{m} \rangle\!\rangle \odot \langle\!\langle \mathsf{n} \rangle\!\rangle$ would describe a mailbox containing both m and n. On the other hand, $E \oplus F$ denotes *choice* between patterns. In particular, it describes that the mailbox is either described by pattern E or by pattern F. Lastly, pattern $E^\star$ describes repeated composition of pattern E. For example, $\langle\!\langle \mathsf{m} \rangle\!\rangle^\star$ denotes a mailbox containing zero or more m messages.

Pattern Semantics. Since patterns describe the contents of an unordered mailbox, multiple patterns can describe the same mailbox. For example, pattern $\langle\!\langle \mathsf{m} \rangle\!\rangle \odot \langle\!\langle \mathsf{n} \rangle\!\rangle$ describes the same mailbox as $\langle\!\langle \mathsf{n} \rangle\!\rangle \odot \langle\!\langle \mathsf{m} \rangle\!\rangle$. Thus, checking equality of mailbox patterns requires a semantic definition. The semantics of mailbox types are usually given by a denotational semantics that map patterns to sets of multisets of atoms [6]. Since we are working with Rocq, which is based on constructive logic, we require a method of constructing these sets; a particular challenge is representing the $E^\star$ pattern whose denotation is an infinite union of multisets and not easily representable in Rocq. Instead, we use a relational approach to connect mailbox configurations to patterns.

Instead of building possibly infinite sets of possible configurations, we relate a mailbox configuration to a pattern, written $m \in E$. A configuration is included in the set induced by a pattern if the configuration can be constructed using the pattern. For example, we have $\langle \mathsf{m} \rangle \uplus \langle \mathsf{n} \rangle \in \langle\!\langle \mathsf{m} \rangle\!\rangle \odot \langle\!\langle \mathsf{n} \rangle\!\rangle$ and $\langle \mathsf{n} \rangle \uplus \langle \mathsf{m} \rangle \in \langle\!\langle \mathsf{m} \rangle\!\rangle \odot \langle\!\langle \mathsf{n} \rangle\!\rangle$, but also $\langle \mathsf{m} \rangle \uplus \langle \mathsf{n} \rangle \in \langle\!\langle \mathsf{m} \rangle\!\rangle \odot \langle\!\langle \mathsf{n} \rangle\!\rangle \odot \mathbb{1}$.

The inference rules for this relation are given in Fig. 3. The first two rules describe that the empty mailbox configuration $\langle\rangle$ is the pattern $\mathbb{1}$ and a configuration containing a single message m is part of pattern $\langle\!\langle \mathsf{m} \rangle\!\rangle$. For the choice operator $E \oplus F$, there are two rules: one for when m is part of E and one for when m is part of F. The rule for composition is the most complex one. If m is part of a composition of patterns E and F, then m is required to be split into two sub-configurations, where one is part of E and one is part of F. Lastly, the rule for $E^\star$ uses the *power* operation (defined in Fig. 2) to state that any mailbox configuration that can be built using a pattern E^n (for some n) is included in $E^\star$.

One important observation to make is that we do not include a rule for pattern $\mathbb{0}$. According to the definition of de'Liguoro and Padovani [6], $\mathbb{0}$ should map to the empty set, containing no configurations. Thus, since we are relating configurations and patterns, there must be no relation between any configuration and $\mathbb{0}$.

We define *pattern inclusion* $E \sqsubseteq F$ as the proposition $\forall m.\; m \in E \Rightarrow m \in F$ ( ). Taking inclusion in both directions yields pattern *equivalence* $E \cong F$ ( ).

Pattern residuals ($\blacktriangleright$) $\boxed{E \setminus \mathsf{m} \triangleq F}$

$$\frac{}{\mathbb{0} \setminus \mathsf{m} \triangleq \mathbb{0}} \qquad \frac{}{\mathbb{1} \setminus \mathsf{m} \triangleq \mathbb{0}} \qquad \frac{}{\langle\!\langle \mathsf{m} \rangle\!\rangle \setminus \mathsf{m} \triangleq \mathbb{1}} \qquad \frac{\mathsf{m} \neq \mathsf{n}}{\langle\!\langle \mathsf{m} \rangle\!\rangle \setminus \mathsf{n} \triangleq \mathbb{0}} \qquad \frac{E \setminus \mathsf{m} \triangleq E'}{E^\star \setminus \mathsf{m} \triangleq E' \odot E^\star}$$

$$\frac{E \setminus \mathsf{m} \triangleq E' \qquad F \setminus \mathsf{m} \triangleq F'}{E \oplus F \setminus \mathsf{m} \triangleq E' \oplus F'} \qquad \frac{E \setminus \mathsf{m} \triangleq E' \qquad F \setminus \mathsf{m} \triangleq F'}{E \odot F \setminus \mathsf{m} \triangleq (E' \odot F) \oplus (E \odot F')}$$

Fig. 4. The definition of pattern residuals.

To verify this formalization has the required properties described by de'Liguoro and Padovani [6], we prove the following properties:

Lemma 1. *The relation $\sqsubseteq$ is a precongruence, i.e. the following properties hold:*

- *Reflexive ( ): $E \sqsubseteq E$*
- *Transitive ( ): if $E \sqsubseteq F$ and $F \sqsubseteq G$, then $E \sqsubseteq G$*
- *Compatible wrt. $\odot$ ( ): if $E_1 \sqsubseteq F_1$ and $E_2 \sqsubseteq F_2$, then $(E_1 \odot E_2) \sqsubseteq (F_1 \odot F_2)$*
- *Compatible wrt. $\oplus$ ( ): if $E_1 \sqsubseteq F_1$ and $E_2 \sqsubseteq F_2$, then $(E_1 \oplus E_2) \sqsubseteq (F_1 \oplus F_2)$*

Lemma 2. *The relation $\cong$ is an equivalence relation, i.e. it is*

- *Reflexive ( ): $E \cong E$*
- *Transitive ( ): if $E \cong F$ and $F \cong G$, then $E \cong G$*
- *Symmetric ( ): if $E \cong F$, then $F \cong E$*

Additionally, we show that we indeed work with a commutative Kleene algebra $(M, \oplus, \odot, {}^\star, \mathbb{0}, \mathbb{1})$, where M is the set of messages ( ).

Pattern Residuals. Mailboxes are dynamic objects, not static. Their content changes dynamically while receiving and consuming messages. For example, when consuming message m from a mailbox described by pattern $\langle\!\langle \mathsf{m} \rangle\!\rangle$ the resulting mailbox should be empty, described by pattern $\mathbb{1}$. To model this behavior, de'Liguoro and Padovani introduce the concept of *pattern residuals* [6] (Fig. 4). In Pat [10], pattern residuals correspond exactly to the Brzozowski derivative of a commutative regular expression [3]. A pattern residual describes the resulting pattern when a message is consumed, i.e. removed from the mailbox.

An important property of residuals is *balancing*. For a configuration described by pattern $\langle\!\langle \mathsf{m} \rangle\!\rangle \odot E$, which is included in a pattern F, E should be included in the residual $F \setminus \mathsf{m} \triangleq F'$. This property is needed for reasoning about the type of a mailbox after a message has been received.

Lemma 3. (Balancing ( ). *If $\langle\!\langle \mathsf{m} \rangle\!\rangle \odot F \sqsubseteq E$ where $F \not\sqsubseteq \mathbb{0}$ and $E \setminus \mathsf{m} \triangleq E'$, then $F \sqsubseteq E'$.*

$$\begin{array}{lll}
\text{Mailbox types (\Pinzatto)} & J, K & ::= \ ?E \mid !E \\
\text{Base types (\Pinzatto)} & C & ::= \ \mathbf{1} \mid \mathsf{Bool} \\
\text{Types (\Pinzatto)} & T, U & ::= \ C \mid J
\end{array}$$

Fig. 5. The syntax of types.

Mechanization. Mailbox configurations mostly rely on the definitions of list permutations already provided by Rocq's standard library, but the formalization of mailbox patterns requires more effort. Describing the semantics of mailbox patterns as a relation between a configuration and a pattern, instead of possibly infinite multisets, yields a mechanization that is adequate to work with. The proofs about pattern equivalence and inclusion are typically inductions over a pattern, but proving balancing (Lemma 3) requires several technical lemmas that rely on proven properties about permutations of mailbox configurations.

When mechanizing the pattern residual relation, we discovered that in the definition of Pat [9] the rule for $\star$ was missing. This issue was consequently fixed in the journal version [8].

2.2 Types

A mailbox type (Fig. 5) consists of a capability and a pattern. A capability is either *input* ? or *output* !. Together, capability and pattern describe what messages are expected to be received from (?) or stored in (!) the mailbox. To build an intuition for mailbox types, consider the following examples: A mailbox with mailbox type $?\langle\!\langle m \rangle\!\rangle$ gives a process the right to receive a message m from that mailbox, while a mailbox with type $!\langle\!\langle m \rangle\!\rangle$ requires the process to send a message m to that mailbox. For a mailbox with mailbox type $!(\langle\!\langle m \rangle\!\rangle \oplus \langle\!\langle n \rangle\!\rangle)$, a process may choose whether to send message m or n, whereas a mailbox with type $?(\langle\!\langle m \rangle\!\rangle \oplus \langle\!\langle n \rangle\!\rangle)$ allows a process to receive either message m or n from that mailbox. The type $?(\langle\!\langle m \rangle\!\rangle \odot \langle\!\langle n \rangle\!\rangle)$ is associated to a mailbox that allows a process to receive both m and n, while a mailbox with mailbox type $!(\langle\!\langle m \rangle\!\rangle \odot \langle\!\langle n \rangle\!\rangle)$ requires a process to send both m and n to the mailbox, in whichever order. Finally, a mailbox with type $!(\langle\!\langle m \rangle\!\rangle^\star)$ allows a process to send an arbitrary number of m messages to the mailbox, while $?(\langle\!\langle m \rangle\!\rangle^\star)$ describes a mailbox from which a process is able to receive an arbitrary number of m messages.

In addition to mailbox types, we also include *base types*. While the unit type $\mathbf{1}$ is required by the type system, additional base types can be added. For demonstration purposes we also include a Boolean type Bool. A type T is then either some base type or a mailbox type.

Type Combination. To model the dynamic nature of mailboxes receiving and sending messages, mailbox types should be able to be combined to create a new mailbox type. Mailbox types need to ensure that sends and receives are matched, i.e. a send is required to have a corresponding receive. For example, given mailbox types $!\langle\!\langle m \rangle\!\rangle$ and $?(\langle\!\langle m \rangle\!\rangle \odot \langle\!\langle n \rangle\!\rangle)$, the resulting type from the type combination should be $?\langle\!\langle n \rangle\!\rangle$.

Pattern permutation (🖐) $\boxed{E \sim F}$ **Type permutation (🖐)** $\boxed{T \sim U}$

$$\frac{}{(E \odot F) \sim (F \odot E)} \qquad \frac{F \sim F'}{E \odot F \sim E \odot F'} \qquad\qquad \frac{}{C \sim C} \qquad \frac{E \sim F}{!E \sim !F}$$

$$\frac{}{E \sim E} \qquad \frac{F \sim E}{E \sim F} \qquad \frac{E \sim F' \quad F' \sim F}{E \sim F} \qquad\qquad \frac{E \sim F}{?E \sim ?F}$$

$$\frac{}{E \odot (F \odot F') \sim (E \odot F) \odot F'}$$

Type combinations (🖐) $\boxed{T \boxplus U = T'}$

$$\frac{}{C \boxplus C = C} \qquad \frac{}{!E \boxplus !F = !(E \odot F)} \qquad \frac{}{!E \boxplus ?(E \odot F) = ?F}$$

$$\frac{}{?(E \odot F) \boxplus !E = ?F} \qquad \frac{T_1' \boxplus T_2' = T_3' \quad T_1 \sim T_1' \quad T_2 \sim T_2' \quad T_3 \sim T_3'}{T_1 \boxplus T_2 = T_3}$$

Fig. 6. The definitions of pattern and type permutations, as well as type combinations.

In the original definitions of type combinations [6,9], types are identified up to commutativity and associativity. In practice, this means that types such as $!(\langle\!\langle \mathsf{m} \rangle\!\rangle \odot \langle\!\langle \mathsf{n} \rangle\!\rangle)$ and $!(\langle\!\langle \mathsf{n} \rangle\!\rangle \odot \langle\!\langle \mathsf{m} \rangle\!\rangle)$ are considered to be equivalent. While this is true from a semantic point of view, syntactically these are different types and assuming equality up to a certain property creates problems when mechanizing such definitions. We require a way to express equivalence up to commutativity and associativity in the context of type combinations. To this end, we define a relation between mailbox types, holding if they are permutations of each other.

The relation $E \sim F$ (Fig. 6) is expressing that two patterns can be rewritten into each other using commutativity and associativity of the $\odot$ operator. Note how these rules do not include the $\oplus$ operator. This is because type combination only considers type composition, and it is not required to include pattern choice in the definition of $\sim$ to achieve the desired properties. Note the difference between the relations $E \sim F$ and $E \cong F$. The former is expressing that E and F can be rewritten into each other by swapping around patterns that appear between the composition operator. The latter relates two semantically equal patterns. For example, consider pattern $\langle\!\langle \mathsf{m} \rangle\!\rangle \odot \langle\!\langle \mathsf{n} \rangle\!\rangle$. Both $\langle\!\langle \mathsf{m} \rangle\!\rangle \odot \mathbb{1} \sim \mathbb{1} \odot \langle\!\langle \mathsf{m} \rangle\!\rangle$ and $\langle\!\langle \mathsf{m} \rangle\!\rangle \odot \mathbb{1} \cong \mathbb{1} \odot \langle\!\langle \mathsf{m} \rangle\!\rangle$ hold, while $\langle\!\langle \mathsf{m} \rangle\!\rangle \odot \mathbb{1} \cong \langle\!\langle \mathsf{m} \rangle\!\rangle$, but $\langle\!\langle \mathsf{m} \rangle\!\rangle \odot \mathbb{1} \not\sim \langle\!\langle \mathsf{m} \rangle\!\rangle$.

The relation $\sim$ is extended to mailbox types by relating the underlying patterns. Base types are always considered to be permutations of each other.

Type combinations model the concurrent interaction between processes acting on the same mailbox. For example, assume processes P_1 and P_2 that both interact with mailbox m. Process P_1 stores some message m, while P_2 stores some message n. Then, mailbox m can be described by the type combination $!\langle\!\langle \mathsf{m} \rangle\!\rangle \boxplus !\langle\!\langle \mathsf{n} \rangle\!\rangle = !(\langle\!\langle \mathsf{m} \rangle\!\rangle \odot \langle\!\langle \mathsf{n} \rangle\!\rangle)$. If instead, we have type $?(\langle\!\langle \mathsf{m} \rangle\!\rangle \odot \langle\!\langle \mathsf{n} \rangle\!\rangle)$, then we get the type combination $!\langle\!\langle \mathsf{m} \rangle\!\rangle \boxplus ?(\langle\!\langle \mathsf{m} \rangle\!\rangle \odot \langle\!\langle \mathsf{n} \rangle\!\rangle) = ?\langle\!\langle \mathsf{n} \rangle\!\rangle$. Figure 7 shows a example

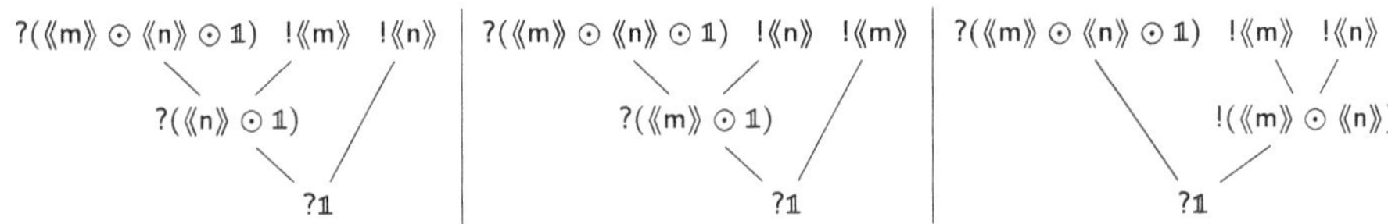

Fig. 7. Example of possible type combinations for three mailbox types. Each top node represents the type of the same mailbox in three different processes that run in parallel. Edges indicate the type combination relation.

with three mailbox types. There are different ways of arranging the combination, but in the end, the result always balances out to an empty mailbox.

Figure 6 shows the definition of the *type combination relation*. Note how there is no rule for type combination of two types with input capabilities. This would be allowing parallel reads of the same mailbox, which is not safe [6], and thus not permitted. The last rule in the definition of type combinations allows us to substitute types for their permutations. Note how the previous definition of pattern equality $E \cong F$ is specifically *not* used in the definition of type combination. The combination operation is a *syntactic* operation, i.e. we can only combine types that are *syntactically equal* to the forms specified by the type combination operation (up to commutativity and associativity). To combine other mailbox types, for example $!\langle\!\langle m \rangle\!\rangle$ and $?(\langle\!\langle m \rangle\!\rangle \oplus \langle\!\langle m \rangle\!\rangle)$ we must firstly use *subtyping* to rewrite the latter mailbox type to $?(\langle\!\langle m \rangle\!\rangle \odot \mathbb{1})$ before using the combination operator. We will discuss subtyping further in Sect. 3.

Mechanization. Our mechanization of mailbox types differs from the original formalizations in that we treat partial operations as relations, and include the notion of pattern and type permutations. This addition allows us to prove desired properties, such as commutativity of type combinations. Naturally, proofs about type combinations become more complex since we have to cover additional cases.

3   The Pat Programming Language

Pat [9] is the first programming language to support mailbox types. In contrast to languages like Erlang or Elixir, where mailboxes are implicit, Pat supports first-class explicit mailboxes. We can express the Future example in Pat as follows:

```
 1   def emptyFuture(self : EmptyFuture) : 1 {
 2     guard self : Put ⊙ Get* {
 3         receive Put[x] from self ↦
 4         fullFuture(self, x)
 5     }
 6   }
 7   def fullFuture(self : FullFuture, value : Int) : 1 {
 8     guard self : Get* {
 9       free ↦ ()
10       receive Get[user] from self ↦
11           user!Reply[value];
12           fullFuture(self, value)
13     }
14   }

15   def client() : 1 {
16     let future = new in
17     spawn emptyFuture(future);
18     let self = new in
19     future!Put[5];
20     future!Get[self];
21     guard self : Reply {
22         receive Reply[result]
23       from self ↦
24         free self;
25         print(intToString(result))
26     }
27   }
```

To support dynamic mailbox creation, new mailboxes are created using the
new keyword and bound to names using **let**-bindings. Pat programs can then
send to mailboxes (e.g., *future*!Put[5] sends a Put message with payload 5 to
mailbox *future*) and receive from mailboxes using the **guard** keyword. A guard
is always accompanied by a mailbox pattern, representing the mailbox's contents,
and contains *guard clauses* including **receive** which receives a message from the
mailbox and binds the payload and new mailbox name; and **free** which is invoked
when a mailbox will not receive any more messages and can be deallocated.

A mechanization of the operational semantics of Pat is outside of the scope
of this paper, but we give an outline of the semantics here for context. Pat's
semantics makes use of a *frame stack* representation that simplifies specifying
inductive invariants for the type preservation proof. There are two reduction relations: a deterministic β-reduction relation on functional terms (like **let**-bindings
and function calls) that is entirely standard, and a nondeterministic reduction
relation on a language of *configurations* that closely resemble processes in the
π-calculus. The communication and concurrency constructs reduce as follows:

– Evaluating the **new** construct creates a fresh runtime mailbox name and
  returns it to the calling thread.
– Evaluating a message send $a!m[v]$ returns the unit value to the calling thread
  and creates an *in-flight* message $a \leftarrow m[v]$.
– Evaluating **spawn** t returns the unit value to the calling thread and evaluates
  t in a new process.
– The behaviour of a **guard** $a : E \; \{\overrightarrow{g}\}$ expression depends on the messages
  that have been sent to mailbox a along with the guards contained in $\overrightarrow{g}$:
  – If there are no messages sent to a; no references to a in other threads;
    and $\overrightarrow{g}$ contains a **free** $\mapsto t$ guard, then mailbox name a will be deleted
    and the thread will run computation t.
  – If there is a message $a \leftarrow m[v]$ and $\overrightarrow{g}$ contains a clause **receive** $m \mapsto t$,
    then the thread will run computation t with bindings for the received
    value and updated mailbox name.

A major problem in Pat is *mailbox name aliasing*, where multiple static names
could be given to the same underlying mailbox name. This could be used to break

Usage annotations $\eta \ ::= \ \circ \mid \bullet$

Usage-annotated types $A, B \ ::= \ C \mid J^\eta$

Type operations
$$\lceil C \rceil = C \qquad \lfloor C \rfloor = C$$
$$\lceil J \rceil = J^\circ \qquad \lfloor J \rfloor = J^\bullet$$
$$\lceil J^\eta \rceil = J^\circ \qquad \lfloor J^\eta \rfloor = J^\bullet$$

Usage-annotated type combinations $\boxed{A \rhd B = A'}$

Usage combinations $\boxed{\eta_1 \rhd \eta_2 = \eta_3}$

$$\overline{C \rhd C = C} \qquad \frac{\eta_1 \rhd \eta_2 = \eta \quad J_1 \boxplus J_2 = K}{J_1^{\eta_1} \rhd J_2^{\eta_2} = K^\eta}$$

$$\circ \rhd \circ = \circ \qquad \circ \rhd \bullet = \bullet$$

Usage subtyping $\boxed{\eta_1 \leq \eta_2}$ **Subtyping** $\boxed{A \leq B}$

$$\eta \leq \eta \qquad \bullet \leq \circ$$

$$\overline{C \leq C} \qquad \frac{E \sqsubseteq F \quad \eta_1 \leq \eta_2}{?E^{\eta_1} \leq ?F^{\eta_2}} \qquad \frac{F \sqsubseteq E \quad \eta_1 \leq \eta_2}{!E^{\eta_1} \leq !F^{\eta_2}}$$

Fig. 8. Definitions of usage-annotated types.

type soundness. The Mailbox Calculus addresses this issue using a dependency graph, which can additionally rule out cyclic dependencies, but this approach does not scale to programming languages (see [9] for a detailed discussion). Instead, Pat uses *quasi-linear typing* [7,14], where types are equipped with *usage annotations*. If a type is defined as *returnable*, it is allowed to appear in the return type of an expression and be returned from an evaluation frame. Otherwise, if a type is defined as *second-class*, it can be used several times, but is never allowed to escape its scope. A returnable occurrence of a mailbox name must be its last lexical usage. Quasilinearity annotations, in combination with syntactic restrictions, eliminates aliasing issues and self-deadlocks.

The authors of Pat present both a *declarative* and an *algorithmic* version of their type system. The algorithmic version (which is needed because the declarative system makes use of environment subtyping and non-deterministic context splits) makes use of *bidirectional typing* and *constraint solving*, and is at the core of Pat's implementation. This paper focuses on the declarative type system.

3.1 Quasi-linear Mailbox Types

Pat uses quasi-linear typing [7,14] to solve the problem of name aliasing and cyclic dependency between mailboxes. To this end, every mailbox type is equipped with a *usage annotation*: either *second class* ($\circ$) or *returnable* ($\bullet$). Values of second class types can be used several times within the scope they are defined, however, they cannot leave that scope. On the other hand, values of returnable types can be let-bound and used as the subject of a guard, but must appear as the last lexical occurrence of the name. Base types are not equipped with usage, as they do not suffer from the aliasing problems.

$$
\begin{array}{lll}
\text{Definition names } (\text{🐦}) & f \\
\text{Function definitions } (\text{🐦}) & d ::= \mathbf{def}\ f(A) : B\ \{t\} \\
\text{Booleans} & b ::= \mathbf{true} \mid \mathbf{false} \\
\text{Values } (\text{🐦}) & v ::= b \mid () \mid \mathsf{Var}\ n \\
\text{Terms } (\text{🐦}) & t ::= v \mid \mathbf{let}\ t_1\ \mathbf{in}\ t_2 \mid f(v) \mid \mathbf{spawn}\ t \\
& \quad\ \mid\ \mathbf{new} \mid v_1!\mathsf{m}[v_2] \mid \mathbf{guard}\ v : E\ \{\vec{g}\} \\
\text{Guards } (\text{🐦}) & g ::= \mathbf{fail} \mid \mathbf{free} \mapsto t \mid \mathbf{receive}\ \mathsf{m} \mapsto t \\
\text{Environments } (\text{🐦}) & \Gamma ::= \emptyset \mid \bot, \Gamma \mid A, \Gamma
\end{array}
$$

Fig. 9. The syntax of Pat.

Figure 8 shows definitions of usage annotations, usage-annotated types and relations on them. We also define operators $\lceil \cdot \rceil$ and $\lfloor \cdot \rfloor$ to turn types into second class and returnable respectively. Additionally, we define a mailbox type to be *unrestricted* (written $\mathsf{un}(A)$) ( ) if it is a base type, or $A = !\mathbb{1}^\circ$.

Usage-annotated Type Combination. We extend type combination to *usage-annotated type combination* by incorporating usage combination. For usage annotations, we have to obey the rule that a $\circ$ variable has to occur before a $\bullet$ variable. Otherwise, we would violate the property that any $\bullet$ variable appears as the final one in a process. Combining two $\bullet$ types is not allowed as there could otherwise be multiple instances of a returnable mailbox name per thread.

Subtyping. Subtyping is needed in mailbox typing to rewrite mailbox types so that they can be combined by the type combination operator. For mailbox types, subtyping is *covariant* for types with receive capability and *contravariant* for types with send capability [6]. Subtyping also allows us to treat returnable types as second-class types.

3.2   Syntax

The Pat syntax we are working with is close to the original definitions by Fowler et al. [9], making use of de Bruijn indices [5] to represent variables. We use de Bruijn indices as they are well-studied for proof assistants, and in particular Rocq [1,19]. We make use of the Rocq library *dblib* [18] that automatically handles de Bruijn indices and operations on them such as shifting.

To ease the burden of proving properties about messages, we restrict messages to only carry a single payload, and consider only functions that take a single argument. We expect that extending our proofs to include arbitrary numbers of payloads and function arguments will not significantly affect the proofs.

Figure 9 shows our syntax of Pat. A value v is either a Boolean value, the unit value (), or a variable $\mathsf{Var}\ n$ represented as a de Bruijn index, with natural number n. Including variables into the definition of values is fairly nonstandard. The inspiration for this approach is the *fine-grain call-by-value* evaluation strategy [16], that makes a syntactic difference between values and computations. Values, including variables that can also represent mailbox names, are immutable and cannot be reduced, while other terms produce values and can be reduced further.

A term is either a value, a let-expression or a function application $f(v)$ of function f on value v. Additionally, there are terms specifically for interacting with mailboxes and processes. The term **spawn** t can be used to create a new process running term t. Dynamic mailbox name creation is done with the **new** keyword, generating a fresh mailbox name. Term $v_1!m[v_2]$ sends message m with payload value v_2 to the mailbox with name v_1. A guard term **guard** $v : E\ \{\overrightarrow{g}\}$ asserts that the mailbox associated with name V has pattern E, and invokes some guard from the list of guards $\overrightarrow{g}$. Guards perform actions on a mailbox: the guard **fail** is triggered when a mailbox receives an unexpected message, and should be evaluated by a well-typed program. In contrast, guard **free** $\mapsto t$ is triggered when a mailbox is empty and not referenced elsewhere in the system; the corresponding mailbox is freed and we proceed with continuation t. Finally, the guard **receive** $m \mapsto t$ is triggered when a mailbox contains the message m. The contents of the message are then available in the continuation t.

A Pat program $\mathcal{P} = (\mathcal{S}, \mathcal{D}, t_0)$ ( ) is a tuple consisting of a signature $\mathcal{S}$ for mapping messages to their payload type, a mapping $\mathcal{D}$ from definition names to function definitions, and an initial term t_0. For simplicity, given a program $\mathcal{P}$, we write $\mathcal{S}_{\mathcal{P}}$ for the signature, and $\mathcal{D}_{\mathcal{P}}$ for the function definitions.

Mechanization. The mechanization of the syntax of Pat is close to its pen-and-paper counterpart, with the exception of using de Bruijn indices. Defining the syntax poses no problem after settling on the representation of variables. While the choice of using de Bruijn indices is standard [1,19,22], it comes with the downside of extensive reasoning about indices and lifting. While *dblib* alleviates some of this burden, a substantial amount of manual work is still required.

Definition names are treated similar to message tags, being represented as an arbitrary type equipped decidable equality.

3.3   Environments

Pat's type system makes use of *environments* for keeping track of types of variables while type checking terms. The implementation of environments depends on how variables are represented. For traditional strings as variables, it is common to use a map, mapping variables to types [17]. In the case of de Bruijn indices, an environment is typically represented as a list of types where a variable indicates the position of its type in the list [17,23]. For Pat, the representation of an environment as a simple list of types is unfortunately not enough, due to its parallel fragment and use of quasilinearity. To illustrate the problem, consider the type derivation of a mailbox calculus term on the left-hand side:

$$\frac{A_1, \emptyset \vdash \mathsf{Var}\ 0 \qquad A_2, \emptyset \vdash \mathsf{Var}\ 1}{A_2, A_1, \emptyset \vdash \mathsf{Var}\ 0 \parallel \mathsf{Var}\ 1} \qquad \frac{\bot, A_1, \emptyset \vdash \mathsf{Var}\ 0 \qquad A_2, \bot, \emptyset \vdash \mathsf{Var}\ 1}{A_2, A_1, \emptyset \vdash \mathsf{Var}\ 0 \parallel \mathsf{Var}\ 1}$$

Environment subtyping (🖐) $\qquad\qquad\qquad\qquad\qquad\qquad\qquad\boxed{\Gamma_1 \leq \Gamma_2}$

$$\frac{}{\Gamma \leq \Gamma} \qquad \frac{\Gamma_1 \leq \Gamma_2 \quad \Gamma_2 \leq \Gamma_3}{\Gamma_1 \leq \Gamma_3} \qquad \frac{\Gamma_1 \leq \Gamma_2}{\bot, \Gamma_1 \leq \bot, \Gamma_2} \qquad \frac{\Gamma_1 \leq \Gamma_2 \quad \mathsf{un}(A)}{A, \Gamma_1 \leq \bot, \Gamma_2} \qquad \frac{\Gamma_1 \leq \Gamma_2 \quad A_1 \leq A_2}{A_1, \Gamma_1 \leq A_2, \Gamma_2}$$

Environment combination (🖐) $\qquad\qquad\qquad\qquad\qquad\qquad\boxed{\Gamma_1 \rhd \Gamma_2 = \Gamma_3}$

$$\frac{}{\emptyset \rhd \emptyset = \emptyset} \qquad \frac{\Gamma_1 \rhd \Gamma_2 = \Gamma_3}{\bot, \Gamma_1 \rhd \bot, \Gamma_2 = \bot, \Gamma_3} \qquad \frac{\Gamma_1 \rhd \Gamma_2 = \Gamma_3}{A, \Gamma_1 \rhd \bot, \Gamma_2 = A, \Gamma_3} \qquad \frac{\Gamma_1 \rhd \Gamma_2 = \Gamma_3}{\bot, \Gamma_1 \rhd A, \Gamma_2 = A, \Gamma_3}$$

$$\frac{A_1 \rhd A_2 = A_3 \quad \Gamma_1 \rhd \Gamma_2 = \Gamma_3}{A_1, \Gamma_1 \rhd A_2, \Gamma_2 = A_3, \Gamma_3}$$

Disjoint environment combination (🖐) $\qquad\qquad\qquad\qquad\boxed{\Gamma_1 + \Gamma_2 = \Gamma_3}$

$$\frac{}{\emptyset + \emptyset = \emptyset} \qquad \frac{\Gamma_1 + \Gamma_2 = \Gamma_3}{\bot, \Gamma_1 + \bot, \Gamma_2 = \bot, \Gamma_3} \qquad \frac{\Gamma_1 + \Gamma_2 = \Gamma_3}{A, \Gamma_1 + \bot, \Gamma_2 = A, \Gamma_3} \qquad \frac{\Gamma_1 + \Gamma_2 = \Gamma_3}{\bot, \Gamma_1 + A, \Gamma_2 = A, \Gamma_3}$$

$$\frac{\Gamma_1 + \Gamma_2 = \Gamma_3}{C, \Gamma_1 + C, \Gamma_2 = C, \Gamma_3}$$

Fig. 10. The definitions of relations on environments.

We assume variable Var 0 has type A_1 and variable Var 1 has type A_2. The term expresses that there are two processes running in parallel, each with only a single variable. Additionally, the current environment consists of $A_2, A_1, \emptyset$. By the typing rules of the mailbox calculus (read bottom-up), given by de'Liguoro and Padovani [6], when typing parallel processes, the environment needs to be split into two. Assuming variable Var 0 has indeed type A_1, the left subtree works without problems. Looking up the type at position Var 0 in environment $A_1, \emptyset$ yields A_1. However, the right subtree poses a problem. There is no type at position Var 1 in environment $A_2, \emptyset$, as it only contains a single element.

One way of solving this issue is the inclusion of entries in the environment representing the absence of a type at a certain position. The example on the right-hand side adds an additional $\bot$-entry, representing an empty position. With this approach, whenever an environment is split, the size of the two new environments is equal to the size of the original one. The *dblib* library we use for managing de Bruijn indices also includes an implementation of environments based on this exact approach. It provides the needed definitions and operations, such as lookup and insertion, together with proofs about properties on environments.

Fowler et al. [9] describe several relations and operations on environments, defined in Fig. 10. Our definitions are essentially equal to the original ones, with modifications to incorporate $\bot$-entries and some corrections that are further discussed at the end of this section. In each relation we add a rule for the case where the first entry in both environments is $\bot$. Similar to partial operations on types, we turn partial operations on environments into relations.

Pattern normal form (📌) $\boxed{E \models F}$

$$\frac{}{E \models \mathbb{0}} \qquad \frac{}{E \models \mathbb{1}} \qquad \frac{E \setminus \mathsf{m} \triangleq E' \quad F \cong E'}{E \models \langle\!\langle \mathsf{m} \rangle\!\rangle \odot F} \qquad \frac{E \models F_1 \quad E \models F_2}{E \models F_1 \oplus F_2}$$

Fig. 11. Pattern normal form.

Pat requires subtyping on *environments* rather than just types in order to rewrite types so that they can be used by the type combination operator. Sequential environment combination $\Gamma_1 \rhd \Gamma_2 = \Gamma$ makes use of type combination and is used when type checking let-expressions. This is the main rule used to ensure that subsequent uses of a mailbox variable "balance out". Additionally, we use *disjoint environment combination* to reason about expressions where subterms may not share mailbox-typed variables (e.g. a variable may not be used as the target of a message send and also be contained in its payload). Environments combined using $+$ are only allowed to share variables of base types and be disjoint otherwise.

As our definition of environments includes $\perp$ entries, it is possible for an environment to be empty without being $\emptyset$, necessitating a new notion of emptiness of environments $\mathsf{Empty}(\Gamma)$ () that holds when Γ only contains $\perp$-entries.

Mechanization. Formalizing environments is, by far, the most complex part of this mechanization. The library *dblib* reduces some of the complexity around environments by proving operations and properties on them. However, reasoning about environment combinations and environment subtyping still is far from trivial. Independent of the representation of environments that were considered, environment splitting and subtyping require dozens of technical lemmas. While the proofs of these properties follow the same general approach, they are lengthy and tedious to perform. For example, for the relation $\Gamma_1 \rhd \Gamma_2 = \Gamma_3$ we have proved that there exists an environment that is the environment combination of both Γ_1 and Γ_2 with the entry at the same position replaced by $\perp$ in both environments ( ). Similar lemmas had to be proven for environment subtyping and disjoint combination. While mechanizing subtyping for environments according to the definition of Pat [9], we noticed that the relation was missing an inference rule, making environment subtyping not transitive. By explicitly including the transitivity rule we were able to prove desired properties of environment subtyping. This issue was subsequently fixed in a revised version [8].

3.4   Pattern Normal Form

When reasoning about the typing of guards, both the Mailbox Calculus and Pat require the type of a mailbox to be in *pattern normal form* (PNF), which is a particular structure of pattern that reflects the subpatterns expected by each guard clause. Specifically, a pattern E is in PNF if it is a sum of subpatterns of the form $\mathbb{0}$ (for a **fail** guard), $\mathbb{1}$ (for a **free** guard) and $\langle\!\langle \mathsf{m} \rangle\!\rangle \odot F$ (for a **receive** guard), where F is equivalent to the residual of E with respect to m. This allows a correct type to be given to a re-bound mailbox name after receiving.

Figure 11 shows the formal definitions for PNF; we write $\models E$ for $E \models E$. The following example derivation shows that pattern $(\langle\!\langle m \rangle\!\rangle \odot 1) \oplus \mathbb{1}$ is in PNF:

$$\dfrac{\dfrac{\langle\!\langle m \rangle\!\rangle \setminus m \triangleq \mathbb{1} \quad \mathbb{1} \setminus m \triangleq 0}{\dfrac{(\langle\!\langle m \rangle\!\rangle \odot 1) \oplus \mathbb{1} \setminus m \triangleq (\mathbb{1} \odot 1) \oplus (\langle\!\langle m \rangle\!\rangle \odot 0) \quad \mathbb{1} \cong (\mathbb{1} \odot 1) \oplus (\langle\!\langle m \rangle\!\rangle \odot 0)}{(\langle\!\langle m \rangle\!\rangle \odot 1) \oplus \mathbb{1} \models (\langle\!\langle m \rangle\!\rangle \odot 1)}} \quad \dfrac{}{(\langle\!\langle m \rangle\!\rangle \odot 1) \oplus \mathbb{1} \models \mathbb{1}}}{(\langle\!\langle m \rangle\!\rangle \odot 1) \oplus \mathbb{1} \models (\langle\!\langle m \rangle\!\rangle \odot 1) \oplus \mathbb{1}}$$

3.5 Typing Rules

We now have all the necessary definitions for specifying the typing rules of Pat. These rules are similar to the original ones by Fowler et al. [9], with a few modifications to fit our definitions of variables, environments and terms.

Figure 12 shows the typing rules for Pat, parameterised by a program $\mathcal{P}$; we omit $\mathcal{P}$ in the rules for readability. We highlight some of the typing rules. Whenever an empty environment is required, we use predicate $\mathsf{Empty}(\Gamma)$ instead of checking for the empty environment $\emptyset$. The insertion operation $[x \mapsto A]\Gamma$ ensures that Γ contains type A at position x.

The SEND rule types a send expression $v_1!m[v_2]$, where message m with payload v_2 is sent to mailbox v_1. The mailbox associated with v_1 has to be of type $!\langle\!\langle m \rangle\!\rangle^\circ$, i.e. it must be capable of sending the message m. Payload v_2 is required to be of the type given by the message's signature with second-class usage. Both derivations for v_1 and v_2 must occur under separate environments Γ_1 and Γ_2, i.e. they are only share base types and their combination yields Γ.

Rule RECEIVE types the receive guard **receive** $m \mapsto t$, retrieving message m from the mailbox, with type B and pattern $\langle\!\langle m \rangle\!\rangle \odot E$. Either Γ must only consist of base types or the payload's type T is a base type. This is a syntactic restriction, ensuring that no existing mailbox name is shadowed by a message's payload. The continuation t must be typeable under Γ extended by $?E^\bullet$ and $[T]$. Type $?E^\bullet$ represents the mailbox after m is consumed. Because of the usage of de Bruijn indices, the order in which the types are inserted into the environment is important. Since inserting a type at position 0 corresponds to simply adding it to the front of the environment, the environment $[0 \mapsto [T]]([0 \mapsto ?E^\bullet]\Gamma)$ is equal to $[T], ?E^\bullet, \Gamma$. Thus, a variable 0 would map to type $[T]$ and a variable 1 would map to type $?E^\bullet$.

The typing relation for a sequence of guards enables us to typecheck each guard individually, while also ensuring the correct pattern structure of the overall expression. In the original definition of typing for guard sequences, Fowler et al. [9] provide only a single rule of the following form:

$$\frac{(\Gamma \vdash g_i : A :: E_i)_i}{\Gamma \vdash \overrightarrow{g} : A :: E_1 \oplus \ldots \oplus E_n}$$

Typing rules for programs and functions (🖐) (🖐) $\boxed{\vdash \mathcal{P}}$ $\boxed{\vdash_{\mathcal{P}} \textbf{def } \mathsf{f}(A) : B \ \{t\}}$

$$\frac{\mathcal{P} = (\mathcal{S}, \mathcal{D}, t_0) \qquad \forall \mathsf{f}.\ \vdash_{\mathcal{P}} \mathcal{D}(\mathsf{f}) \qquad \emptyset \vdash t_0 : \mathbf{1}}{\vdash \mathcal{P}}$$

$$\frac{A, \emptyset \vdash t : B}{\vdash_{\mathcal{P}} \textbf{def } \mathsf{f}(A) : B \ \{t\}}$$

Typing rules for terms (🖐) $\boxed{\Gamma \vdash_{\mathcal{P}} t : A}$

$$\text{VAR} \quad \frac{\text{Empty}(\Gamma)}{[x \mapsto A]\Gamma \vdash \textsf{Var } x : A}$$

$$\text{BOOL} \quad \frac{\text{Empty}(\Gamma)}{\Gamma \vdash b : \textsf{Bool}}$$

$$\text{UNIT} \quad \frac{\text{Empty}(\Gamma)}{\Gamma \vdash () : \mathbf{1}}$$

$$\text{APP} \quad \frac{\mathcal{D}_{\mathcal{P}}(\mathsf{f}) = \textbf{def } \mathsf{f}(A) : B \ \{t\} \qquad \Gamma \vdash v : A}{\Gamma \vdash \mathsf{f}(v) : B}$$

$$\text{LET} \quad \frac{\Gamma_1 \rhd \Gamma_2 = \Gamma \qquad \Gamma_1 \vdash t_1 : \lfloor A \rfloor \qquad [0 \mapsto \lfloor A \rfloor]\Gamma_2 \vdash t_2 : B}{\Gamma \vdash \textbf{let } t_1 \textbf{ in } t_2 : B}$$

$$\text{NEW} \quad \frac{\text{Empty}(\Gamma)}{\Gamma \vdash \textbf{new} : ?\mathbf{1}^{\bullet}}$$

$$\text{SEND} \quad \frac{\mathcal{S}_{\mathcal{P}}(\mathsf{m}) = T \qquad \Gamma_1 \vdash v_1 : !\langle\!\langle\mathsf{m}\rangle\!\rangle^{\circ} \qquad \Gamma_2 \vdash v_2 : \lceil T \rceil \qquad \Gamma_1 + \Gamma_2 = \Gamma}{\Gamma \vdash v_1!\mathsf{m}[v_2] : \mathbf{1}}$$

$$\text{GUARD} \quad \frac{E \sqsubseteq F \qquad \models F \qquad \Gamma_1 \vdash v : ?F^{\bullet} \qquad \Gamma_2 \vdash \vec{g} : A :: F \qquad \Gamma_1 + \Gamma_2 = \Gamma}{\Gamma \vdash \textbf{guard } v : E \ \{\vec{g}\} : A}$$

$$\text{SUB} \quad \frac{\Gamma \leq \Gamma' \qquad A \leq B \qquad \Gamma' \vdash t : A}{\Gamma \vdash t : B}$$

$$\text{SPAWN} \quad \frac{\lceil \Gamma \rceil = \Gamma' \qquad \Gamma' \vdash t : \mathbf{1}}{\Gamma \vdash \textbf{spawn } t : \mathbf{1}}$$

Typing rules for guard sequences (🖐) $\boxed{\Gamma \vdash_{\mathcal{P}} \vec{g} : A :: E}$

$$\frac{\Gamma \vdash g : A :: E}{\Gamma \vdash \{g\} : A :: E} \ \text{SINGLE} \qquad \frac{\Gamma \vdash g : A :: E \qquad \Gamma \vdash \vec{g_s} : A :: E'}{\Gamma \vdash \{g, \vec{g_s}\} : A :: E \oplus E'} \ \text{SEQ}$$

Typing rules for guards (🖐) $\boxed{\Gamma \vdash_{\mathcal{P}} g : A :: E}$

$$\text{FAIL} \quad \frac{}{\Gamma \vdash \textbf{fail} : A :: \mathbb{0}}$$

$$\text{FREE} \quad \frac{\Gamma \vdash t : A}{\Gamma \vdash \textbf{free} \mapsto t : A :: \mathbb{1}}$$

$$\text{RECEIVE} \quad \frac{\mathcal{S}_{\mathcal{P}}(\mathsf{m}) = T \qquad \text{base}(\mathsf{T}) \vee \text{base}(\Gamma) \qquad [0 \mapsto \lceil T \rceil]([0 \mapsto ?E^{\bullet}]\Gamma) \vdash t : B}{\Gamma \vdash \textbf{receive } \mathsf{m} \mapsto t : B :: \langle\!\langle\mathsf{m}\rangle\!\rangle \odot E}$$

Fig. 12. Pat typing rules.

By splitting this single rule into two distinct ones (SINGLE and SEQ), we provide a recursive definition for typing of sequences. This avoids using lists of well-typed relations as a premise in the rule, and in turn, Rocq is able to automatically come up with appropriate inductive schemes.

Mechanization. The mechanization of Pat's typing rules closely follows the pen-and-paper definitions. However, proving properties about well-typed terms requires technical lemmas, such as inversion lemmas or canonical forms of terms. For example, we had to prove that every well-typed Boolean value under environment Γ implies that Γ is a subenvironment of an empty environment ( ). These types of proofs would usually be omitted in classical pen-and-paper proofs, but in our case, even these kinds of proofs required technical lemmas such as properties about environment subtyping.

3.6 Substitution

The call-by-value operational semantics of Pat ensures that substitution only needs to replace a variable with a value. However, since Pat enforces a syntactic separation of values and computations (following *fine-grain call-by-value* [16]), variables are classed as values, which makes the proof of substitution nontrivial.

The Rocq library *dblib* [18], which we use for de Bruijn indices, provides a definition of substitution. To use it, a user defines substitution as a *traverse* function ( ) over terms. It applies a function f at every variable and provides f with the number of binders that have been visited. To use the substitution operation, several lemmas about the traverse function need to be proven.

Lemma 4. (Substitution ( ). *If* $[x \mapsto A]\Gamma_1 \vdash t : B$ *and* $\Gamma_2 \vdash v : A'$, *with* $A \leq A'$ *and* $\Gamma_1 + \Gamma_2 = \Gamma$, *then* $\Gamma \vdash \{v/x\}t : B$.

Mechanization. Originally, the proof of this lemma was assumed to be standard [6,9]. The mechanization revealed the opposite to be the case, and the proof is by far the most complex and largest in the mechanization. One of the most complex parts of the proof is the LET case, which requires extensive reasoning about variable lifting and environment combination. Additionally, due to quasi-linear typing, environment combinations and environment subtyping, one has to consider more cases than initially expected. Although *dblib* alleviates some of the proof burden, manual work is still required. Since variables are considered values in Pat, reasoning about substituting one variable for another is required. While *dblib* provides tactics for automatically proving some of these properties, it often would not be able to do so. We are unsure as to why this is the case.

4 Related Work

Since little research exists on mailbox types, we discuss related work with a focus on mechanizations of the π-calculus and session types [12]. These are tailored to languages that make use of *communication channels* rather than mailboxes.

Ambal et al. [1] present a Rocq formalization of a higher-order π-calculus, where messages are able to carry processes. Their work focuses on the representation of binders in name restrictions of processes. The authors provide four versions of their mechanization, each with a different representation of variables. They conclude that their de Bruijn formalization is the most concise, but requires complex manipulation of de Bruijn indices and intricate proofs about renaming lemmas. This fact can also be observed in our work.

Goto et al. [11] provide a mechanization of polymorphic session types for the π-calculus in Rocq. Their mechanization uses the locally-nameless [4] approach for variables. Similar to our work, the authors first provide their definitions for processes and types independently. They are able to prove that their type system guarantees preservation and safety properties.

Thiemann [21] presents a mechanization of session types in Agda. In contrast to other mechanizations, his approach makes use of *intrinsically* typed terms, meaning that only well-typed terms can be constructed. As is common with intrinsically typed mechanizations, variables are represented by de Bruijn indices [23]. The preservation and progress properties are proven by construction. Intrinsic typing can lead to reduced proof sizes and fewer lemmas [23]. Whether such a representation would also work for Pat is worth exploring.

Tirore et al. [22] provide a mechanization of multiparty asynchronous session types in Rocq. They rely on the original definitions by Honda et al. [13]. During their mechanization they discovered flaws with the original definitions, such that type preservation does not hold in that system. They propose a new type system for which preservation and other properties hold, formally proving this claim. To manage the complexity of variables, they use the *Autosubst2* library [19], which generates Rocq code based on the de Bruijn representation. In contrast to our formalization, the authors choose to represent environments as a list of pairs, with name and type. They claim that this representation, in particular, simplified context splitting for parallel composition.

Zalakain and Dardha [24] present a mechanization of a type system for the π-calculus in Agda. Their approach facilitates *leftover typing*, where the typing judgment includes a second leftover environment. The leftover environment contains types not used in the typing of the term, leaving them available for parallel processes. This technique eliminates the need for environment splits but would likely be difficult to use due to the need for type combination.

5   Conclusion and Future Work

In this paper, we have described the first mechanization of mailbox types and their semantics, as well as the syntax and semantics of the Pat programming language, in the Rocq Prover. We show that mechanizing Pat is nontrivial: in particular, environment combinations and subtyping pose a big challenge due to the numerous technical lemmas needed. Our work successfully provides a significant number of machine-checked proofs for various properties about mailbox types and Pat's static semantics. During the mechanization process, we also identified and fixed multiple oversights in the original definitions and proofs.

The next step for future work is the mechanization of the operational semantics, which would allow us to formulate machine-checked proofs of properties such as preservation and progress. Initial work has shown that a primary difficulty in formalizing Pat's operational semantics is the constant manipulation of de Bruijn indices. While tedious, previous work [24] was able to successfully formalize a similar semantics with this representation of variables. Alternatively, we could make heavier use of Rocq's dependent types. In some mechanizations of the π-calculus [1], the type system keeps track of available channel endpoints for each process, which could potentially reduce the proofs regarding de Bruijn indices.

Acknowledgements. We thank the anonymous reviewers for their helpful comments. Fowler was supported by EPSRC grant EP/T014628/1 (STARDUST).

References

1. Ambal, G., Lenglet, S., Schmitt, A.: HOπ in Coq. J. Autom. Reason. **65**(1), 75–124 (2020). https://doi.org/10.1007/s10817-020-09553-0
2. Armstrong, J.: Making reliable distributed systems in the presence of software errors. Ph.D. thesis, Royal Institute of Technology, Stockholm, Sweden (2003). https://nbn-resolving.org/urn:nbn:se:kth:diva-3658
3. Brzozowski, J.A.: Derivatives of regular expressions. J. ACM **11**(4), 481–494 (1964). https://doi.org/10.1145/321239.321249
4. Charguéraud, A.: The locally nameless representation. J. Autom. Reason. **49**(3), 363–408 (2012). https://doi.org/10.1007/s10817-011-9225-2
5. de Bruijn, N.G.: Lambda calculus notation with nameless dummies, a tool for automatic formula manipulation, with application to the Church-Rosser theorem. Indagationes Mathematicae (Proc.) **75**(5), 381–392 (1972). https://doi.org/10.1016/1385-7258(72)90034-0
6. de'Liguoro, U., Padovani, L.: Mailbox Types for Unordered Interactions. LIPIcs, Vol. 109, ECOOP 2018 **109**, 15:1–15:28 (2018). https://doi.org/10.4230/LIPICS.ECOOP.2018.15
7. Ennals, R., Sharp, R., Mycroft, A.: Linear Types for Packet Processing. In: Schmidt, D. (ed.) ESOP 2004. LNCS, vol. 2986, pp. 204–218. Springer, Heidelberg (2004). https://doi.org/10.1007/978-3-540-24725-8_15
8. Fowler, S., Attard, D.P., Marshall, D., Gay, S.J., Trinder, P.: Special Delivery: Programming with Mailbox Types (Extended Version) (2025). https://doi.org/10.48550/arXiv.2306.12935
9. Fowler, S., Attard, D.P., Sowul, F., Gay, S.J., Trinder, P.: Special delivery: programming with mailbox types. Proc. ACM Program. Lang. **7**(ICFP), 78–107 (2023). https://doi.org/10.1145/3607832
10. Fowler, S., Attard, D.P., Sowul, F., Gay, S.J., Trinder, P.: Special Delivery: Programming with Mailbox Types (Extended Version) (Jun 2023). https://doi.org/10.48550/arXiv.2306.12935
11. Goto, M., Jagadeesan, R., Jeffrey, A., Pitcher, C., Riely, J.: An extensible approach to session polymorphism. Math. Struct. Comput. Sci. **26**(3), 465–509 (2016). https://doi.org/10.1017/S0960129514000231
12. Honda, K.: Types for dyadic interaction. In: Best, E. (ed.) CONCUR 1993. LNCS, vol. 715, pp. 509–523. Springer, Heidelberg (1993). https://doi.org/10.1007/3-540-57208-2_35
13. Honda, K., Yoshida, N., Carbone, M.: Multiparty asynchronous session types. J. ACM **63**(1), 9:1–9:67 (2016). https://doi.org/10.1145/2827695
14. Kobayashi, N.: Quasi-linear types. In: Proceedings of the 26th ACM SIGPLAN-SIGACT Symposium on Principles of Programming Languages. pp. 29–42. POPL '99, Association for Computing Machinery, New York, NY, USA (1999). https://doi.org/10.1145/292540.292546
15. Leroy, X.: Formal verification of a realistic compiler. Commun. ACM **52**(7), 107–115 (2009). https://doi.org/10.1145/1538788.1538814

16. Levy, P., Power, J., Thielecke, H.: Modelling environments in call-by-value programming languages. Inf. Comput. **185**(2), 182–210 (2003). https://doi.org/10.1016/S0890-5401(03)00088-9
17. Pierce, B.C.: Types and Programming Languages. MIT Press, Cambridge, Mass (2002)
18. Pottier, F., Orr, K.: Dblib (2021). https://github.com/rocq-community/dblib. commit: 25469872c0ba99b046f7e5b8608205eeea5ac077
19. Stark, K.: Mechanising Syntax with Binders in Coq, Ph.D. thesis. Saarbrücken, Germany (2019)
20. Team, T.R.D.: The Rocq Prover. Zenodo (2025). https://doi.org/10.5281/zenodo.15149629
21. Thiemann, P.: Intrinsically-Typed Mechanized Semantics for Session Types. In: Proceedings of the 21st International Symposium on Principles and Practice of Declarative Programming, pp. 1–15. PPDP '19, Association for Computing Machinery, New York, NY, USA (2019). https://doi.org/10.1145/3354166.3354184
22. Tirore, D., Bengtson, J., Carbone, M.: Multiparty asynchronous session types: a mechanised proof of subject reduction. In: Aldrich, J., Silva, A. (eds.) 39th European Conference on Object-Oriented Programming (ECOOP 2025). Leibniz International Proceedings in Informatics (LIPIcs), vol. 333, pp. 31:1–31:30. Schloss Dagstuhl – Leibniz-Zentrum für Informatik, Dagstuhl, Germany (2025). https://doi.org/10.4230/LIPIcs.ECOOP.2025.31
23. Wadler, P., Kokke, W., Siek, J.G.: Programming Language Foundations in Agda (2022). https://plfa.inf.ed.ac.uk/22.08/
24. Zalakain, U., Dardha, O.: π with Leftovers: A Mechanisation in Agda. In: Peters, K., Willemse, T.A.C. (eds.) FORTE 2021. LNCS, vol. 12719, pp. 157–174. Springer, Cham (2021). https://doi.org/10.1007/978-3-030-78089-0_9

Deductive Verification of Legal Contracts

Reiner Hähnle[1] and Cosimo Laneve[2]

[1] Department of Computer Science, TU Darmstadt, Darmstadt, Germany
reiner.haehnle@tu-darmstadt.de
[2] DISI, University of Bologna, Bologna, Italy
cosimo.laneve@unibo.it

Abstract. We enable deductive verification for *Stipula*, a domain-specific language for legal contracts, by systematically translating contracts into Java programs annotated with Java Modeling Language specifications, and subsequently proving them using a deductive verification tool. A central challenge of the translation lies in representing event-driven and time-dependent behaviour within a static specification framework. To address this, we introduce a dispatch table that records schedulable events together with their triggering times. The technique is presented for acyclic *Stipula* contracts. We also extend the proposed technique to cyclic contracts, outlining the additional challenges and the conditions under which the approach remains applicable.

Keywords: Formal Verification · Stipula Language · Translation-based Verification · Deductive Verification

1 Introduction

Stipula is a domain-specific programming language designed to model legal contracts with formally enforceable properties, particularly those governing asset transfers, obligations, and time-dependent rights [8]. Contracts written in *Stipula* combine declarative clauses with executable semantics, yielding models whose behaviour evolves dynamically over time. To facilitate the contract lifecycle, a supporting toolchain has been developed that has been integrated into a unified workbench, enabling legal practitioners and developers in writing, testing, debugging, and managing legal contracts [13, 21]. While this infrastructure provides practical support for contract development and experimentation, it currently lacks advanced deductive verification capabilities.

This paper complements the existing *Stipula* workbench with a formal verification layer capable of establishing both partial and total correctness properties of legal contracts. Our approach relies on a systematic translation of *Stipula* contracts into Java programs annotated with Java Modeling Language (JML) specifications, thereby reducing the verification of legal contracts to the discharge of proof obligations within a mature and well-established formal methods framework. Concretely, we use KeY [4] as a general-purpose deductive verification system.

© IFIP International Federation for Information Processing 2026
Published by Springer Nature Switzerland AG 2026
R. Casadei and F. Ghassemi (Eds.): COORDINATION 2026, LNCS 16590, pp. 218–239, 2026.
https://doi.org/10.1007/978-3-032-28358-0_11

A central challenge in this setting is achieving sufficient precision in the representation of execution behaviour. Legal contracts typically exhibit *dynamic* features – notably the scheduling of events at future times – while JML specifications are inherently *static*. Modelling time and deferred events within a deductive verification framework, therefore, requires an explicit and carefully structured representation of the contract's temporal evolution. Unlike our preliminary study [11], where time and events were treated in an abstract manner, the present work fully incorporates timed events into the translation. This is challenging because the underlying semantic models of *Stipula* contracts are infinite-state due to the unbounded progression of time and the generation of future events.

To represent the behaviour of *Stipula* using static method contracts, we exploit the finite-state structure defined by the contract's underlying automaton, in line with *Stipula*'s state-based programming style. Starting from this automaton, we systematically construct all sequences of clauses that are legally admissible according to the contract specification. This construction yields an explicit representation of the contract's behavioural space, abstracting away from concrete executions while preserving the permitted control-flow structures. A key component of this process is the dispatch table, which records the events that can be scheduled together with their trigger times. This representation plays a central role in verification: the soundness and completeness of the properties that can be established depend directly on how precisely the admissible execution paths are captured.

We first present the technique for acyclic *Stipula* contracts. In this setting, we formally define the translation, describe the construction of the dispatch table and the generation of execution paths, and show how partial-correctness properties of contracts can be reduced to proof obligations discharged automatically by KeY. For acyclic contracts, the behavioural space is finite and can be represented with high precision.

We subsequently extend our approach to cover cyclic contracts. The translation devised for the acyclic setting can be generalised to contracts featuring *separate cycles*: cycles are not nested, even if multiple paths between their entry/exit states are permitted. Here, each cycle is mapped to a bounded Java loop iteration, whose termination is enforced through an explicit counter and a predetermined upper bound. This encoding makes the verification task possible for a deductive verification tool, while deliberately introducing a controlled over-approximation of the contract's potentially unbounded behaviour. As customary in deductive verification, the presence of loop iterations requires suitable invariants. Accordingly, while the structural aspects of the translation are fully automated, the user may be required to provide contract-specific invariants to enable KeY to complete the proof obligations generated by cyclic constructs.

Overall, the main contributions of this work are as follows:

- *A principled encoding of time-dependent contractual behaviour.* We devise a novel and adequate data structure, the *dispatch table*, for representing time constraints and event scheduling within a deductive verification setting.

```
stipula C {
    assets h̄
    fields x̄
    agreement(Ā) {
        Ā₁ : x̄₁
        ...
        Āₙ : x̄ₙ
    } ⇒ @Q
    F
}
```

$$
\begin{aligned}
\textit{Functions} \quad & F ::= \quad \_ \quad | \quad \texttt{@Q A}: \texttt{f}(\overline{\texttt{y}})[\overline{\texttt{k}}]\,(E)\{\,S\,;\,W\,\} \Rrightarrow \texttt{@Q}'\,F \\
\textit{Prefixes} \quad & P ::= \quad E \rightarrow \texttt{x} \quad | \quad E \rightarrow \texttt{A} \quad | \quad E \multimap \texttt{h},\texttt{h}' \\
& \qquad\quad | \quad E \multimap \texttt{h},\texttt{A} \\
\textit{Statements} \quad & S ::= \quad \_ \quad | \quad P\,S \quad | \quad \textbf{if}\,(E)\,\{\,S\,\}\,\textbf{else}\,\{\,S\,\}\,S \\
\textit{Events} \quad & W ::= \quad \_ \quad | \quad \textbf{now} + \texttt{t} \gg \texttt{@Q}\,\{\,S\,\} \Rrightarrow \texttt{@Q}'\,W \\
\textit{Expressions} \quad & E ::= \quad v \quad | \quad \textbf{now} \quad | \quad X \quad | \quad E\,\textsf{op}\,E \quad | \quad \textsf{nop}\,E
\end{aligned}
$$

Fig. 1. Syntax of *Stipula*

– *A systematic and extensible translation framework.* We define a formal, fully specified translation from legal contracts written in *Stipula* into Java programs annotated with JML specifications. The translation is not limited to acyclic interaction patterns, but also covers separate (non-nested) cycles, thereby addressing a wide range of realistic contractual behaviour.
– *A sound verification methodology based on mainstream deductive technology.* We establish the soundness of the translation, ensuring that properties verified on the generated JML/Java code by a state-of-the-art deductive verification system such as KeY correctly reflect the semantics of the original contract.

The paper is organised as follows. Section 2 contains the necessary background about *Stipula* and KeY. Section 3 defines the translation function for *Stipula* contracts; the translation covers both acyclic contracts and those with cycles. Sect. 4 analyses the management of timed events with the dispatch table and the generation of execution paths; Sect. 5 extends the analysis to cyclic behaviour. Section 6 briefly reviews related efforts in formal verification of legal contracts and Sect. 7 concludes the paper and outlines directions for future work.

2   Background

To set the stage for our translation-based verification method, we briefly review the relevant background. Section 2.1 presents the *Stipula* language, emphasising its constructs for assets, states, and timed events. Section 2.2 introduces the KeY system, which we employ as the verification backend.

2.1   *Stipula*

A *Stipula* contract consists of a set of parties, states, assets, fields, and a set of functions and events. The declaration of a contract is defined in Fig. 1, where C is the name of the contract, $\overline{\texttt{h}}$ and $\overline{\texttt{x}}$ are the *assets* and *fields*, respectively, $\overline{\texttt{A}}$ are the *parties*. The **agreement** construct declares the parties that set the initial value of the fields. For example, if the agreement has three parties $\texttt{A}_1, \texttt{A}_2, \texttt{A}_3$ and the contract has two fields $\texttt{x}_1, \texttt{x}_2$, if it declares $\texttt{A}_1 : \texttt{x}_1$ and $\texttt{A}_2, \texttt{A}_3 : \texttt{x}_2$ then $\texttt{x}_1$ will be set by A_1 and x_2 will be set upon agreement on the value between A_2 and A_3. When the agreement is concluded, the initial state of the contract is set and the parties may invoke a function in F.

A *function* f declared as @Q A : $f(\overline{y})[\overline{k}]\,(E)\{\,S;\,W\,\}$ ⇒ @Q$'$ can be invoked by a party A if the contract is in state Q and the guard E is *true*. The names $\overline{y}$ and $\overline{k}$ are the formal parameters of f; they are kept separate because $\overline{y}$ are *field* values while $\overline{k}$ are *asset* quantities.

Function bodies are *statements S* followed by *events W*. The former include value transfers, asset movements, conditional logic, and field assignments. *Stipula* distinguishes between different transfer operations: field updates and messages use the symbol $\rightarrow$ with the usual semantics of assignment, while asset transfers, called *moves*, use the linear operator $\multimap$ to emphasise the conservation semantics. For instance, an expression like "1 $\multimap$ wallet, Seller" denotes exclusive transfer of a unit in wallet to the Seller and, *at the same time*, the decrease by 1 of wallet. In contrast "wallet $\rightarrow$ Seller" specifies that the value currently stored in wallet is communicated to Seller, while leaving the state of wallet unchanged. It is common practice in *Stipula* to use the abbreviations h $\multimap$ h$'$ and h $\multimap$ A, which stand for h $\multimap$ h, h$'$ and h $\multimap$ h, A, respectively.

Events **now** + t $\gg$ @Q$\{\,S\,\}$ ⇒ @Q$'$ define a statement S to be executed if, *after* t time units from the current execution, the contract is in the state Q. The expression t is either a non-negative number or a variable (a formal parameter or a field) or a variable plus a non-negative number. If the event is executed, the contract will transit to the state Q$'$. The expression **now** + t is called *time guard*. Functions and events are generically called *clauses*.

Expressions E include integer constant values v, the keyword **now** (that stands for a non-negative integer value), names of assets, fields and parameters generically ranged over by X, standard arithmetic and Boolean operations op (binary) and nop (unary). Booleans are encoded by integers in the usual way. Actually, *Stipula* has a richer set of values (reals, strings, time and asset values). For the time being, we stick to integer arithmetic, where deductive verification systems exhibit a high degree of automation. Other datatypes require corresponding support in automated theorem provers and SMT solvers: experimentation is needed to determine what is possible. We also want to keep the presentation simple.

The semantics of *Stipula* is defined operationally by means of a transition relation between *configurations* $\mathbb{C}, \mathbb{t}$, where $\mathbb{t}$ is a positive integer value representing the system's global clock and $\mathbb{C}$ is a tuple $C(\mathbb{Q}, \ell, \Sigma, \Psi)$, where:

- C is the *Stipula* contract name;
- $\mathbb{Q}$ is the contract's current state: either _ (for no state) or a contract state Q;
- ℓ maps names (parties, fields, assets, function parameters) to values;
- Σ is the (possibly empty) residual of a function body or of an event handler, *i.e.* Σ is either _ or a term $S\,W$ ⇒ @Q;
- Ψ is a (possibly empty) multiset of *pending events* to be executed. We let Ψ be _ when there are no pending events, or

$$\mathbb{t}_1 \gg_{\mathsf{ev}_1} @Q_1\{\,S_1\,\} ⇒ @Q_1' \quad | \quad \cdots \quad | \quad \mathbb{t}_n \gg_{\mathsf{ev}_n} @Q_n\{\,S_n\,\} ⇒ @Q_n' \,, \qquad (1)$$

Table 1. The control transition rules of *Stipula*

[FUNCTION]

$$\dfrac{\begin{array}{c}\texttt{@Q A}:\texttt{f}(\overline{y})\,[\overline{k}]\ (E)\ \{\,S\,W\,\}\Rrightarrow\texttt{@Q}'\in\texttt{C}\\[2pt]\Psi\ ,\ \mathbb{t}\nrightarrow\\[2pt]\ell(\texttt{A})=A\quad \ell'=\ell[\overline{y}\mapsto\overline{u},\overline{k}\mapsto\overline{v}]\quad [\![E]\!]_{\ell'}\neq 0\end{array}}{\texttt{C}(\texttt{Q},\ell,\,\_\,,\Psi)\ ,\ \mathbb{t}\ \xrightarrow{A:\texttt{f}(\overline{u})[\overline{v}]}\ \texttt{C}(\texttt{Q},\ell',\,S\,W\Rrightarrow\texttt{@Q}',\Psi)\ ,\ \mathbb{t}}$$

[STATE-CHANGE]

$$\dfrac{[\![W\{^{\mathbb{t}}/_{\texttt{now}}\}]\!]_{\ell}=\Psi'}{\begin{array}{c}\texttt{C}(\texttt{Q},\ell,\,\_\,W\Rrightarrow\texttt{@Q}',\Psi)\ ,\ \mathbb{t}\\[2pt]\longrightarrow\texttt{C}(\texttt{Q}',\ell,\,\_\,,\Psi'\mid\Psi)\ ,\ \mathbb{t}\end{array}}$$

[EVENT-MATCH]

$$\dfrac{\Psi=\mathbb{t}\gg_{\mathbf{ev}_\kappa}\texttt{@Q}\ \{\,S\,\}\Rrightarrow\texttt{@Q}'\mid\Psi'}{\texttt{C}(\texttt{Q},\ell,\,\_\,,\Psi)\ ,\ \mathbb{t}\ \xrightarrow{\mathbf{ev}_\kappa}\ \texttt{C}(\texttt{Q},\ell,\,S\Rrightarrow\texttt{@Q}',\Psi')\ ,\ \mathbb{t}}$$

[TICK]

$$\dfrac{\Psi\ ,\ \mathbb{t}\nrightarrow}{\begin{array}{c}\texttt{C}(\texttt{Q},\ell,\,\_\,,\Psi)\ ,\ \mathbb{t}\\[2pt]\longrightarrow\texttt{C}(\texttt{Q},\ell,\,\_\,,\Psi\downarrow_{\mathbb{t}})\ ,\ \mathbb{t}+1\end{array}}$$

where $\mathbb{t}_i$ are the values of the expressions **now** $+\ \mathsf{t}_i$ of the corresponding events. The indices $\mathbf{ev}_i$ are introduced by rule [FUNCTION] when the body of a function is incorporated into the configuration and denotes a unique identifier statically assigned to the event.

The transition relation of *Stipula* is $\mathbb{C},\mathbb{t}\xrightarrow{\mu}\mathbb{C}',\mathbb{t}'$, where μ may be empty, or an initial agreement, or $A:\texttt{f}(\overline{u})[\overline{v}]$ (in case of function invocations) or an event. Its formal definition is given in Table 1 for the control transition rules, see [8] for the agreement and statement rules. The former rule set requires a specific JML/Java encoding, whereas the latter are translated in a standard way and are inessential for the understanding of this paper.

The formal definition of $\mathbb{C},\mathbb{t}\xrightarrow{\mu}\mathbb{C}',\mathbb{t}'$ uses the following auxiliary predicates and functions:

- $[\![E]\!]_\ell$ is a *partial function* returning the value of E in memory ℓ.
- $[\![W\{^{\mathbb{t}}/_{\texttt{now}}\}]\!]_\ell$ is the multiset of scheduled events obtained from the sequence W by replacing every **now** by $\mathbb{t}$ and evaluating every expression in the time guards.
- $\Psi\ ,\ \mathbb{t}\nrightarrow$ is a predicate that is *true* whenever Ψ is as in Eq. (1) and, for every $1\leqslant i\leqslant n$, $\mathbb{t}_i\neq\mathbb{t}$. It is *false* otherwise.
- $\Psi\downarrow_{\mathbb{t}}$ removes from Ψ every event with time value less or equal to $\mathbb{t}$.

We explain the rules in Table 1. Rule [FUNCTION] defines invocations: the label specifies party A performing the invocation of a function named $\texttt{f}$ with the actual parameters. The transition may occur provided (i) the contract is in the state $\texttt{Q}$, admitting invocations of $\texttt{f}$ from A, (ii) the contract is *idle*, *i.e.* the contract has no statement to execute (presence of $\_$ in the left configuration), (iii) the precondition E is satisfied, and no event can be triggered (premise $\Psi\ ,\ \mathbb{t}\nrightarrow$). In particular, the final constraint expresses that events *have precedence* on possible function invocations. For example, if a payment deadline is reached and, at the same time, the payment arrives, it will be refused in favour of the event managing the deadline. We use two notations for party identifiers: A and A. The former denotes the formal name used in the contract specification, whereas A refers to the concrete party name instantiated and fixed when the agreement is concluded.

Rule [STATE-CHANGE] says that a contract changes state when the execution of the statement in the function body terminates. At this stage, the sequence of events W is added to the multiset of pending events once their time expressions have been evaluated, in particular now is replaced by the current value of the clock. Rule [EVENT-MATCH] specifies that event handlers may run provided there is no statement to perform and the time guard of the event has exactly the value of $\mathfrak{t}$. Rule [TICK] defines the elapsing of time, which may happen when there is no statement to perform and no event can be triggered.

In this paper we use the state transition models of *Stipula* contracts, called the *underlying automata*. The states of these automata are those of the *Stipula* contract. The transitions correspond to clauses and are labelled either with the function name (the party name is always omitted, for simplicity's sake we assume that function names are pairwise different) or with a uniquely numbered event. By definition, these automata are *finite models*; Figs. 2 and 3 show the two underlying automata of the contracts Licence and Deposit. These contracts are drawn from [11] with minor modifications, which are discussed below.

Example 1. Figure 2 defines the License contract regulating a licensing transaction between a Licensor and a Licensee, with a 30 days trial period and the possibility to purchase or decline the license. The field code stores the information for the trial period access, the asset token grants the licence. If the Licensee does not purchase the license before the trial period expires, the contract terminates and the token is automatically returned to the Licensee. The **agreement**

```
1   stipula License {
2       assets balance, token
3       fields cost, code
4       agreement (Licensor, Licensee)(cost) {
5           Licensor, Licensee : cost
6       } ⇒ @Init
7       @Init Licensor: offer(x)[n] {
8           n ⊸ token
9           x → code
10          now + 1 ≫ @Prop { token ⊸ Licensor } ⇒ @End
11      } ⇒ @Prop
12      @Prop Licensee: activate()[b] (b == cost) {
13          b ⊸ balance
14          code → Licensee ;
15          now + 30 ≫ @Trial {
16                  balance ⊸ Licensee
17                  token ⊸ Licensor
18                  } ⇒ @End
19      } ⇒ @Trial
20      @Trial Licensee: buy()[] {
21          balance ⊸ Licensor
22          token ⊸ Licensee
23      } ⇒ @End
24  }
```


Fig. 2. The License contract in *Stipula* and its underlying automaton.

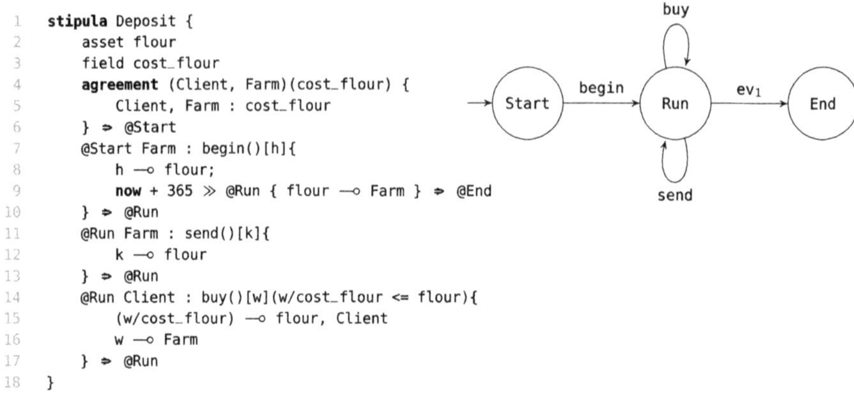

```
1   stipula Deposit {
2       asset flour
3       field cost_flour
4       agreement (Client, Farm)(cost_flour) {
5           Client, Farm : cost_flour
6       } ⇒ @Start
7       @Start Farm : begin()[h]{
8           h ⊸ flour;
9           now + 365 ≫ @Run { flour ⊸ Farm } ⇒ @End
10      } ⇒ @Run
11      @Run Farm : send()[k]{
12          k ⊸ flour
13      } ⇒ @Run
14      @Run Client : buy()[w](w/cost_flour <= flour){
15          (w/cost_flour) ⊸ flour, Client
16          w ⊸ Farm
17      } ⇒ @Run
18  }
```


Fig. 3. The Deposit contract in *Stipula* and its underlying automaton

in Line 2 allows the parties to agree on the license cost. Upon agreement, the first state is @Init where

the Licensor may invoke offer, transferring a token (representing the license) into escrow and a trial code. A scheduled event is simultaneously registered after 1 day to reclaim the token if the Licensee fails to start the trial period. The contract then moves to Prop. If no function is called in this state, then time is advanced, eventually triggering the event at line 2. In Prop, the Licensee can activate the trial by paying the cost (observe that b is an asset of the Licensee), which is transferred to the contract's balance: the contract acts as a notary for assets that are not finally disposed. Now the license code is revealed to the Licensee and another event is scheduled to handle the expiration of the trial period: if the license is not purchased before 30 days, the balance is refunded, the token returned to the Licensor. The license purchase is done by the buy function, which finalises the transaction by transferring the balance to the Licensor and assigning the token permanently to the Licensee. In the corresponding contract in [11], the start and end of the trial period are defined during the agreement, whereas here, for simplicity, they are hard-coded in the contract.

Example 2. Figure 3 defines the Deposit contract that models the interactions between a Farm and a Client. The Farm deposits flour, while the Client purchases and withdraws the corresponding amount at an agreed price. The contractual terms are enforced over a validity period of 365 days. The clause send allows the Farm to deposit flour into the contract's stock; the operation h⊸flour implements the deposit in the asset flour. Actual delivery occurs only with buy()[w], where (w/cost_flour)⊸flour, Client transfers flour from the contract's stock to the Client (hence w/cost_flour must not be greater than flour) and w⊸Farm represents the payment to the Farm. In [11], the Deposit contract does not allow buy and send to start and end in the same state, as the underlying theory does not cover this case. Consequently, a more convoluted contract was required. In contrast, the definition of `Deposit` presented here is simpler, as it relies on a more expressive theoretical framework.

`License` and `Deposit` represent paradigmatic interaction patterns that frequently arise in legal contracts and that are clearly reflected in their underlying automata. The behavioural structure of `License` is *acyclic*: no state is revisited during execution. In contrast, `Deposit` exhibits a *cyclic* pattern, as it includes functions that may be invoked repeatedly, leading to repeated traversals of certain states. It is important to observe that, while the semantics of *Stipula* admits potentially infinite cyclic behaviour (for example, `Deposit` allows an unbounded number of interactions in a fixed time window of 365 days), in practice only finitely many transactions can realistically occur. In Sect. 5, we use this observation to obtain bounded encoding of cycles in the translated contracts.

Definition 1 (Cyclic Contract, Separate Cycle). *A Stipula contract is* cyclic *if its underlying automaton has a* cycle: *a sequence* $Q_1 \xrightarrow{\nu_1} Q_2 \xrightarrow{\nu_2} \cdots \xrightarrow{\nu_{\ell-1}} Q_\ell \xrightarrow{\nu_\ell} Q_1$ *where* $Q_1, \ldots, Q_\ell$ *are pairwise different and* ν_i *are either function names or events. A contract has* separate cycles *if any two cycles either have no state in common or share their initial state only. A contract is* acyclic *if it has no* cycle.

The contract `License` is acyclic, while `Deposit` has separate cycles. In what follows, we first consider acyclic contracts and then turn to separate cyclic ones. This progression allows us to introduce the complexities of the translation into `JML`/`Java` in a gradual manner.

2.2 Deductive Verification with the KeY System

The KeY system [2,4] is a deductive verification framework for `Java` that combines symbolic execution, invariant reasoning, and method contracts[1] on top of a calculus for an expressive program logic. The main use case of KeY is formal verification of Java programs annotated with specifications written in `JML`. It provides an interactive user environment, where one can construct correctness proofs of `Java` methods against their `JML` contracts. Method contracts typically include preconditions (**requires**), postconditions (**ensures**), frame conditions (**assignable**), class invariants, and auxiliary annotations such as loop invariants and assertions. Given a `JML`-annotated `Java` class, KeY translates the specifications into logical proof obligations and attempts to discharge them using its symbolic execution engine. The details of the verification process are irrelevant for the purpose of this paper: KeY is used as a *black box*, the input is a `JML`-annotated Java file that results from translation of a *Stipula* contract. In principle, *any* deductive verification system with a sufficient coverage of `JML`/`Java` can be used, for example, Krakatoa [9] or OpenJML [7], although we did not try that. In general, KeY is

---

[1] Not to be confused with *Stipula* contracts. In this paper, both kinds of contract are featured, but it should be obvious from the context when we mean *Stipula* contracts and when `JML`/`Java` method contracts.

used in interactive or auto-active mode, however, for all case studies discussed below, the verification is *fully automatic.*

3   Translation Approach

To enable formal verification of a *Stipula* contract with KeY, we define a systematic translation into `Java` code annotated with `JML` specifications. As discussed in [11], *Stipula* contracts are translated into classes where functions and events are modelled by stateful `Java` methods, assets and fields are modelled by suitable `Java` fields. The definition of the translation is given in Listing 1.

We begin by analysing the declaration component of the translation. As mentioned in Sect. 2.1, we assume all *Stipula* fields, assets, and auxiliary variables are of type `int` which preserves the operational semantics of the original contracts.[2] Verification involves a trade-off between precision and generality: parameters may be assigned concrete values, thereby analysing a specific execution scenario, or left symbolic to reason about all possible executions. The translation in Listing 1 adopts the former approach, targeting a single scenario. Accordingly, fields $\overline{x}$ are initialised to constant values $\overline{u}$ (the values the fields have after the agreement), and formal parameters of functions are likewise instantiated to fixed values $(\overline{y_1} = \overline{v_1}, \overline{k_1} = \overline{v'_1}, \ldots, \overline{y_n} = \overline{v_n}, \overline{k_n} = \overline{v'_n})$.

```
TRANSLATE( stipula C { assets h̄ fields x̄ agreement( Ā ) { ··· } ⇒ @Q F )  ≝
  public final class C {
      public static int Ā, h̄, (A_h)^{A∈Ā,h∈h̄} ;
      public static int x̄ = ū ;
                    // ū are the values the fields x̄ have after the agreement
      public static int now = 0 ;
      public static int u_Q1, ..., u_Qm, w_Q1, ..., w_Qm ;
                    // auxiliary variables: Q1, ..., Qm are the states of C
      public static int[] DT = new int[N] ;
                    // DT is the dispatch table, N is the number of events in C
      public static int ȳ1 = v̄1, k̄1 = v̄'1, ..., ȳn = v̄n, k̄n = v̄'n ;
                    // formal parameters of functions and their initialization
      public static invariant ASSET_INVC ;
      public static invariant 1 <= w_Q1 <= max_Q1 && ··· && 1 <= w_Qm <= max_Qm ;
        // max_Q1,...,max_Qm are the number of functions starting at Q1,...,Qm
      public static invariant 0 <= u_Q1 <= max_tv && ··· && 0 <= u_Qm <= max_tv ;
                    // max_tv is a constant, see Section 4
  TRANSLATE(F)


      /*@ public normal_behaviour
        @ requires h̄ == 0 ; DT[0] == -1 && ... && DT[N-1] = -1 ;
          // assets of C are initially 0, DT is empty (encoded by value -1)
        @ requires OTHER PRE-CONDITIONS ;
        @ ensures THE POST-CONDITION ;        // the property we want to prove
```

---

[2] *Stipula* itself is type-free: concrete types (e.g., integers, doubles, strings, Booleans) are inferred statically and at run time [8].

```
@*/

    public final static void behaviour(){  GEN_C(Q) }
}
```

Listing 1. The TRANSLATE function for a *Stipula* contract

The translation introduces auxiliary variables: The dispatch table DT is an array of size N, where N is the number of events in the contract. For each contract state Q1, ..., Qm, the variable u_Qi tracks time progression and ranges over non-negative values bounded by max_tv, the largest constant (plus one) appearing in time expressions (in principle, a single variable would suffice). For each state Qi, the variable w_Qi counts function invocations and ranges between 0 and max_Qi (the number of functions whose initial state is Qi).

Assets satisfy a non-duplication property: *the total amount of a given asset in the system – that is, in the contract and in all the parties – must remain constant.* To enforce this property, we introduce a field A_h for every party A and every asset h in class C. Moreover, we enforce a static invariant ASSET_INV_C that holds for every method in C as follows:

$$ASSET\_INV_C \overset{\text{def}}{=}$$
$$h_1 + A_1\_h_1 + \cdots + A_k\_h_1 == \backslash\text{old}(h_1) + \backslash\text{old}(A_1\_h_1) + \cdots + \backslash\text{old}(A_k\_h_1)$$
$$\&\& \cdots \&\&$$
$$h_r + A_1\_h_r + \cdots + A_k\_h_r == \backslash\text{old}(h_r) + \backslash\text{old}(A_1\_h_r) + \cdots + \backslash\text{old}(A_k\_h_r)$$

In JML the **old** construct is used to refer to the values of fields *prior to method execution.* This allows us to precisely relate the post-state of a method to its pre-state, which is essential for enforcing the non-duplication property. For example, ASSET_INV_License, the invariant of the License contract is

```
balance + Licensor_balance + Licensee_balance ==
    \old(balance) + \old(Licensor_balance) + \old(Licensee_balance)
&& token + Licensor_token + Licensee_token ==
    \old(token) + \old(Licensor_token) + \old(Licensee_token)
```

When assets are transferred directly from one party to another without being stored in a contract's asset (for example, the buy function in the Deposit contract), we also add the invariant

$$A_1 + \cdots + A_k = \backslash\text{old}(A_1) + \cdots + \backslash\text{old}(A_k)$$

modeling that, in these cases, assets are transferred directly to the party's identifier (which was introduced for this purpose).[3]

Functions and events are modeled as static Java methods annotated with JML specifications consisting of three clauses. Consider a *Stipula* function declared as @Q A : f($\overline{y}$)[$\overline{k}$] (E) { $S\,W$ } ⇒ @Q′. Its translation, defined in Listing 2, includes:

---

[3] In [11], assets are classified as *divisible* (*e.g.*, digital currencies) or *indivisible* (*e.g.*, non-fungible tokens), thus generating appropriate invariants to enforce the intended asset semantics. Here, for simplicity, we assume that every asset is divisible.

- A **requires** clause expressing that guard E that must hold in the initial state for the function to execute.
- An **ensures** clause specifying the resulting state transition, including field updates and asset transfers. This clause is defined via the strongest post-condition STRONG_POSTCOND(E, S) computed from the pre-state (see [4] for details about strong post-conditions).
- An **assignable** clause listing the variables that may be modified, determined by a simple static "writes-to" analysis LHSVAR$_\mathtt{A}(S)$.

The body of each method corresponding to a *Stipula* function invoked by a party $\mathtt{A}$, as well as the bodies of events declared within that function, are generated via the function STIPULA2JAVA$_\mathtt{A}(S)$. This function maps a *Stipula* statement S to a sequence of Java statements, yielding a compositional encoding of the function's operational semantics into executable Java code.

```
TRANSLATE( @Q A : f(ȳ)[k̄] (E) { S W } ⇒ @Q' )  ≝
 /*@ public normal_behaviour
   @ requires E ;
   @ ensures   STRONG_POSTCOND(E, S) && ENSUREDTf ;
   @ assignable LHSVARA(S), DT ;
   @*/
 public final static void f(int̄ y, int̄ k) {
     Stipula2JavaA(S)
     UPDATEDT(W)
}
 /*@ public normal_behaviour          // for every now + tᵢ ≫ @Qᵢ { Sᵢ } ⇒ @Q'ᵢ ∈ W
   @ ensures   STRONG_POSTCOND(true, Sᵢ) ;
   @ assignable LHSVARA(Sᵢ) ;
   @*/
 public final static void event_i() {
     Stipula2JavaA(Sᵢ)
}
```

Listing 2. The TRANSLATE function for Stipula functions and events

The definition of STIPULA2JAVA$_\mathtt{A}(S)$ follows a well-established and standard formulation. For readability, the definition is relegated to the Addendum A at the end of the paper.

The discussion about the function GEN$_\mathtt{C}(\mathtt{Q})$ (in Listing 1) and the functions UPDATEDT(W) and ENSUREDT$_\mathsf{f}$ (in Listing 2) are deferred to the next section, as they rely on the dispatch table mechanism.

4   The Dispatch Table and Generation of Execution Paths

To complete the translation, we encode the behaviour of a *Stipula* contract. We use three key mechanisms:

1. Event declarations are collected into a *dispatch table*, recording enabled events and their execution times.
2. *Symbolic execution* implicitly enumerates admissible scenarios via non-deterministic function and event selection;
3. Time progression in a state Q is bounded by a constant `max_tv`, defined as the maximum constant (plus one) occurring in time expressions, and tracked through the symbolic variable `u_Q` $\in [0..$`max_tv`$]$. Advancing time beyond this bound is unnecessary, as no pending event can be executed past that deadline unless generated by a subsequent function invocation.

The dispatch table, introduced in Listing 1, is an array `DT` of size `N`, where `N` is the number of events in the contract. The i-th entry corresponds to the i-th event `now` + t_i $\gg$ `@`Q_i $\{S_i\}$ $\Rightarrow$ `@`Q'_i. The value `DT[i]` is `-1` if the event has not been created; otherwise, it stores the scheduled execution time `now` + t_i, where `now` denotes the time at which the event was generated.

Events declared in a function are inserted in Listing 2 into the dispatch table by UPDATEDT(W). If a function `f` declares events indexed by $\mathrm{ev}_{J_1}, \ldots, \mathrm{ev}_{J_{N_f}}$ with time expressions `now` + t_{J_i}, then UPDATEDT(W) assigns the corresponding computed times to the entries `DT[`ev_{J_i}`]`. In other words, it updates exactly those positions associated with the events generated by `f`. Entries of `DT` not corresponding to events in W remain unchanged, while the relevant entries are updated to `now` + t_{J_i} using the current value of `now`. The formalisation of this behaviour in `JML` is done by the predicate ENSUREDT$_f$. Thus, the specification guarantees that precisely the events declared in `f` are scheduled, relative to the current time `now`, and that no other dispatch table entries are affected. (The formal definition of UPDATEDT(W) and ENSUREDT$_f$ is omitted, because it is straightforward.)

To obtain the possible behaviour of a *Stipula* contract, the dispatch table will be queried to identify one of the events that can be enabled next. To this end, we introduce the auxiliary `Java` method

$$\texttt{int minTimeEntry(\{ev}_1\texttt{,}\ldots\texttt{, ev}_m\texttt{\}) .}$$

The method returns the index in the dispatch table entry corresponding to an event in $\{\mathrm{ev}_1, \ldots, \mathrm{ev}_m\}$ whose associated time value is minimal, provided that such an event exists; otherwise, it returns `-1`. The method is non-deterministic, as multiple events may share the same minimal time value in the dispatch table. In this case, any one of these events may be selected, thereby allowing the symbolic execution to explore all admissible scheduling choices. The implementation of the method `minTimeEntry()` is omitted. Instead, we provide its `JML` specification that defines the essential semantic properties required for verification, which is sufficient for KeY to reason symbolically about the method's behaviour:

```
/*@ public normal_behaviour // specification of int minTimeEntry({ev_1,..., ev_m})
  @ ensures ( \exists i; 0 <= i < N; (i ∈ {ev_1, ..., ev_m} && DT[i] >= now) )
              ⇒ \result ∈ {ev_1, ..., ev_m} && DT[\result] >= now &&
                \forall j; 0 <= j < N; (j ∈ {ev_1, ..., ev_m} && DT[j] >= now)
                                          ⇒ DT[j] >= DT[\result] ;
  @ ensures ( \forall i; 0 <= i < N; i ∈ {ev_1, ..., ev_m} ⇒ DT[i] < now)
              ⇒ \result == -1;
  @ assignable \nothing;
  @*/
```

The first **ensures** clause says that when there is an index in $\{ev_1, \ldots, ev_m\}$ such that its time value in DT is greater or equal to now, then such an index is returned. There can be more than one such index. This causes symbolic execution to branch over all indices \result such that DT[\result] >= now. The second **ensures** clause covers the case when no entry is found. In this case \result is -1.

$$\text{GEN}_C(\mathsf{Q}) \stackrel{\text{def}}{=}$$

```
    int entry = minTimeEntry({ev_1,..., ev_m}) ;
    if ((entry == -1) || (DT[entry] > now && w_Q > 0)) { // call a function
       if (entry == -1) now = now + u_Q ; else now = min(DT[entry]-1, now+u_Q) ;
       if (w_Q == 1) { f_1(ȳ_1, k̄_1) ; GEN_C(Q_1) }
       else if (w_Q == 2) { f_2(ȳ_2, k̄_2) ; GEN_C(Q_2) }
       ...
       else { f_n(ȳ_n, k̄_n) ; GEN_C(Q_n) } // max_Q == n, see Listing 1
    } else { // trigger an event
       now = DT[entry] ;
       if (entry == 1) { event_1() ; DT[entry] = -1 ; GEN_C(Q'_1) }
       else if (entry == 2) { event_2() ; DT[entry] = -1 ; GEN_C(Q'_2) }
       ...
       else { event_m() ; DT[entry] = -1 ; GEN_C(Q'_m) } // entry == m
    }
```

Listing 3. The function $\text{GEN}_C(\mathsf{Q})$; the $f_1, \ldots, f_n$ and **event_1**,…,**event_m** are the functions and events that start in Q and end in $\mathsf{Q}_1, \ldots, \mathsf{Q}_n$ and $\mathsf{Q}'_1, \ldots, \mathsf{Q}'_m$, respectively.

We can now complete the definition of TRANSLATE (Listing 2) by specifying the function $\text{GEN}_C(\mathsf{Q})$ (Listing 3). Assume that in state Q functions $f_1, \ldots, f_n$ can be called and events $\text{event}_1, \ldots, \text{event}_m$ can be triggered. The *Stipula* semantics is non-deterministic. To model this, we use two symbolic variables that were declared in Listing 1: $\text{w\_Q} \in [0..\text{max\_Q}]$, for selecting a function in the state Q, and $\text{u\_Q} \in [0..\text{max\_tv}]$, for controlling time progression. The behaviour is as follows:

1. *Enabled events at current time.* If minTimeEntry(...) returns an index whose time equals now, the corresponding event *must* execute (events preempt functions). After execution, the event is removed from DT. (This removal is actually unnecessary since the automaton is acyclic, it cannot occur again.)
2. *Pending future events.* If one of the earliest scheduled events occurs at a time entry > now, then two cases arise: either time advances, but not until

entry, i.e. at most to `min(DT[entry]-1, now+u_Q)` and a function is executed
(`w_Q > 0`); otherwise, time advances *exactly* to `t` and the event is executed
(`w_Q = 0`).

3. *No pending events.* If no event from `Q` remains to be scheduled, a function must eventually execute. Time progression is bound by `max_tv`, defined as the largest constant (plus one) appearing in time expressions. Assigning `u_Q ∈ [0..max_tv]` ensures a finite, yet sound exploration of all relevant execution scenarios.

Now that the translation is complete, it becomes possible to define and verify meaningful properties for *Stipula* contracts translated to `JML`/`Java` by filling in the slots for `OTHER PRE-CONDITION` and `THE POST-CONDITION`, respectively, in Listing 1. For example, one can prove with KeY the following property of the `License` contract:

```
requires Licensor_balance >= 0 && Licensee_balance > 0 &&
         Licensor_token > 0    && Licensee_token == 0 ;
ensures  (Licensor_balance == \old(Licensor_balance)+cost && Licensor_token == 0
         && Licensee_balance == \old(Licensee_balance)-cost
         && Licensee_token == \old(Licensor_token)
         ) || (
         Licensor_balance == \old(Licensor_balance) &&
         Licensor_token == \old(Licensor_token) &&
         Licensee_balance == \old(Licensee_balance) &&
         Licensee_token == \old(Licensee_token)
         ) ;
```

The contract expresses that, upon termination, either the licensing transaction succeeded (the `Licensee` purchased the license and the `Licensor` obtained the money) or the `Licensee` is withdrawn and no `token` was delivered.

Theorem 1 (Soundness). *Let* C *be an acyclic* *Stipula* *contract and let*

$$\mathbb{C}, 0 \xrightarrow{(\overline{A},\, \overline{A_i : \overline{v_i}}^{\,i \in 1..\ell})} {}^* \; \mathbb{C}_1, \mathbb{t}_1 \xrightarrow{\mu_1} {}^* \; \mathbb{C}_2, \mathbb{t}_2 \xrightarrow{\mu_2} {}^* \cdots \xrightarrow{\mu_{n+1}} {}^* \; \mathbb{C}_{n+1}, \mathbb{t}_{n+1}$$

where Q_i *are the states of* $\mathbb{C}_i$, *with* $i \in 1..n+1$, Q_{n+1} *is the final state of the underlying automaton, and* μ_i *are either function invocations* $A_i{:}f_i(\overline{v_i})[\overline{v_i'}]$ *or events* ev_i. *Then the above computation may be traced in the code of* $\mathrm{GEN}_C(\cdot)$ *as follows. Consider* $\mathbb{C}_i, \mathbb{t}_i \xrightarrow{\mu_i} {}^* \; \mathbb{C}_{i+1}, \mathbb{t}_{i+1}$; *if, in the code of* $\mathrm{GEN}_C(Q_i)$,

1. $\mathbf{now} = \mathbb{t}_i$ *if* μ_i *is an event;* $\mathbf{now} \leqslant \mathbb{t}_i$ *if* μ_i *is a function;*
2. *if the multiset of pending events in* $\mathbb{C}_i$ *is*

$$\mathbb{t}_{J_1} \gg_{\mathsf{ev}_{J_1}} @Q_{J_1}\{S_{J_1}\} \Rightarrow @Q'_{J_1} \mid \cdots \mid \mathbb{t}_{J_k} \gg_{\mathsf{ev}_{J_k}} @Q_{J_k}\{S_{J_k}\} \Rightarrow @Q'_{J_k}$$

and the dispatch table $\mathrm{DT}[\mathsf{ev}_{J_i}] = \mathbb{t}_{J_i}$, *with* $i \in 1..k$.

Then, whenever $\mu_i = A_i{:}f_i(\overline{v_i})[\overline{v_i'}]$ *it is possible to execute the method* $f_i(\overline{v_i}, \overline{v_i'})$ *and if* $\mu_i = \mathsf{ev}_{J_i}$, *it is possible to execute method* $\mathsf{event}\ _{J_i}(\ )$ *and obtain a state where (1.) and (2.) hold for* $\mathbb{C}_{i+1}$, $\mathbb{t}_{i+1}$.

Therefore, every computation of an acyclic *Stipula* contract is faithfully represented within the `Java` code generated by our translation (the proof is omitted, it is technical, but not difficult). Consequently, when the program is analysed with KeY, each legally admissible behaviour of the original contract is systematically explored. This guarantees that the verification process is sound with respect to the contract's operational semantics in the acyclic setting, as no admissible execution is omitted. We further conjecture that the translation is complete in the acyclic case, in the sense that every behaviour of the generated `Java` program corresponds to a computation that is admissible in the original *Stipula* contract. Establishing such a result formally, however, would require a formalisation of `Java` semantics, which lies beyond the scope of the present paper.

5   Cyclic Behaviour and Its Translation

The technique of Sects. 3 and 4 extends to cyclic contracts with separate cycles such as `Deposit`. Here we examine the additional challenges posed by cycles and clarify the resulting loss of precision.

In `Deposit`, the `Farm` and the `Client` may repeatedly invoke `send` and `buy`, forming a cycle in the contract underlying automaton (Fig. 3). The cycle is exited through a dedicated event executed at most once. This reflects a common contractual pattern: (*i*) cycles have a unique entry/exit state and contain only function invocations; (*ii*) cycles are not nested; (*iii*) events occur outside cycles and typically enforce their termination. As a consequence, each event is executed at most once, even in the presence of cyclic behaviour.

This observation allows us to reuse the dispatch table mechanism developed for acyclic contracts, since the set of events remains finite. However, events generated inside cycles require special care: although they share the same index, different iterations may assign them different time values. To handle this, we assign such events an *abstract* clock value, encoded as `-2`. Rather than reasoning about their precise scheduling time, we only record that they have been generated. We illustrate the resulting loss of precision with an example. Consider the cyclic *Stipula* function declaration:

```
@Q f()[] {
    now + 1 ≫ @Q {} ⇒ @Q1
    now + 2 ≫ @Q {} ⇒ @Q2
} ⇒ @Q
```

According to the *Stipula* semantics, the second event is never triggered, because the first one always precedes it, so state `@Q2` is unreachable. But since the events occur in a cycle, both are given the abstract clock value `-2`, enabling an infeasible execution in the `JML`/`Java` model that triggers the second event and reaches `@Q2`.

For modeling cycles in `JML` we refine UPDATEDT(W) and distinguish whether the generating function of an event lies inside or outside a cycle. If it belongs to a cycle, the events in W are inserted into the dispatch table with the abstract time value `-2`, instead of a concrete timestamp. Accordingly, the predicate ENSUREDT$_f$

is adapted to enforce that *exactly* the events generated by f are assigned the value -2, while all other entries of DT remain unchanged. The structure of the specification remains the same as in the acyclic case, differing only in the assigned time value. The remaining definitions in Sect. 4 are omitted, because they are straightforward.

The crucial adaptation concerns the extension of $\textsc{gen}_\mathtt{C}(\mathtt{Q})$ (Listing 3) to states within cycles. For such states, we use the notation $\textsc{gen}_\mathtt{C}^{\mathtt{Q},\mathtt{count}}(\mathtt{Q}')$, where Q denotes the entry/exit state of the cycle and count is the iteration counter introduced by the translation (see Listing 4). Each cycle is translated into a dedicated Java **while** loop whose body encodes all possible traversals of the cycle. A counter tracks the number of iterations, bounded by a cycle-specific constant $\mathtt{MAX\_ITE}_\mathtt{Q}$. This bound becomes a parameter of the behaviour method in Listing 1 with precondition **requires** $\mathtt{MAX\_ITE}_\mathtt{Q} \geqslant 0$ and provides a natural abstraction: although *Stipula* allows unbounded cyclic behaviour (*e.g.*, in Deposit), only finitely many interactions occur in practice. Finally, the time-progress variable u_Q used in the acyclic case is omitted for cyclic states, since events generated within cycles carry an undetermined time value and do not require explicit clock advancement.

From a deductive verification perspective, finding suitable loop invariants is a very difficult task in formal program verification and usually not amenable to automation. For this reason our translation technique leaves the supply of post condition-specific invariants to the verification engineer. For example, in the case of Deposit, using the following invariant (v_s is the actual value of the parameters h and k in begin and send; v_b is the value of w in buy) it is possible to derive in KeY the property that all the flour acquired by the Client has been paid to the Farm at agreed cost.

```
loop_invariant (Client_flour == \old(Client_flour) && flour == \old(flour)+vₛ) ||
               (Client_flour == \old(Client_flour)+vᵦ/cost_flour &&
                Farm == \old(Farm)+vᵦ) ;
```

Another limitation of our current encoding is that function parameters are treated as symbolic constants throughout a loop, meaning all iterations are analysed under a single symbolic instantiation (e.g., v_s and v_b). While *Stipula* allows parameters to vary between iterations, verifying this non-determinism would require loop invariants over sequences of iteration-dependent values, which tools like KeY cannot currently handle automatically. Supporting such cases is theoretically possible with user-supplied invariants and interactive proofs, but will further reduce the automation of our approach.

For the cyclic case, we can prove a soundness theorem for the contracts analysed here, assuming constraints on repeated function calls with identical arguments and on the number of iterations.

Theorem 2 (Soundness). *Let C be a Stipula contract with separate cycles and events that are outside cycles. Let*

$$\mathtt{C},0 \xrightarrow{(\overline{A},\, \overline{A_i:\overline{u_i}}^{\,i\in 1..\ell})} {}^* \mathtt{C}_1,\mathbb{t}_1 \xrightarrow{\mu_1} {}^* \mathtt{C}_2,\mathbb{t}_2 \xrightarrow{\mu_2} {}^* \cdots \xrightarrow{\mu_{n+1}} {}^* \mathtt{C}_{n+1},\mathbb{t}_{n+1}$$

where Q_i are the states of $\mathbb{C}_i$, with $i \in 1..n+1$, and μ_i are either function invocations $A_i{:}f_i(\overline{v_i})[\overline{v_i'}]$ or events ev_i. Additionally, if μ_i and μ_j are invocations of the same function then $\mu_i = \mu_j$ (the invocations have the same actual values). Then, the above computation may be traced in the code of $\mathrm{GEN}_C(\cdot)$ as follows. Consider $\mathbb{C}_i, \mathbb{t}_i \xrightarrow{\;\mu_i\;}{}^* \mathbb{C}_{i+1}, \mathbb{t}_{i+1}$ and assume that, in the code of $\mathrm{GEN}_C(Q_i)$ or of $\mathrm{GEN}_C^{Q,\mathrm{count}}(Q_i)$ (when Q_i is part of a cycle),

1. *$\mathbf{now} = \mathbb{t}_i$ if μ_i is an event not generated inside a cycle; $\mathbf{now} \leqslant \mathbb{t}_i$, otherwise;*
2. *if the multiset of pending events in $\mathbb{C}_i$ is*

$$\mathbb{t}_{J1} \gg_{\mathsf{ev}_{J1}} @Q_{J1}\{S_{J1}\} \Rrightarrow @Q_{J1}' \mid \cdots \mid \mathbb{t}_{J\kappa} \gg_{\mathsf{ev}_{J_k}} @Q_{J_k}\{S_{J_k}\} \Rrightarrow @Q_{J_k}'$$

and the dispatch table is such that $\mathrm{DT}[\mathsf{ev}_{J_i}] \in \{\mathbb{t}_{J_i}, -2\}$, with $i \in 1..k$.

There are two cases:

(1) Q is the entry/exit state of a cycle; $f_1, \ldots, f_n$ and $\mathsf{ev}_{J1}, \ldots, \mathsf{ev}_{Jm}$ are functions with initial state Q and final states $Q_1, \ldots, Q_n$ and $Q_1', \ldots, Q_m'$, respectively.

```
GEN_C(Q) =def=
    int entry = minTimeEntry({ev_J1, ··· , ev_Jm}) ;
    if ((entry == -1) || (DT[entry] > now && w_Q > 0)) {
      int count = 0 ;
      /*@ loop_invariant 0 <= count <= MAX_ITE_Q ; // bounds
        @ loop_invariant ... ; // assets, fields, and DT invariants
        @ decreases MAX_ITE_Q - count ; // termination expression
        @*/
      while (count < MAX_ITE_Q) {
        if (w_Q == 1) { f_1(x_1,k_1) ; if (Q != Q_1) GEN_C^{Q,count}(Q_1) }
        else if (w_Q == 2) { f_2(x_2,k_2) ; if (Q != Q_2) GEN_C^{Q,count}(Q_2) }
        ...
        else { f_n(x_n,k_n) ; if (Q != Q_n) GEN_C^{Q,count}(Q_n) } // max_Q == n
        count = count + 1 ;
      }
      entry = minTimeEntry({ev_J1,···,ev_Jm}) ; // we are back in state Q
      if (DT[entry] > now || DT[entry] == -2) {
        if (DT[entry] > now) now = DT[entry] ;
        if (entry == ev_J1) { event_J1() ; GEN_C(Q_1') }
        else if (entry == ev_J2) { event_J2(); GEN_C(Q_2') }
        ...
        else { event_Jm() ; GEN_C(Q_m') } // entry == ev_Jm
      }
    } else { if (DT[entry] > now) now = DT[entry] ;
      if (entry == ev_J1) { event_J1() ; GEN_C(Q_1') }
      else if (entry == ev_J2) { event_J2(); GEN_C(Q_2') }
      ...
```

```
    else { event_jm() ; GEN_C(Q'_m) } // entry == ev_jm
}
```

(2) Q' is a state of a cycle that is *not* the entry/exit state. Let $f_1, \ldots, f_\ell$ be the functions whose final states $Q_1, \ldots, Q_\ell$ are in the cycle.

$$\mathrm{GEN}_C^{Q,count}(Q') \overset{\mathrm{def}}{=} \texttt{if (w\_Q' == 1) \{ } f_1(\overline{x_1}, \overline{k_1}) \texttt{ ; if (Q != Q}_1\texttt{) } \mathrm{GEN}_C^{Q,count}(Q_1)$$
$$\hookrightarrow \texttt{ \}}$$
$$\texttt{else if (w\_Q' == 2) \{ } f_2(\overline{x_2}, \overline{k_2}) \texttt{ ; if (Q != Q}_2\texttt{)}$$
$$\hookrightarrow \mathrm{GEN}_C^{Q,count}(Q_2) \texttt{ \}}$$
$$\ldots$$
$$\texttt{else \{ } f_\ell(\overline{x_\ell}, \overline{k_\ell}) \texttt{ ; if (Q != Q}_\ell\texttt{) } \mathrm{GEN}_C^{Q,count}(Q_\ell) \texttt{ \}}$$

Listing 4. The function $\mathrm{GEN}_C^{Q,count}(Q')$.

Then, if $\mu_i = A_i{:}f_i(\overline{v_i})[\overline{v'_i}]$ it is possible to execute the method $f_i(\overline{v_i}, \overline{v'_i})$ and if $\mu_i = \mathbf{ev}_{j_i}$, it is possible to execute method $\texttt{event\_}j_i(\ )$ and obtain a state where (1.) and (2.) hold for $\mathbb{C}_{i+1}$, $\mathbb{t}_{i+1}$.

This result crucially depends on the values of $\texttt{MAX\_ITE}_Q$. If reliable upper bounds on the number of possible iterations are known, the analysis carried out with KeY is guaranteed to explore all the legally admissible behaviour of the contract. However, in contrast to the acyclic setting, completeness can no longer be claimed. As discussed at the beginning of the section, the introduction of over-approximations, specifically, assigning the abstract time value -2 to events generated inside cycles, may lead the translated Java program to exhibit behaviour not admissible by the semantics of *Stipula*. As a consequence, the verification performed by KeY may encounter spurious executions, potentially preventing the proof of properties that do hold in the original contract.

6   Related Work

Legal modeling frameworks like Ergo [19], OpenLaw [18], Lexon [14], and Accord [1] embed contracts into broader systems, but they lack a precise formal semantics. While Catala [15] formalizes legislative logic and has a runtime environment, it does not address contract verification. In contrast, *Stipula* offers an operational model with explicit permissions, assets, and timed clauses and has a comprehensive suite of tools, including a visual code editor for intuitive contract authoring, an interpreter for automatic execution, and a number of analyzers for verifying several legally relevant properties (unreachability of clauses, absence of frozen assets, etc.) [13].

Closer to our work, prior efforts explored translation-based verification: OCL-to-Java with JML [12], and Circus-to-Java for formal reasoning [10]. Our approach applies this paradigm to legal contracts, preserving their normative and temporal semantics.

More recent work models blockchain smart contracts (by hand) in a modeling language designed for verification which is then automatically translated to EVM bytecode [20], for example, Dafny-to-EVM [6] or Why3-to-EVM [16]. This is the *reverse* direction of our approach. While it makes verification easier, *validation* becomes harder.

While the current *Stipula* runtime is realized by compilation to Java [21], the language is implementation-agnostic and could be compiled to blockchain smart contracts like Solidity [20] or Obsidian [17]. This path is promising, as our verification approach using KeY [2] can build on established work that already applies the system to blockchain platforms like Hyperledger Fabric [5] and Solidity [3] by embedding them into Java.

7   Conclusion

The formal modeling and verification of digital contracts is gaining momentum at the intersection of legal informatics, programming languages, and formal methods. This work contributes by connecting the contract language *Stipula* with a deductive verification system (KeY) via a translation to JML-annotated Java.

We focus on two recurring interaction patterns in legal contracts: acyclic behaviour and non-nested cyclic behaviour consisting only of function calls. We also impose other technical restrictions which might be lifted in the future. Maximising automation has been our guiding principle. In the acyclic case, verification is fully automatic once the contract is specified. For cyclic behaviour, where stronger reasoning is needed, we aim to minimise additional annotations and proof guidance to preserve usability and scalability. From a theoretical perspective, the most challenging problem is the precise handling of clock values in events originating from cycles. It would require a generalisation of dispatch tables that precisely describes event generation for an *unbounded* number of iterations. A systematic, experimentally driven investigation of the trade-offs between coverage and precision constitutes an important direction for future work. Table 2 summarises the current restrictions and to which extent they could be dropped.

Table 2. Restrictions to *Stipula* and motivations

Restriction	Motivation/How to Lift
Fields, assets and variables are of type integer, see Sect. 2.1	Increase degree of automation; can be lifted by dedicated automated reasoners
Cycles in contracts are separate and event-free, see Sects. 2.1 and 5	General cycles are rare in legal contracts and significantly complicate the translation, because they cannot be modeled by loops
Events generated in cycles get abstract clock value, see Sect. 5	Precise treatment requires dynamic and unbounded extension of dispatch table
Cycle iterations are analysed under a single symbolic instantiation of the formal parameters, see Sect. 5	Requires more complex loop invariants that might be hard to find

In general, a systematic empirical evaluation, especially for large and structurally complex cyclic contracts remains to be done. Preliminary results are promising but concern an earlier version of the translation without dispatch tables [11]. A comprehensive assessment of the current framework remains essential.

A   Addendum: The Function STIPULA2JAVA

The definition of $\mathrm{STIPULA2JAVA}_{\mathsf{A}}(S)$ follows.

- $\mathrm{STIPULA2JAVA}_{\mathsf{A}}(\_) \overset{\mathsf{def}}{=} \varepsilon$, where ε is the empty string.
- $\mathrm{STIPULA2JAVA}_{\mathsf{A}}(E \to \mathtt{x}\ \ S) \overset{\mathsf{def}}{=} \mathtt{x} = E$; $\mathrm{STIPULA2JAVA}_{\mathsf{A}}(S)$.
- $\mathrm{STIPULA2JAVA}_{\mathsf{A}}(E \to \mathtt{B}\ \ S) \overset{\mathsf{def}}{=} \mathrm{STIPULA2JAVA}_{\mathsf{A}}(S)$. The value of E is irrelevant in our examples. If the value of E is relevant, we declare an *ad hoc* field, say `B_transmitted`, for storing the value.
- $\mathrm{STIPULA2JAVA}_{\mathsf{A}}(E \multimap \mathtt{h}, \mathtt{h}'\ \ S)$. There are two cases: (i) both $\mathtt{h}$ and $\mathtt{h}'$ are assets of the contract or
  (ii) $\mathtt{h}$ is a formal parameter and $\mathtt{h}'$ is an asset of the contract. The code for case (i) and (ii) is (`tmp` is a fresh variable):

<table>
<tr><td>

```
int tmp = E ;
//@ assert h-tmp >= 0 ;
h = h-tmp ; h' = h'+tmp ;
STIPULA2JAVA_A(S)
```

Case *(i)*

</td><td>

```
int tmp = E ;
//@ assert h-tmp >= 0 && A_h'-tmp >= 0 ;
h = h-tmp ; A_h' = A_h'-tmp ;
h' = h'+tmp ;
STIPULA2JAVA_A(S)
```

Case *(ii)*

</td></tr>
</table>

According to the `JML` **assert** semantics, verification can only succeed provided that `h-tmp >= 0`, which is exactly what the *Stipula* semantics requires. In addition, in case (ii), the formal parameter `h` represents (part of) the asset `A_h'` that the caller `A` transfers to the contract upon invocation. Consequently, the decrease in `h` must be reflected in the caller's asset rather than in the contract state. This semantic correspondence motivates the assignment `A_h' = A_h'-tmp;` which correctly accounts for the transfer of the asset from the caller to the contract.

- $\mathrm{STIPULA2JAVA}_{\mathsf{A}}(E \multimap \mathtt{h}, \mathtt{B}\ \ S)$. Again, there are two cases. Either (i) `h` is an asset or (ii) it is a formal parameter. The code of cases (i) and (ii) is:

<table>
<tr><td>

```
int tmp = E ;
//@ assert h-tmp >= 0 ;
h = h-tmp ;
B_h = B_h+tmp ;
STIPULA2JAVA_A(S)
```

Case *(i)*

</td><td>

```
int tmp = E ;
//@ assert h-tmp >= 0 && A-tmp >= 0 ;
h = h-tmp ; A = A-tmp ;
B = B+tmp ;
STIPULA2JAVA_A(S)
```

Case *(ii)*

</td></tr>
</table>

In case (ii), we decrease and increase the assets `A` and `B`, respectively, where `tmp` is a fresh variable. In case (i), we assume that `h` is an asset, not a formal parameter. This allows us to determine what asset of `B` must be increased by the move (the general case is dealt with *ad hoc* annotations).

238   R. Hähnle and C. Laneve

- $\textsc{Stipula2Java}_{\mathsf{A}}(\mathbf{if}\,(E)\,\{\,S'\,\}\,\mathbf{else}\,\{\,S''\,\}\,S) \stackrel{\text{def}}{=}$
$$\begin{aligned}&\mathtt{if\,(}E\mathtt{)\,\{}\ \textsc{Stipula2Java}_{\mathsf{A}}(S')\ \mathtt{\}}\\&\mathtt{else\,\{}\ \textsc{Stipula2Java}_{\mathsf{A}}(S'')\ \mathtt{\}}\\&\textsc{Stipula2Java}_{\mathsf{A}}(S)\end{aligned}$$

The semantics of the conditional is obvious: we simply use the corresponding `Java` statement.

Regarding the shortcuts $\mathbf{h} \multimap \mathbf{h}'$ and $\mathbf{h} \multimap \mathsf{A}$, we generate optimized `Java` code, to avoid the declaration of the auxiliary variable `tmp`:

$$\textsc{Stipula2Java}_{\mathsf{A}}(\mathbf{h} \multimap \mathbf{h}') \stackrel{\text{def}}{=}\ \texttt{h' = h'+h ; h = 0 ;}\ \textit{// h and h' assets}$$

$$\textsc{Stipula2Java}_{\mathsf{A}}(\mathbf{h} \multimap \mathbf{h}') \stackrel{\text{def}}{=}\ \begin{aligned}&\texttt{//@ assert A\_h'-h >= 0 ;}\ \textit{// h formal param., h' asset}\\&\texttt{h' = h'+h ;}\\&\texttt{A\_h'= A\_h'-h ;}\\&\texttt{h = 0 ;}\end{aligned}$$

and $\textsc{Stipula2Java}_{\mathsf{A}}(\mathbf{h} \multimap \mathsf{B}) \stackrel{\text{def}}{=}\ \texttt{B\_h = B\_h+h ; h = 0 ;}\ \textit{// h asset}$

$$\textsc{Stipula2Java}_{\mathsf{A}}(\mathbf{h} \multimap \mathsf{B}) \stackrel{\text{def}}{=}\ \begin{aligned}&\texttt{//@ assert A-h >= 0 ;}\ \textit{// h formal parameter}\\&\texttt{B = b+h ; h = 0 ;}\end{aligned}$$

References

1. The Accord Project: Open source software tools for smart legal contracts. https://accordproject.org. Accessed 31 Mar 2026
2. Ahrendt, W., Beckert, B., Bubel, R., Hähnle, R., Schmitt, P.H., Ulbrich, M. (eds.): Deductive Software Verification: The KeY Book. LNCS, vol. 10001. Springer, Cham (2016). https://doi.org/10.1007/978-3-319-49812-6
3. Ahrendt, W., Bubel, R.: Functional verification of smart contracts via strong data integrity. In: Margaria, T., Steffen, B. (eds.) ISoLA 2020. LNCS, vol. 12478, pp. 9–24. Springer, Cham (2020). https://doi.org/10.1007/978-3-030-61467-6_2
4. Beckert, B., et al.: The Java verification tool KeY: a tutorial. In: Platzer, A., Rozier, K.Y., Pradella, M., Rossi, M. (eds.) FM 2024. LNCS, vol. 14934, pp. 597–623. Springer, Cham (2024). https://doi.org/10.1007/978-3-031-71177-0_32
5. Beckert, B., Herda, M., Kirsten, M., Schiffl, J.: Formal specification and verification of hyperledger fabric chaincode. In: 3rd Symposium on Distributed Ledger Technology (SDLT), Gold Coast, Australia, 12 November 2018, pp. 44–48. Institute for Integrated and Intelligent Systems (2018)
6. Cassez, F., Fuller, J., Quiles, H.M.A.: Deductive verification of smart contracts with Dafny. Int. J. Softw. Tools Technol. Transf. **26**(2), 131–145 (2024). https://doi.org/10.1007/S10009-024-00738-1
7. Cok, D.R.: JML and OpenJML for Java 16. In: Cok, D.R. (ed.) FTfJP 2021: Proceedings of 23rd ACM International Workshop on Formal Techniques for Java-like Programs, Virtual Event, Denmark, pp. 65–67. ACM (2021). https://doi.org/10.1145/3464971.3468417
8. Crafa, S., Laneve, C., Sartor, G., Veschetti, A.: Pacta sunt servanda: legal contracts in Stipula. Sci. Comput. Program. **225**, 102911 (2023). https://doi.org/10.1016/j.scico.2022.102911

9. Filliâtre, J.-C., Marché, C.: The Why/Krakatoa/Caduceus platform for deductive program verification. In: Damm, W., Hermanns, H. (eds.) CAV 2007. LNCS, vol. 4590, pp. 173–177. Springer, Heidelberg (2007). https://doi.org/10.1007/978-3-540-73368-3_21

10. Freitas, A., Cavalcanti, A.: Automatic translation from *Circus* to Java. In: Misra, J., Nipkow, T., Sekerinski, E. (eds.) FM 2006. LNCS, vol. 4085, pp. 115–130. Springer, Heidelberg (2006). https://doi.org/10.1007/11813040_9

11. Hähnle, R., Laneve, C., Veschetti, A.: Formal verification of legal contracts: a translation-based approach. In: Damiani, F., Farrell, M. (eds.) IFM 2025. LNCS, vol. 16194, pp. 59–78. Springer, Cham (2025).https://doi.org/10.1007/978-3-032-10794-7_4

12. Hamie, A., Haddad, H., Omicini, A., Wainwright, R.L.: Translating the object constraint language into the java modelling language. In: Liebrock, L.M. (ed.) Proceedings of the ACM Symposium on Applied Computing (SAC), pp. 1531–1535. ACM, Nicosia, Cyprus (2004). https://doi.org/10.1145/967900.968206

13. Laneve, C.: The stipula platform: a workbench for programming and analyzing legal contracts. In: Journeys Between Formal Methods and the Railway Industry: Essays Dedicated to Alessandro Fantechi on the Occasion of His 70th Birthday. LNCS, vol. 16470, pp. 160–177. Springer (2026)

14. Lexon Foundation. https://gitlab.com/lexon-foundation. Accessed 31 Mar 2026

15. Merigoux, D., Chataing, N., Protzenko, J.: Catala: a programming language for the law. Proc. ACM Program. Lang. **5**(ICFP), 1–29 (2021). https://doi.org/10.1145/3473582

16. Nehaï, Z., Bobot, F.: Deductive proof of industrial smart contracts using why3. In: Sekerinski, E., et al. (eds.) FM 2019. LNCS, vol. 12232, pp. 299–311. Springer, Cham (2020). https://doi.org/10.1007/978-3-030-54994-7_22

17. Obsidian: A safer blockchain programming language. http://obsidian-lang.com/. Accessed 31 Mar 2026

18. OpenLaw: Real world contracts for Ethereum. https://www.openlaw.io. Accessed 31 Mar 2026

19. Roche, N., Hernandez, W., Chen, E., Siméon, J., Selman, D.: Ergo – a programming language for smart legal contracts. arXiv CoRR (2021). https://doi.org/10.48550/arXiv.2112.07064

20. Solidity Documentation: State Machine Common Pattern. https://docs.soliditylang.org/en/v0.8.35-pre.1/common-patterns.html#state-machine. Accessed 31 Mar 2026

21. The Stipula Project. https://github.com/stipula-language. Accessed 31 Mar 2026

Formal Verification in Coordination Languages

Simulation and Analysis
of Indoor-Air-Quality Measuring Devices
with YODA

Riccardo Petracci, Nicola Del Giudice[✉], Diletta Romana Cacciagrano, and Michele Loreti

University of Camerino, Via Madonna delle Carceri 9, 62032 Camerino, Italy
{riccardo.petracci,nicola.delgiudice,diletta.cacciagrano,
michele.loreti}@unicam.it

Abstract. Collective Adaptive Systems (CAS) are groups of heterogeneous components that interact to achieve local and global goals. One way to view CAS is to consider them as intelligent agents that operate according to a behaviour based on observations and a state. Internet-of-Things (IoT) ecosystems provide a natural application domain for agent-based solutions to support modelling and analysis, as they share many architectural similarities. In this paper, we show how one of the recently proposed agenda-based languages, named YODA, can be used to support the design and engineering of an IoT system designed to measure indoor air quality and warn if it falls below a given threshold. The proposed model has been simulated using the tool Sibilla to forecast how battery life, coverage, and overall Indoor Air Quality evolve with the number of people in a building. In the paper, we show how the proposed methodology can be used during the design phase to support developers and engineers and aid their decision-making, without relying on real-world deployment.

Keywords: Collective Systems · Multi-Agent Systems · IoT · Indoor Air Quality

1 Introduction

Collective Adaptive Systems (CAS) [15] are defined as groups of heterogeneous components that interact with each other and the surrounding environment to achieve local and global goals. In this kind of system, components act without centralised control, and their behaviour adapts to changes in the surrounding environment. As interactions among components can become intricate, it is crucial to understand how these components evolve over time. Under these circumstances, we need to use rigorous methodologies and tools to specify and simulate CAS and verify their correct functioning.

This paper has been partially supported by the project SIMBA, funded by Regione Marche under the initiative "Dottorati Innovativi" (CUP B14E24001160009).

R. Casadei and F. Ghassemi (Eds.): COORDINATION 2026, LNCS 16590, pp. 243–264, 2026.
https://doi.org/10.1007/978-3-032-28358-0_12

One way to see CAS is to consider them as groups of *agents*, or, to be more precise, *intelligent agents* [28]. These computational entities can support complex interactions and adapt their behaviour as the whole system evolves. If these agents operate and interact with each other, we are considering a Multi-Agent System (MAS) [23,25,27], which is defined as "*a loosely coupled network of problem-solving entities (agents) that work together to find answers to problems that are beyond the individual capabilities or knowledge of each entity (agent)*".

Internet-of-Things (IoT) ecosystems provide a natural playground for working with MAS. As IoT systems rely on the three layers of Perception, Network, and Application, it is natural to think of them as agent-based systems. Many examples of this union can be found in the literature, spanning from smart home environments [13] to smart cities [21] or smart manufacturing [1]. MAS can also help understand and predict how energy behaves and evolves over time through distributed communication and control. Specifying and simulating such systems in a digital environment can help us optimise real ones, without wasting important resources [12,24].

In this paper, we analyse the evolution of a smart ecosystem considering a set of IoT devices and different people walking around. In this scenario, the devices analyse the Indoor Air Quality (IAQ), which is influenced by the number of people around each device. Devices can identify people and measure carbon dioxide levels in a room. As in Sibilla, the system evolves at fixed times, and agents operate synchronously, at every scheduled time, the device reads the CO_2 levels and calculates the IAQ. The goal of this paper is to develop a model that can forecast system behaviour to measure parameters such as each device's battery life, changes in area coverage over time due to people movement, and the general IAQ index.

The proposed model mimics a real part of a university building, abstracted into nine equal-sized rooms with low ventilation. These are organised into a main hall connected to five rooms and a secondary hall connected to three rooms and to the main hall itself. IAQ is modelled exclusively through CO_2 concentration, and each device operates according to a timer-based strategy. They read at regular intervals, but they are also forced whenever a person enters a room or when the IAQ index drops below a given critical threshold. The dynamic activation and deactivation of devices are governed by an adaptive mechanism that considers the number of people in the room and the IAQ index, allowing the system to balance battery consumption and to analyse the percentage of devices not in energy-saving mode. The entire ecosystem is modelled leveraging the YODA [8] MAS language and simulated with the Sibilla [10] forecasting tool. Different scenarios are evaluated by varying the number of people across rooms and the IAQ threshold values to assess their impact on device lifetime, coverage, and air quality.

The main goal of the paper is to present a methodology for use during the design phase of an IoT ecosystem. As we will see later in Sect. 2, many methods are based on technical deployment and specific cases. Instead, our approach aims to provide simulation results that inform early decision-making processes, where it is fundamental to make architectural and system choices. In fact, the ultimate objective of this research is to provide a methodology, through an experiential approach, for critically analysing the evolution of an IoT environment. This methodology can enable developers and engineers to implement resources without wasting either resources or time.

The remainder of the paper is structured as follows. In Sect. 2, we review some similar works and how they deal with MAS and IoT. Section 3 introduces the tools used to develop the presented approach. In Sect. 4, the actual specification of the proposed case study is presented. Section 5 presents the simulation of our IoT system and discusses the results. Finally, we conclude the paper with some remarks for future iterations in Sect. 6.

2   Related Works

As IoT systems become increasingly prevalent in our lives, it is crucial to provide methods for modelling such systems and analysing the resulting data. An example is the *ACOSO* framework [11], where all smart objects are modelled as agents that run across three architectural layers. Agents operate across the application, transport, and network/physical layers, interacting directly with sensors, actuators, and networking components. Here, the authors emphasise the system's design and implementation, leaving aside its macro-level emergent properties. This decision implies that each object (or agent) must handle its own resource management and communication, and that if an ecosystem increment becomes large, the number of agents and the complexity of their interfaces increase significantly.

FIoT [20] is an example of a MAS-based framework for developing an IoT application that can self-adapt and self-organise. This framework combines MAS agents and machine learning techniques such as neural networks and evolutionary algorithms. The authors demonstrate the framework's practical application through two real-world scenarios: Quantified Things (i.e., smart agriculture) and self-organising smart street lights, using neuronal algorithms to enable autonomous decision-making. Compared with our approach, this framework includes the concept of different agents and device roles. They still require engineers to define and tune agents for devices, controllers, and learning algorithms. In contrast, the present proposal operates at an aggregate level with greater abstraction capabilities, able to take global properties, thus avoiding complexity and scalability limitations.

Brandão et al. [4] present an approach based on Belief-Desire-Intention (BDI) agents and the JaCaMo framework. JaCaMo [3] is a platform for developing MAS that integrates three key programming dimensions called *Ja*son (agents), *Ca*rtago (environment), and *Mo*ise (organisation). The combination of BDI and JaCaMo introduces multiple agents that must manage hardware, such as sensors and actuators, as well as communication and general tasks. In this way, they do not prefer the server placement, but the hardware interfaces, message formats, and edge. The solution proposed by Brandão et al. involves compromises and highlights bottlenecks. The abstraction presents problems related to the growth in complexity with increasing device count, because there is a correlation between the agent and the device that creates an agent-per-device granularity.

The approach presented by Dähling et al. in [6] highlights the problem of building large-scale, fault-tolerant MAS in the IoT, where this scenario is often characterised by thousands or even millions of devices. They present a modern multi-agent platform based on cloud-computing techniques to solve the problem. The solution does not raise the modelling abstraction, as agents still represent individual devices or services that interact via message passing. The approach of [6] requires specifying agents for each sensor or actuator, along with their respective communication protocols. Aspects related to network configuration management and implementation should also be specifically modelled. This lacks abstract modelling capable of combining all system components and considering possible increases in the number of agents per device in large-scale ecosystems.

Some examples focused on behaviour and the formal modelling of IoT environments can be considered high-level. The approach used by Batool et al. is based on Cognitive Agent-Based Computing (CABC) [2] and proposes a framework for simulating complex IoT networks. To model the environment, they combine complex networks and agent-based models where agents represent nodes in topologies and are used to study network-level properties. The authors argue that packet-level simulators are not suitable for large IoT environments, so they motivate the need for an agent-based model as a high-level alternative. However, the abstraction of this approach links an agent to a node, and there is no aggregation or language based on the field that can collect behaviour information.

Another approach is based on the Bigraphical Agent (BiAgent) [18], which aims to define a model for IoT applications. This model has been developed to support the structural aspects of IoT application modelling. Additionally, the model incorporates agents responsible for specifying analytics and decision-making aspects. In their work based on the BiAgents model, Souad M. et al. [17] propose a formal description of the structure and behaviour of IoT systems. Additionally, the specification is encoded into the Maude language, thereby facilitating the automatic execution of behaviours intrinsic to IoT systems. Using BiAgents and rewriting logic to provide a formal description of the IoT structure yields a mathematically precise and executable model, but the modeller controls the explicit structure and rules. However, like others, this work lacks a macro-programming perspective on global collective behaviours.

The gap that emerges with the existing works is that existing MAS and IoT frameworks excel at engineering and deployment, but they need a modeller who thinks about single agents (or devices). The low-level granularity also makes scalability challenging. Regarding agent-based models for IoT, the abstraction is raised above the packet and hardware levels, but there is no collective high-level or aggregate language. They treat agents (nodes) explicitly, without tailoring to IoT properties such as spatial coverage or battery evolution across a large population.

3 A Short Introduction of **YODA** and **Sibilla**

To design and predict the behaviour of CAS systems, we need tools that allow researchers to specify that behaviour. An ideal candidate for this task is the **YODA** [8] framework. **YODA** is an agent-based specification language developed for describing the behaviour of computational entities based on possible actions that can be performed. **YODA** allows us to interact with and sense the surrounding environment, which is a fundamental aspect in the IoT context, especially when the main goal is to measure IAQ. In fact, this task is more difficult to achieve with tools like Actor Models, because they rely on messages rather than actively sensing the environment. The language is equipped with a computational model that defines how each component of **YODA** interacts with the others. In a **YODA** model, we need to define three elements: 1) the types of *agents* operating in the system, 2) the *environment* where the agents operate, and 3) the possible *initial configurations*. An agent is defined in terms of observations and state, which in turn is divided into internal state, defining attributes known only to the agent, and features, defining environmental attributes. The agent operates by selecting one of the available actions based on its internal state and the observations gathered from the environment. Upon selecting an action, the agent's internal state is updated accordingly. A key feature of **YODA** is the possibility to model the enclosing environment. The latter is responsible for informing agents about what they can observe and updating their feature attributes. The latter are updated according to the performed action. In this way, we can model even agent mobilities and possible interactions with IoT devices, which have their own spatial characteristics. To make these concepts explicit, a specification language has been developed. This is a high-level language for describing MAS according to the **YODA** paradigm, which has been used to design the IAQ-measuring ecosystem described in this paper.

To simulate and analyse our scenario, we use the **Sibilla** [10] simulation tool. **Sibilla** is a Java tool for simulating Collective Systems. The tool has been conceived as modular software that serves as a container for different specification formalisms, allowing us to overcome the limitations of language-based tools. In fact, the key feature of **Sibilla** is its customizability. Indeed, it is already equipped with a set of languages to design collective systems, such as **YODA**, and other specification languages can be integrated. The tool is also equipped with APIs for 1) *simulating systems*, thus forecasting systems' behaviour, 2) *performing transient analysis* to prove correctness of models via statistical model checking, and 3) *modelling different CASs*, to define various types of systems. This choice allows us to provide an even more abstract solution that simulates complex IoT scenarios during the design phase, helping IoT ecosystem designers make preliminary choices about how to arrange the devices.

4 Modelling IoT for Indoor Air Quality

In this section, we present the rationale for the modelling of the proposed IAQ scenario. First, we described the scenario from a general point of view and explained how we abstracted some parameters. After, we enter the model specification, presenting respectively i) the parameters and constants, ii) the IAQ measuring devices specification, and iii) the human agents specification. Finally, we conclude the section with the system configuration, which is later used to initialise the agent during the simulation process.

4.1　IAQ Scenario Abstraction

The model we want to represent[1] depicts a type of dynamic interaction within embedded systems equipped with various types of sensors that form a distributed network. The distributed network consists of nodes that interface with each other, and their behaviour is influenced by the stochastic behaviour of the N human occupants within a room R.

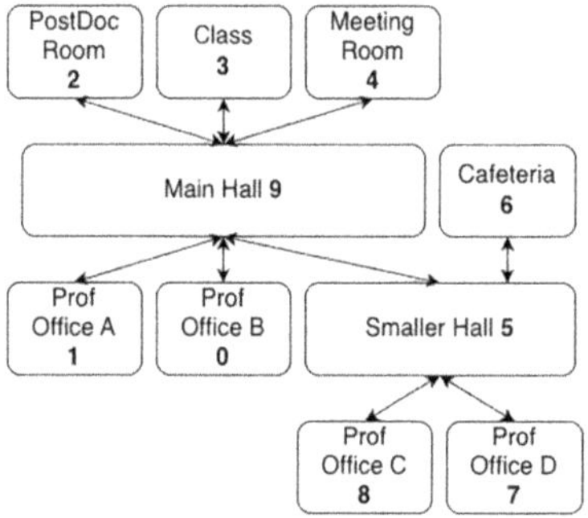

Fig. 1. Scheme of the University environment of our scenario.

This type of model is used in simulation to analyse the system's ability to cope with, overcome, and reorganise its work and energy consumption. This means maintaining a constant work regime over time while providing adequate coverage of the area to be monitored, even in conditions of limited resources when nodes are shut down. The difference between this environment and classic statistical models lies in how the environment is treated. It is a living ecosystem in which the data recorded by the sensors is determined by human presence. In our scenario, we represent an abstraction of the university's room arrangement, as shown in Fig. 1.

The topological representation is a simplified model designed to mirror a real-world scenario within our institute. This topology is scalable and can be generalised to accommodate an arbitrary number of N rooms. To maintain the consistency of the system logic, the *Main Hall* and the *Smaller Hall* must remain the central hubs to which all rooms are attached. The indexing convention is defined as follows:

---

[1] The whole model specification is available at https://github.com/quasylab/sibilla/wiki/YODA#indoor-air-quality.

- **Main Hall (MH) Connections:** Rooms connected to the Main Hall are assigned indices ranging from 0 to $nRoom_{MH} - 1$.
- **Smaller Hall (SH) Indexing:** The Smaller Hall itself is assigned the index $nRoom_{MH}$. The rooms connected to the Smaller Hall have indices ranging from $nRoom_{MH} + 1$ to $nRoom_{MH} + nRoom_{SH}$.
- **Main Hall Index:** The final index for the Main Hall is calculated as
$$Index_{MH} = nRoom_{MH} + nRoom_{SH} + 1$$

This structure ensures that the core logic remains functional regardless of the total number of rooms added to the system.

The system works by detecting human presence and performing its tasks based on the "wake-on-demand" philosophy. Based on this philosophy, devices within a room remain in an idle state to consume less energy and only increase their activity when people are detected in the room, thanks to motion sensors [5, 16]. The device's energy efficiency takes a back seat when people are in the room, as the priority becomes controlling the air quality. For this reason, the device will have to work harder to monitor air quality data and send the data to the server, at the expense of increased energy consumption. IAQ [26] of a closed room is affected by different pollutants that can be correlated by human presence (i.e., CO_2, VOCs, PM2.5, PM10) and other pollutants not strictly related to their presence (i.e., CO, NH_3, NO2) [7,22]. IAQ is critical for health, comfort, and productivity, as most of the population nowadays spends more than 80% of their time indoors, and pollutants can be up to 5 times higher indoors than outdoors. The low quality of indoor air can be hazardous to human health, causing symptoms such as headaches, allergies, and fatigue. On the other hand, maintaining good IAQ helps people enhance cognitive functions, improve sleep quality, and increase productivity in workplaces (e.g., schools, offices) [7].

In general, the model specified in Sect. 4.3 is a self-organising environment in which IoT devices equipped with sensors can analyse the situation and perform different actions based on the information they retrieve. Functioning is subject to modification in response to human interaction with the environment. The interaction of humans with their environment begins with elementary movement or occupancy, and subsequently progresses to the introduction of a contaminant. Each human introduces pollutants into the rooms (abstracted as small offices) with scarce ventilation, so the air recycle is possible only when no humans are inside the room, thanks to the mass balance law [14].

4.2   IAQ Scenario Parameters and Constants

To properly set up our scenario, we need to declare constants and parameters. Concerning the first, we declare eight constants that represent the different devices' status through numerical values (`idle`, `reading`, `sending`, `battSave`, `exhausted`), the minimum and maximum CO_2 that can be inside a room (`CO2min` equals to 600 and `CO2max` to 3000), and the Nepero constant approximated with 3 decimal digits (`nepero`).

For the parameters, we declare a set used to model the CO_2 concentration in a room, the devices, and the humans who sojourn in various rooms. The parameters `CO2out` (outdoor CO_2), `CO2ph` (average CO_2 produced by a human), and `ventilation` (ventilation coefficient of the room) are used to compute the CO_2 concentration in a room. We decided to perform our abstraction and simulation using only the CO_2 pollutant, as it is the most relevant parameter for calculating a general concentration. Using only this pollutant is reductive for a real scenario because to calculate the IAQ, we should also collect other information (i.e., VOC, NO_x, CH_2O, PM2.5, PM10, etc.), but performing these assumptions requires a higher effort, assuming real scenarios with different humans, possible external conditions, and indoor rooms characteristics. The battery of devices loses percentage points based on activities done, which also affects the status, and to equalise the context, the consumption in mA of all devices is parametrised (`idleCons`, `readCons`, and `sendCons`). Two parameters (`sendTimer` and `readTimer`) regulate the duty cycle of a device that monitors air quality and sends information to the server. Another important parameter is the battery capacity (`initMaxBatteryCapacity`), which helps determine which battery is most suitable to use. Since each simulation step represents one minute, the capacity, usually expressed in mAh (milliampere-hours), is here expressed in mAmin (milliampere-minutes), where $1mA$ is equivalent to $60mAmin$ of cumulative discharge.

We declare different parameters to model human behaviour and orchestrate how they move between rooms. In a system, there are different humans (`nHuman`) who have a sojourn time to stay in a room before moving to another one, and this is decided by randomly choosing between a minimum and maximum sojourn time (`maxST`, `minST`), making the movement of the various agents random. Moreover, two other parameters link the human behaviour and the device one, using two different thresholds (`threshold`, `minH`). It is possible to define how many humans can be accommodated in a room by a human, and the minimum number of humans required to activate the device's reading routine. This means that if there are too many people in a room, it is marked as crowded and they need to be moved to another room. With the other threshold, it is possible to regulate the device's sensitivity, which ignores the timer and instead analyses the air quality in the room. To tweak the number of satellite rooms of the two halls, `nSatellitesMainHall` and `nSatellitesSmallHall` are used.

4.3   IAQ Device Specification

Each agent `Device` has to analyse the CO_2 inside the corresponding room. From a general point of view, these agents sense the presence of people in the room and measure the level of carbon dioxide, thereby calculating the IAQ of the room. If the IAQ is no longer acceptable, the `Device` sends a message to a hypothetical server. This process is repeated throughout the simulation, and when the battery is low, an alarm LED is activated. In the proposed example, humans can't replace the battery, and when it's drained, it simply turns off. Listing 1.1 shows the specification of said agent.

```
agent Device =
  state:
    int status = 0;
    real batteryPerc = 100.0;
    real batteryCapacity = 10000.00;
    int saving = 1;
    real registeredIAQ = 100.0;
    real savedCO2 = 600.0;
    int minutes = 0;
  features:
    bool lowChargeLed = false;
    real numOfRoom = 0.0;
    real roomCO2 = 600.0;
  observations:
    real numOfHuman = 0;
    real registeredCO2 = 600.0;
  actions:
    goIdle [
      status <- idle;
      batteryCapacity <- batteryCapacity - idleCons;
      batteryPerc <- 100 * (batteryCapacity - idleCons) /
    initMaxBatteryCapacity;
      registeredIAQ <- 100 * (CO2max - registeredCO2) / (CO2max - CO2min);
      savedCO2 <- registeredCO2;
      minutes <- minutes + 1;
    ]
    read [
      status <- reading;
      batteryCapacity <- batteryCapacity - (readCons + idleCons);
      batteryPerc <- 100 * (batteryCapacity - (readCons + idleCons)) /
    initMaxBatteryCapacity;
      registeredIAQ <- 100 * (CO2max - registeredCO2) / (CO2max - CO2min);
      savedCO2 <- registeredCO2;
      minutes <- minutes + 1;
    ]
    send [
      status <- sending;
      batteryCapacity <- batteryCapacity - (sendCons + idleCons);
      batteryPerc <- 100 * (batteryCapacity - (sendCons + idleCons)) /
    initMaxBatteryCapacity;
      registeredIAQ <- 100 * (CO2max - registeredCO2) / (CO2max - CO2min);
      savedCO2 <- registeredCO2;
      minutes <- minutes + 1;
    ]
    save [
      status <- battSave;
      saving <- 2;
      batteryCapacity <- batteryCapacity - idleCons;
      batteryPerc <- 100 * (batteryCapacity - idleCons) /
    initMaxBatteryCapacity;
      registeredIAQ <- 100 * (CO2max - registeredCO2) / (CO2max - CO2min);
      savedCO2 <- registeredCO2;
      minutes <- minutes + 1;
    ]
    turnOff [
      status <- exhausted;
      batteryCapacity <- 0;
      batteryPerc <- 0;
    ]
  behaviour:
    when batteryPerc <= 0 -> [turnOff:1;]
    orwhen (batteryPerc <= 30) && (saving == 1) -> [save:1;]
    orwhen (minutes%(sendTimer*saving)) == 0 -> [send:1;]
    orwhen ((minutes%(readTimer*saving)) == 0) || (numOfHuman>minH) || (
    registeredIAQ <85) -> [read:1;]
    otherwise [goIdle:1;]
end
```

Listing 1.1. IAQ Scenario: Device agent

Regarding the internal state, we can include the `status`, initialised to idle mode by default, and the `batteryCapacity`, which is initially set to the parameter `initMaxBatteryCapacity`. We also keep track of time passing with the `minutes` attribute. With the `saving` attribute, we manage the device's battery-saving status, which is used both as a multiplier and a controller. Indeed, it avoids setting the battery save status more than once, and when it is changed, it also acts as a multiplier, changing from 1 to another value (in our case, 2). This increases the time before performing actions that drain the battery more quickly, like sending a message. Then we have to consider the indoor air quality, which is strictly related to CO_2 levels in a room. The `registeredIAQ` represents the last IAQ index registered by the device, which reads the actual CO_2 (`savedCO2`) in the room, and performs the formula. As features, we consider the physical LED of a device, which helps indicate when it is close to discharge. The use of the `lowChargeLed` function indicates that the device has reached a percentage of 30% or less. This configuration enables the device to enter a state of battery conservation, characterised by an increase in the time interval between scans or the time between data transmissions to the server. We use the `numOfRoom` to define the room where the device is located. The CO_2 produced by a human is a feature in a room that is collected by a device to obtain the room's IAQ index. Then, we can observe the number of humans present in the room (`numOfHuman`) and the CO_2 registered by the device (`registeredCO2`).

This agent has five different actions available for selection. Actions are responsible for changing an agent's state attributes. The first one is the `goIdle`, which allows the agent to set the device in idle mode and calculate the remaining battery during this phase with low energy consumption (`idleCons`). The battery capacity (`batteryCapacity` and `batteryPerc`) is calculated based on idle consumption parameters. The `read` and `send` actions increase the device's battery consumption. In the first one, a `reading` status is established, and consumption increases due to sensor activation and the use of resources to monitor environmental pollution. In the other one, we set the device to the `sending` status. Here, the consumption is higher due to the activation of communication protocols with the hypothetical server. These actions have parameters (`sendTimer`, `readTimer`) that are analysed within the behaviour and help the agent manage the device's duty cycle. These two timers schedule how often the device must read data and send it to the server. It is also possible to configure these parameters to observe how agents' behaviour can change. The fourth action emulates a battery-saving status. It differs mainly from the other actions in that it changes the `saving` attribute. This attribute allows the agent to perform the `save` action only once and to double the time required to perform the `read` and `send` actions. Finally, the `turnOff` action sets the device to `exhausted` and the battery-related attributes are set to 0. In general, all actions update the consumption based on three parameters (`timeIdle`, `timeRead`, `timeSend`), which represent the estimated times the device takes to perform the various actions. The consumption considered with the parameters is an instantaneous average that must be averaged over time. When considering a one-minute time slice, we must bear in mind that the idle state lasts for 60 s, while the other actions last for the same amount of time as an idle state, but without the time required for reading or sending. This is because sensors and communication components consume the device's battery power only when they are in use, optimising battery consumption, not all the time.

Regarding the agent's behaviour, actions are performed based on the battery percentage and elapsed time, with a timer regulating the duty cycle of `read` and `send` actions. The first check is on the battery: if the `batteryPerc` is equal to 0, it means that the device is exhausted, but if the `batteryPerc` is between 0 and 30, it means the device is close to exhausting the battery, and triggers the `save` action. Then it is checked whether sufficient time has passed to perform another sensor reading, or whether it is time to send data to the server. If none of these rules is met, the `goIdle` action is performed as the default action. The behaviour of a device is deterministic, which means that, given the same conditions, the probability of doing the related action is 100%.

```
environment:
   sensing:
      Device [
         let  nh = #Human[roomPos == it.numOfRoom]
         and  neperoK = nepero ^ ((-ventilation)/60)
         in
               numOfHuman <- nh;
            let  newCO2  = CO2out+(((CO2ph*nh)/ventilation)*(1-neperoK))+
                              ((roomCO2-CO2out)*neperoK)
            in
               if (newCO2 >= CO2min) then
                     registeredCO2 <- newCO2;
               else
                     registeredCO2 <- CO2min;
               endif
            endlet
         endlet
      ]
      ...
   dynamic:
      Device [
         lowChargeLed <- batteryPerc <= 30;
         roomCO2 <- savedCO2;
      ]
      ...
end
```

Listing 1.2. IAQ Scenario: Device Sensing and Dynamic Functions

The environmental updates of the *Device*, which are listed in Listing 1.2, allow us to change its observations and features. Within the sensing function, observations are recorded on the quantity of human presence and the registered levels of carbon dioxide. The CO_2 in a room is calculated considering a simplified concentration formula that requires parameters such as the Nepero number, the ventilation coefficient, the approximated carbon dioxide produced by a human, and the carbon dioxide already in that room. Then, the features of the agent that represent the low battery charge level and the carbon dioxide in the room are computed within the `dynamic` of the environment.

4.4   Human Specification

The behaviour of the `Human` agent is modelled according to the rooms configuration seen in Fig. 1. Humans are directly responsible for the degradation of the air quality in a room, and their movement among available spaces is fundamental to understanding how quickly the batteries of IoT devices run out of energy. Moreover, we modelled the human agent to tolerate a given number of its similar in the same room: when the room is crowded (or its sojourn time has ended), the `Human` moves to another room.

```
agent Human =
  state :
     real  movingTowards = 0;  int  sojournTime = 10;
  features :
     real  roomPos = 0.0;
  observations :
     bool  isCrowded = false;  real  currentRoom = 0.0;
  actions :
    moveFromHall [movingTowards <- floor(U[0,(nSatellitesMainHall+1)]);
    sojournTime <- U[minST, maxST];]
    moveToHall [movingTowards <- (nSatellitesMainHall+
    nSatellitesSmallHall+1); sojournTime <- U[minST, maxST];]
    moveFromCorridor [movingTowards <- ceil(U[nSatellitesMainHall,(
    nSatellitesMainHall+nSatellitesSmallHall+1)]); sojournTime <- U[
    minST, maxST];]
    moveToCorridor [movingTowards <- nSatellitesMainHall; sojournTime <-
      U[minST, maxST];]
    stop [movingTowards <- currentRoom; sojournTime <- sojournTime - 1;]
  behaviour :
    when (isCrowded || (sojournTime<=0)) && (currentRoom == (
    nSatellitesMainHall+nSatellitesSmallHall+1)) -> [moveFromHall:0.90;
    stop:0.10;]
    orwhen (isCrowded || (sojournTime<=0)) && (currentRoom <
    nSatellitesMainHall) -> [moveToHall:0.90; stop:0.10;]
    orwhen (isCrowded || (sojournTime<=0)) && (currentRoom ==
    nSatellitesMainHall) -> [moveFromCorridor:0.90; stop:0.10;]
    orwhen (isCrowded || (sojournTime<=0)) && ((currentRoom >
    nSatellitesMainHall) && (currentRoom<=8)) -> [moveToCorridor:0.90;
    stop:0.10;]
    otherwise [stop:1;]
end
```

Listing 1.3. IAQ Scenario: Human agent

In Listing 1.3, we display the specification of the `Human` agent. The agent's internal state is based on the `movingTowards` variable, which specifies the room the agent is intended to move to, and the `sojournTime`, representing the maximum time that an agent can spend in a room. The feature `roomPos` identifies the room where the agent is located at the end of a simulation step. Finally, a `Human` can perform two observations. First, it checks if the room it is located in is too crowded (hence the boolean variable `isCrowded`). Then it looks at the rooms where it is located (`currentRoom`). The two variables referring to the agent's position (`roomPos` and `currentRoom`) have been separated for responsibility reasons: in the first case, we specify the agent's spatial characteristics, while the other is used by the agent to reason about its behaviour.

In actions, we specify five possible movements the agent can take, based on the rooms it can move to. As `nSatellitesMainHall` and `nSatellitesSmallHall` are set to 5 and 3, respectively, the rooms have been indexed accordingly. Indeed, the actions `moveFromHall` and `moveFromCorridor` allow the agent to move to one of the adjacent rooms (namely from 0 to 5 in the first case, from 6 to 9 in the second case). On the other hand, the actions `moveToHall` and `moveToCorridor` allow the agent to return, respectively, to the main hall (indexed as 9) and the corridor (indexed as 5). If any of these four actions is performed, the `sojournTime` is reset according to a parameter called `maxSojournTime`. Obviously, the agent can also perform the `stop` action, where the `movingTowards` variable does not change, and the `sojournTime` is decreased by 1.

Concerning the `Human` behaviour, it is mainly based on the observation attributes `isCrowded` and `currentRoom`, and the state variable `sojournTime`. Any of the four room change actions is actuated if the actual room is too crowded or the agent can no longer stay in that room (`sojournTime` less than or equal to 0). Then, the action is chosen according to the index of its actual room. To avoid everyone leaving a room at once when it is crowded, we included the `stop` action among the possible actions with a low probability. Finally, if any of the previous behavioural rules aren't met, the agent simply stops in the room.

```
environment:
  sensing:
    ...
    Human [
      isCrowded <- ((#Human[roomPos == it.roomPos]/#Human)*100 >
      threshold);
      currentRoom <- it.roomPos;
    ]
  dynamic:
    ...
    Human [
      roomPos <- movingTowards;
    ]
end
```

Listing 1.4. IAQ Scenario: Human Sensing and Dynamic Functions

The environmental updates of the `Human`, which are listed in Listing 1.4, allow us to change its observations and features. In the sensing function, the attribute `isCrowded` is updated according to the percentage of `Human` agents in the same room. If this ratio is higher than a given `threshold` parameter, the attribute is set to `true`. On the other hand, the `currentRoom` observation is done by looking at the agent's actual room through the command `it.roomPos`. The latter is updated in the dynamic function through the `movingTowards` state attribute.

4.5   System Configuration

To initialise a YODA system, we need to configure the agents specified above. In the system configuration, we overwrite the default values to characterise each agent. In Listing 1.5, the full configuration specification is displayed.

```
configuration Main:
  for i from 0 to (nSatellitesMainHall+nSatellitesSmallHall+2) do
    Device[numOfRoom = i; batteryCapacity = initMaxBatteryCapacity; ]
  endfor
  for j sampled distinct nHuman time from U[0, (nSatellitesMainHall+
    nSatellitesSmallHall+1)] do
```

```
Human[roomPos = floor(j);  currentRoom = floor(j);  movingTowards =
    floor(j);]
  endfor
end
```

Listing 1.5. IAQ Scenario: Configuration

Each of the ten rooms is assigned to a single `Device` with an iterative process. Moreover, we initialise each `Device` using the parameter `initMaxBatteryCapacity`, which can be adjusted to simulate different battery types.

`Human` agents are simply initialised by declaring the room they are located in. The room is chosen randomly from the ten available rooms, and the process is repeated `nhuman` times, where `nhuman` is a parameter specifying the number of `Human` agents we want in the system. For this agent, we don't need to initialise any other attributes, as the sensing function for both agent types is based on the positions of humans.

5   Simulation and Results

In this section, we present the results from simulating the proposed IAQ scenario[2]. The analysis of the scenario is performed using two methods, both embedded in Sibilla. The first method simulates the scenario for a given number of replicas. The final result is deduced by *aggregating* the single results of each replica. In the other method, we can perform a single replica and analyse the evolution *trace* of each agent (of both types).

For this paper, we consider three cases based on the number of humans inside the building and the acceptable threshold for them. The first case (*C1*) considers 10 persons with a threshold of 2. The second one (*C2*) considers 20 people with the same threshold. Finally, the last case (*C3*), an exaggerated scenario, involves 60 persons with a threshold of 6.

The three chosen cases are related to the abstract environment. During the analysis, we observed that the critical number of people for this environment was around 60. Starting from the limit case (*C3*), we profiled the other two cases with fewer people, demonstrating that a ratio of one person per room has a low impact on AIQ. For the medium case (*C2*), we doubled the number of people in the low-impact case while maintaining the same threshold. Regarding the threshold, we maintained a ratio of 10 ($nHumans/threshold$) per room to avoid people becoming trapped in a room. In alternative scenarios, the number of human participants in the environment and the associated threshold can be selected, as is feasible with the tool. These scenarios are considered to be the most pertinent.

Sibilla permits simulating with different front-ends. For basic operations, a Command Line Interpreter, called Sibilla Shell, was developed. However, it requires installing the tool. For this example, we considered using the Python

---

[2] The tool used to simulate the scenario, a video demo of it, and the appendix on how we derive the IAQ calculation formula are available at https://doi.org/10.5281/zenodo.19405833.

front-end instead. Using a Python-based interface does not require any installation, and the commands available in Google Colab, accessible from the Sibilla GitHub wiki, are already set up to let users start playing with our tool.

The section concludes with final remarks on the presented approach and how the simulation can be influenced by the number of agents and entities initialised in the model.

5.1   Using the Simulate Command

YODA encompasses ways to perform quantitative measurement within the model specification. Using the `measure` command, we can analyse how specific aspects of the model evolve. In our case, we are interested in measuring the building's coverage, the average battery percentage, and the average IAQ, as shown in Listing 1.6.

```
measure  coverage = (#Device[( batteryPerc >= 30)]/#Device)*100;
measure  averageBattery = mean Device.batteryPerc;
measure  averageIAQ = mean Device.registeredIAQ;
```

Listing 1.6. IAQ Scenario: Measures

The first measure, `coverage`, is based on the percentage of devices with batteries over 30%. The specification shows that we use the ratio of agents that satisfy the guard to the total number of `Device` agents. The `averageBattery` measure is calculated on the `mean` value of all of the `batteryPerc` of every `Device`. Similarly, the `averageIAQ` measure is calculated.

These measures can be used by Sibilla to simulate the system. The IAQ Scenario is simulated with the *Sibilla Runtime* with different commands by loading the YODA module, and configuring the parameters (*threshold, nHuman, initMaxBatteryCapacity*). Subsequently, the time for a *deadline* is to be determined, along with the number of *replicas* to be created for the purpose of aggregating files.

After fetching the Sibilla runtime module, we use it to perform all the simulation commands. First, we define the language module we will use, which in our case is YODA, and the specification file. Then, the configuration is selected from the available options. In our case, only one is specified (the `Main` configuration). At this point, we can change the parameters we defined in our scenario. As shown in the listing, we decided to change `threshold`, `nHuman`, and `initMaxBatteryCapacity`. Before starting the simulation, we define the simulation parameters. In the example, we want to analyse all the measures declared above. Then, we declare, respectively, the maximum simulation deadline, the delta for each timestamp, and the number of replicas.

Figure 2 shows the aggregated results of the three measures we captured during the simulations. Each graph includes how the measure evolves under the three case scenarios. Considering *C1*, we see that the average battery of this scenario, shown in Fig. 2a, drains more slowly than the other two cases. The light flexion around 850 min is due to the savings policy discussed in the specification. Of course, as the number of persons increases, the battery drain curve is lower.

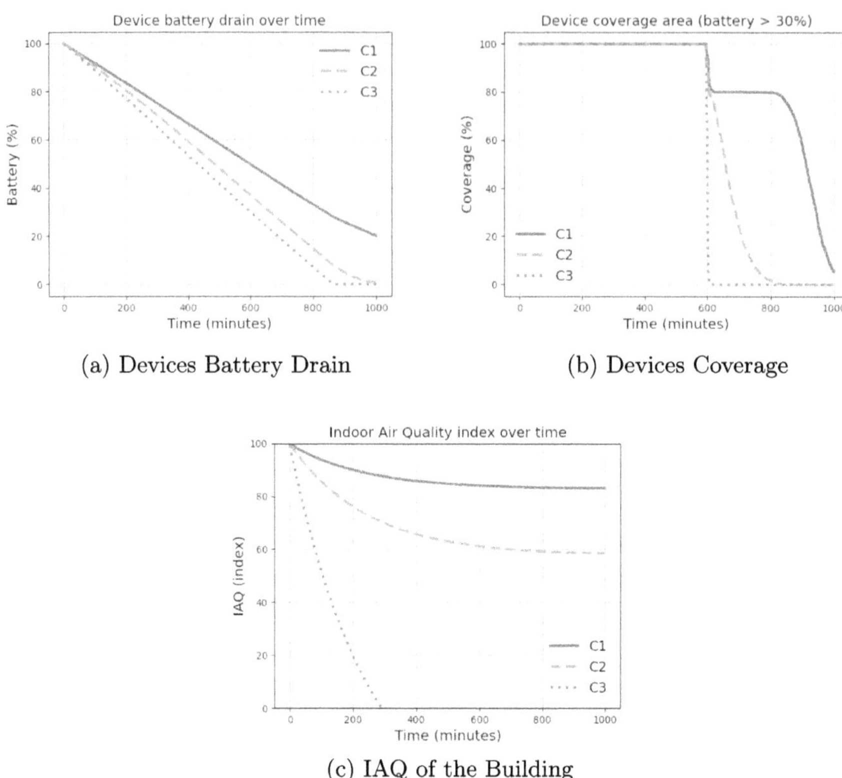

(a) Devices Battery Drain

(b) Devices Coverage

(c) IAQ of the Building

Fig. 2. Simulation aggregates of the three case scenarios.

The coverage shown in Fig. 2b reflects the behaviour of the battery drainage. As the time reaches 600 min, we can see that, for *C3*, the average battery is lower than or equal to 30%, which means that the minimal condition of the coverage can't be met: that is why we see in the coverage graph that the related curve drops abruptly. The IAQ index presented in Fig. 2c evolves in the same way as the previous trends. Generally, the IAQ index stabilises over time. The steepness of the trend is influenced by the number of `Human` agents. As our model only considers the number of people to calculate the CO_2 in a room, it is clear that the more people are present (and spend time in a room), the less time each room has to ventilate. Each room, and generally the building, has no time to ventilate. In fact, if we consider the *C3* trend line, we see that the IAQ index is dangerously low (even going below zero) while *C1* and *C2* present acceptable air quality levels.

5.2   Using the Trace Command

We can gain insight into the individual simulation runs for each agent using the *Trace* command. This command was originally implemented to capture the movement of agents inside a physical environment. Indeed, the related specification includes the XYZ axes and attributes that represent the direction and the physical format. However, we can exploit this by assigning the attributes from the IAQ scenario specification, i.e. `x = batteryPerc;` and `y = registeredIAQ;`. The latter instructions are saved in a special file (`iaq.trc`) used by different commands. Here, unlike in the simulation, we run a single *replica*, so we do not use `set_replica`. The main change is on command `sr.trace` rather than `sr.simulate`, which also requires the trace file rather than the simulation file.

The use of the *Trace* command enables us to observe the device's battery behaviour and indoor air quality under different scenarios. We decided to consider different scenarios with high, medium, and low population density representing *Main Hall* (Fig. 3), *Smaller Hall* (Fig. 4), and *Office Room* (Fig. 5). It is possible to observe in the *C1* that, also with a low population density (10 humans) in the environment, the *Main Hall* (Fig. 3a) and the *Small Hall* (Fig. 4a) present air quality degradation. The motivation is associated with the configuration of the rooms, which function as passageways facilitating movement between different areas. This configuration differs from that of an *Office Room* (Fig. 5a), which maintains good air quality over time with a low-density population. In a scenario with 20 humans in the environment (*C2*), the *Office room* (Fig. 5b) maintains almost good air quality, with a slight degradation over time. The *Small Hall* (Fig. 4b) presents a high increase of CO_2 inside the room that decreases the quality of the air, but it is not as drastic as the situation exhibited in the *Main Hall* (Fig. 3b), where the quality of the air decreases faster. The last scenario (*C3*) presents an exaggeration in which a high-density population of 60 humans is present in the environment. It is possible to observe how the *Main Hall* and *Small Hall* (Figs. 3c and 4c) curve is steep, and the air quality decreases fast. In contradistinction to the other rooms, the *Office Room* (Fig. 5c) exhibits a less precipitous curve and nevertheless attains a hazardous index of IAQ.

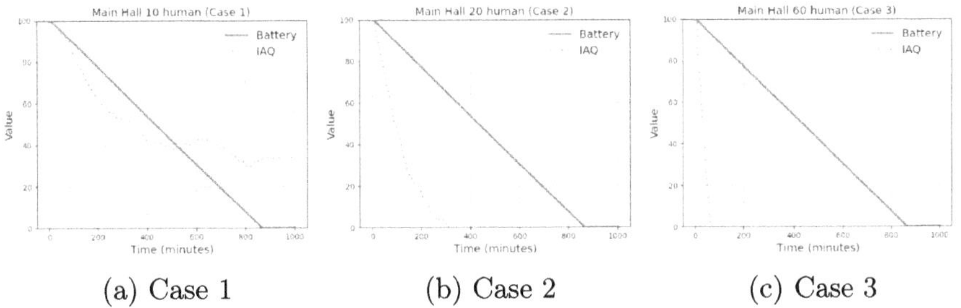

(a) Case 1   (b) Case 2   (c) Case 3

Fig. 3. Device Battery and IAQ of the Main Hall (Room 9).

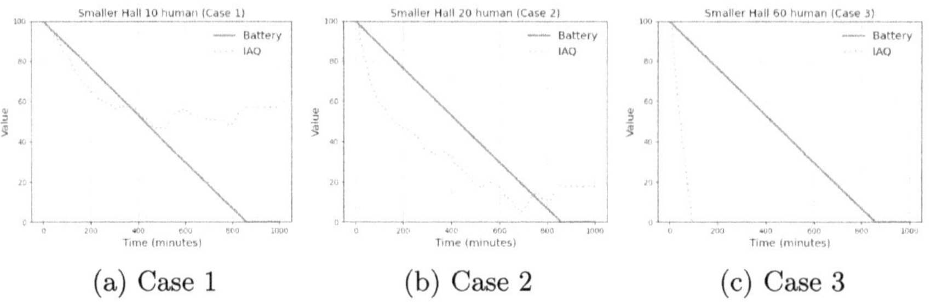

(a) Case 1   (b) Case 2   (c) Case 3

Fig. 4. Device Battery and IAQ of the Smaller Hall (Room 5).

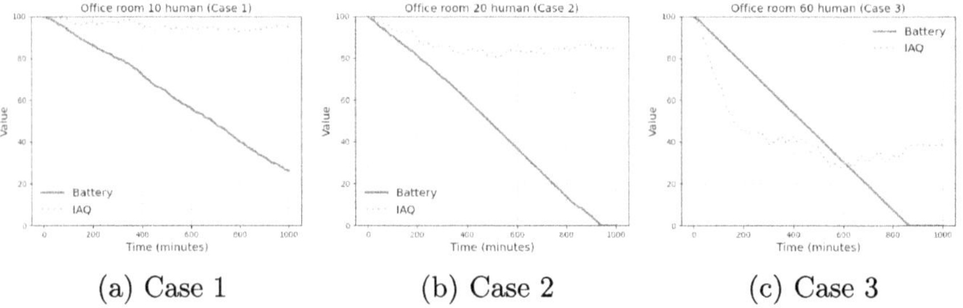

(a) Case 1   (b) Case 2   (c) Case 3

Fig. 5. Device Battery and IAQ of the Office Room (Room 0).

5.3   Final Remarks

The results presented in the previous sections show that as the number of people in the environment increases, battery life decreases rapidly. Furthermore, a lower IAQ threshold, which triggers more frequent pollution readings, significantly increases the devices' overall energy consumption. Coverage, defined as the percentage of devices retaining more than 30% of their battery life, showed a consistent pattern across all cases. It has an initial stable phase followed by a first noticeable decline around a coverage of 80%. This marks the first time the battery has fallen below the threshold. In scenarios with the highest population density (60 humans), coverage degrades continuously, ultimately reaching complete absence. In contrast, scenarios exhibiting lower population density demonstrate a more gradual decline. Notably, the case with 20 humans experienced a temporary slowdown in coverage loss before dropping sharply. In contrast, the lower-density population case (10 humans) exhibited stable coverage close to 80% for most of the observed time window, without reaching zero. The building's IAQ shows how strongly it is influenced by population density. The first two cases, with low- and moderate-density populations of 10 and 20 humans, show a moderate decrease in air quality. Conversely, in the third case, where 60 humans are present, it is evident that a high-density population significantly increases CO_2 concentration in the rooms. This phenomenon leads to a significant deterioration in air quality and a substantial decline in IAQ. These considerations

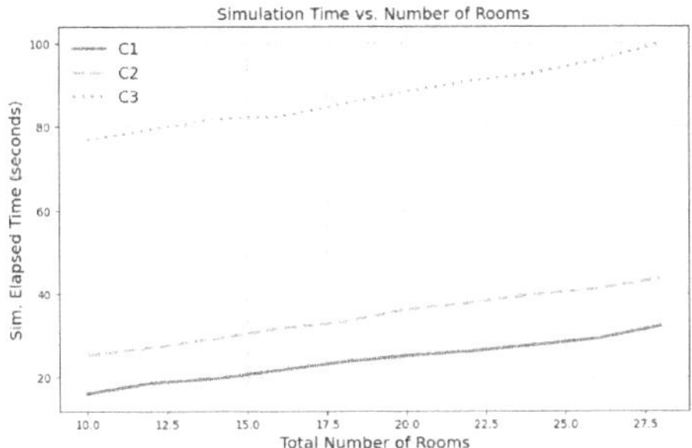

Fig. 6. Simulation Time.

demonstrate how our approach can be a useful tool for informing and guiding decision-making during the design phase of an IoT environment. By analysing the evolution of the simulated scenario, we can avoid deploying the scenario in the real world. Additionally, the proposed approach allows us to scale it up to more complex scenarios, or even unexpected ones (as in the case of 60 people).

We can finally observe that all the analyses presented in this paper can be completed in a reasonable amount of time. Indeed, Fig. 6 shows that if we increase the number of rooms, the simulation time increases linearly.

6 Conclusions and Future Work

In this paper, we analysed the evolution of a smart IoT ecosystem designed for IAQ monitoring and simulated within a university-inspired building environment. This was achieved using the YODA MAS language and the Sibilla simulation tool.

We plan to extend our work in two different directions. First, we aim to further improve the model. As of now, the proposed scenario is an example of how YODA can be used to design an IoT ecosystem more abstractly. However, we can further increase the model's complexity (and precision) by accounting for more details about room locations and capacities, or by considering different people's movement patterns in the building. To simplify this task, we plan to extend YODA with new primitives and constructs specifically thought to describe and constrain the movement of agents over a physical space.

Moreover, we plan to integrate the proposed model into a monitoring system that can compare real data collected from a building with simulation-generated data. This approach will allow us, on the one hand, to tune the model and evaluate its accuracy relative to the real system, and, on the other hand, to build a *digital twin* that the monitor can use to anticipate unwanted or dangerous situations. To tune the model, we plan to use parameter synthesis [19] integrated in Sibilla, while unwelcome computations can be identified using formal tools for runtime verification. Indeed, Sibilla integrates the *GLoTL* temporal logic [9], which allows us to determine whether the model satisfies properties at the global and local levels. This tool can be used to determine whether, for example, the device's coverage is satisfied for a given period, or whether the IAQ in one of the rooms is acceptable over an interval.

Acknowledgements. The authors thank the anonymous reviewers for their constructive comments and suggestions, which helped to improve the quality of this paper.

References

1. Alzubaidi, L.H., et al.: Multi-Agent systems for distributed control in IoT-enabled smart manufacturing. In: 2024 International Conference on IoT, Communication and Automation Technology (ICICAT), pp. 1324–1328. IEEE (2024). https://doi.org/10.1109/ICICAT62666.2024.10923025
2. Batool, K., Niazi, M.A.: Modeling the internet of things: a hybrid modeling approach using complex networks and agent-based models. Complex Adapt. Syst. Model. **5**, 4 (2017). https://doi.org/10.1186/S40294-017-0043-1
3. Boissier, O., Bordini, R.H., Hübner, J.F., Ricci, A., Santi, A.: Multi-Agent oriented programming with JaCaMo. Sci. Comput. Program. **78**(6), 747–761 (2013). https://doi.org/10.1016/J.SCICO.2011.10.004
4. Brandão, F.C., Lima, M.A.T., Pantoja, C.E., Zahn, J., Viterbo, J.: Engineering approaches for programming agent-based IoT objects using the resource management architecture. Sensors **21**(23), 8110 (2021). https://doi.org/10.3390/S21238110
5. Chaudhari, P., Xiao, Y., Cheng, M.M., Li, T.: Fundamentals, algorithms, and technologies of occupancy detection for smart buildings using IoT sensors. Sensors **24**(7), 2123 (2024). https://doi.org/10.3390/S24072123
6. Dähling, S., Razik, L., Monti, A.: Enabling scalable and fault-tolerant multi-agent systems by utilizing cloud-native computing. Auton. Agents Multi Agent Syst. **35**(1), 10 (2021). https://doi.org/10.1007/S10458-020-09489-0
7. Das, R., Acharyya, A., Majumdar, S.: Influences of human presence on the indoor air quality of educational institutions: concurrent multi-pollutant sensing approach. IEEE Open J. Instrum. Meas. (2025). https://doi.org/10.1109/OJIM.2025.3583294
8. Del Giudice, N., Loreti, M.: YODA: yet another agent description language. In: Casadei, R., Nitto, E.D., et al. (eds.) IEEE International Conference on Autonomic Computing and Self-Organizing Systems Companion, ACSOS-C 2022, Virtual, CA, USA, September 19-23, 2022, pp. 82–87. IEEE (2022). https://doi.org/10.1109/ACSOSC56246.2022.00038
9. Del Giudice, N., Loreti, M., Quadrini, M., Rehman, A.: Monitoring local and global properties of collective adaptive systems. In: Margaria, T., Steffen, B. (eds.) Leveraging Applications of Formal Methods, Verification and Validation. Rigorous Engineering of Collective Adaptive Systems - 12th International Symposium, ISoLA 2024, Crete, Greece, October 27-31, 2024, Proceedings, Part II. Lecture Notes in Computer Science, vol. 15220, pp. 281–296. Springer (2024). https://doi.org/10.1007/978-3-031-75107-3_17
10. Del Giudice, N., Matteucci, L., Quadrini, M., Rehman, A., Loreti, M.: Sibilla: a tool for reasoning about collective systems. Sci. Comput. Program. **235**, 103095 (2024). https://doi.org/10.1016/J.SCICO.2024.103095

11. Fortino, G., Russo, W., Savaglio, C., Shen, W., Zhou, M.: Agent-oriented coopera-tive smart objects: from IoT system design to implementation. IEEE Trans. Syst. Man Cybern. Syst. **48**(11), 1939–1956 (2018). https://doi.org/10.1109/TSMC.2017.2780618

12. González-Briones, A., De La Prieta, F., Mohamad, M.S., Omatu, S., Cor-chado, J.M.: Multi-Agent systems applications in energy optimization problems: a state-of-the-art review. Energies **11**(8), 1928 (2018). https://doi.org/10.3390/en11081928

13. Harrabi, A., Hassen, H., Alsulbi, K.A., Zouai, M.: IoT environment based on multi agent system in smart home. In: Barolli, L. (ed.) Advanced Information Networking and Applications - Proceedings of the 38th International Conference on Advanced Information Networking and Applications (AINA-2024), Kitakyushu, Japan, 17–19 April 2024, Volume 5. Lecture Notes on Data Engineering and Communications Technologies, vol. 203, pp. 415–426. Springer (2024). https://doi.org/10.1007/978-3-031-57931-8_40

14. Hernandez-Cruz, P., Vicente-Gómez, N., Azkorra-Larrinaga, Z., Pérez-Orozco, R., Erkoreka-Gonzalez, A.: Applicability and accuracy of physical CO2 mass balance in multi-zone mechanically ventilated office buildings to estimate real-time occu-pancy. Build. Environ. **289**, 114099 (2026). https://doi.org/10.1016/j.buildenv.2025.114099

15. Hölzl, M.M., Rauschmayer, A., Wirsing, M.: Engineering of software-intensive sys-tems: state of the art and research challenges. In: Wirsing, M., Banâtre, J., Hölzl, M.M., Rauschmayer, A. (eds.) Software-Intensive Systems and New Computing Paradigms - Challenges and Visions, Lecture Notes in Computer Science, vol. 5380, pp. 1–44. Springer (2008). https://doi.org/10.1007/978-3-540-89437-7_1

16. Lasla, N., Doudou, M., Djenouri, D., Ouadjaout, A., Zizoua, C.: Wireless energy efficient occupancy-monitoring system for smart buildings. Pervasive Mob. Com-put. **59** (2019). https://doi.org/10.1016/J.PMCJ.2019.101037

17. Marir, S., Belala, F., Hameurlain, N.: Formal modeling IoT systems on the basis of biagents* and maude. In: 4th International Conference on Advanced Aspects of Software Engineering, ICAASE 2020, Constantine, Algeria, November 28-30, 2020. pp. 1–7. IEEE (2020). https://doi.org/10.1109/ICAASE51408.2020.9380126

18. Marir, S., Kitouni, R., Benzadri, Z., Belala, F.: Biagent-Based model for IoT appli-cations - case of a collision avoidance system. In: Braubach, L., et al. (eds.) Service-Oriented Computing - ICSOC 2017 Workshops - ASOCA, ISyCC, WESOACS, and Satellite Events, Málaga, Spain, November 13-16, 2017, Revised Selected Papers. Lecture Notes in Computer Science, vol. 10797, pp. 111–123. Springer (2017). https://doi.org/10.1007/978-3-319-91764-1_9

19. Matteucci, L., Quadrini, M., Loreti, M.: Synthesis tool suite for large stochastic model. In: Gribaudo, M., Iacono, M., Sarvestani, S.S. (eds.) Performance Eval-uation Methodologies and Tools - 17th EAI International Conference, VALUE-TOOLS 2024, Milan, Italy, December 12–13, 2024, Proceedings. Lecture Notes of the Institute for Computer Sciences, Social Informatics and Telecommunications Engineering, vol. 663, pp. 369–390. Springer (2024). https://doi.org/10.1007/978-3-032-06818-7_19

20. do Nascimento, N.M., de Lucena, C.J.P.: FIoT: an agent-based framework for self-adaptive and self-organizing applications based on the internet of things. Inf. Sci. **378**, 161–176 (2017). https://doi.org/10.1016/J.INS.2016.10.031

21. Nezamoddini, N., Gholami, A.: A survey of adaptive multi-agent networks and their applications in smart cities. Smart Cities **5**(1), 318–347 (2022). https://doi.org/10.3390/smartcities5010019
22. Prek, M., Butala, V.: Comparison between fanger's thermal comfort model and human exergy loss. Energy **138**, 228–237 (2017). https://doi.org/10.1016/j.energy.2017.07.045
23. Rocha, J., Boavida-Portugal, I., Gomes, E.: Introductory chapter: multi-agent systems. In: Rocha, J. (ed.) Multi-Agent Systems, chap. 1. IntechOpen, Rijeka (2017). https://doi.org/10.5772/intechopen.70241
24. Sadeeq, M.A., Zeebaree, S.R.: Design and analysis of intelligent energy management system based on multi-agent and distributed IoT: DPU case study. In: 2021 7th International Conference on Contemporary Information Technology and Mathematics (ICCITM), pp. 48–53. IEEE (2021). https://doi.org/10.1109/ICCITM53167.2021.9677679
25. Stone, P., Veloso, M.M.: Multiagent systems: a survey from a machine learning perspective. Auton. Robots **8**(3), 345–383 (2000). https://doi.org/10.1023/A:1008942012299
26. Tsang, T.W., Mui, K.W., Wong, L.T., Chan, A.C.Y., Chan, R.C.W.: Real-Time Indoor Environmental Quality (IEQ) monitoring using an IoT-based wireless sensing network. Sensors **24**(21), 6850 (2024). https://doi.org/10.3390/s24216850
27. Wooldridge, M.: An introduction to multiagent systems. John Wiley & sons (2009)
28. Wooldridge, M.J., Jennings, N.R.: Intelligent agents: theory and practice. Knowl. Eng. Rev. **10**(2), 115–152 (1995). https://doi.org/10.1017/S0269888900008122

High-Fidelity Simulation of Aggregate Computing Systems with Collektivity

Filippo Gurioli, Martina Baiardi(✉), Angela Cortecchia,
and Danilo Pianini

Department of Computer Science and Engineering, University of Bologna,
Cesena, Italy
`filippo.gurioli@studio.unibo.it,`
`{m.baiardi,angela.cortecchia,danilo.pianini}@unibo.it`

Abstract. The verification and validation of collective adaptive systems is a challenging task, typically tackled through a combination of approaches including formal analysis, simulation, Hardware-in-the-Loop, and real-world experimentation. One critical aspect of simulation concerns the trade-off between realism and scalability. A typical validation pipeline involves initial simulation of large-scale scenarios with simplified models of the world, and detail is gradually increased in subsequent steps, introducing more realistic physical and environmental dynamics. An underexplored opportunity in this context lies in leveraging game development platforms to achieve high-fidelity simulations. In this work, we explore the integration of an existing implementation of aggregate programming, a common paradigm for engineering collective adaptive systems, with Unity, a widely used game development platform. We show that this integration is feasible even though the two systems were not designed to work together, we discuss the technical challenges that were encountered and the limitations of the approach, while highlighting the potential for such integration to enhance simulation realism in the study of collective adaptive systems.

Keywords: Aggregate Programming · Aggregate Computing ·
Collektive · Unity

1 Introduction

Collective Adaptive Systems (CASs) [9] are composed of a large number of interacting devices that can adapt their behavior based on local interactions and environmental changes. Examples of CASs include swarms of robots [3], sensor networks [22, 27], and Internet of Things (IoT) applications [4].

M. Baiardi is supported by "WOOD4.0 - Woodworking Machines for Industry 4.0", (CUP E69J22007520009) Emilia-Romagna regional project, call 2022, art. 6 L.R. N. 14/2014.

R. Casadei and F. Ghassemi (Eds.): COORDINATION 2026, LNCS 16590, pp. 265–283, 2026.
https://doi.org/10.1007/978-3-032-28358-0_13

The verification of such systems is a daunting task, due to their inherent complexity, emergent behaviors, and the need for scalability. Typically, a combination of approaches is employed [2,16], including formal analysis [25], simulation with multiple levels of detail [31,34,35] (as a trade-off exists between realism and scalability), Hardware-in-the-Loop (HIL) testing [38], and real-world experimentation [43,46]. Among these approaches, simulation is particularly critical, as different levels of abstraction can be used to model various aspects of the system, ranging from high-level behaviors to low-level physical dynamics. While lower-fidelity, large-scale simulators are common [10], high-fidelity simulations that accurately capture physical dynamics and environmental interactions are less explored, despite their potential to provide more realistic insights into system behavior before moving to more costly HIL or real-world experiments. Part of the reason for this gap is that developing high-fidelity simulators from scratch can be resource-intensive and may require expertise from communities other than those traditionally involved in CAS research, e.g., to model complex physics, render realistic environments, or handle large-scale interactions efficiently [39,45].

From this observation stems the motivation for our work: relying on game development platforms, such as Unity and Unreal Engine, to create high-fidelity simulations of CASs. We contribute to this vision by proposing Collektivity, a toolchain that integrates aggregate programming (using Collektive [14] as the runtime implementation), with Unity, demonstrating the feasibility of this approach and discussing the technical challenges and limitations encountered.

The remainder of the paper is structured as follows. Section 2 provides background on simulation techniques for CASs, and the use of game engines as simulation platforms. Section 3 describes the design and implementation of Collektivity. Section 4 presents some exemplars of the use of Collektivity in a simple three-dimensional space and in a richer environment. Finally, Sect. 5 summarizes the contribution and future work.

2   Background and Related Work

In this section, we briefly review the background and related work on CASs, aggregate programming, simulation techniques for CASs, and the use of game development platforms for simulation.

2.1   Collective Adaptive Systems and Aggregate Programming

Collective Adaptive Systems are typically characterized by *(i)* a large number of spatially situated devices, *(ii)* predominantly local interactions (e.g., short-range wireless communication and sensing), *(iii)* dynamism in both the environment and the network (mobility, failures, intermittent connectivity), and *(iv)* an *open* setting where components can appear and disappear over time. In such conditions, the desired behaviour is naturally expressed at the *collective* level (e.g., "estimate a spatial distribution", "form a pattern", "route information towards a region"), while the actual execution is performed by individual devices with local knowledge. This gap between global intent and local execution is one of the core difficulties in engineering and assuring CASs: small changes in topology, density, or timing may lead to qualitatively different emergent outcomes.

A common response to these challenges is to adopt *macro-programming* [11] approaches, where developers program the system as a whole instead of explicitly orchestrating each device [42]. *Aggregate programming* [7] is a macro-programming paradigm specifically tailored to spatially distributed collectives, in which the programmer specifies the global behaviour of the system as a computation over a *computational field* [6]—intuitively, a function mapping each device (and time) to a value. The field abstraction promotes composability and reuse: complex collective behaviours can be obtained by functional composition of simpler field transformations [41].

In this landscape, *Collektive* [14] is a concrete framework for aggregate programming, implemented in Kotlin and designed to be portable across multiple backends. Operatively, each device repeatedly executes the same program in asynchronous rounds. In each round, a device: *(i)* reads local sensor values and the messages received from its neighbours; *(ii)* computes the shared aggregate program against the previous state (if any), and the inputs of the previous step, producing a new state and a message to be sent to neighbours; and *(iii)* sends the message to its neighbours and retains the new state for the next round.

Building on the field calculus, *aggregate computing* organizes theory and practice into layers: a formal core [6] (to reason about correctness and compositionality), reusable libraries of collective operators [41], and runtime/tooling to execute programs on real or simulated platforms [5,12,33]. This layered view is particularly useful for CASs because it separates concerns: local execution and communication are handled by the runtime, while developers program at the level of collective information flow and spatial structure. Aggregate programs are inherently *situated*: neighbour relations, sensing, and actuation depend on the physical environment and on the embodied dynamics of devices. As a consequence, the credibility of simulation results depends on how faithfully the simulator reproduces motion, sensing, communication constraints, and environmental interactions. This motivates the exploration of higher-fidelity simulation platforms for aggregate programming (and CASs in general).

2.2   Simulation Techniques for CASs

Simulation is a cornerstone of CAS engineering because it enables controlled, repeatable experimentation at scales and costs that are typically impractical with purely physical deployments, while supporting systematic assessment of design alternatives under uncertainty and stochasticity [28,36]. In CASs, simulation is rarely monolithic: different concerns (e.g., decision-making, networking, sensing, and physics) often require different modelling abstractions, which naturally leads to heterogeneous simulation pipelines and staged increases in model detail [19]. This section summarizes the main simulation techniques adopted in the CAS literature, emphasizing the recurring trade-off between realism and scalability [37].

Agent-Based Simulation and Macro-level Models. A common choice for CASs is Agent-Based Modelling and Simulation (ABMS) [1], where system-level phenomena emerge from local agent rules and interactions, matching the typical decentralization and adaptivity assumptions of CASs. ABMS platforms and toolkits are widely used to explore collective behaviours [26,30], to run large parameter sweeps [32], and to support model evolution across iterative design cycles [31].

Embodied and Physics-Based Simulation for Robotic CASs. When CASs components are embodied (e.g., mobile robots), physical dynamics can critically shape emergent outcomes, making physics-based simulation important for credible evaluation prior to field tests [8,10]. To span the realism–scalability continuum, the literature includes both *(i)* scalable multi-robot simulators targeting large populations via simplified physics and efficient execution [34], and *(ii)* higher-fidelity simulators targeting accurate contact dynamics, perception, and environment interaction [24]. Comparative studies [17,35] show that simulator choice (and configuration) measurably impacts performance, accuracy, and the transferability of results across settings.

Multi-level, Hybrid, and Co-simulation. Because CASs often couple processes operating at different temporal/spatial scales (e.g., fast physics vs. slower decision adaptation), hybrid approaches that combine paradigms such as ABMS and system dynamics are used to capture complementary aspects within a single study [29]. More generally, co-simulation [19] coordinates multiple specialized simulators (or model components) through explicit coupling, allowing heterogeneous models to interoperate while preserving tool specialization. These techniques are particularly relevant when networking, control, and physics must be represented with different fidelity assumptions, or when parts of the system are replaced incrementally to refine realism without discarding prior results [28].

Hardware-in-the-Loop and Mixed Reality. To mitigate the limits of purely simulated evaluation (including model uncertainty and the "reality gap"), the literature explores experiments where simulated components and real hardware interact [38], enabling progressive realism while keeping costs manageable. Mixed reality and HIL setups support testing of sensing/communication constraints and partial deployment scenarios, and can be used to validate whether behaviours observed in simulation persist when real components are introduced.

2.3   Game-Engine-Based Simulation Platforms

Modern game engines (e.g., Unity, Unreal Engine, CryEngine) provide an integrated toolchain for interactive 3D worlds, combining real-time rendering, rigid-body physics, collision handling, animation, and support for heterogeneous Input/Output devices. Originally developed for entertainment, these platforms have been increasingly adopted in cyber-physical and robotics contexts to obtain visually rich environments and fast iteration cycles, especially when perception, human interaction, or environmental complexity are central to the study [13].

One example is the use of the Unity game engine as a visualization tool for externally generated collective-system simulation traces [18], while another is the integration of the Menge crowd-simulation framework with Unity for visual authoring and rendering [15]. However, in these works the collective logic is not executed natively within the game engine itself; rather, the game engine is primarily a visualization support. As a result, they only partially explore the potential of game engines as high-fidelity simulation platforms for CASs.

Use in Robotics Simulation and Digital-Twin Workflows. Robotics researchers have explored game engines as an alternative (or complement) to robotics-oriented simulators, typically by coupling the engine to robotic middleware and control stacks. Comparative studies [17,35,44] report that Unity-based pipelines can simplify scene construction and yield high-quality visualization, while robotics-specific simulators may provide more direct support for standard robot models and established integration patterns; the trade-off depends on the target task and on the required balance between graphical realism, physics fidelity, and tooling overhead. Game engines are also increasingly used as a front-end for digital-twin experiences, where the virtual replica must be both interactive and connected to (or synchronized with) a physical asset, again highlighting the need to balance visual immersion with model accuracy and system integration [40].

High-Fidelity Perception and Data Generation. A key driver for adopting game engines in robotics is the possibility of producing visually rich and complex environmental effects, supporting better dissemination and synthetic-data generation. Representative examples include Unreal-Engine-based simulation environments for autonomous vehicles and robots, explicitly targeting high-fidelity visual and physical simulation and dataset generation [39,45]. Such use cases are closely related to the broader sim-to-real problem: even with improved rendering, transferring learned or tuned behaviours to the real world remains challenging, and typically requires dedicated mitigation strategies beyond the choice of simulator alone [23].

Bridging the Reality Gap with Mixed Reality and Incremental Realism. Game engines also align naturally with staged validation pipelines, where realism is increased progressively and parts of the system may be replaced by real components. Mixed-reality and hardware-in-the-loop [38] approaches can exploit the rendering and interaction capabilities of game engines to connect simulated environments with physical devices, helping to expose integration issues earlier and to narrow the reality gap.

Implications for Aggregate-Computing Simulation. For aggregate programming and CASs, game engines are attractive primarily as a high-fidelity *environment layer*: they can provide realistic geometry, motion, and sensor/actuation interfaces, while the aggregate runtime remains responsible for neighbour interaction, distributed rounds, and collective logic. This separation suggests a pragmatic integration strategy: use the engine for embodied dynamics and scene management, and couple it to the aggregate platform through a well-defined interface for sensing, actuation, and neighbourhood exchange. The feasibility and limitations of this approach motivate our integration of an aggregate programming implementation with Unity, discussed in the remainder of the paper.

3   Collektivity: Running Collektive on Top of Unity

In this section, we describe Collektivity, our proposed integration of the Collektive aggregate programming runtime with a game engine to enable high-fidelity physics-based simulation of collective behaviours. We discuss the integration requirements, the design strategies and implementation nuances, and the challenges encountered in bridging these two distinct platforms.

3.1   Requirements and Domain Analysis

A general-purpose, high-fidelity environment for the simulation of CASs, must be designed to support a wide range of scenarios and use cases, while ensuring that the integration does not introduce prohibitive overheads or limit the expressiveness of the programming model. With this in mind, we identified the following key requirements for the integration of Collektive with a game engine:

R1 Agnosticism to the case study: the integration layer should not be tailored towards any specific CAS case study. Instead, it must provide a general framework where diverse sensing, actuation and information exchange structures can be defined, without requiring any review of the integration interface.

R2 Bidirectional Communication: the interaction between the aggregate program and the game engine is inherently bidirectional: the engine must provide the aggregate program with the necessary sensory data (which, as per R1, may vary widely across use cases), while the aggregate program must send actuation commands back to the engine to drive the evolution of the simulation.

R3 High-Performance: simulation scalability is a primary concern, hence the communication bridge between the two platforms must minimize latency. Although adding realism will inevitably impact on scalability, the system should be capable to scale to the order of hundreds of deployed devices (compared to the order of thousands or tens of thousands that are typically targeted by lower-fidelity simulators).

Target Game Engine: Unity Among the available game-engine options, we selected Unity because it combines mature real-time 3D rendering, integrated physics, broad support for external plugins, and deployment across multiple target platforms. These characteristics have made Unity a common choice in robotics, XR, and digital-twin applications, where visual fidelity, interactive scene authoring, and rapid prototyping are central requirements [13]. In addition, comparative studies in robotics simulation report that Unity-based tools can deal with large environments, visual quality, and real-time perception-oriented workloads are important, while still supporting integration with robotics middleware and custom simulation components [35,40,44]. Although our implementation targets Unity, the architectural principles discussed here are not inherently engine-specific and could be adapted to other game engines offering comparable extensibility and runtime services.

Technical Challenges. The integration must contend with the technical constraints imposed by the two platforms. This is a general challenge when integrating systems that were not designed to work together, and in this case it is a prominent issue. In fact, Unity is meant for *game designers* to quickly create and animate interactive 3D worlds, with no clear mechanism to load or use external code. At the same time, Collektive is designed to support a certain degree of flexibility when building a compatible runtime and is, to a certain extent, designed to be executable in simulated environments; however, it provides an abstraction (`interface Mailbox`) that is meant to be implemented by the integration layer provider, and it is not aware of any specific requirement for bidirectional communication with a game engine.

On top of these general challenges, there are specific technical issues related to the different technological stacks and runtime environments of the two platforms. Collektive, being built on Kotlin Multiplatform, inherits the set of targets supported by the Kotlin toolchain itself. As a result, it is designed to be portable across different platforms and runtimes by naturally supporting multiple backends (Java Virtual Machine (JVM), JavaScript (JS), WebAssembly (WASM), native code for Windows, Linux x64 and ARM64, and MacOS x64 and ARM64). Unfortunately, Unity's runtime is based on a custom .NET implementation that is not natively supported by Collektive's existing backends. Therefore, Collektive cannot be executed within Unity through any existing Kotlin Multiplatform target.

3.2   Architecture

Requirements R1 and R2 induce an architecture where data that flows between the two platforms is structured according to a shared schema, which must be flexible enough to accommodate different use cases. Since the device behavior is defined by the aggregate program, while the environment behavior (including physics, position in the world, and neighborhood relationships) pertain to the game engine, the natural division of responsibilities is to have the game engine provide sensory data to the aggregate program, while the aggregate program computes the actuation commands back to the engine.

This architectural choice implication is that, when designing new case studies, users must, as first step, define the data types that represent sensors and actuators. These must constitute an *agnostic* layer, expressed in a platform-agnostic format, that must, in turn, generate bindings that enable communication between the two platforms.

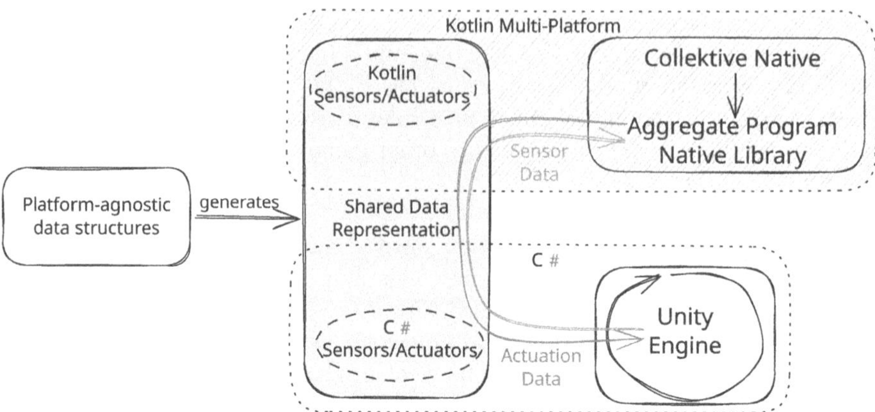

Fig. 1. High-level architecture of the integration between Collektive and Unity. The Unity game engine provides Sensor Data to the Collektive aggregate program, which computes Actuation Data that is sent back to the engine. The Shared Data Representation layer allows users to define Sensors and Actuators data schema using platform-agnostic data structures, which are then used to automatically generate concrete data types for both platforms (i.e., Kotlin for Collektive and C# for Unity), thus enabling direct communication.

Architecturally, Unity is designed as an active component hosting a game loop, while Collektive is designed to be executable in a purely functional style (indeed, every aggregate program is a pure function from previous state, sensor inputs, and neighbour messages to new state, actuation commands, and outgoing messages): this clearly suggests that Unity should drive the execution, and Collektive should be invoked as a library to compute the next state and actuation commands at each step of the game loop.

The architecture resulting from these considerations is illustrated in Fig. 1: the agnostic layer generates bindings for C# and Kotlin, plus a shared schema for the data that flows between the two platforms. Unity is the active component, which, at each step of the game loop, *(i)* collects sensory data from the environment *(ii)* calls Collektive providing the data as input, and *(iii)* applies the actuation commands based on the data returned by Collektive.

3.3   Integration Design

This section details the design of the integration layer that couples Unity's execution model with the Collektive runtime. The design follows the architectural decomposition in Fig. 2, separating *(i)* the *environment layer* (Unity), *(ii)* the *aggregate layer* (Collektive), and *(iii)* an *agnostic data layer* that defines what information flows between the two.

Agnostic Data Layer: Sensors and Actuators. Requirements R1 and R2 imply that the integration cannot hard-code any specific notion of sensing or

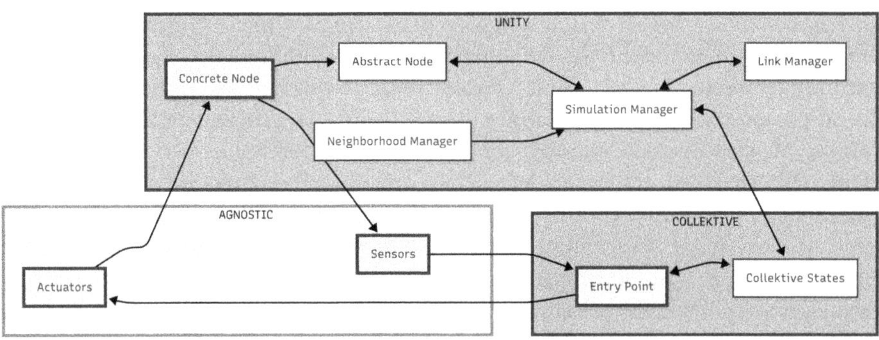

Fig. 2. Design of the integration layer between Collektive and Unity. Components highlighted in yellow must be implemented by the final user. (Color figure online)

actuation. Instead, Collektivity exposes a thin, platform-independent contract expressed as two families of data types: *Sensors* (from Unity to Collektive) and *Actuators* (from Collektive to Unity). From this contract, the toolchain generates strongly typed bindings for both C# and Kotlin, plus the marshaling code needed to exchange values across runtimes. Practically, this is realized via an Interface Description Langage (IDL)-driven workflow: users describe the schema once, and code generation produces compatible representations on both sides. This choice keeps the interface stable while allowing each case study to tailor the exchanged data to its needs.

The agnostic data layer must, in the general case, be provided by the user, as it is scenario-specific; however, since most scenarios will likely share common sensing and actuation patterns (e.g., position, velocity, proximity, light intensity, etc.), in the future a library of common schemas and bindings could be provided to reduce the initial overhead for new users.

Unity-Side Runtime. Collektivity follows Unity's composition model, where behavior is defined by attaching `MonoBehaviour` components to *game objects*. The integration provides three core components. `SimulationManager` centralizes reproducibility concerns (e.g., deterministic initialization via explicit seeds) and exposes an API to create and manage links. `AbstractNode` marks a game object as a Collektive device. It defines the extension points that are scenario-specific: how sensor data is sampled from the Unity world, and how actuator commands are applied. Concrete scenarios are implemented by subclassing `AbstractNode` (e.g., `ConcreteNode` in Fig. 2) and providing the domain logic for sensing and actuation, while reusing the integration-provided communication and execution machinery. `LinkManager` is a visualization-oriented singleton that maintains and renders the current network links (when enabled), decoupling debugging/inspection concerns from simulation logic.

Aggregate programs depend on neighbor exchange, but the definition of *who is a neighbor* is inherently situated and environment-dependent. In Collektivity, neighborhood construction is handled by Unity, which creates and removes directed or bidirectional links through the `SimulationManager` Application Programming Interface (API). This enables multiple strategies, ranging from geometric proximity to occlusion-aware connectivity. An efficient pattern leverages Unity's physics system and trigger colliders; for instance, a connection rule component that automatically subscribes/unsubscribes links when other nodes enter/exit a proximity volume can be implemented by annotating the implementing class with an attribute, whose `OnTriggerEnter` and `OnTriggerExit` methods call the appropriate link-management API to maintain the neighborhood structure. By delegating neighborhood dynamics to Unity, the integration can directly reuse engine-level facilities (collisions, triggers, layers, and spatial partitioning), while keeping the Collektive runtime agnostic of the specific spatial model.

At each simulation tick, Unity performs the following steps for each node: *(i)* sample sensors from the world state, *(ii)* invokes the Collektive adapter, which evaluates the aggregate program provided the most recent messages from current neighbors and the last device state, returning actuation commands, and *(iii)* apply actuators to Unity objects. This design preserves the functional structure of aggregate rounds while fitting Unity's imperative update loop, and provides a single place (`SimulationManager`) to enforce scheduling policies (e.g., fixed-rate stepping) and to coordinate message delivery.

Collektivity provides the implementation for the `SimulationManager`, the `AbstractNode`, and the `LinkManager`, plus the code-generation workflow for Sensors/Actuators. Scenario developers provide: *(i)* the sensor/actuator schema, *(ii)* concrete node components that interpret the schema and implement sensing/actuation, and *(iii)* neighborhood rules implemented as Unity components that call the link-management API.

Collective-Side Collective-Side API. On the Collektive side, Collektivity exposes a minimal API that wraps the execution engine and presents it as a stateful service to the Unity runtime. This API has two goals: *(i)* provide Unity with a stable entry point to advance the aggregate computation for each device, and *(ii)* internalize all program-dependent artifacts (in particular, neighbor message contents and device state), so that the Unity integration remains independent of the specific aggregate program.

In aggregate computing, the shape of the messages exchanged among neighbors is not an application-level design choice: it is induced by the program structure and by the compilation strategy of the underlying calculus [6]. Consequently, modeling messages as part of the Unity-side schema would undermine R1: every change in the aggregate program could require regenerating schemas and bindings and revising Unity-side code, which is not sustainable for iterative development and experimentation. For this reason, Collektivity treats neighbor messaging as an internal concern of the Collektive runtime, not as part of the Sensors/Actuators contract. Thus, the collective-side API maintains, for each simulated device: *(i)* the latest *device state* produced by the aggregate program

Table 1. Performance comparison between the native (FFI) and socket-based backends. Times are in nanoseconds (ns), lower is better. Speedup is reported as Socket/-Native (higher is worse for sockets).

Metric	Overhead Collektive-side			End-to-end (ns)		
	FFI	**Socket**	**Speedup**	**Native**	**Socket**	**Speedup**
count	970	969	–	969	968	–
median	13830	137857	11.20×	550600	200001950	363.32×
mean	13175	170269	13.86×	484754	199963813	456.26×
p95	16597	348890	28.02×	612140	200560775	719.35×
p99	36306	456583	41.25×	850520	202753798	747.95×
std	4843	265368	–	141814	3265095	–

(used to support stateful constructs across rounds), *(ii)* the most recent *inbound messages* received from current neighbors, and *(iii)* the *outbound messages* generated in the last round, which will be delivered to neighbors according to the topology provided by Unity. In addition, it stores the association between Unity node identifiers and Collektive engine instances, so that Unity can refer to devices through stable handles.

At each simulation tick, Unity invokes the collective-side API to advance each device by one round. For a given device, the API evaluates the aggregate program against *(i)* the stored device state, *(ii)* the current sensor snapshot provided by Unity, and *(iii)* the inbound messages buffered from neighbors. The evaluation produces a new device state, a set of outbound messages, and the actuator commands. Unity then applies the returned actuators to update the game objects, and uses its current link graph to determine how outbound messages are routed to neighbor buffers before the next tick. This division of responsibilities matches the architecture in Fig. 2: Unity owns the environment and the topology, while Collektive owns the distributed computation semantics.

3.4   Implementation Strategy

In this section, we describe the practical construction of Collektivity, discussing the technological choices that realize the design outlined in Sect. 3.3. The implementation of Collektivity is publicly available[1] and archived for future reference [20], and has the form of a repository template. The purpose of the template is to provide a starting point for researchers and practitioners interested in integrating experimenting with aggregate programs in Unity.

As first step to head into implementation, we built an experimental prototype with 12 nodes to compare the performance of two communication strategies through a simple benchmark that simulates the core communication pattern of Collektive programs: *(i)* a socket-based backend, where Unity and Collektive run

---

[1] https://github.com/pslab-unibo/collektivity.

as separate processes and exchange data through TCP sockets, and *(ii)* a native backend, where Collektive is compiled to a shared library and directly invoked by Unity through FFI. We expected better performance for the latter, but the former has the advantage of being more flexible, as any Collektive target could be used, instead of limiting the support to the native compilation targets. The benchmark is publicly available[2] and archived for future reference [21]. Table 1 summarizes the results. The performance difference is stark: the socket-based backend is, on average, over 450x slower than the native backend, with a worst-case slowdown of over 700x. Provided the relevance of R3, we adopted the native compilation strategy for the integration, and we designed the agnostic data layer to support it.

Data Model. Collektive and Unity use different type systems and memory layouts. As discussed in Sect. 3.3, a shared data model representation, expressed in a platform-agnostic format, is essential to enable communication between the two platforms while maintaining flexibility and extensibility. *Protocol Buffers*[3] (`protobuf`) is a language-neutral, platform-neutral mechanism for serializing structured data. Protocol Buffers defines data models using a declarative syntax (`.proto` files) that describes their structure in an implementation-agnostic way. From a single `.proto` definition, the `protoc` compiler can generate serialization source code for multiple languages automatically, including C#, Kotlin, Java, and many others. Protocol Buffers data structures are defined as `messages`, which are composed of fields with a type and a unique identifier (tag). In our use case, we always have exactly two messages: one for `Sensors` and one for `Actuators` (indeed, the `messages` of protocol buffers are *not* the messages that aggregate programs exchange, rather, they describe the data that is exchanged with Unity). Each field can be a primitive type (e.g., integer, string, boolean) or a user-defined message type, allowing for nested and complex data structures. The tag is used to identify fields in the binary format, enabling efficient serialization and deserialization. This makes Protocol Buffers fit for bridging complex data model representation for Kotlin and C# runtimes. In Collektivity, users define `Sensors` and `Actuators` data schema using Protocol Buffers, the latter will then generate the necessary bindings for both platforms. A minimal example of a Protocol Buffers schema for Sensors and Actuators is shown in Listing 1.1. Depending on the specific requirements of the application, users can define more complex data structures.

Listing 1.1. Example of Protocol Buffers schema for Sensors and Actuators. `sourceIntensity` is a `double` field used by the aggregate program to determine the direction of movement towards the destination. `Vector3` maps a Unity 3D vector, which in this example represents the current position of the device and the target position computed by the aggregate program. `repeated Vector3` represents a list of 3D vectors, which in this example represent obstacles positions. The integer tags (e.g., = 1) are used to identify fields in the binary format.

```
message Actuators {
  Vector3 targetPosition = 1;
}
message Sensors {
  double sourceIntensity = 1;
  Vector3 currentPosition = 2;
  repeated Vector3 obstacles = 3;
}
```

FFI interaction and Engine API. Collektivity extends the Collektive runtime to support execution within the Unity environment, to do so, it provides an **Engine** (Listing 1.2) that defines the contract between the aggregate program and the Unity environment—i.e., the operations that Unity can invoke on the Collektive runtime to execute the aggregate program and retrieve the resulting state and actuation commands. **Engine** is the Collektive interface that Unity invokes to execute the aggregate computation at each simulation tick, i.e. each update cycle in the Unity execution loop triggers the invocation of the **step()** function in the **Engine**. This function is invoked by Unity via Engine for each simulation node, which identifier is specified during invocation along with **Sensors** data structure. The result returned by Collektive is an **Actuators** data structure, which is then used by Unity to update the simulation environment accordingly. **Sensors** and **Actuators** are defined in the agnostic data layer, and their schema is defined by the user (c.f., Sect. 3.4).

Listing 1.2. Engine API definition for Collektive library.

```
interface Engine {
    fun step(id: Int, sensorData: Sensors): Actuators
    fun subscribe(node1: Int, node2: Int): Boolean
    fun unsubscribe(node1: Int, node2: Int): Boolean
    fun addNode(id: Int): Boolean
    fun removeNode(id: Int): Boolean
}
```

Along with the **step()** function, **Engine** also defines methods for *(i)* register a node for being neighbor of another node (i.e., using **subscribe()**), *(ii)* unregister a node from being neighbor of another node (i.e., using **unsubscribe()**), *(iii)* add a node to the simulation (i.e., using **addNode()**), and *(iv)* remove a node from the simulation (i.e., using **removeNode()**). This infrastructure is then compiled using Collektive-native, and it is directly invoked by Unity via FFI.

4   Exemplars

In this section, we show a simple and a richer exemplar that we include with Collektivity to demonstrate its capabilities and to provide a starting point for users interested in experimenting with aggregate programming in Unity. In both exemplars, we deploy devices that must navigate towards a source of interest while avoiding obstacles, which is a common pattern in CASs and is relevant for a wide range of applications (e.g., search and rescue). They do so through a gradient ascent strategy, with no cooperative logic is implemented for obstacle avoidance. All nodes execute synchronous rounds at a fixed frequency of $20Hz$, in which they perceive the local "intensity" of the source of interest (based on the distance) and detect obstacles in their vicinity. Vicinities and communication between nodes are established through a distance-based neighborhood model: two nodes are considered neighbors if their separation is within 10 units, which defines the connectivity graph for the aggregate computation. They exchange this information with their neighbors to compute their next movement direction, computing a vector that points to the direction of higher source intensity and away from nearby obstacles (including other devices). Gradient computations are performed through the standard library in Collektive, which provides implementations for all the building blocks in [41].

4.1 Simple 3D Space

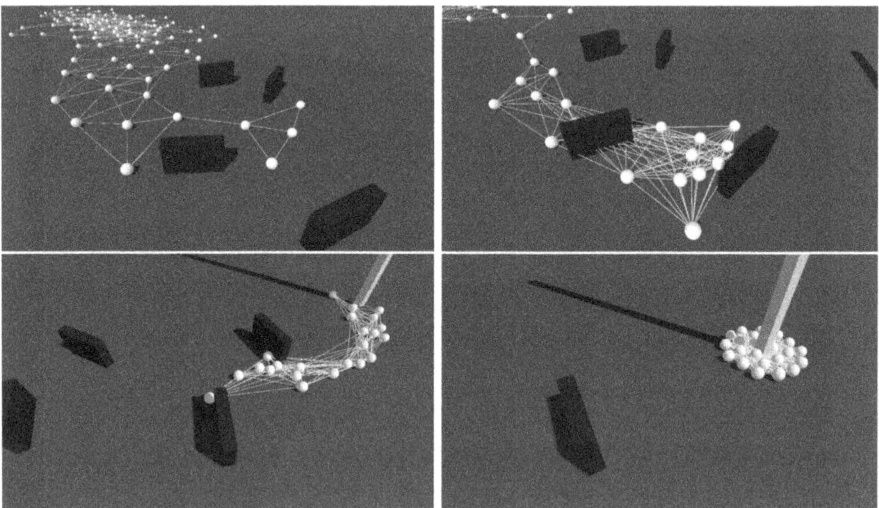

Fig. 3. Snapshots of the simple 3D space scenario with 100 nodes.

Here, we consider a simple arena with four parallelepipedic obstacles that physically obstruct the movement towards the source. The environment contains of $1 \times 3 \times 5$ units. Devices are represented by spheres that can move in the 3D space, and the arena is a flat plane with a source of interest located at a fixed position. We tested the scenario with different numbers of nodes. Laptops with integrated graphics could achieve reasonable real-time performance with up to 50 nodes, while we easily scaled to 100 nodes on a desktop with a dedicated GPU (nVidia GTX 4070). Snapshots in Fig. 3 show the evolution of the system with 100 nodes.

4.2   Richer Environment

Fig. 4. Snapshots of the Oasis scenario with 100 nodes.

To showcase the potential of this integration, we ran the same experiment in one of Unity's built-in environments (i.e., "Oasis"). In this scenario, obstacles are represented by trees, bushesh, and rocks, and the source of interest is located inside a tent located on the opposite side of the arena with respect to the initial placement of the nodes. Snapshots in Fig. 4 show the evolution of the system with 100 nodes. This scenario had to be executed on the better equipped desktop to retain real-time performance, as the increased complexity of the environment (e.g., more complex geometry, more detailed rendering, and more complex physics interactions) significantly impacted the performance of the simulation.

5   Conclusion and Future Work

In this work we presented Collektivity, a toolchain for the execution of aggregate programs written in Collektive on top of the Unity game engine. This integration enables to leverage Unity's physics capabilities to create realistic and general-purpose simulations for testing and validating CASs.

To achieve this integration, we designed an architecture to unify the execution model of Unity with the functional nature of aggregate programs, we extended the Unity engine to support the direct invocation of Collektive computations through FFI, while using a shared platform-agnostic data model using Protocol Buffer. To guide the design and implementation of Collektivity, we conducted a benchmark to compare the performance of FFI and socket-based communication strategies, which informed our decision to adopt FFI for the integration. Finally, we show two examples of unity applications that demonstrates the opportunities of running Collektive on top of Unity, both of them provided as a starting point for users interested in experimenting with aggregate programming in Unity.

As future work, we plan to provide additional example scenarios that showcase more complex aggregate computations, also including larger populations (e.g., 1,000 and 10,000 nodes) to demonstrate the scalability of the integration. This will offer users a broader reference set of examples for building their own simulations, thereby lowering the entry barrier for experimenting with aggregate programming in Unity. We also plan to compare the current implementation with an Entity Component System (ECS)-based one, which is a design pattern widely adopted in game development and recently supported by Unity through its Data-Oriented Technology Stack (DOTS) framework[4].

As discussed in Sect. 3.1, the main technical and design challenges encountered in the integration are expected to recur, at least in part, in other game engines. To assess this hypothesis, we plan to integrate Collektive with another game engine, such as Unreal Engine or Godot. This would help evaluate the generality of the proposed design and identify which aspects transfer across engines and which require engine-specific solutions.

References

1. Abar, S., Theodoropoulos, G.K., Lemarinier, P., O'Hare, G.M.P.: Agent based modelling and simulation tools: a review of the state-of-art software. Comput. Sci. Rev. **24**, 13–33 (2017)
2. Abeywickrama, D.B., et al.: Autonomous robotic swarms: A corroborative approach for verification and validation. In: 2025 IEEE Engineering Reliable Autonomous Systems (ERAS), pp. 1–8. IEEE (2025).https://doi.org/10.1109/eras63351.2025.11135547
3. Aguzzi, G., et al.: A field-based approach for runtime replanning in swarm robotics missions. In: IEEE International Conference on Autonomic Computing and Self-Organizing Systems, ACSOS 2025, Tokyo, Japan, September 29 - Oct. 3, 2025, pp. 1–10. IEEE (2025). https://doi.org/10.1109/ACSOS66086.2025.00017
4. Aguzzi, G., Casadei, R., Pianini, D., Viroli, M.: Dynamic decentralization domains for the internet of things. IEEE Internet Comput. **26**(6), 16–23 (2022)
5. Audrito, G., Torta, G.: FCPP to aggregate them all. Sci. Comput. Program. **231**, 103026 (2024). https://doi.org/10.1016/J.SCICO.2023.103026
6. Audrito, G., Viroli, M., Damiani, F., Pianini, D., Beal, J.: A higher-order calculus of computational fields. ACM Trans. Comput. Log. **20**(1), 5:1–5:55 (2019). https://doi.org/10.1145/3285956
7. Beal, J., Pianini, D., Viroli, M.: Aggregate programming for the internet of things. IEEE Comput. (2015). https://doi.org/10.1109/MC.2015.261
8. Brambilla, M., Ferrante, E., Birattari, M., Dorigo, M.: Swarm robotics: a review from the swarm engineering perspective. Swarm Intell. **7**(1), 1–41 (2013)
9. Bucchiarone, A., Mongiello, M.: Ten years of self-adaptive systems: from dynamic ensembles to collective adaptive systems. In: ter Beek, M.H., Fantechi, A., Semini, L. (eds.) From Software Engineering to Formal Methods and Tools, and Back. LNCS, vol. 11865, pp. 19–39. Springer, Cham (2019). https://doi.org/10.1007/978-3-030-30985-5_3

---

[4] https://unity.com/dots.

10. Calderón-Arce, C., Brenes-Torres, J.C., Solis-Ortega, R.: Swarm robotics: simulators, platforms and applications review. Comput. **10**(6), 80 (2022)
11. Casadei, R.: MacroProgramming: concepts, state of the art, and opportunities of macroscopic behaviour modelling. ACM Comput. Surv. **55**(13s), 275:1–275:37 (2023). https://doi.org/10.1145/3579353
12. Casadei, R., Viroli, M., Aguzzi, G., Pianini, D.: Scafi: A scala DSL and toolkit for aggregate programming. SoftwareX **20**, 101248 (2022)
13. Coronado, E., Itadera, S., Ramirez-Alpizar, I.G.: Integrating virtual, mixed, and augmented reality to human–robot interaction applications using game engines: a brief review of accessible software tools and frameworks. Appl. Sci. **13**(3), 1292 (2023)
14. Cortecchia, A.: Multiplatform self-organizing systems through a Kotlin-MP implementation of aggregate computing. In: IEEE International Conference on Autonomic Computing and Self-Organizing Systems, ACSOS 2024 - Companion, Aarhus, Denmark, September 16-20, 2024, pp. 155–157. IEEE (2024). https://doi.org/10.1109/ACSOS-C63493.2024.00048
15. Diamanti, M., Vilhjálmsson, H.H.: Extending the Menge crowd simulation framework: visual authoring in unity. In: Intelligent Virtual Agents. Association for Computing Machinery (2022). https://doi.org/10.1145/3514197.3549698
16. Dixon, C., Winfield, A.F.T., Fisher, M., Zeng, C.: Towards temporal verification of swarm robotic systems. Robotics Auton. Syst. **60**(11), 1429–1441 (2012)
17. Farley, A., Wang, J., Marshall, J.A.: How to pick a mobile robot simulator: A quantitative comparison of coppeliasim, gazebo, MORSE and webots with a focus on accuracy of motion. Simul. Model. Pract. Theory **120**, 102629 (2022). https://doi.org/10.1016/J.SIMPAT.2022.102629
18. Giudice, N.D., Cruciani, F.M., Loreti, M.: Visualisation of collective systems with sequit and sibilla. In: Castellani, I., Tiezzi, F. (eds.) Coordination Models and Languages - COORDINATION 2024, vol. 14676, pp. 277–294. Springer (2024). https://doi.org/10.1007/978-3-031-62697-5_15
19. Gomes, C., Thule, C., Broman, D., Larsen, P.G., Vangheluwe, H.: Co-simulation: a survey. ACM Comput. Surv. **51**(3), 49:1–49:33 (2018). https://doi.org/10.1145/3179993
20. Gurioli, F., Baiardi, M., Cortecchia, A., Pianini, D.: pslab-unibo/collektivity: Release 1.1.1 (2026). https://doi.org/10.5281/ZENODO.18761590
21. Gurioli, F., Baiardi, M., Cortecchia, A., Pianini, D.: pslab-unibo/experiment-2026-coordination-collektive-unity-benchmark: Release 1.0.0 (2026). https://doi.org/10.5281/ZENODO.18717594
22. Ingelrest, F., Barrenetxea, G., Schaefer, G., Vetterli, M., Couach, O., Parlange, M.: SensorScope: application-specific sensor network for environmental monitoring. ACM Trans. Sens. Networks **6**(2), 17:1–17:32 (2010). https://doi.org/10.1145/1689239.1689247
23. Ju, H., Juan, R., Gomez, R., Nakamura, K., Li, G.: Transferring policy of deep reinforcement learning from simulation to reality for robotics. Nat. Mac. Intell. **4**(12), 1077–1087 (2022)
24. Koenig, N.P., Howard, A.: Design and use paradigms for gazebo, an open-source multi-robot simulator. In: 2004 IEEE/RSJ International Conference on Intelligent Robots and Systems, Sendai, Japan, September 28 - October 2, 2004, pp. 2149–2154. IEEE (2004). https://doi.org/10.1109/IROS.2004.1389727
25. Konur, S., Dixon, C., Fisher, M.: Analysing robot swarm behaviour via probabilistic model checking. Robotics Auton. Syst. **60**(2), 199–213 (2012)

26. Luke, S., Cioffi-Revilla, C., Panait, L., Sullivan, K., Balan, G.C.: MASON: a multiagent simulation environment. Simul. **81**(7), 517–527 (2005)
27. Mainwaring, A.M., Culler, D.E., Polastre, J., Szewczyk, R., Anderson, J.: Wireless sensor networks for habitat monitoring. In: Raghavendra, C.S., Sivalingam, K.M. (eds.) Proceedings of the First ACM International Workshop on Wireless Sensor Networks and Applications, WSNA 2002, Atlanta, Georgia, USA, September 28, 2002, pp. 88–97. ACM (2002). https://doi.org/10.1145/570738.570751
28. Mittal, S., Risco-Martín, J.L.: Simulation-based complex adaptive systems, pp. 127–150. Springer International Publishing (2017).https://doi.org/10.1007/978-3-319-61264-5_6
29. Nguyen, L.K.N., Howick, S., Megiddo, I.: A framework for conceptualising hybrid system dynamics and agent-based simulation models. Eur. J. Oper. Res. **315**(3), 1153–1166 (2024)
30. North, M.J., et al.: Complex adaptive systems modeling with repast simphony. Complex Adapt. Syst. Model. **1**(1) (2013). https://doi.org/10.1186/2194-3206-1-3
31. Pianini, D., Montagna, S., Viroli, M.: Chemical-oriented simulation of computational systems with ALCHEMIST. J. Simulation **7**(3), 202–215 (2013)
32. Pianini, D., Sebastio, S., Vandin, A.: Distributed statistical analysis of complex systems modeled through a chemical metaphor. In: International Conference on High Performance Computing & Simulation, HPCS 2014, Bologna, Italy, 21-25 July, 2014, pp. 416–423. IEEE (2014). https://doi.org/10.1109/HPCSIM.2014.6903715
33. Pianini, D., Viroli, M., Beal, J.: Protelis: practical aggregate programming. In: Wainwright, R.L., Corchado, J.M., Bechini, A., Hong, J. (eds.) Proceedings of the 30th Annual ACM Symposium on Applied Computing, Salamanca, Spain, April 13-17, 2015, pp. 1846–1853. ACM (2015). https://doi.org/10.1145/2695664.2695913
34. Pinciroli, C., et al.: ARGoS: a modular, parallel, multi-engine simulator for multi-robot systems. Swarm Intell. **6**(4), 271–295 (2012)
35. Platt, J., Ricks, K.: Comparative analysis of ROS-unity3D and ros-gazebo for mobile ground robot simulation. J. Intell. Robotic Syst. **106**(4), 80 (2022)
36. Sargent, R.G.: Verification and validation of simulation models. J. Simulation **7**(1), 12–24 (2013)
37. Schut, M.C.: On model design for simulation of collective intelligence. Inf. Sci. **180**(1), 132–155 (2010)
38. Sende, M., Raffelsberger, C., Bettstetter, C.: Bridging the reality gap in drone swarm development through mixed reality. Autono. Rob. **48**(7) (2024). https://doi.org/10.1007/s10514-024-10169-1
39. Shah, S., Dey, D., Lovett, C., Kapoor, A.: AirSim: high-fidelity visual and physical simulation for autonomous vehicles. In: Hutter, M., Siegwart, R. (eds.) Field and Service Robotics, Results of the 11th International Conference, FSR 2017, Zurich, Switzerland, 12-15 September 2017. Springer Proceedings in Advanced Robotics, vol. 5, pp. 621–635. Springer (2017). https://doi.org/10.1007/978-3-319-67361-5_40
40. Singh, M., et al.: Comparative study of digital twin developed in unity and gazebo. Electronics **14**(2), 276 (2025)
41. Viroli, M., Audrito, G., Beal, J., Damiani, F., Pianini, D.: Engineering resilient collective adaptive systems by self-stabilisation. ACM Trans. Model. Comput. Simul. **28**(2), 16:1–16:28 (2018). https://doi.org/10.1145/3177774
42. Viroli, M., Beal, J., Damiani, F., Audrito, G., Casadei, R., Pianini, D.: From distributed coordination to field calculus and aggregate computing. J. Log. Algebraic Meth. Program. **109** (2019). https://doi.org/10.1016/J.JLAMP.2019.100486

43. Werfel, J., Petersen, K., Nagpal, R.: Designing collective behavior in a termite-inspired robot construction team. Science **343**(6172), 754–758 (2014)
44. Wijaya, G.D., Caesarendra, W., Petra, M.I., Królczyk, G., Glowacz, A.: Comparative study of gazebo and unity 3D in performing a virtual pick and place of universal robot UR3 for assembly process in manufacturing. Simul. Model. Pract. Theory **132**, 102895 (2024)
45. Wolf, P., Groll, T., Hemer, S., Berns, K.: Evolution of robotic simulators: using UE 4 to enable real-world quality testing of complex autonomous robots in unstructured environments. In: Proceedings of the 10th International Conference on Simulation and Modeling Methodologies, Technologies and Applications, pp. 271–278. SCITEPRESS - Science and Technology Publications (2020). https://doi.org/10.5220/0009911502710278
46. Zhou, X., et al.: Swarm of micro flying robots in the wild. Sci. Robotics **7**(66) (2022). https://doi.org/10.1126/SCIROBOTICS.ABM5954

Author Index

GPSR Compliance
The European Union's (EU) General Product Safety Regulation (GPSR) is a set
of rules that requires consumer products to be safe and our obligations to
ensure this.

If you have any concerns about our products, you can contact us on

ProductSafety@springernature.com

In case Publisher is established outside the EU, the EU authorized
representative is:

Springer Nature Customer Service Center GmbH
Europaplatz 3
69115 Heidelberg, Germany